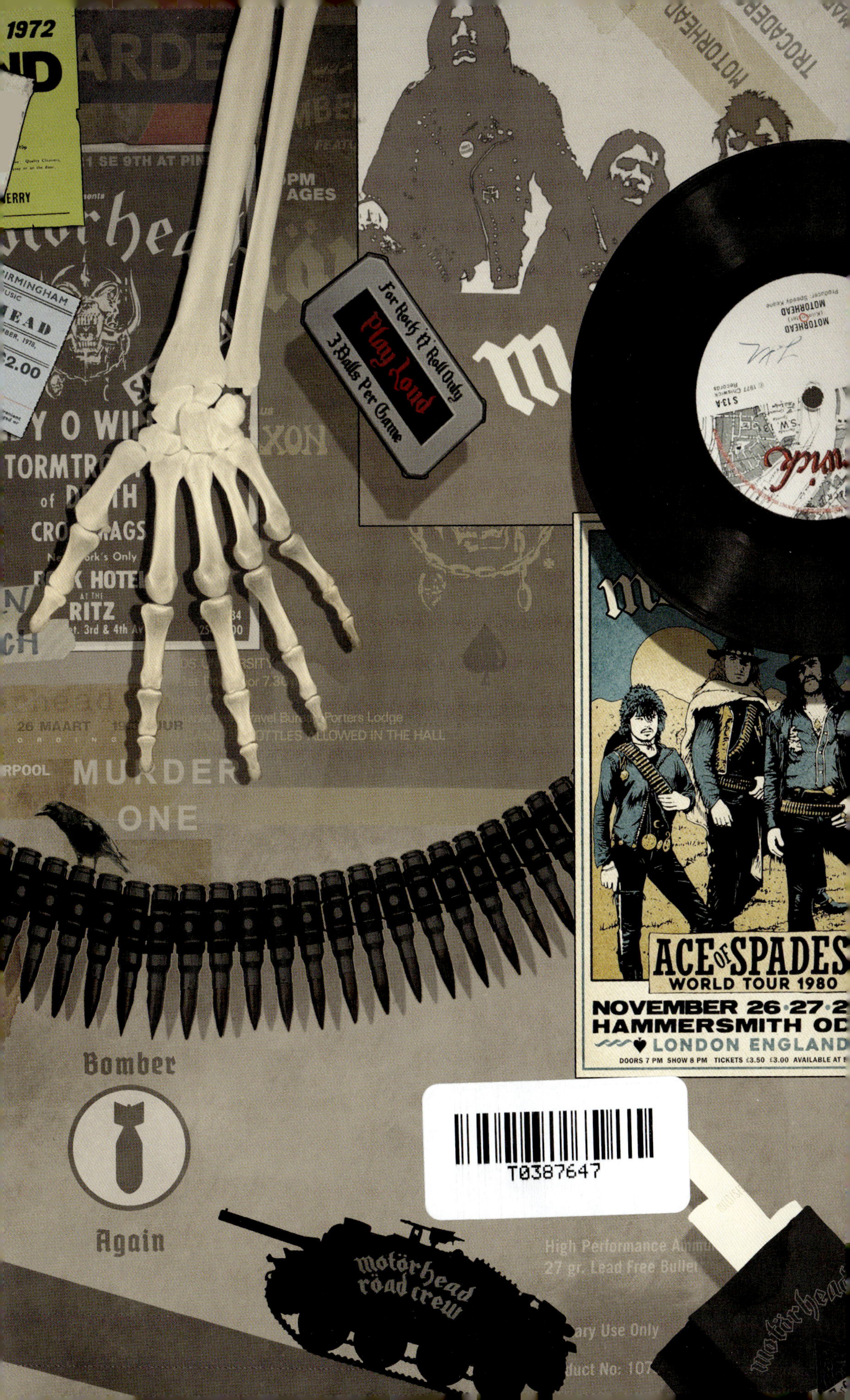
1972
MOTORHEAD
TROCADERO
For Rock 'n' Roll Only
Play Loud
3 Balls Per Game
MOTORHEAD
Producer: Speedy Keane
S 13 A
STORMTR
CROW
ROCK HOTEL
AT THE
RITZ
MURDER
ONE
Bomber
Again
ACE OF SPADES
WORLD TOUR 1980
NOVEMBER 26·27·2
HAMMERSMITH OD
LONDON ENGLAND
DOORS 7 PM SHOW 8 PM TICKETS £3.50 £3.00 AVAILABLE AT
T0387647
High Performance Ammu
27 gr. Lead Free Bullet
motörhead
röad crew
motörhead

THIS
BOOK IS
DEDICATED
TO THE AMAZING
LIFE
OF

lemmy kilmister

1945 ~ 2015

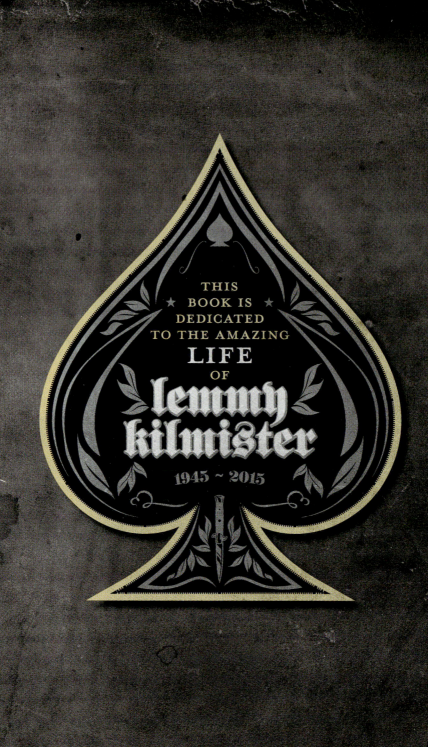

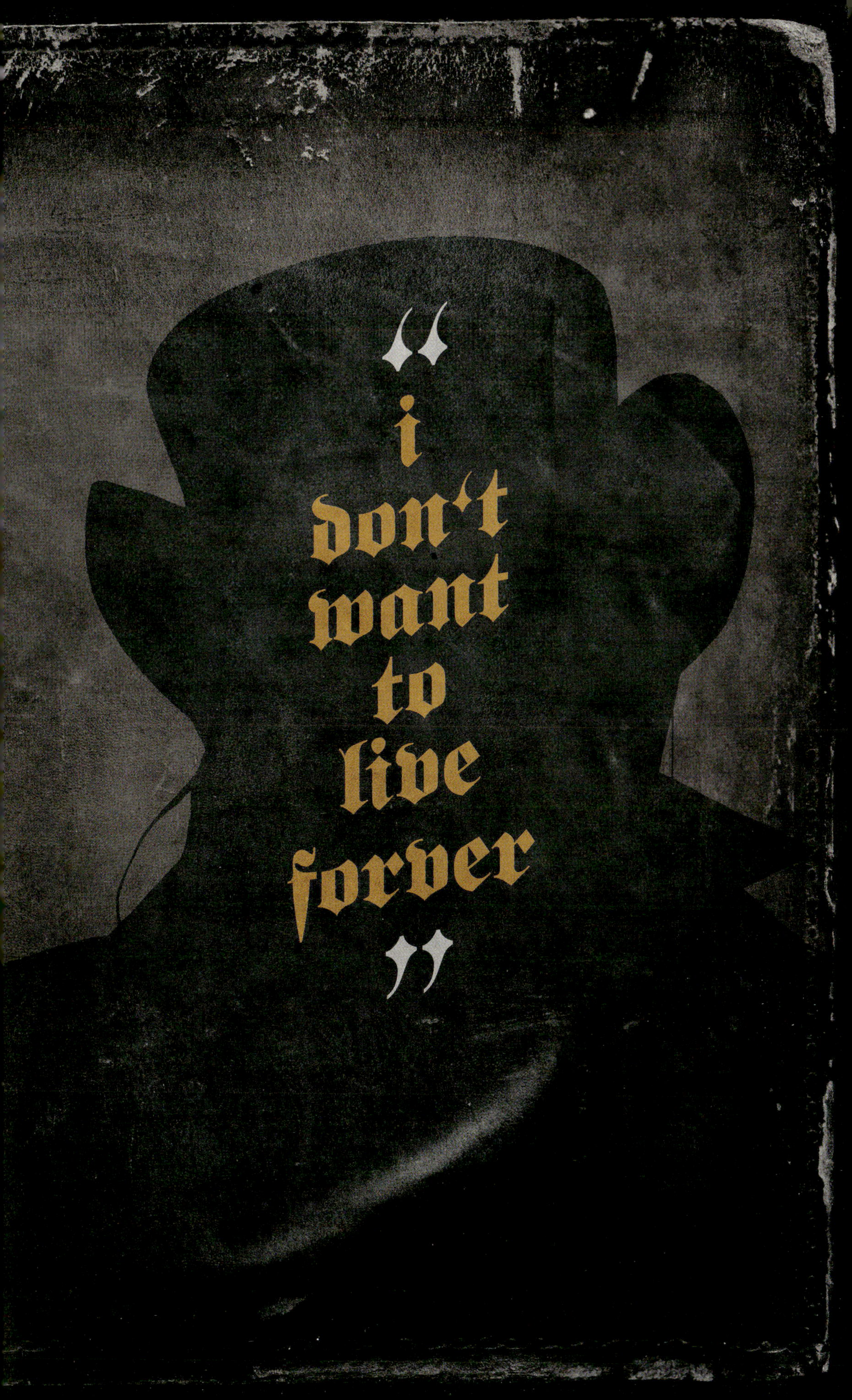
"i don't want to live forver"

PUBLISHER
sridhar reddy

CHIEF EXECUTIVE OFFICER
kevin meek

PRESIDENT
josh bernstein

EDITOR IN CHIEF
rantz hoseley

V.P., BUSINESS
anthony lauletta

EDITOR
jasminne saravia

MARKETING DESIGNER
darren vogt

FULFILLMENT
clarence head

©2024 Motörhead. All rights reserved. All characters featured in this graphic novel and the distinctive names and likenesses thereof, and all related indicia are property of [rightsholder]. No similarity between any of the names, characters, persons, and/or institutions in this graphic novel with those of any living or dead person or institution is intended, and any such similarity which may exist is purely coincidental. No part of this publication may be copied, reproduced, stored in a retrieval system or transmitted in any form or any means, electronic, mechanical, photocopying, recording or otherwise, without prior written permission of Motörhead. Printed in Lithuania. For mature audiences only.

The Illustrated ★ True ★ Stories of

lemmy kilmister and motörhead

With a foreword by

dave gröhl

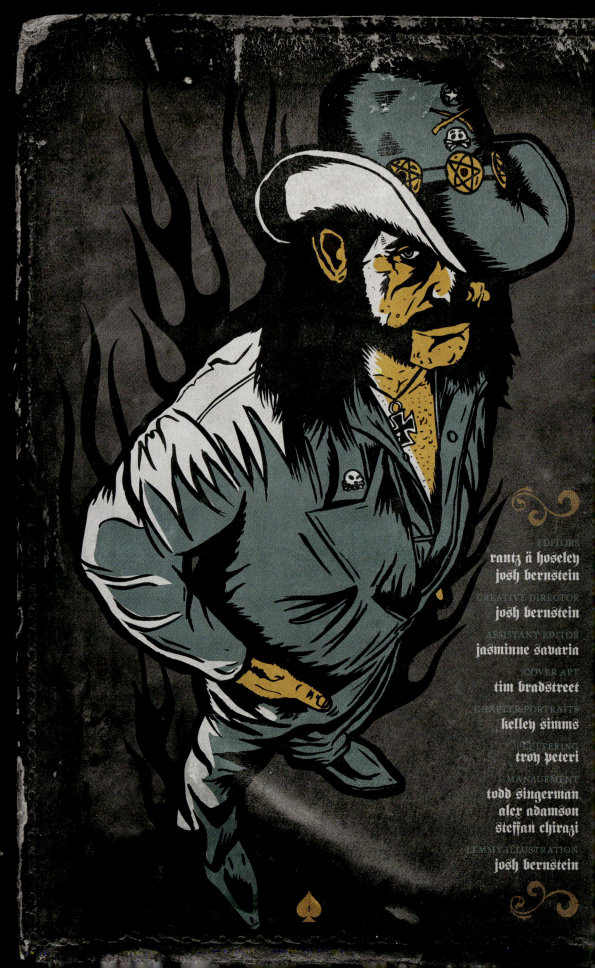

EDITORS
rantz ä hoseley
josh bernstein

CREATIVE DIRECTOR
josh bernstein

ASSISTANT EDITOR
jasminne savaria

COVER ART
tim bradstreet

CHAPTER PORTRAITS
kelley simms

LETTERING
troy peteri

MANAGEMENT
todd singerman
alex adamson
steffan chirazi

LEMMY ILLUSTRATION
josh bernstein

table öf contents

ALL STORIES HERE ARE FROM
FIRST-PERSON ENCOUNTERS WITH
lemmy kilmister

06 FOREWORD BY
dave grohl

166 AFTERWORD BY
ozzy osbourne

neil warnock 08
ART BY PIOTR KOWALSKI

wayne kramer 14
ART BY PAT MORIARITY

michael moorcock 22
ART BY JOHN BERGIN

phil campbell 30
ART BY JOHN BIVENS

chrissie hynde 36
ART BY CHRIS VISIONS

kim mcauliffe 40
ART BY FRED HARPER

slim jim phantom 46
ART BY BOB FINGERMAN

lars ulrich 52
ART BY STEVE CHANKS

neil gaiman 56
ART BY DAVE CHISHOLM

dee snider 62
ART BY JAYJAY JACKSON

slash 68
ART BY FELIPE SOBREIRO

steffan chirazi 74
ART BY GIDEON KENDALL

lita ford 80
ART BY RON JOSEPH

riki rachtman 86
ART BY STEVE KURTH

92 **penelope spheeris**
ART BY SHANE PATRICK WHITE

98 **dave navarro**
ART BY JIM MAHFOOD

104 **mikkey dee**
ART BY LUKE McGARRY

110 **chuck billy**
ART BY RYAN DUNLAVEY

116 **mikeal maglieri jr.**
ART BY KOREN SHADMI

120 **todd singerman**
ART BY JEFF McCLELLAND + JEFF McCOMSEY

126 **lars frederiksen**
ART BY WES HARGIS

132 **dave grohl**
ART BY BRENT ENGSTROM

140 **triple h**
ART BY ERIK RODRIGUEZ

144 **matt pinfield**
ART BY SEAN PRYOR

148 **josh bernstein**
ART BY JOSH BERNSTEIN

152 **steve luna**
ART BY FRANK POWERS

158 **corey graves**
ART BY TONY PARKER

172 **the road crew**
ART BY KELLEY SIMMS

"we are motörhead and we play rock & roll"

FOREWORD BY dave gröhl
ILLUSTRATION BY erik rödriguez

THIS SIMPLE DECLARATION, DELIVERED IN LEMMY KILMISTER'S unmistakable growl at an ear-shattering 130 decibels (the same volume as a jet taking off or a gunshot fired at close range) served as a simple, but most apropos introduction to the nuclear, boogie-woogie, speed-freak stomp of Motörhead's countless legendary live performances. ♠ Standing onstage with a Rickenbacker bass slung around his outlaw frame like a World War II soldier shouldering an machine gun, Lemmy carved a most frightening, though beautifully iconic, figure. An Apocalyptic Whiskey Cowboy Christ. And he wasn't fucking kidding, either. Within seconds of this menacing proclamation, the band would launch into a relentless, bone rattling repertoire of exactly that: Rock and Roll. A virtual sound bath from hell.

OVER THE YEARS, many have classified Motörhead's sound as hard rock. Others have called it heavy metal. Some have even dared to label it punk rock. Call it what you want, but the truth is that Motörhead's roots were always deeply buried in the swing and swagger of the original architects of rock and roll. Little Richard's piercing screams, The Everly Brothers eternal cool, and The Beatles flawless backbeat (a band that Lemmy saw perform at Liverpool's Cavern Club at the the tender age of 16) can all be found between the grooves of any Motörhead album. Take a listen to songs like *No Class*, *I'll Be Your Sister* or *Bomber* and you'll undoubtedly hear the chords and rhythms from legends past that formed this man's undying love of rock and roll... although at breakneck speed. (Pun intended)

The rockers loved them. The headbangers loved them. The punks loved them. And they can all squabble and debate the origins of Motörhead's monstrous musical mastery until their denim jackets fall off, but at the end of the day, the heart of all things Motörhead was not the work of others. It was the work one man: Lemmy.

"If we moved in next door to you, your lawn would die..." he once said. Was he referring to the ear-splitting volume that only he and his merry band of hooligans were capable of conjuring? The quantities of chemicals that only they could consume? The legions of die-hard fans that would undoubtedly flock to their master's humble dwelling in droves as some sort of mandatory Motörhead mecca, mowing down everything in their path? We may never know, but it's clear that beneath Lemmy's dark and sinister persona lied a wickedly brilliant, passionate, and outrageously funny man. With a Marlboro cigarette in one hand and a Jack and Coke in the other, Lemmy could charm his way into (or out of) any situation. He was a messenger, a seer, a villain, a wolf, a guardian, an angel. But to most, Lemmy was a hero, and his influence is forever immeasurable.

We were all given a gift that day of December 24, 1945. A Capricorn was born somewhere in the West Midlands of the United Kingdom and lived to become a King. His crown? A battered, black hat pulled below his sniper gaze. His kingdom? Rock and roll. His army?

You and me.

Long live the King.

dave gröhl
1-19-24

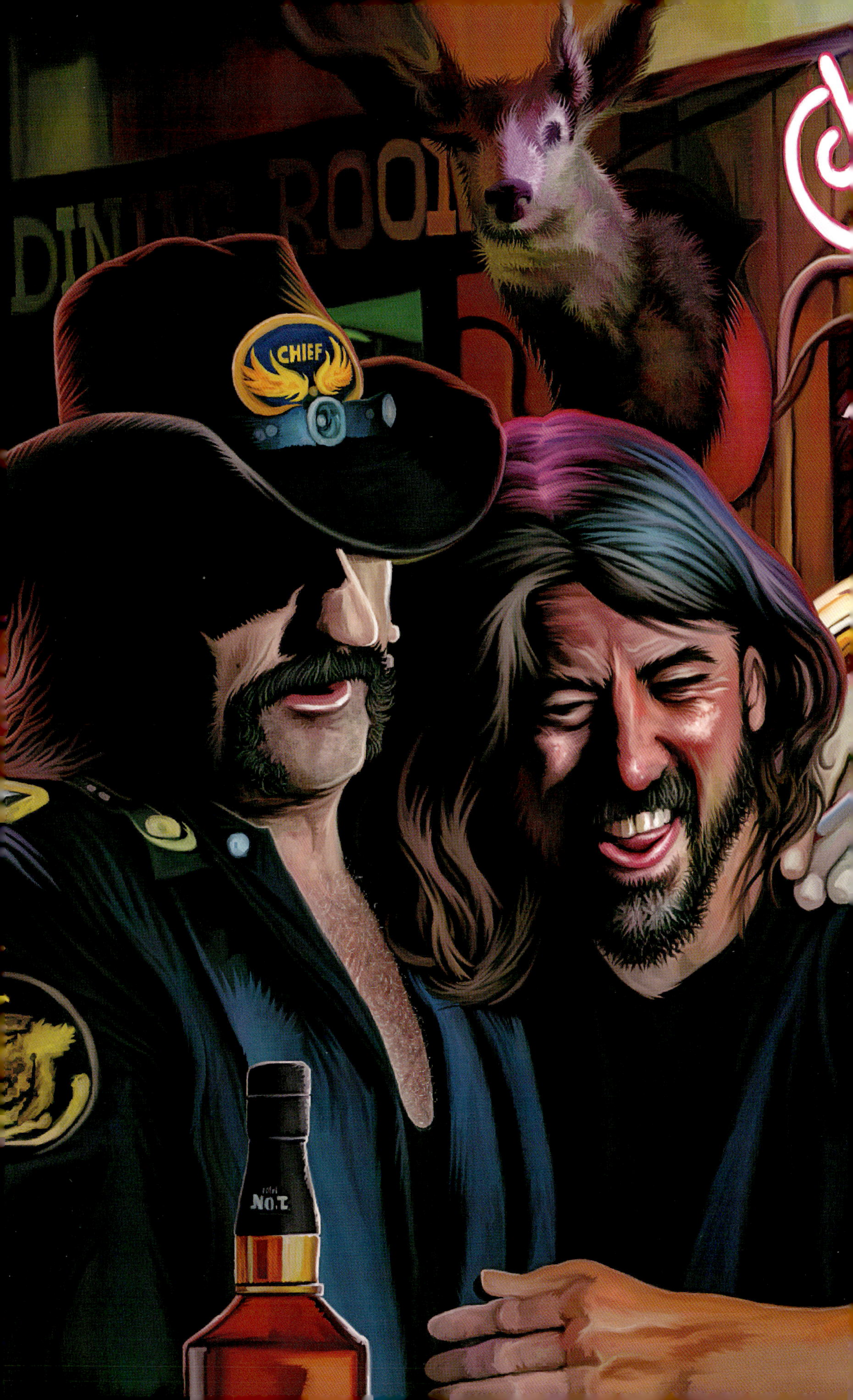
CHIEF

"I'd be up with the crack of a Sparrow's fart and Lemmy would still be at the bar telling stories!"

FIRST MET LEMMY IN 1964

neil warnock

AN MBE + THE HEAD OF UTA AND EARLY HAWKWIND AGENT

STORY ILLUSTRATED BY PIOTR KOWALSKI

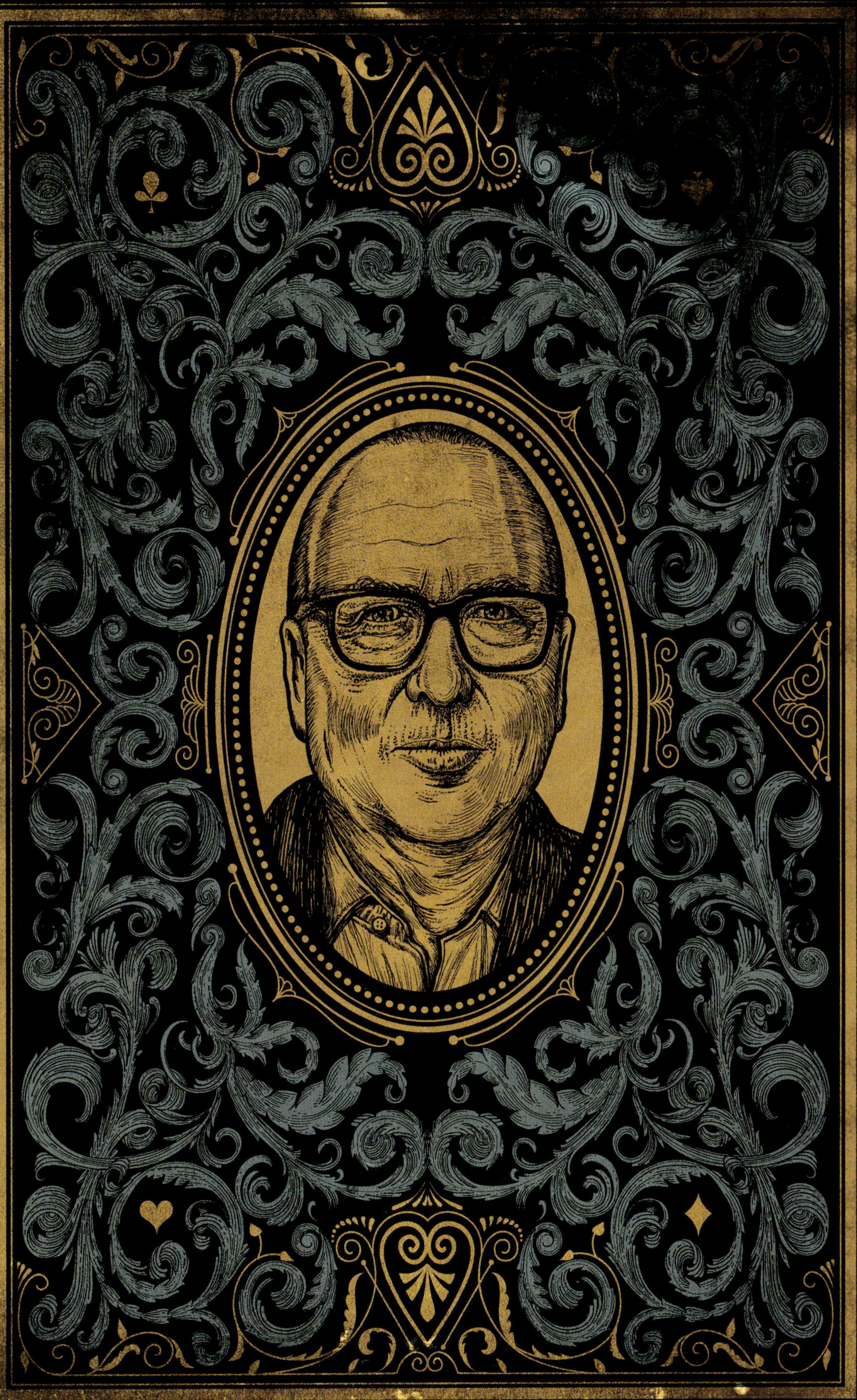

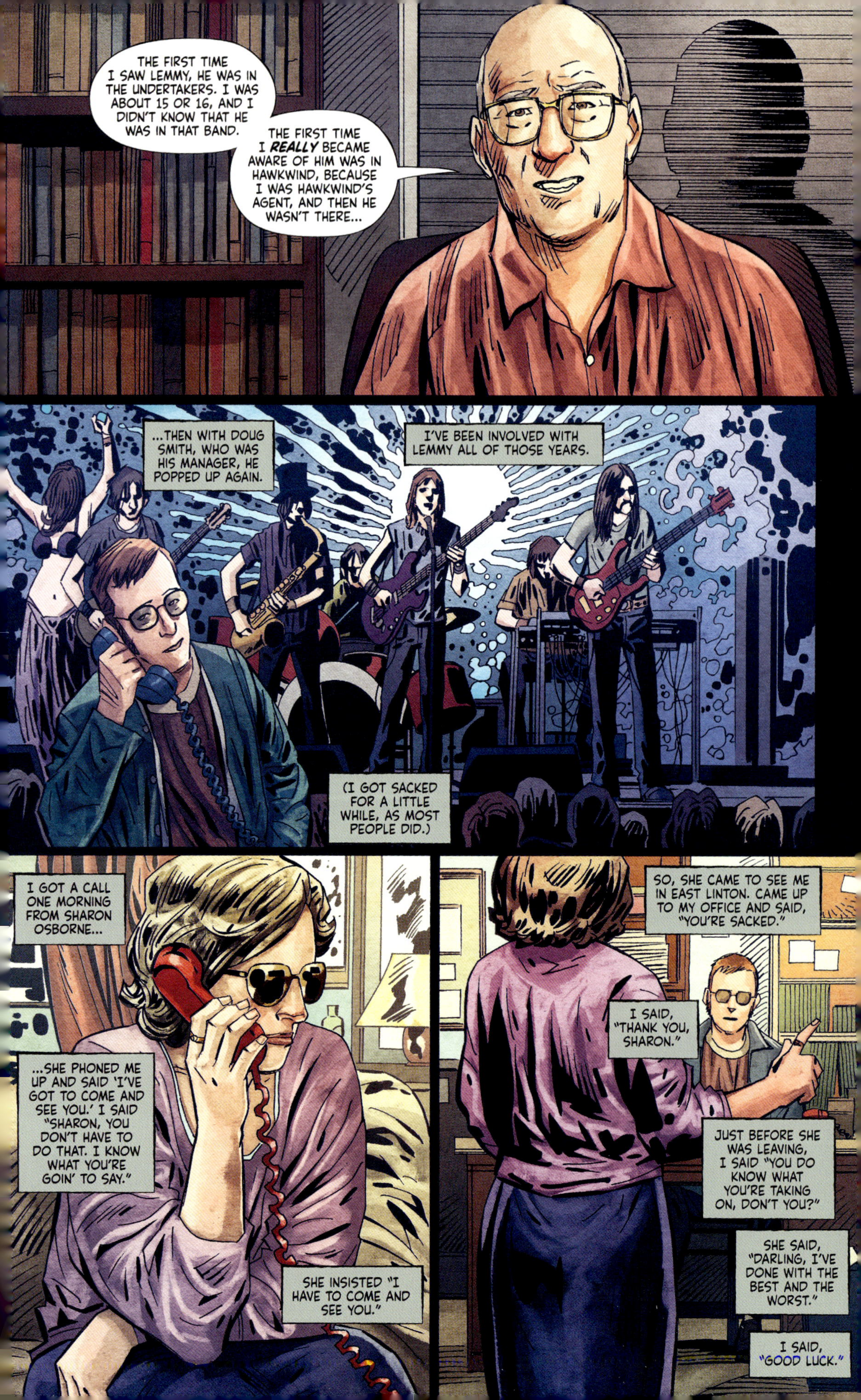
THE FIRST TIME I SAW LEMMY, HE WAS IN THE UNDERTAKERS. I WAS ABOUT 15 OR 16, AND I DIDN'T KNOW THAT HE WAS IN THAT BAND.
THE FIRST TIME I *REALLY* BECAME AWARE OF HIM WAS IN HAWKWIND, BECAUSE I WAS HAWKWIND'S AGENT, AND THEN HE WASN'T THERE...
...THEN WITH DOUG SMITH, WHO WAS HIS MANAGER, HE POPPED UP AGAIN.
I'VE BEEN INVOLVED WITH LEMMY ALL OF THOSE YEARS.
(I GOT SACKED FOR A LITTLE WHILE, AS MOST PEOPLE DID.)
I GOT A CALL ONE MORNING FROM SHARON OSBORNE...
...SHE PHONED ME UP AND SAID 'I'VE GOT TO COME AND SEE YOU.' I SAID "SHARON, YOU DON'T HAVE TO DO THAT. I KNOW WHAT YOU'RE GOIN' TO SAY."
SHE INSISTED "I HAVE TO COME AND SEE YOU."
SO, SHE CAME TO SEE ME IN EAST LINTON. CAME UP TO MY OFFICE AND SAID, "YOU'RE SACKED."
I SAID, "THANK YOU, SHARON."
JUST BEFORE SHE WAS LEAVING, I SAID "YOU DO KNOW WHAT YOU'RE TAKING ON, DON'T YOU?"
SHE SAID, "DARLING, I'VE DONE WITH THE BEST AND THE WORST."
I SAID, "GOOD LUCK."

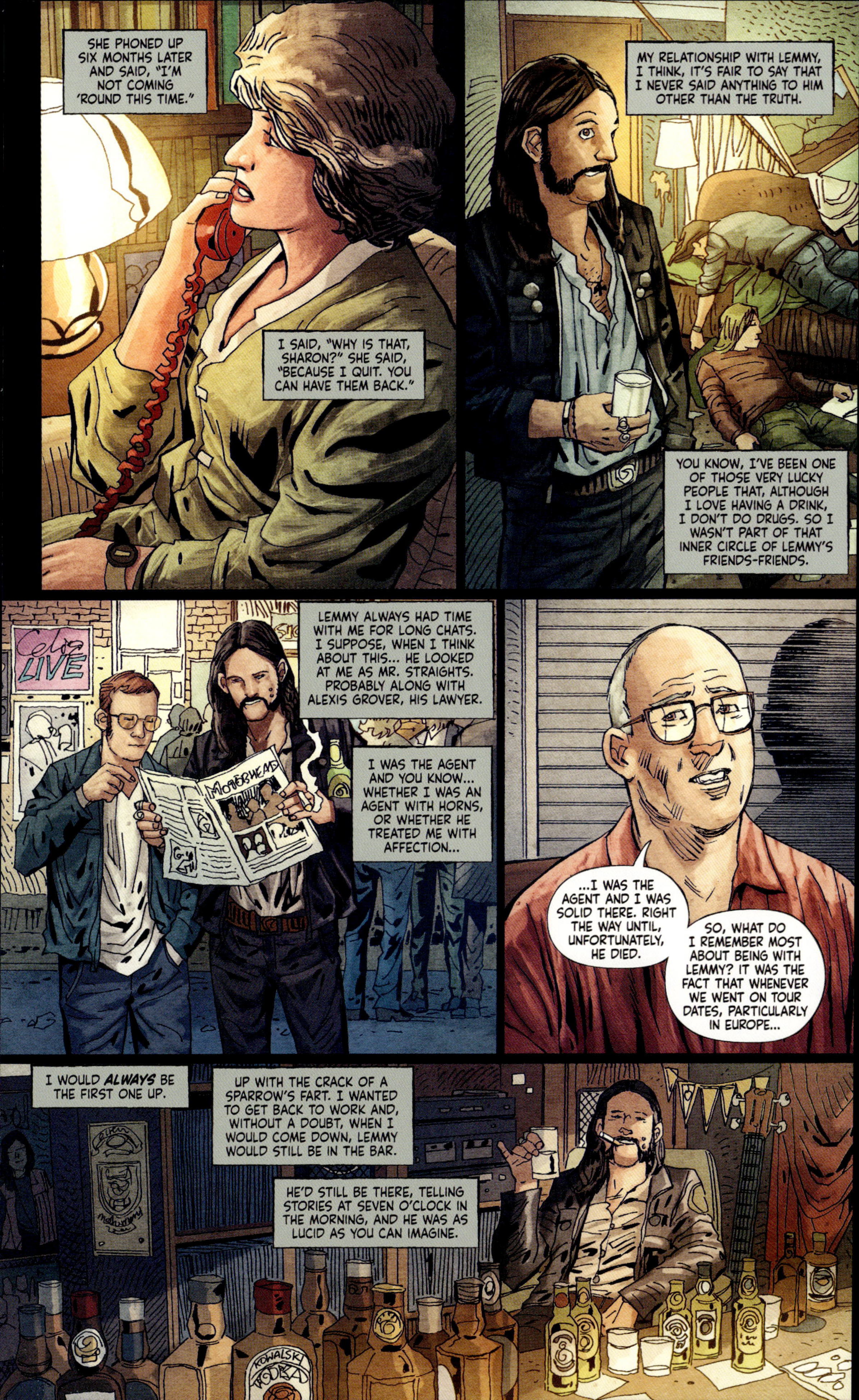

SHE PHONED UP SIX MONTHS LATER AND SAID, "I'M NOT COMING 'ROUND THIS TIME."
I SAID, "WHY IS THAT, SHARON?" SHE SAID, "BECAUSE I QUIT. YOU CAN HAVE THEM BACK."
MY RELATIONSHIP WITH LEMMY, I THINK, IT'S FAIR TO SAY THAT I NEVER SAID ANYTHING TO HIM OTHER THAN THE TRUTH.
YOU KNOW, I'VE BEEN ONE OF THOSE VERY LUCKY PEOPLE THAT, ALTHOUGH I LOVE HAVING A DRINK, I DON'T DO DRUGS. SO I WASN'T PART OF THAT INNER CIRCLE OF LEMMY'S FRIENDS-FRIENDS.
LIVE
LEMMY ALWAYS HAD TIME WITH ME FOR LONG CHATS. I SUPPOSE, WHEN I THINK ABOUT THIS... HE LOOKED AT ME AS MR. STRAIGHTS. PROBABLY ALONG WITH ALEXIS GROVER, HIS LAWYER.
MOTÖRHEAD
I WAS THE AGENT AND YOU KNOW... WHETHER I WAS AN AGENT WITH HORNS, OR WHETHER HE TREATED ME WITH AFFECTION...
...I WAS THE AGENT AND I WAS SOLID THERE. RIGHT THE WAY UNTIL, UNFORTUNATELY, HE DIED.
SO, WHAT DO I REMEMBER MOST ABOUT BEING WITH LEMMY? IT WAS THE FACT THAT WHENEVER WE WENT ON TOUR DATES, PARTICULARLY IN EUROPE...
I WOULD *ALWAYS* BE THE FIRST ONE UP.
UP WITH THE CRACK OF A SPARROW'S FART. I WANTED TO GET BACK TO WORK AND, WITHOUT A DOUBT, WHEN I WOULD COME DOWN, LEMMY WOULD STILL BE IN THE BAR.
HE'D STILL BE THERE, TELLING STORIES AT SEVEN O'CLOCK IN THE MORNING, AND HE WAS AS LUCID AS YOU CAN IMAGINE.
KOWALSKI VODKA

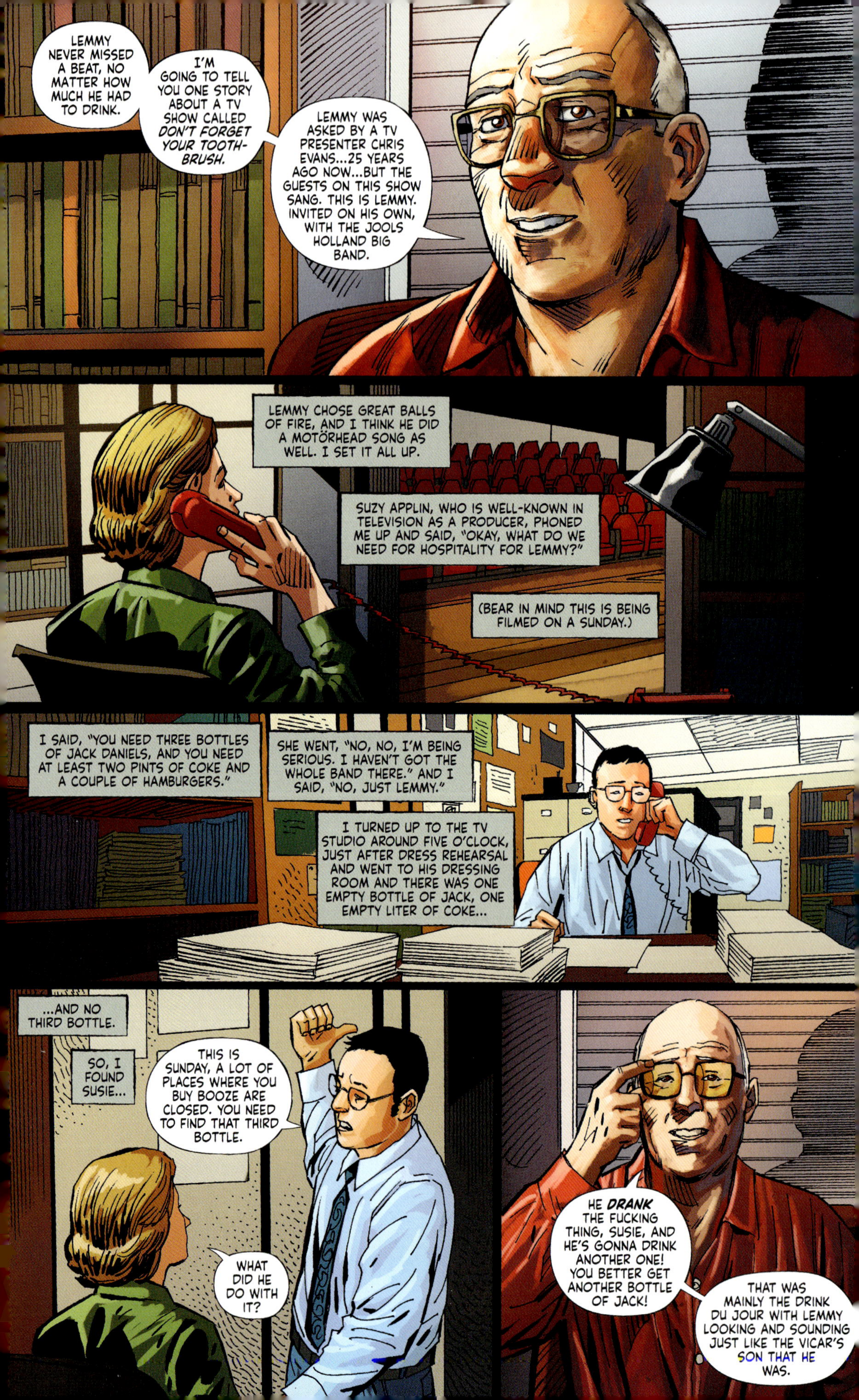
LEMMY NEVER MISSED A BEAT, NO MATTER HOW MUCH HE HAD TO DRINK.
I'M GOING TO TELL YOU ONE STORY ABOUT A TV SHOW CALLED *DON'T FORGET YOUR TOOTH-BRUSH.*
LEMMY WAS ASKED BY A TV PRESENTER CHRIS EVANS...25 YEARS AGO NOW...BUT THE GUESTS ON THIS SHOW SANG. THIS IS LEMMY. INVITED ON HIS OWN, WITH THE JOOLS HOLLAND BIG BAND.
LEMMY CHOSE GREAT BALLS OF FIRE, AND I THINK HE DID A MOTÖRHEAD SONG AS WELL. I SET IT ALL UP.
SUZY APPLIN, WHO IS WELL-KNOWN IN TELEVISION AS A PRODUCER, PHONED ME UP AND SAID, "OKAY, WHAT DO WE NEED FOR HOSPITALITY FOR LEMMY?"
(BEAR IN MIND THIS IS BEING FILMED ON A SUNDAY.)
I SAID, "YOU NEED THREE BOTTLES OF JACK DANIELS, AND YOU NEED AT LEAST TWO PINTS OF COKE AND A COUPLE OF HAMBURGERS."
SHE WENT, "NO, NO, I'M BEING SERIOUS. I HAVEN'T GOT THE WHOLE BAND THERE." AND I SAID, "NO, JUST LEMMY."
I TURNED UP TO THE TV STUDIO AROUND FIVE O'CLOCK, JUST AFTER DRESS REHEARSAL AND WENT TO HIS DRESSING ROOM AND THERE WAS ONE EMPTY BOTTLE OF JACK, ONE EMPTY LITER OF COKE...
...AND NO THIRD BOTTLE.
SO, I FOUND SUSIE...
THIS IS SUNDAY, A LOT OF PLACES WHERE YOU BUY BOOZE ARE CLOSED. YOU NEED TO FIND THAT THIRD BOTTLE.
WHAT DID HE DO WITH IT?
HE ***DRANK*** THE FUCKING THING, SUSIE, AND HE'S GONNA DRINK ANOTHER ONE! YOU BETTER GET ANOTHER BOTTLE OF JACK!
THAT WAS MAINLY THE DRINK DU JOUR WITH LEMMY LOOKING AND SOUNDING JUST LIKE THE VICAR'S SON THAT HE WAS.

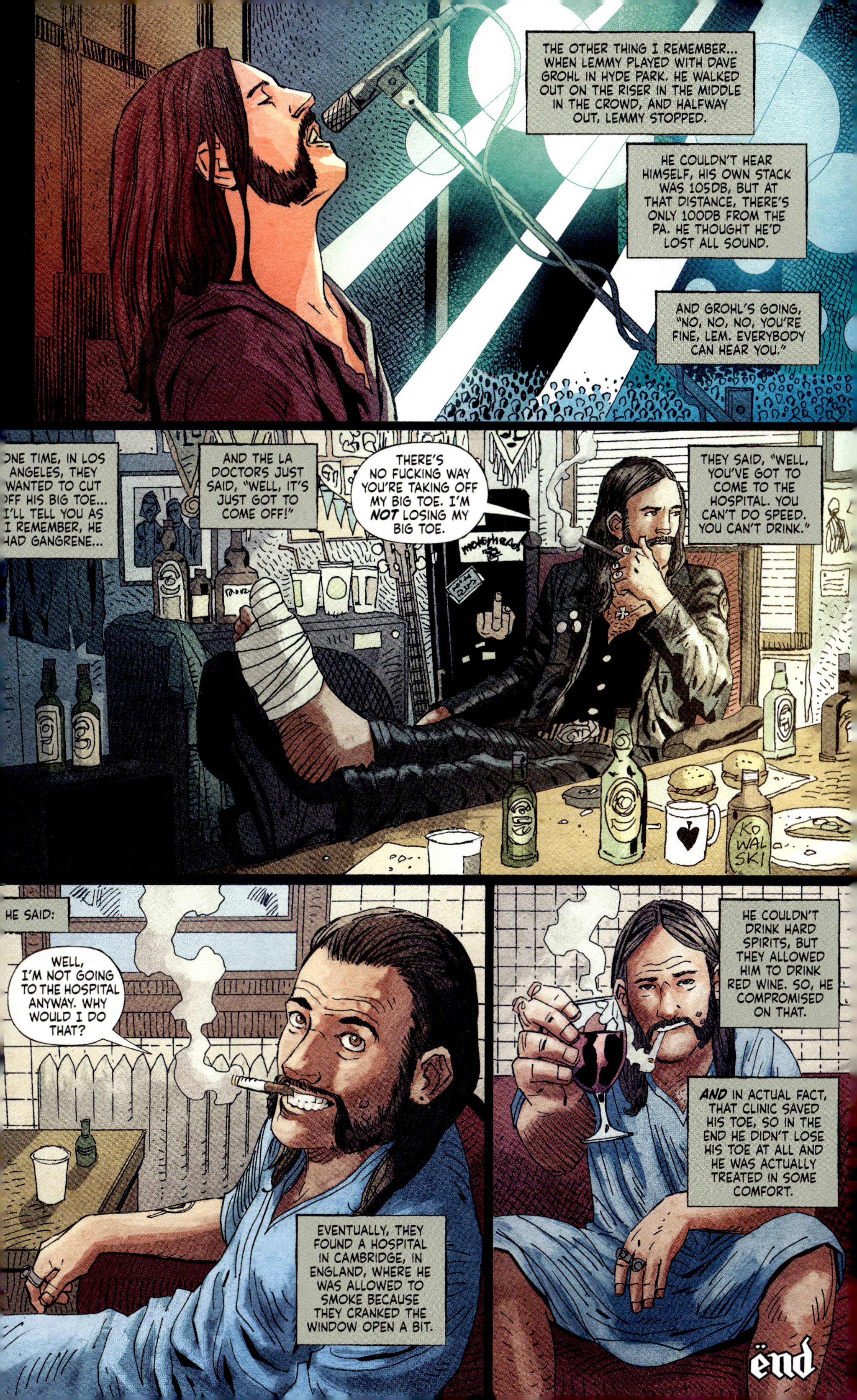

THE OTHER THING I REMEMBER... WHEN LEMMY PLAYED WITH DAVE GROHL IN HYDE PARK. HE WALKED OUT ON THE RISER IN THE MIDDLE IN THE CROWD, AND HALFWAY OUT, LEMMY STOPPED.
HE COULDN'T HEAR HIMSELF, HIS OWN STACK WAS 105DB, BUT AT THAT DISTANCE, THERE'S ONLY 100DB FROM THE PA. HE THOUGHT HE'D LOST ALL SOUND.
AND GROHL'S GOING, "NO, NO, NO, YOU'RE FINE, LEM. EVERYBODY CAN HEAR YOU."
ONE TIME, IN LOS ANGELES, THEY WANTED TO CUT OFF HIS BIG TOE... I'LL TELL YOU AS I REMEMBER, HE HAD GANGRENE...
AND THE LA DOCTORS JUST SAID, "WELL, IT'S JUST GOT TO COME OFF!"
THERE'S NO FUCKING WAY YOU'RE TAKING OFF MY BIG TOE. I'M ***NOT*** LOSING MY BIG TOE.
THEY SAID, "WELL, YOU'VE GOT TO COME TO THE HOSPITAL. YOU CAN'T DO SPEED. YOU CAN'T DRINK."
KO WAL SKI
HE SAID:
WELL, I'M NOT GOING TO THE HOSPITAL ANYWAY. WHY WOULD I DO THAT?
EVENTUALLY, THEY FOUND A HOSPITAL IN CAMBRIDGE, IN ENGLAND, WHERE HE WAS ALLOWED TO SMOKE BECAUSE THEY CRANKED THE WINDOW OPEN A BIT.
HE COULDN'T DRINK HARD SPIRITS, BUT THEY ALLOWED HIM TO DRINK RED WINE. SO, HE COMPROMISED ON THAT.
AND IN ACTUAL FACT, THAT CLINIC SAVED HIS TOE, SO IN THE END HE DIDN'T LOSE HIS TOE AT ALL AND HE WAS ACTUALLY TREATED IN SOME COMFORT.
ënd

"Lemmy's defiance served him well. Whatever the trend was, he was against it, which I appreciate."

FIRST MET LEMMY IN 1970

wayne kramer

FOUNDER / GUITARIST OF THE MC5 + WHITE PANTHER PARTY

STORY ILLUSTRATED BY PAT MORIARITY

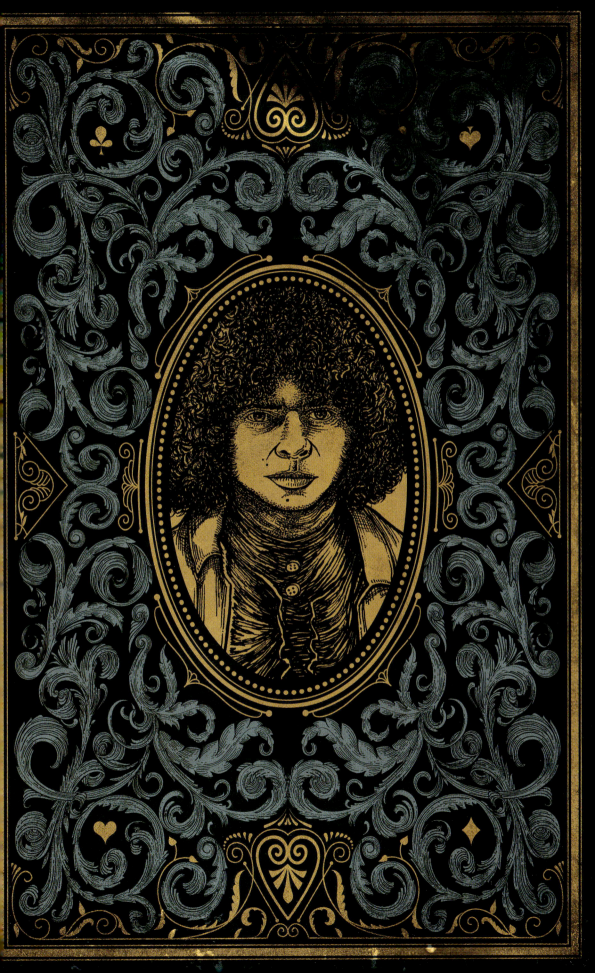

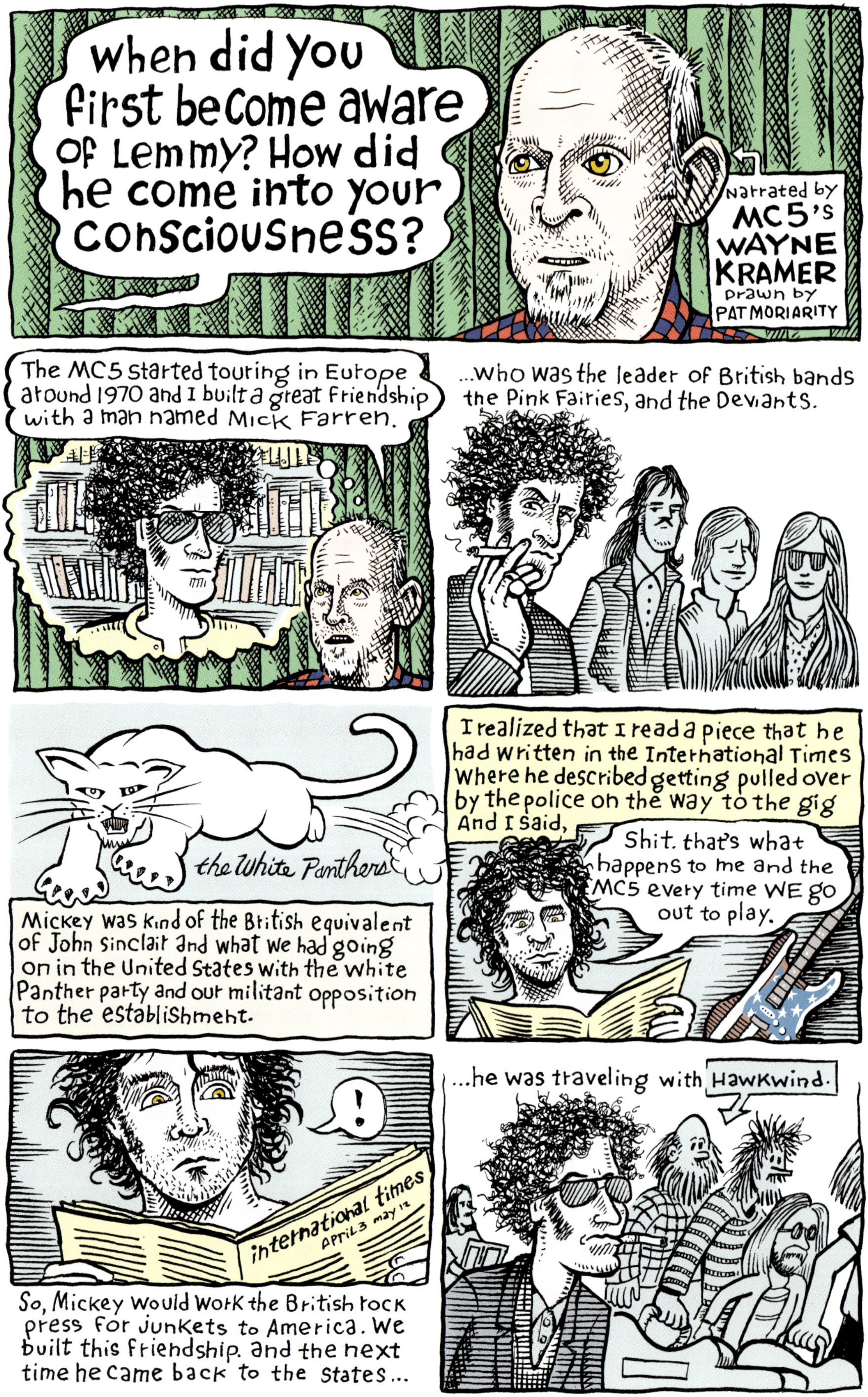
When did you first become aware of Lemmy? How did he come into your consciousness?
Narrated by MC5's WAYNE KRAMER
Drawn by PAT MORIARITY
The MC5 started touring in Europe around 1970 and I built a great friendship with a man named Mick Farren.
...who was the leader of British bands the Pink Fairies, and the Deviants.
the White Panthers
Mickey was kind of the British equivalent of John Sinclair and what we had going on in the United States with the White Panther party and our militant opposition to the establishment.
I realized that I read a piece that he had written in the International Times where he described getting pulled over by the police on the way to the gig and I said,
Shit. that's what happens to me and the MC5 every time WE go out to play.
!
international times
APRIL 3 MAY 12
So, Mickey would work the British rock press for junkets to America. We built this friendship. and the next time he came back to the states...
...he was traveling with Hawkwind.

So I went down to the hotel to meet up with him and have some drinks and he had this skinny young kid with him whose name was Lemmy.

He was the roadie for the band.

...he was kind of shy and quiet and kind of stayed in the background.

Then... of course, the MC5 imploded and my life went down the drain.

I went to the penitentiary for a few years.

"Mickey was involved with a management/publishing group. A guy named Doug Smith and Wayne Bardell, his partner."

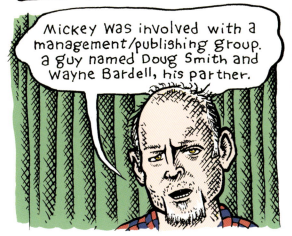

I liked him RIGHT OFF. I thought, yeah, he's a sweet kid, you know? And, uh..

Then the next time Hawkwind came to Detroit Lemmy was the BASS PLAYER in the band. So he had escalated his position.

And when I came back, I went back to London to look Mickey up and some old friends and see if I could generate any interest in someone wanting to make a Wayne Kramer record.

So, I went over and met with them and we talked about music and what I wanted to do.

2

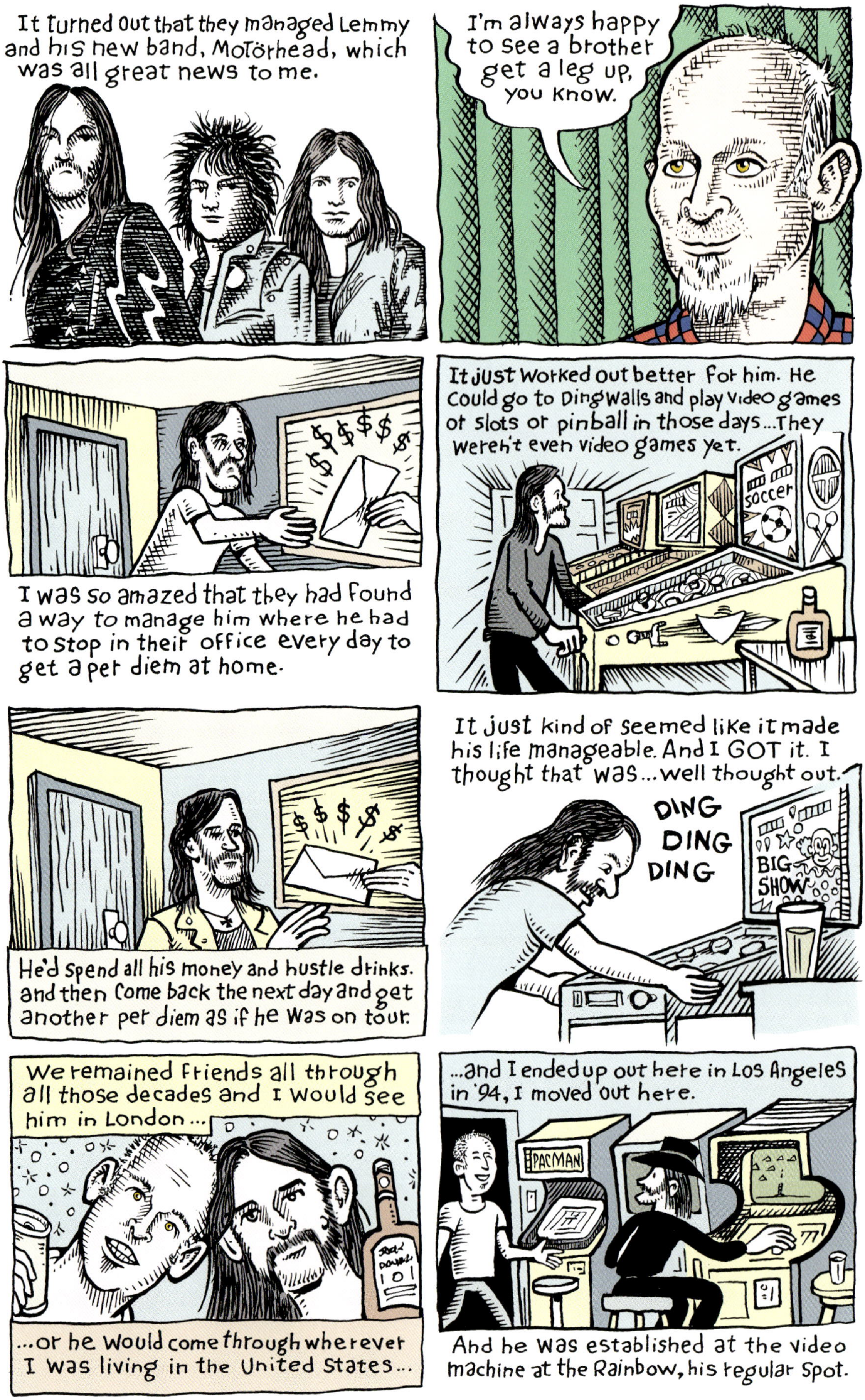
It turned out that they managed Lemmy and his new band, Motörhead, which was all great news to me.
I'm always happy to see a brother get a leg up, you know.
I was so amazed that they had found a way to manage him where he had to stop in their office every day to get a per diem at home.
It just worked out better for him. He could go to Dingwalls and play video games or slots or pinball in those days...They weren't even video games yet.
Soccer
He'd spend all his money and hustle drinks. and then come back the next day and get another per diem as if he was on tour.
It just kind of seemed like it made his life manageable. And I GOT it. I thought that was...well thought out.
DING
DING
DING
BIG SHOW
We remained friends all through all those decades and I would see him in London...
...or he would come through wherever I was living in the United States...
...and I ended up out here in Los Angeles in '94, I moved out here.
PACMAN
And he was established at the video machine at the Rainbow, his regular spot.

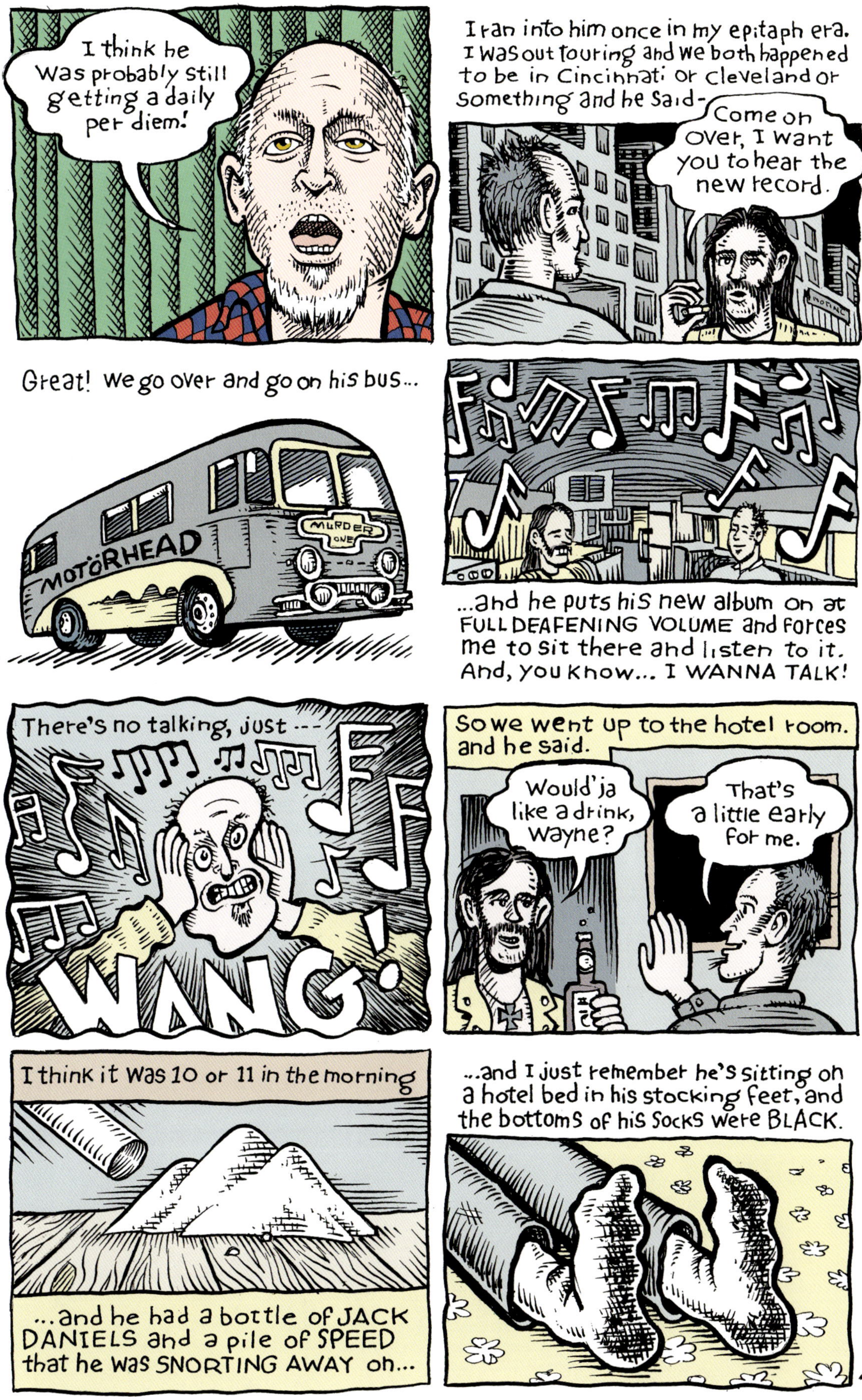
I think he was probably still getting a daily per diem!
I ran into him once in my epitaph era. I was out touring and we both happened to be in Cincinnati or Cleveland or something and he said-
Come on over, I want you to hear the new record.
Great! we go over and go on his bus...
MOTÖRHEAD
MURDER ONE
...and he puts his new album on at FULL DEAFENING VOLUME and forces me to sit there and listen to it. And, you know... I WANNA TALK!
There's no talking, just ---
WANG!
So we went up to the hotel room. and he said.
Would'ja like a drink, Wayne?
That's a little early for me.
I think it was 10 or 11 in the morning
...and he had a bottle of JACK DANIELS and a pile of SPEED that he was SNORTING AWAY on...
...and I just remember he's sitting on a hotel bed in his stocking feet, and the bottoms of his socks were BLACK.

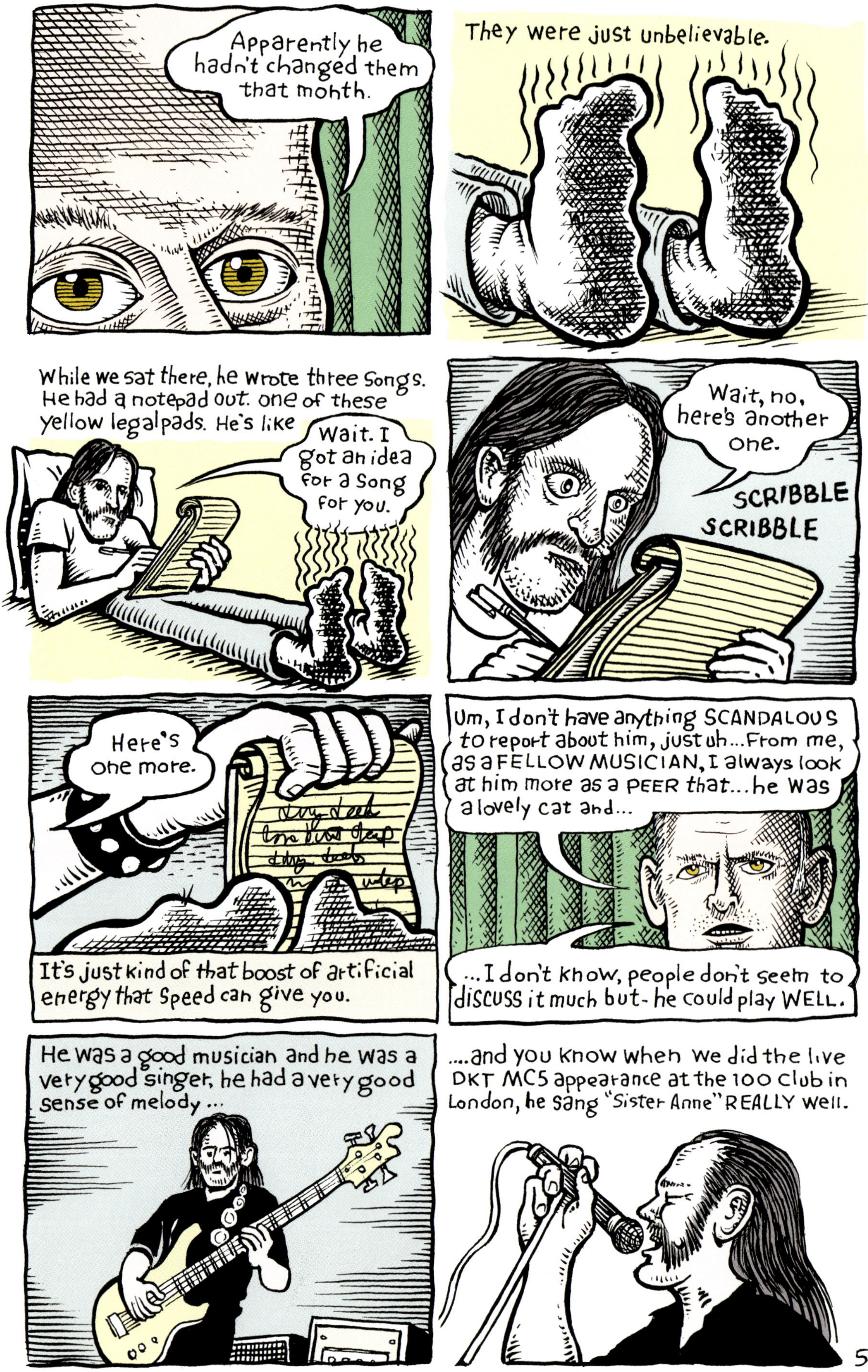
Apparently he hadn't changed them that month.
They were just unbelievable.
While we sat there, he wrote three songs. He had a notepad out. one of these yellow legalpads. He's like
Wait. I got an idea for a Song for you.
Wait, no, here's another one.
SCRIBBLE SCRIBBLE
Here's one more.
It's just kind of that boost of artificial energy that Speed can give you.
Um, I don't have anything SCANDALOUS to report about him, just uh...From me, as a FELLOW MUSICIAN, I always look at him more as a PEER that...he was a lovely cat and...
...I don't know, people don't seem to discuss it much but- he could play WELL.
He was a good musician and he was a very good singer, he had a very good sense of melody...
....and you know when we did the live DKT MC5 appearance at the 100 club in London, he sang "Sister Anne" REALLY well.

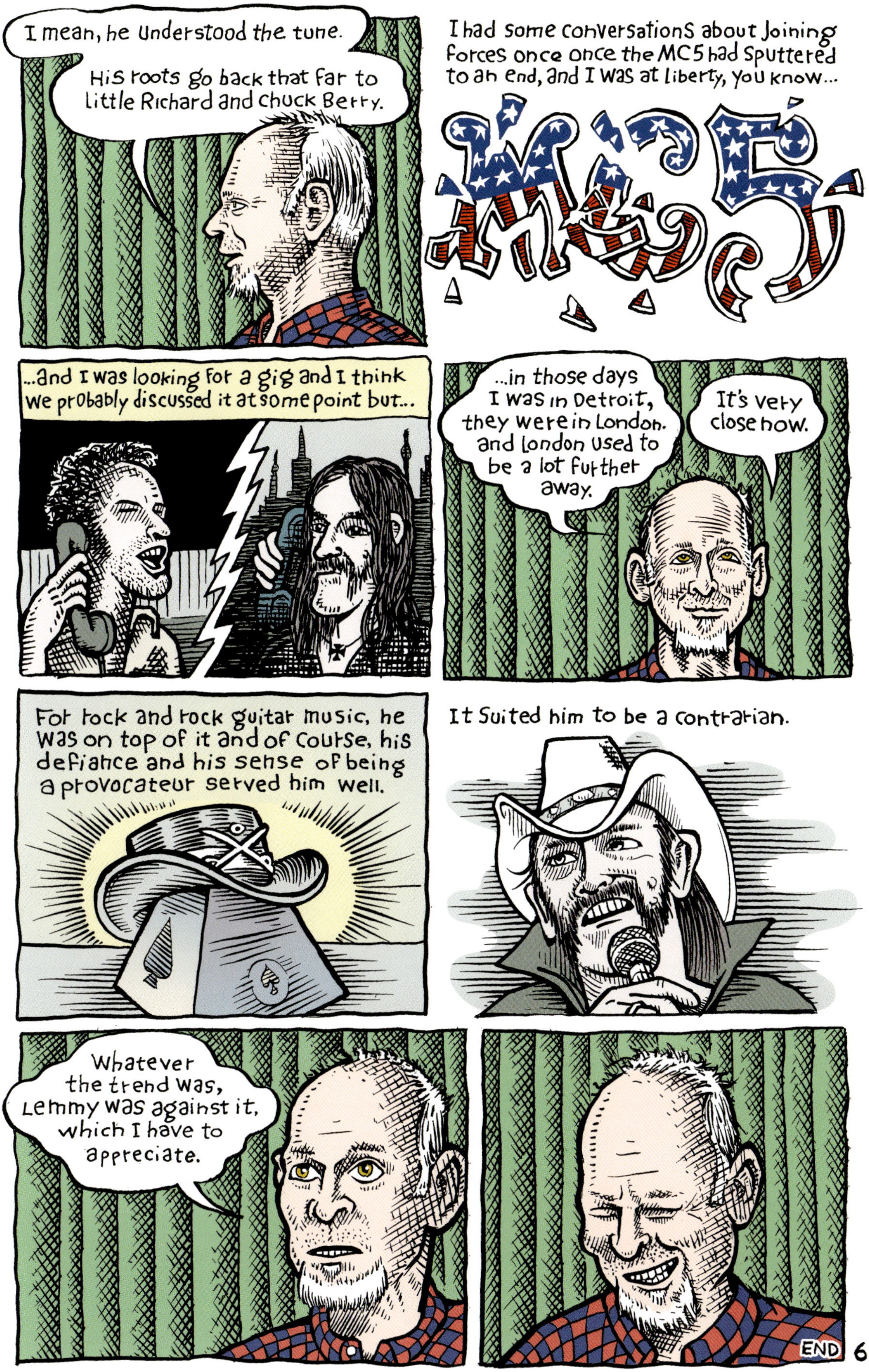

I mean, he understood the tune.
His roots go back that far to Little Richard and Chuck Berry.
I had some conversations about joining forces once once the MC5 had sputtered to an end, and I was at liberty, you know...
MC5
...and I was looking for a gig and I think we probably discussed it at some point but...
...in those days I was in Detroit, they were in London. and London used to be a lot further away.
It's very close now.
For rock and rock guitar music, he was on top of it and of course, his defiance and his sense of being a provocateur served him well.
It suited him to be a contrarian.
Whatever the trend was, Lemmy was against it, which I have to appreciate.
END

"Lemmy put on all that sort of leather gear and motorbike shit as a kind of armor."

FIRST MET LEMMY IN 1970

michael moorcock

FAMED SCIENCE FICTION WRITER AND HAWKWIND BANDMATE

STORY ILLUSTRATED BY JOHN BERGIN

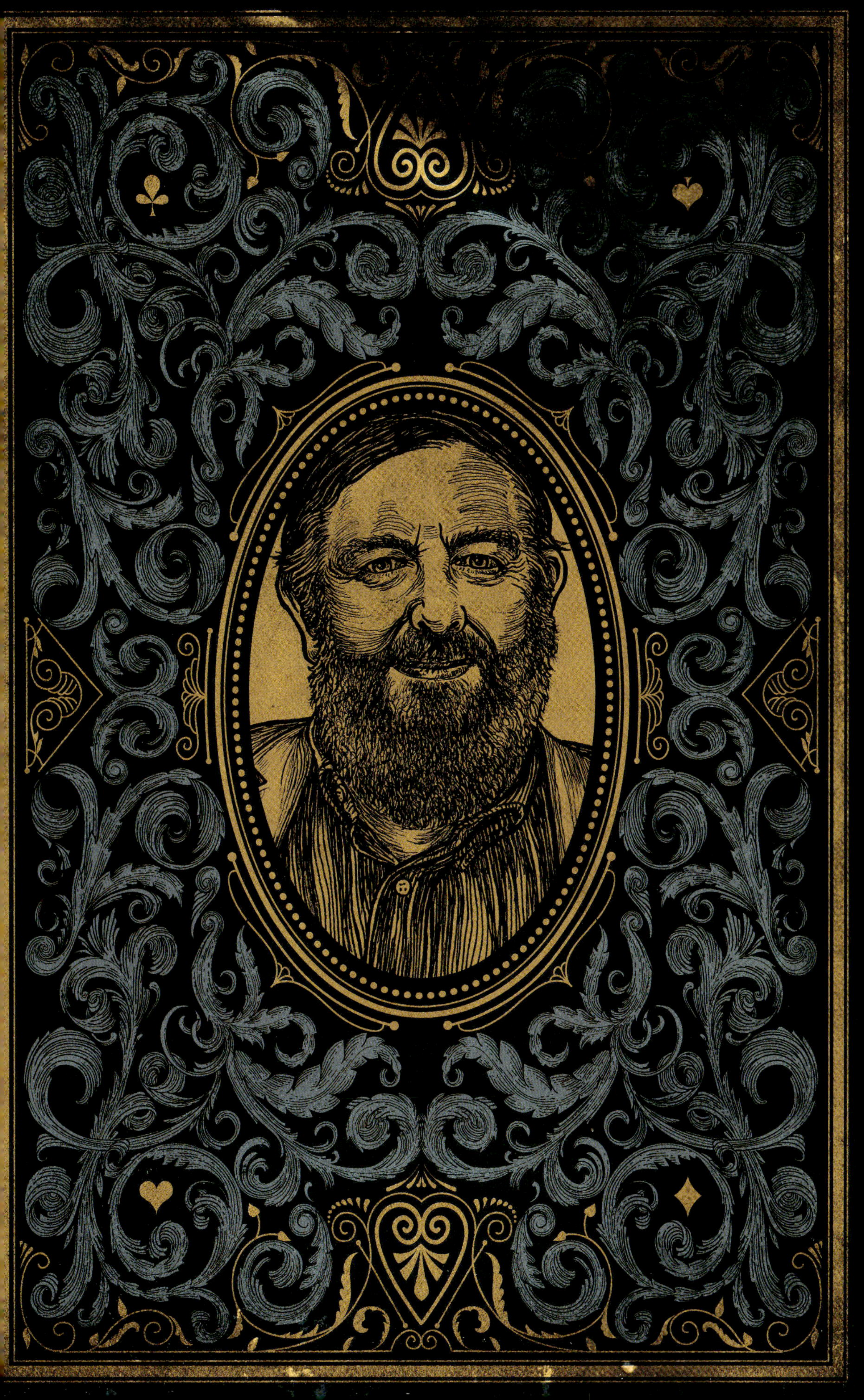

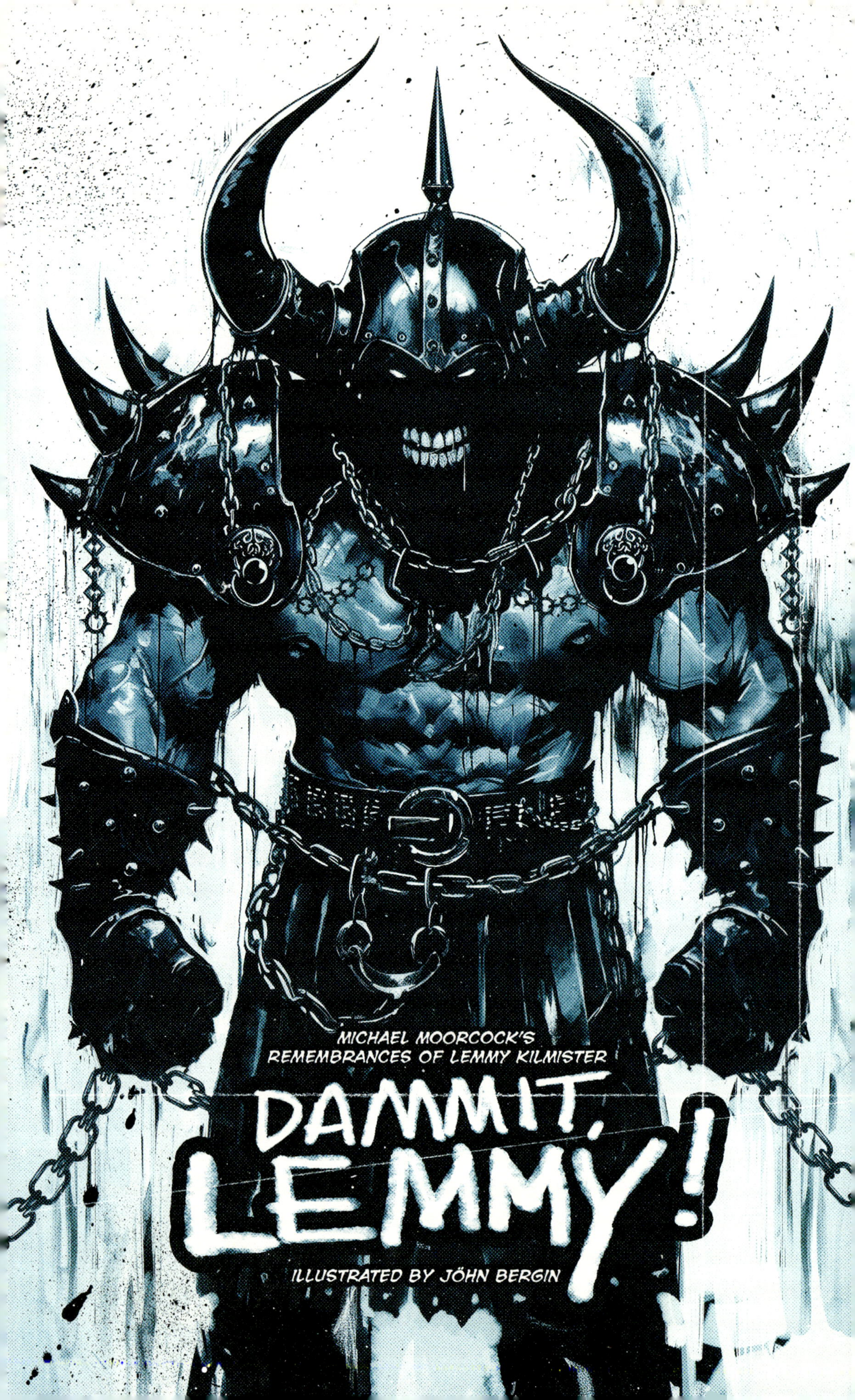
MICHAEL MOORCOCK'S
REMEMBRANCES OF LEMMY KILMISTER
DAMMIT, LEMMY!
ILLUSTRATED BY JÖHN BERGIN

I FIRST ENCOUNTERED ***LEMMY*** AT THE FIRST AUDITION HE DID FOR ***HAWKWIND***.

I WENT DOWN THERE WITH ANOTHER BASS PLAYER NAMED CURTIS. CURTIS WAS GOING TO AUDITION FOR THE JOB, TOO, BUT WHEN WE GOT THERE, ***LEMMY WAS ALREADY THERE,*** AND DAVE SAID, "SORRY MATE, WE'VE ALREADY GOT IT! BASS THERE!" IT WAS IN THE MIDDLE OF RECORDING AND REHEARSAL, AND THAT WAS IT.

FROM THEN ON, WE HIT IT OFF.

I BECAME ***GOOD FRIENDS*** WITH LEMMY, EVEN THOUGH HE ***CONSTANTLY*** SEEMED TO SUGGEST THAT I WAS SOME KIND OF ***UPPER-CLASS TWIT...***

BUT THAT WAS REALLY OUR RELATIONSHIP.

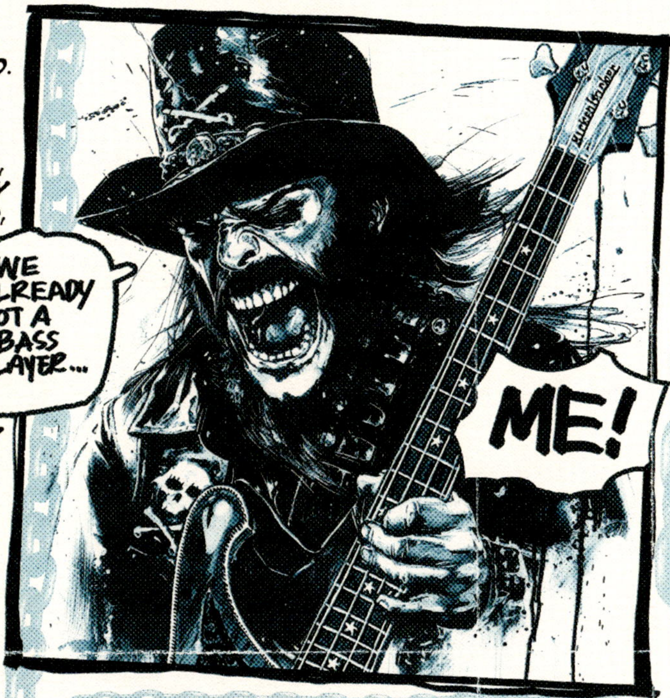
WE ALREADY GOT A BASS PLAYER...
ME!

I DIDN'T DO MUCH IN HAWKWIND. I JUST DID WHAT WAS ESSENTIALLY SOME OF MY OWN STUFF. I HAD A ***DEAL*** WITH BOB CALVERT. HE WAS IN AND OUT OF THE ***LOONY BIN***, SO HE WORRIED THAT WHEN I TOOK OVER FOR HIM, I'D ***TAKE HIS JOB OFF HIM***. SO I ***PROMISED*** HIM THAT AS SOON AS HE CAME OUT OF ***THE BIN*** AND WAS BACK TO WORK, I WOULD ***BACK OFF***. AND THAT'S WHAT I DID. ESSENTIALLY, THE BAND WOULD CALL ME WHEN THEY NEEDED ME.

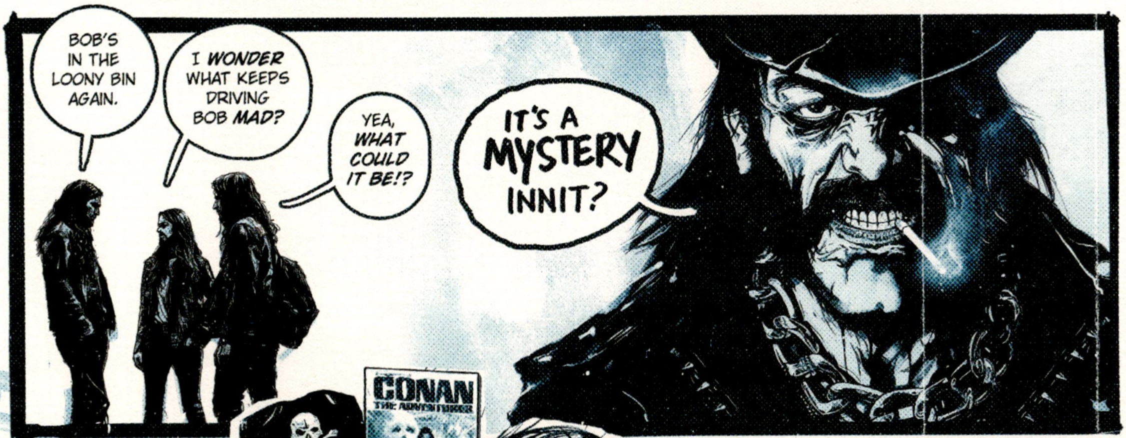
BOB'S IN THE LOONY BIN AGAIN.
I WONDER WHAT KEEPS DRIVING BOB MAD?
YEA, WHAT COULD IT BE!?
IT'S A MYSTERY INNIT?

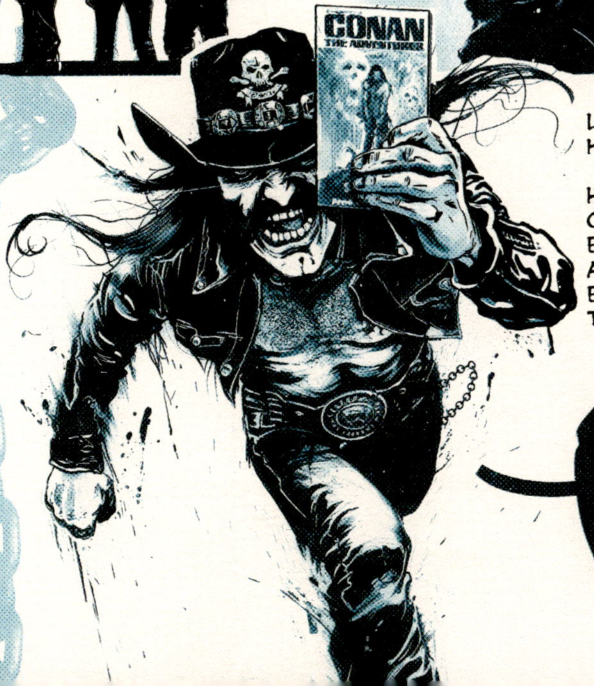
CONAN
IT'S MINE NOW, BY CROM!

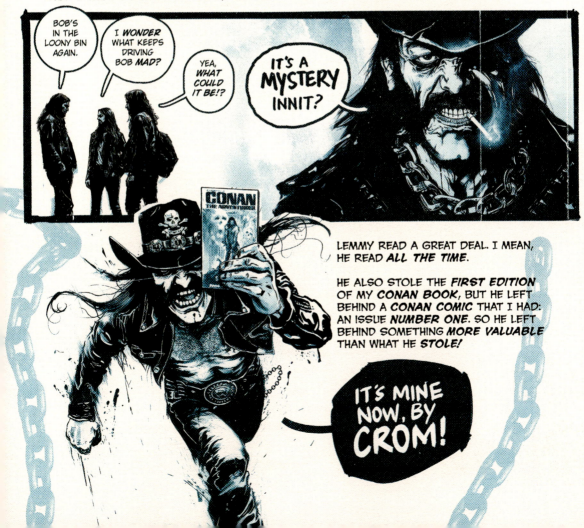

LEMMY READ A GREAT DEAL. I MEAN, HE READ ***ALL THE TIME***.

HE ALSO STOLE THE ***FIRST EDITION*** OF MY ***CONAN BOOK***, BUT HE LEFT BEHIND A ***CONAN COMIC*** THAT I HAD: AN ISSUE ***NUMBER ONE***. SO HE LEFT BEHIND SOMETHING ***MORE VALUABLE*** THAN WHAT HE ***STOLE!***

WHEN THE BAND WAS COMING UP, MY FIRST WIFE AND I HAD A ***BIG HOUSE*** IN YORKSHIRE NEAR LANCASTER. WE WERE DOING A GIG IN LANCASTER, SO THE BAND DECIDED TO ***STAY AT MY PLACE*** BECAUSE WE HAD ENOUGH SPACE, AND MY WIFE AT THE TIME WAS RATHER ***WORRIED ABOUT LEMMY***, YOU KNOW, WHAT HE MIGHT ***GET UP TO***.

SO SHE ***WORRIED*** A BIT ABOUT IT.

BUT THEN THE BAND TURNED UP, AND EVERYTHING WAS ALL RIGHT.

THE FIRST THING SHE SAW THE NEXT MORNING WAS ***LEMMY*** LAYING THE FIRE IN THE FIREPLACE TO MAKE IT READY FOR EVERYBODY ELSE WHEN THEY GOT UP, AND HE ***MADE TEA*** FOR EVERYBODY.

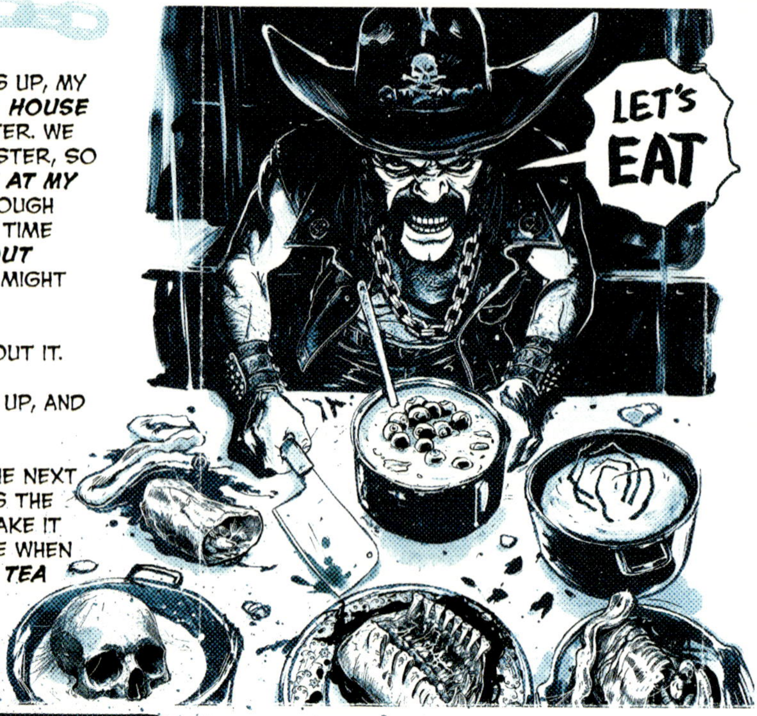
LET'S EAT

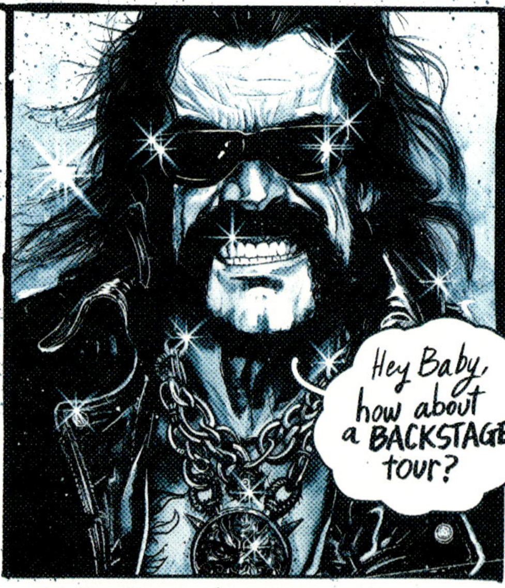
Hey Baby, how about a BACKSTAGE tour?

LATER, AFTER I MARRIED LINDA, I REMEMBER WE WERE GOING TO DO A ***REUNION CONCERT***. SOME SORT OF SPECIAL – MAYBE A CHRISTMAS CONCERT AT HAMMERSMITH, ODEON. LINDA WAS COMING WITH ME, AND SHE SAID SHE HAD THIS IDEA OF ***LEMMY*** BEING THIS SORT OF ***"MACHO"*** GUY.

I DIDN'T SAY ANYTHING. I THOUGHT I'D JUST WAIT, YOU KNOW, AND LET HER MAKE UP HER OWN MIND BECAUSE I ***KNEW*** WHAT WOULD HAPPEN.

SO WE GET THERE, AND THE ***FIRST THING*** LEMMY DOES IS SORT OF ***BOW*** AND ***CLICK HIS HEELS*** AND ***KISS HER HAND*** AND, YOU KNOW, SAY SOMETHING ***PLEASANT***. THE NEXT THING HE'S ***CRACKING JOKES***. SHE JUST ***LOVED*** HIM AFTER THAT, ALMOST IMMEDIATELY.

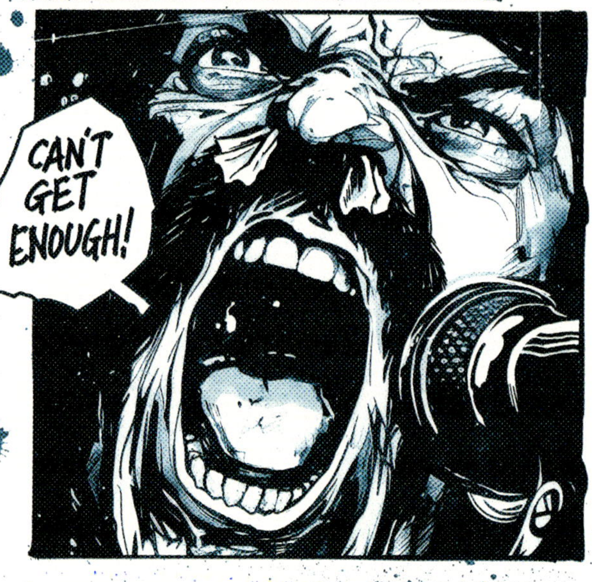
CAN'T GET ENOUGH!

LEMMY WAS ALSO RATHER ***NERVOUS*** ABOUT ***GOING BACK*** WITH HAWKWIND AFTER SOME TIME FOR THIS SHOW.

AND HE HAD A ***NOSE BLEED*** (A LOT OF FOLKS HAD 'NOSE BLEEDS' AROUND THAT TIME, YOU KNOW) AND HERE LINDA IS, HELPING HIM ***STUFF KLEENEX*** UP HIS NOSE TO STOP THE ***BLEEDING*** BEFORE HE GOES ON. LEMMY'S SAYING, "I DON'T KNOW WHETHER I CAN DO IT!"

AND HE ACTUALLY PULLED IT OFF ***MARVELOUSLY***. I MEAN, HE WAS A VERY GOOD MUSICIAN AND ***PARTICULARLY GOOD*** WITH DAVE BROCK. THE TWO OF THEM REALLY DID BLEND ***PERFECTLY*** AND BOUNCED OFF EACH OTHER ALL THE TIME.

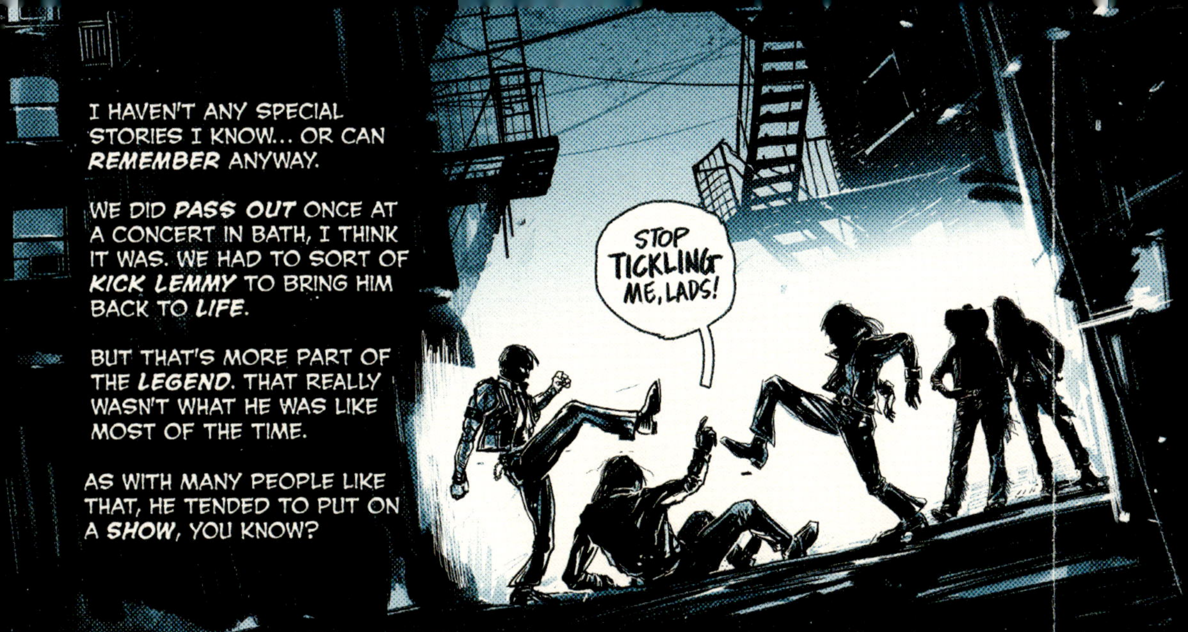
I HAVEN'T ANY SPECIAL STORIES I KNOW... OR CAN *REMEMBER* ANYWAY.
WE DID *PASS OUT* ONCE AT A CONCERT IN BATH, I THINK IT WAS. WE HAD TO SORT OF *KICK LEMMY* TO BRING HIM BACK TO *LIFE*.
BUT THAT'S MORE PART OF THE *LEGEND*. THAT REALLY WASN'T WHAT HE WAS LIKE MOST OF THE TIME.
AS WITH MANY PEOPLE LIKE THAT, HE TENDED TO PUT ON A *SHOW*, YOU KNOW?
STOP TICKLING ME, LADS!

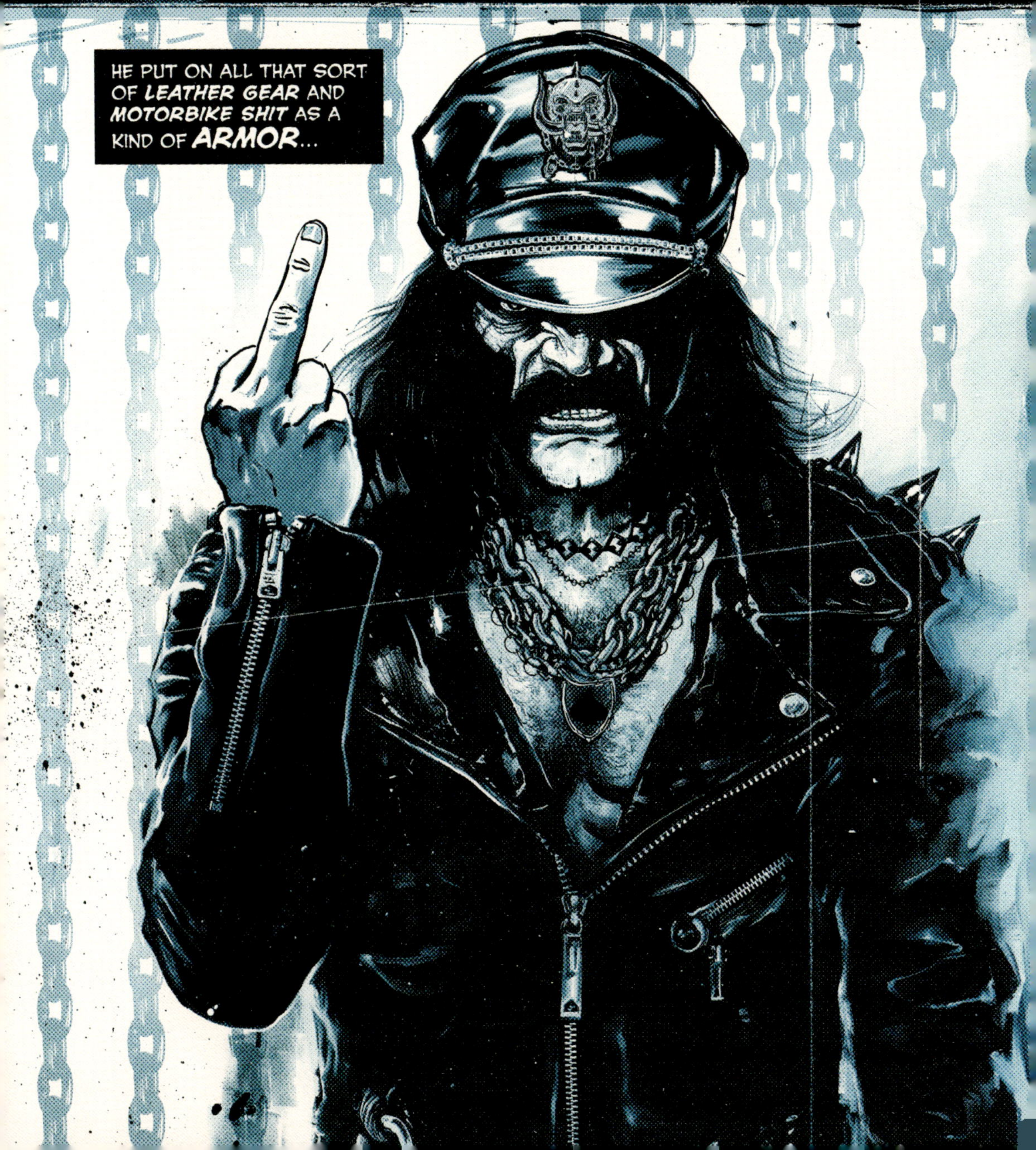
HE PUT ON ALL THAT SORT OF *LEATHER GEAR* AND *MOTORBIKE SHIT* AS A KIND OF *ARMOR*...

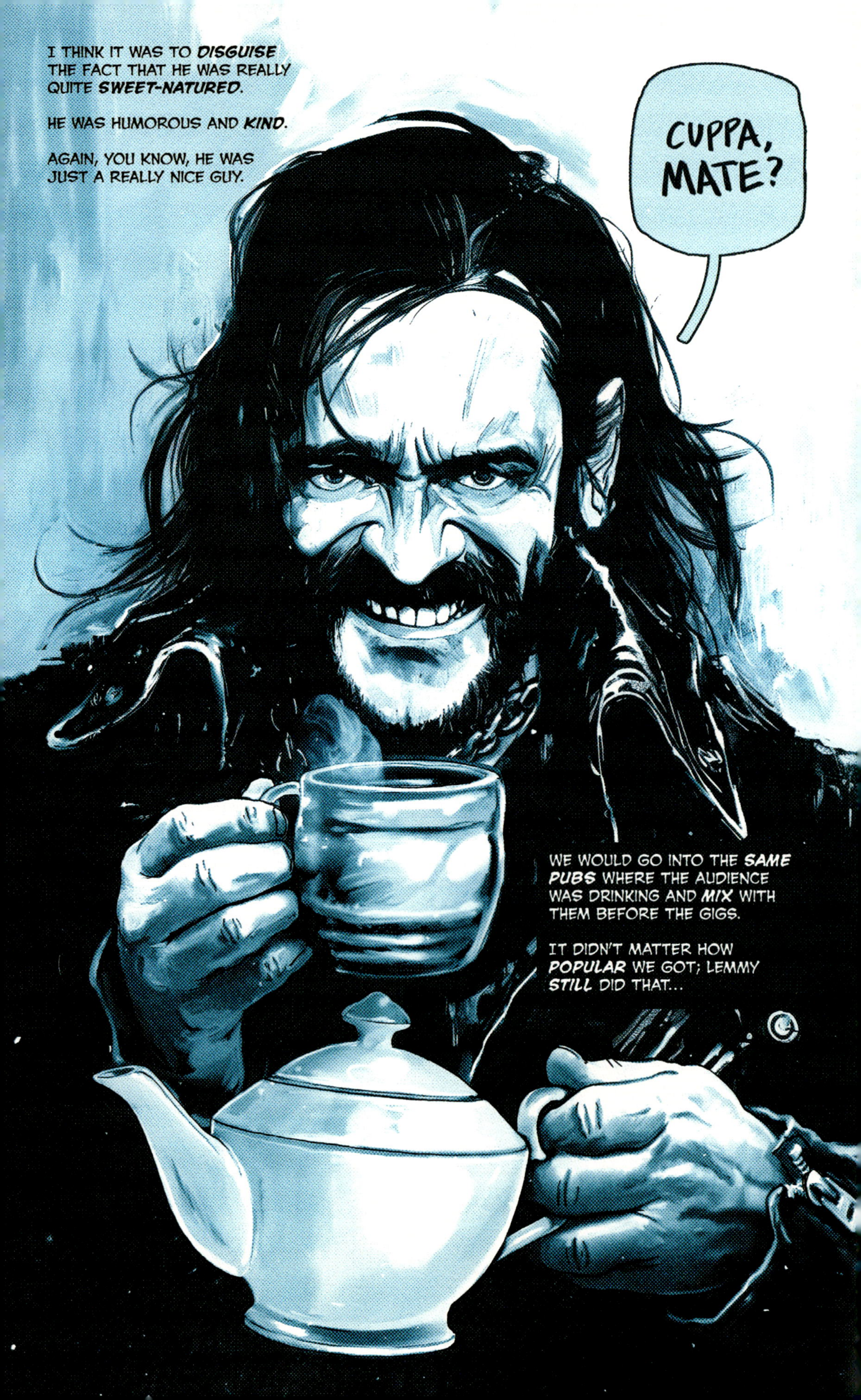
I THINK IT WAS TO DISGUISE THE FACT THAT HE WAS REALLY QUITE SWEET-NATURED.
HE WAS HUMOROUS AND KIND.
AGAIN, YOU KNOW, HE WAS JUST A REALLY NICE GUY.
CUPPA, MATE?
WE WOULD GO INTO THE SAME PUBS WHERE THE AUDIENCE WAS DRINKING AND MIX WITH THEM BEFORE THE GIGS.
IT DIDN'T MATTER HOW POPULAR WE GOT; LEMMY STILL DID THAT...

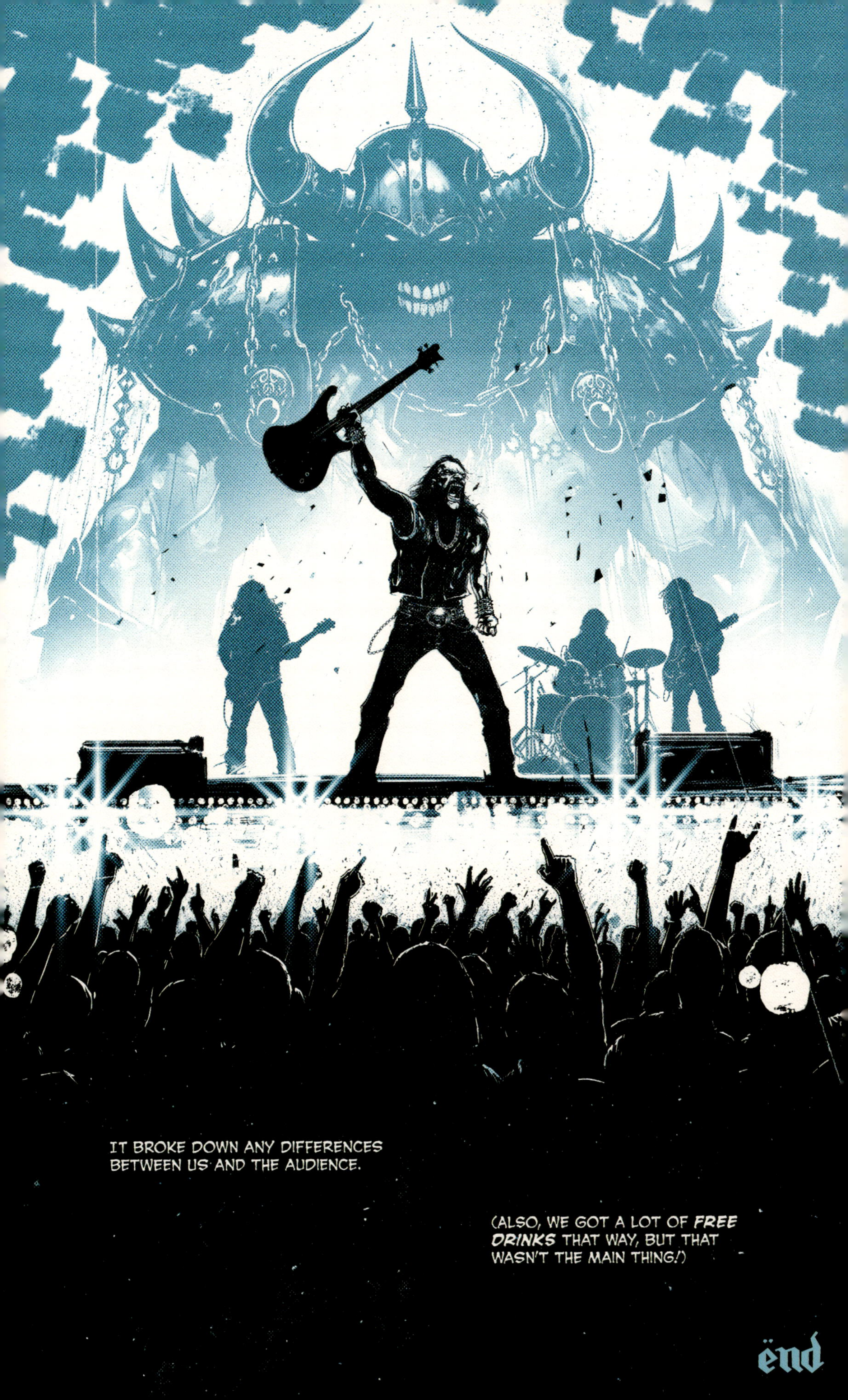
IT BROKE DOWN ANY DIFFERENCES BETWEEN US AND THE AUDIENCE.
(ALSO, WE GOT A LOT OF *FREE DRINKS* THAT WAY, BUT THAT WASN'T THE MAIN THING!)
ënd

"When I was 12, I went to see Hawkind. Lemmy was the only one that came outside and signed my program."

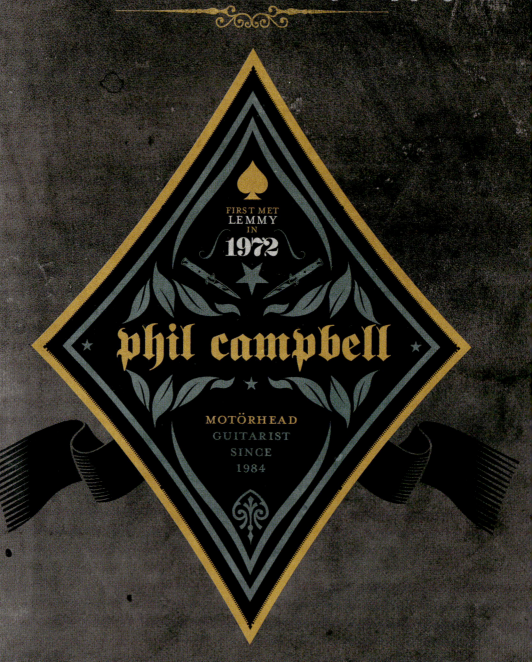

FIRST MET LEMMY IN 1972

phil campbell

MOTÖRHEAD GUITARIST SINCE 1984

STORY ILLUSTRATED BY JOHN BIVENS

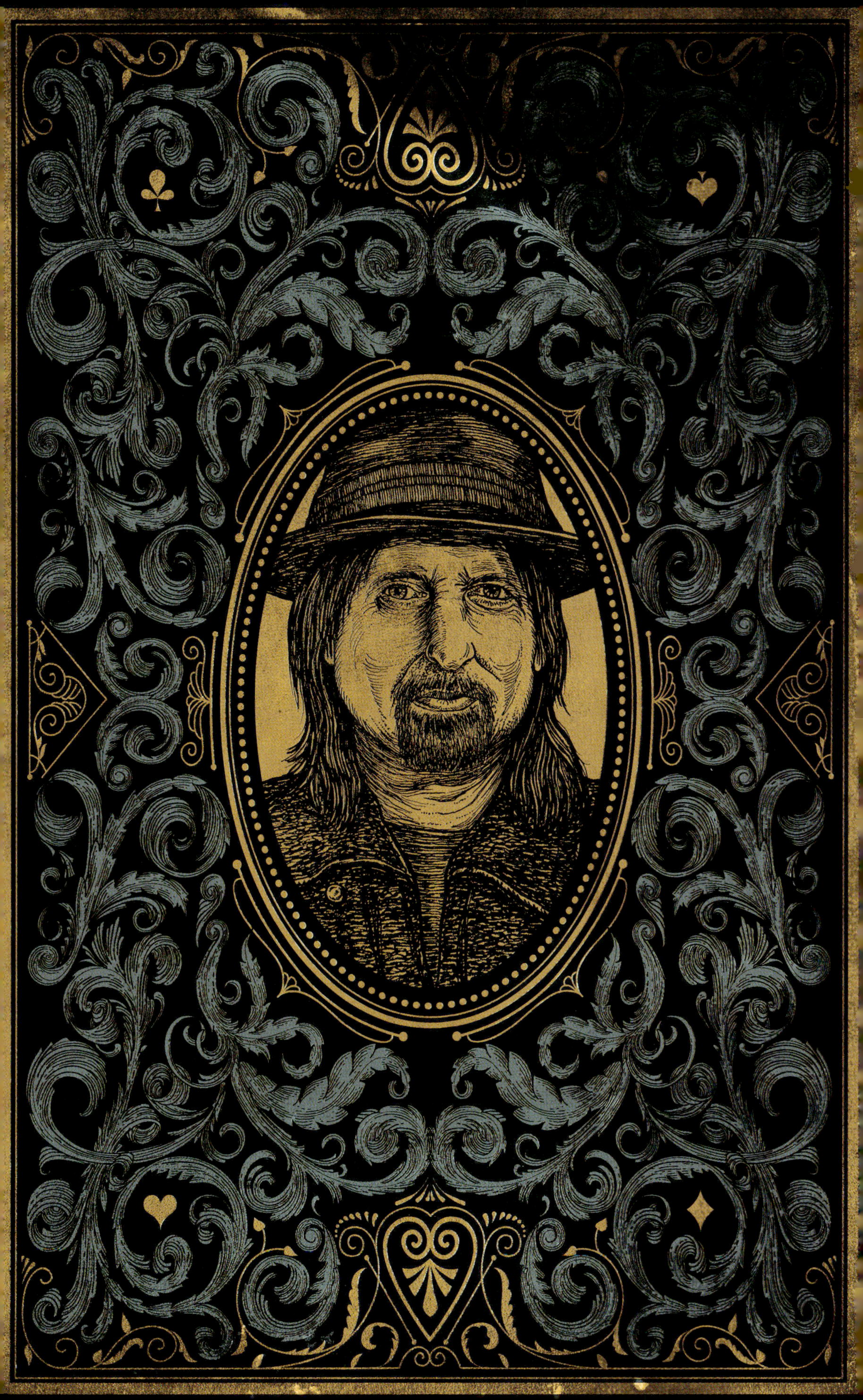

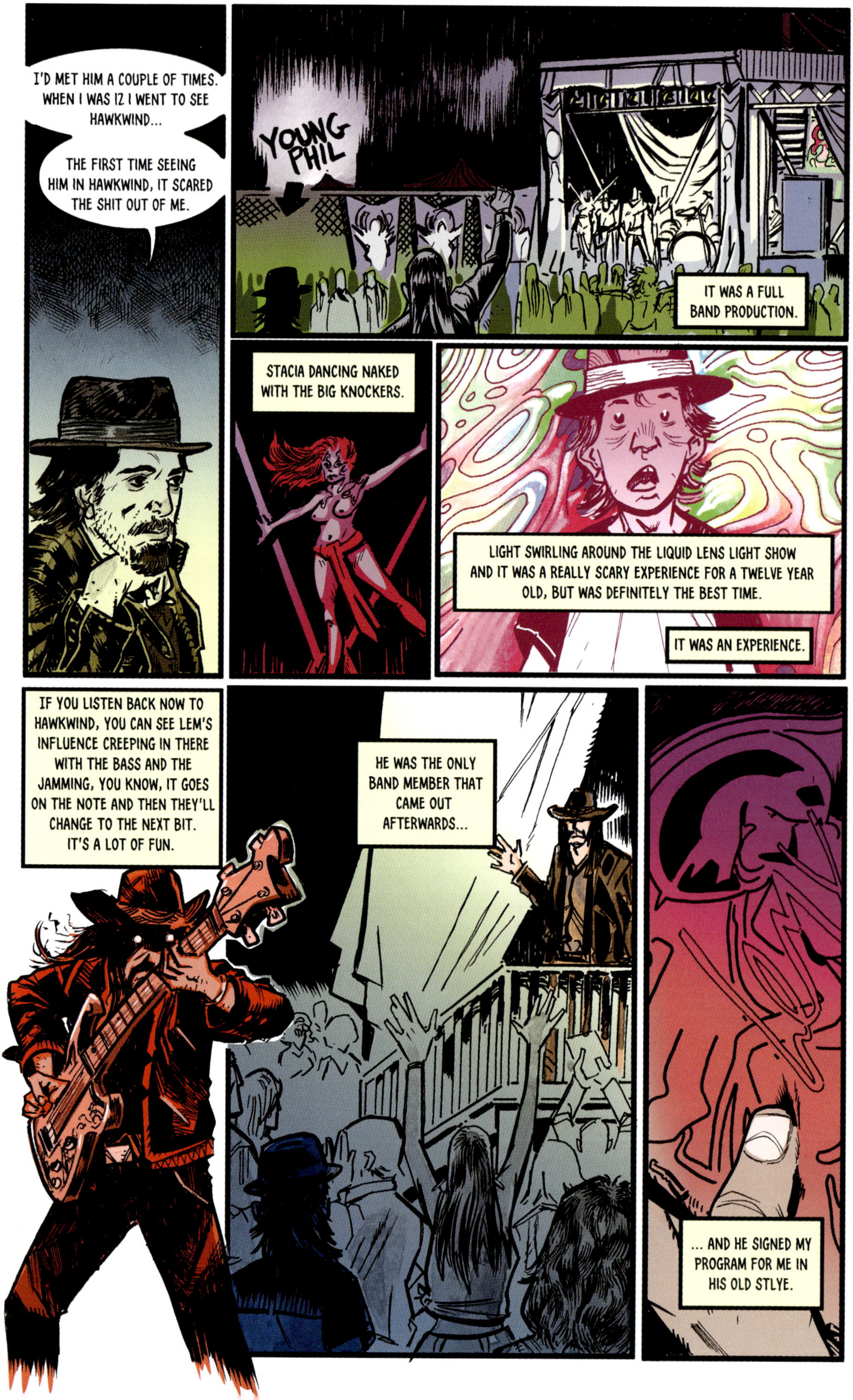

I'D MET HIM A COUPLE OF TIMES. WHEN I WAS 12 I WENT TO SEE HAWKWIND...
THE FIRST TIME SEEING HIM IN HAWKWIND, IT SCARED THE SHIT OUT OF ME.
YOUNG PHIL
IT WAS A FULL BAND PRODUCTION.
STACIA DANCING NAKED WITH THE BIG KNOCKERS.
LIGHT SWIRLING AROUND THE LIQUID LENS LIGHT SHOW AND IT WAS A REALLY SCARY EXPERIENCE FOR A TWELVE YEAR OLD, BUT WAS DEFINITELY THE BEST TIME.
IT WAS AN EXPERIENCE.
IF YOU LISTEN BACK NOW TO HAWKWIND, YOU CAN SEE LEM'S INFLUENCE CREEPING IN THERE WITH THE BASS AND THE JAMMING, YOU KNOW, IT GOES ON THE NOTE AND THEN THEY'LL CHANGE TO THE NEXT BIT. IT'S A LOT OF FUN.
HE WAS THE ONLY BAND MEMBER THAT CAME OUT AFTERWARDS...
... AND HE SIGNED MY PROGRAM FOR ME IN HIS OLD STLYE.

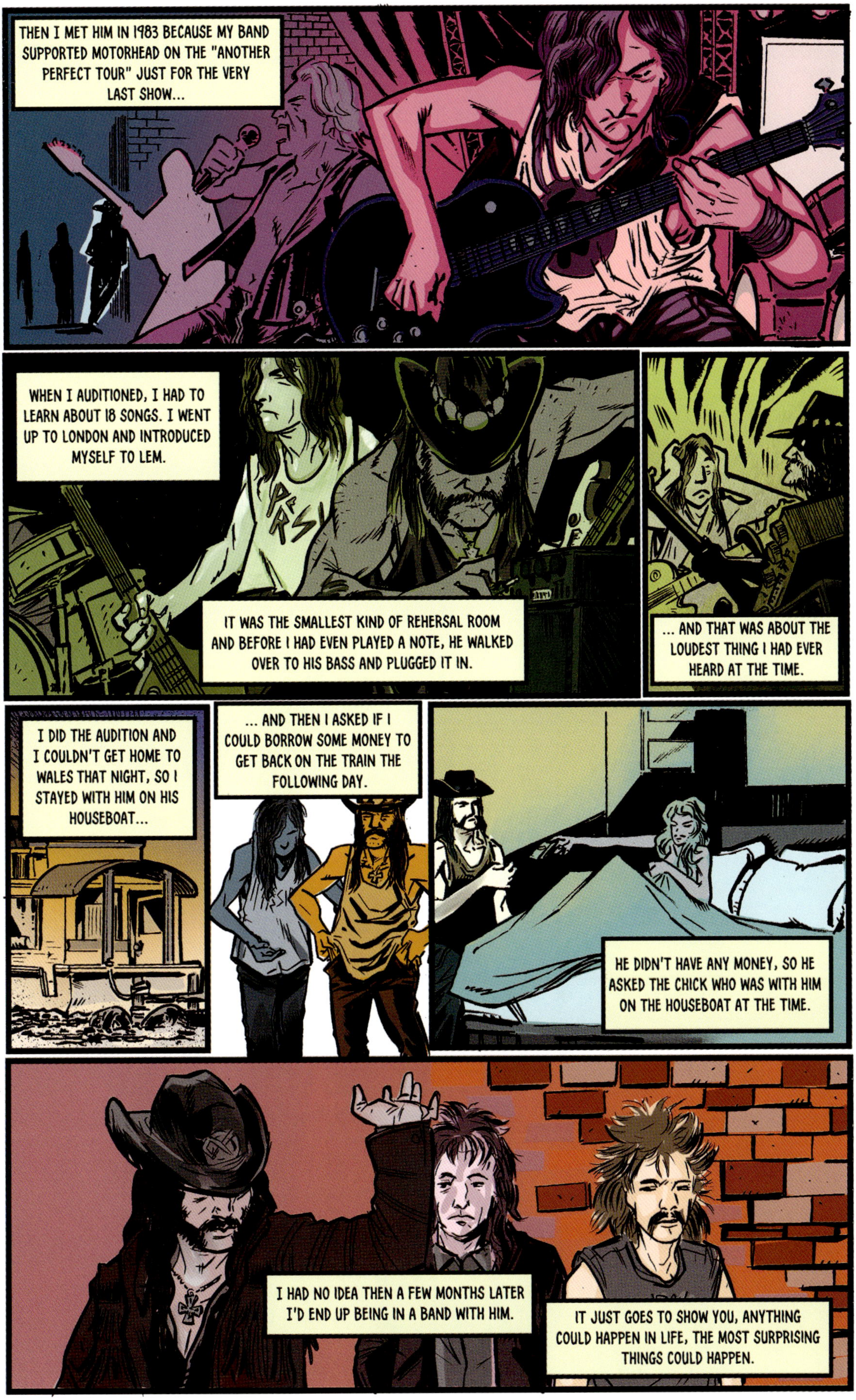
THEN I MET HIM IN 1983 BECAUSE MY BAND SUPPORTED MOTORHEAD ON THE "ANOTHER PERFECT TOUR" JUST FOR THE VERY LAST SHOW...
WHEN I AUDITIONED, I HAD TO LEARN ABOUT 18 SONGS. I WENT UP TO LONDON AND INTRODUCED MYSELF TO LEM.
IT WAS THE SMALLEST KIND OF REHERSAL ROOM AND BEFORE I HAD EVEN PLAYED A NOTE, HE WALKED OVER TO HIS BASS AND PLUGGED IT IN.
... AND THAT WAS ABOUT THE LOUDEST THING I HAD EVER HEARD AT THE TIME.
I DID THE AUDITION AND I COULDN'T GET HOME TO WALES THAT NIGHT, SO I STAYED WITH HIM ON HIS HOUSEBOAT...
... AND THEN I ASKED IF I COULD BORROW SOME MONEY TO GET BACK ON THE TRAIN THE FOLLOWING DAY.
HE DIDN'T HAVE ANY MONEY, SO HE ASKED THE CHICK WHO WAS WITH HIM ON THE HOUSEBOAT AT THE TIME.
I HAD NO IDEA THEN A FEW MONTHS LATER I'D END UP BEING IN A BAND WITH HIM.
IT JUST GOES TO SHOW YOU, ANYTHING COULD HAPPEN IN LIFE, THE MOST SURPRISING THINGS COULD HAPPEN.

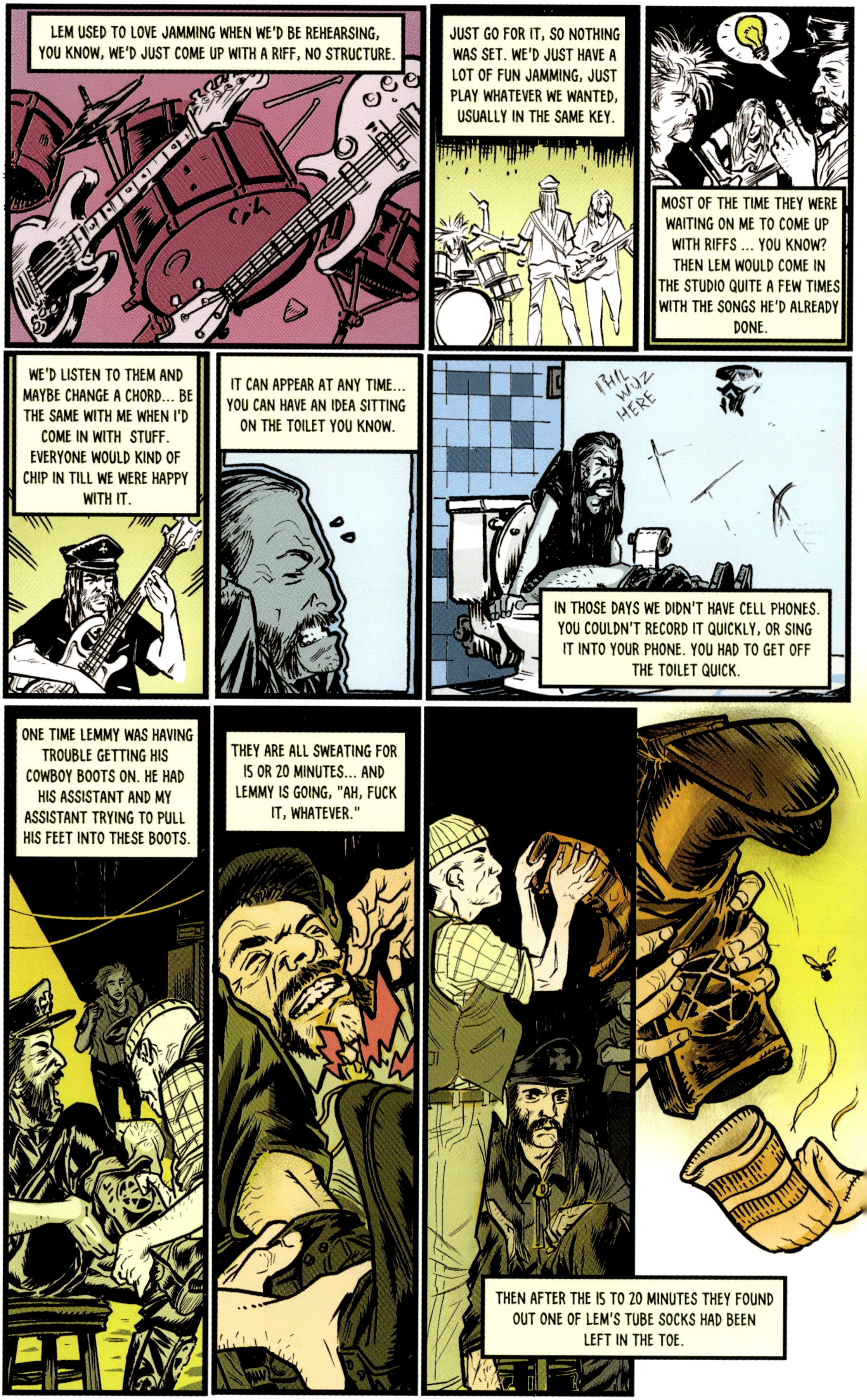
LEM USED TO LOVE JAMMING WHEN WE'D BE REHEARSING, YOU KNOW, WE'D JUST COME UP WITH A RIFF, NO STRUCTURE.
JUST GO FOR IT, SO NOTHING WAS SET. WE'D JUST HAVE A LOT OF FUN JAMMING, JUST PLAY WHATEVER WE WANTED, USUALLY IN THE SAME KEY.
MOST OF THE TIME THEY WERE WAITING ON ME TO COME UP WITH RIFFS ... YOU KNOW? THEN LEM WOULD COME IN THE STUDIO QUITE A FEW TIMES WITH THE SONGS HE'D ALREADY DONE.
WE'D LISTEN TO THEM AND MAYBE CHANGE A CHORD... BE THE SAME WITH ME WHEN I'D COME IN WITH STUFF. EVERYONE WOULD KIND OF CHIP IN TILL WE WERE HAPPY WITH IT.
IT CAN APPEAR AT ANY TIME... YOU CAN HAVE AN IDEA SITTING ON THE TOILET YOU KNOW.
PHIL WUZ HERE
IN THOSE DAYS WE DIDN'T HAVE CELL PHONES. YOU COULDN'T RECORD IT QUICKLY, OR SING IT INTO YOUR PHONE. YOU HAD TO GET OFF THE TOILET QUICK.
ONE TIME LEMMY WAS HAVING TROUBLE GETTING HIS COWBOY BOOTS ON. HE HAD HIS ASSISTANT AND MY ASSISTANT TRYING TO PULL HIS FEET INTO THESE BOOTS.
THEY ARE ALL SWEATING FOR 15 OR 20 MINUTES... AND LEMMY IS GOING, "AH, FUCK IT, WHATEVER."
THEN AFTER THE 15 TO 20 MINUTES THEY FOUND OUT ONE OF LEM'S TUBE SOCKS HAD BEEN LEFT IN THE TOE.

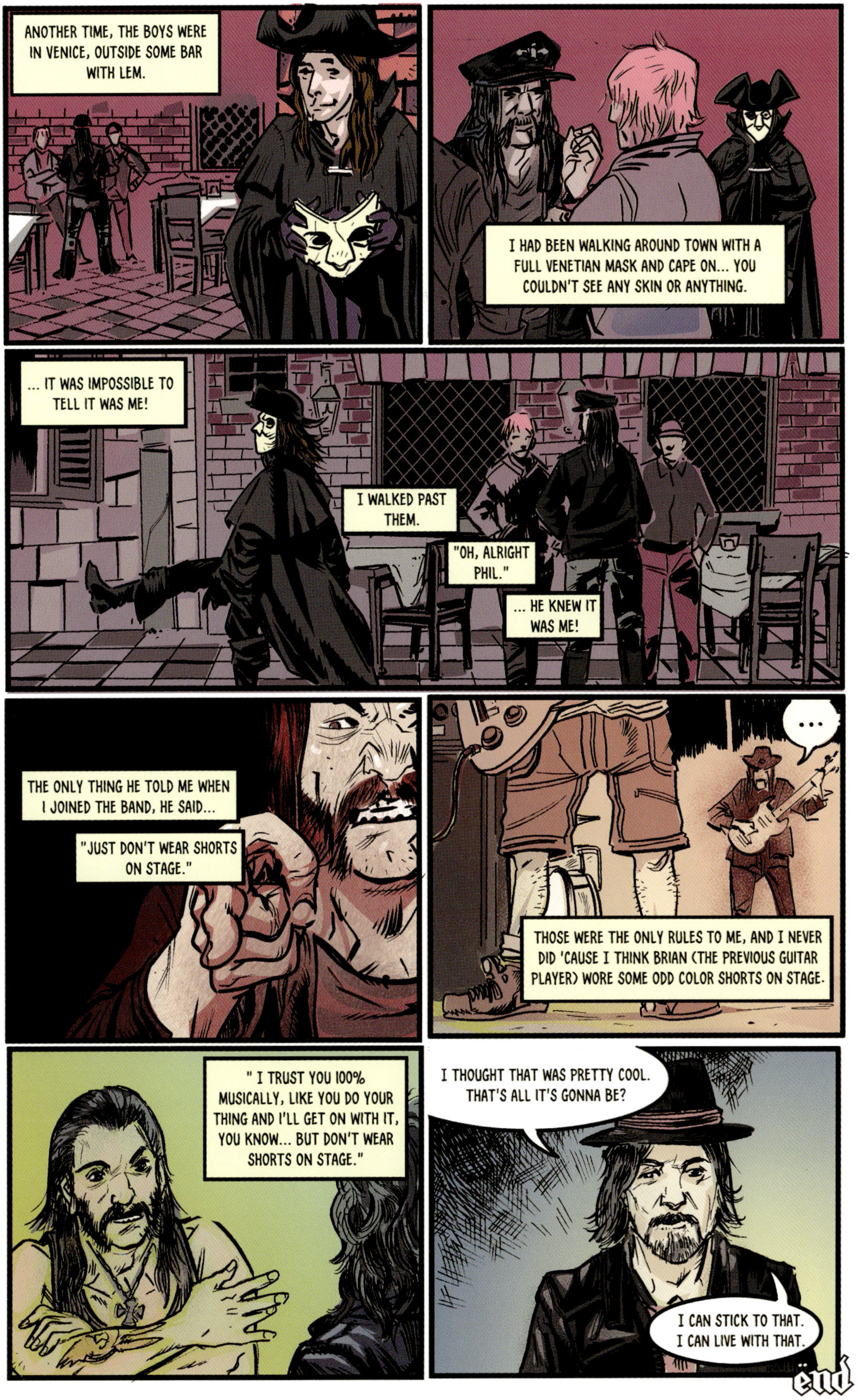
ANOTHER TIME, THE BOYS WERE IN VENICE, OUTSIDE SOME BAR WITH LEM.
I HAD BEEN WALKING AROUND TOWN WITH A FULL VENETIAN MASK AND CAPE ON... YOU COULDN'T SEE ANY SKIN OR ANYTHING.
... IT WAS IMPOSSIBLE TO TELL IT WAS ME!
I WALKED PAST THEM.
"OH, ALRIGHT PHIL."
... HE KNEW IT WAS ME!
THE ONLY THING HE TOLD ME WHEN I JOINED THE BAND, HE SAID...
"JUST DON'T WEAR SHORTS ON STAGE."
...
THOSE WERE THE ONLY RULES TO ME, AND I NEVER DID 'CAUSE I THINK BRIAN (THE PREVIOUS GUITAR PLAYER) WORE SOME ODD COLOR SHORTS ON STAGE.
" I TRUST YOU 100% MUSICALLY, LIKE YOU DO YOUR THING AND I'LL GET ON WITH IT, YOU KNOW... BUT DON'T WEAR SHORTS ON STAGE."
I THOUGHT THAT WAS PRETTY COOL. THAT'S ALL IT'S GONNA BE?
I CAN STICK TO THAT. I CAN LIVE WITH THAT.
end

"Lemmy was very instrumental in my history. Without him, the Pretenders wouldn't have happened."

FIRST MET LEMMY IN 1976

chrissie hynde

FOUNDER
SINGER/GUITARIST
THE PRETENDERS

STORY ILLUSTRATED BY CHRIS VISIONS

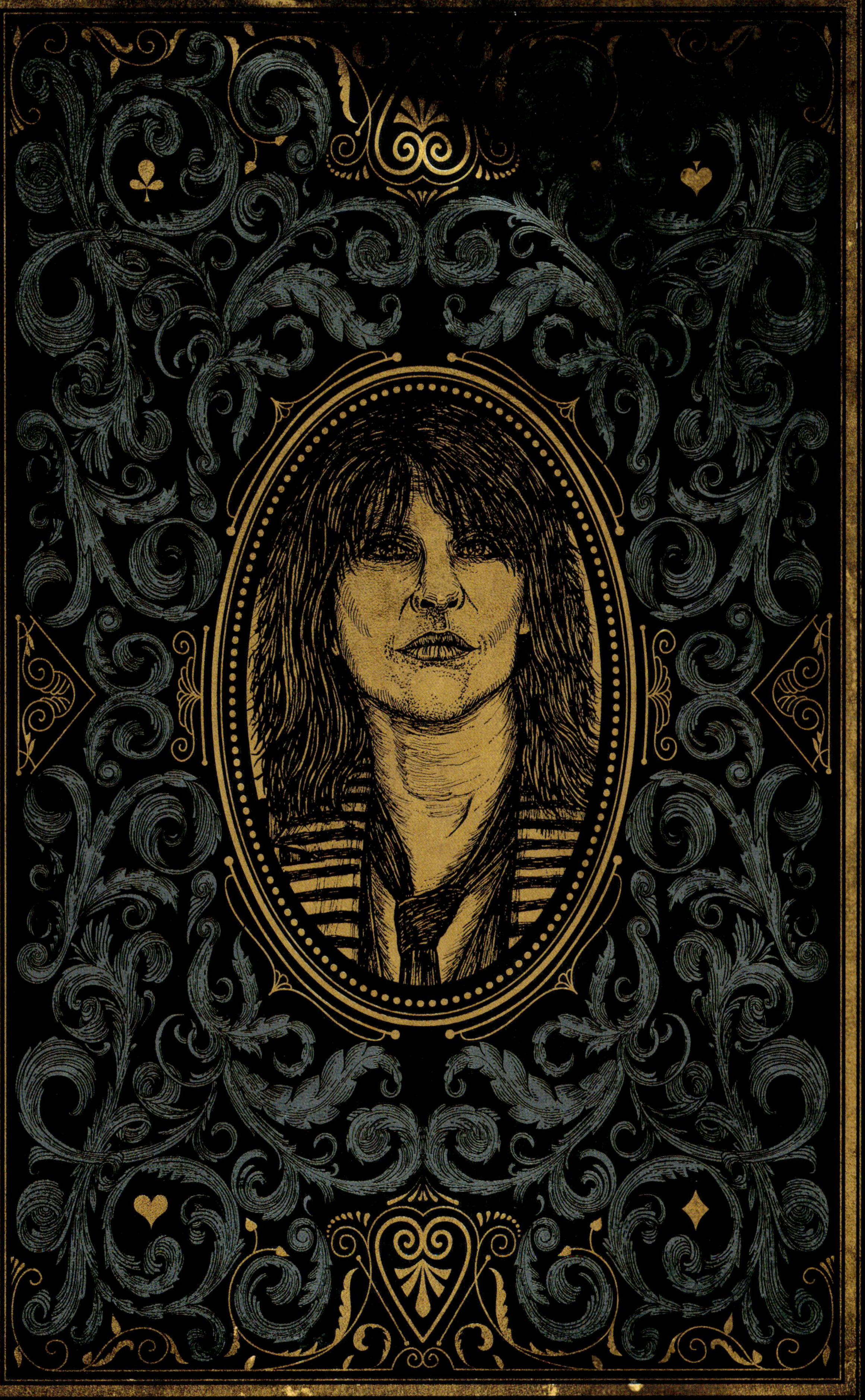

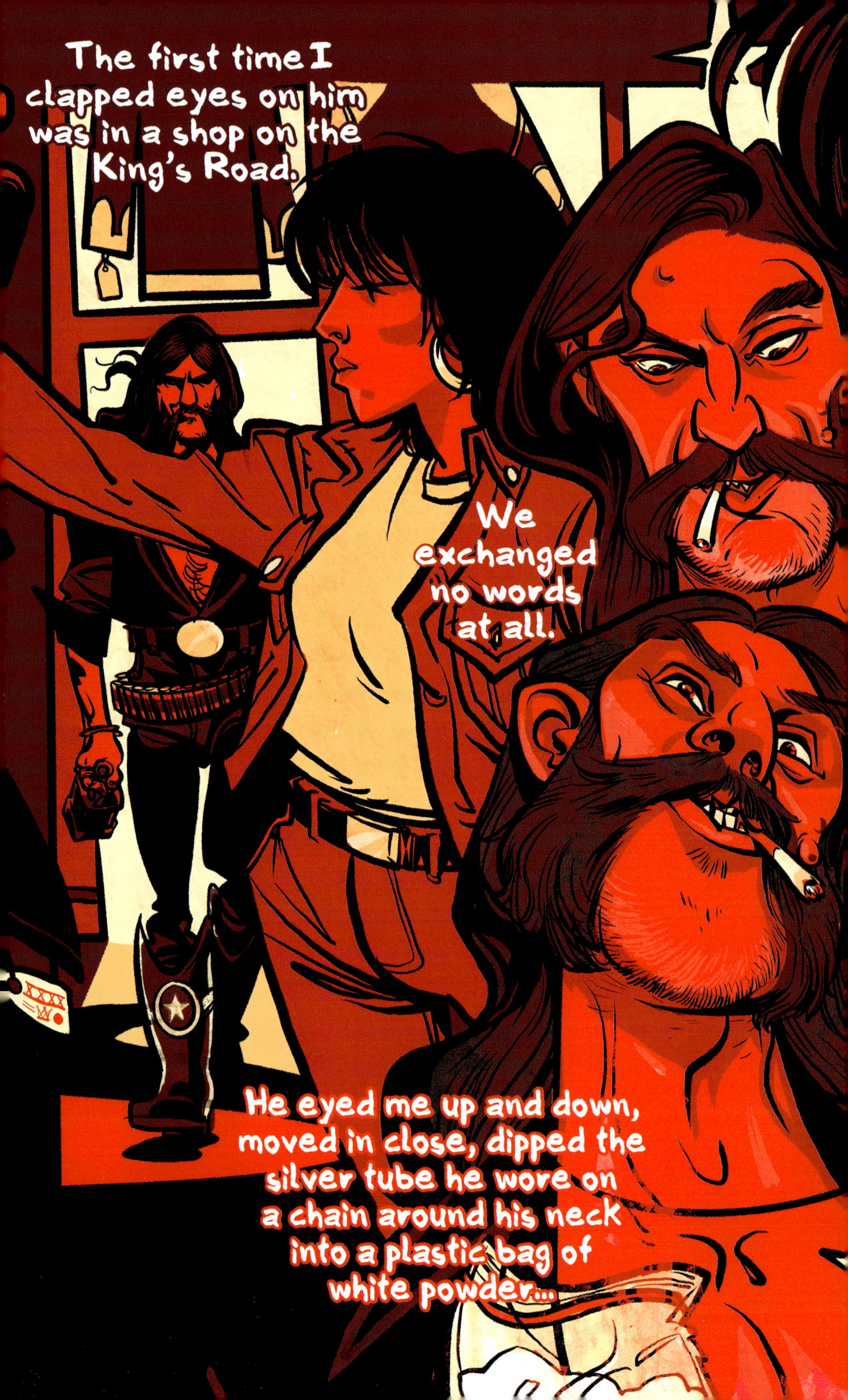
The first time I clapped eyes on him was in a shop on the King's Road.
We exchanged no words at all.
He eyed me up and down, moved in close, dipped the silver tube he wore on a chain around his neck into a plastic bag of white powder...

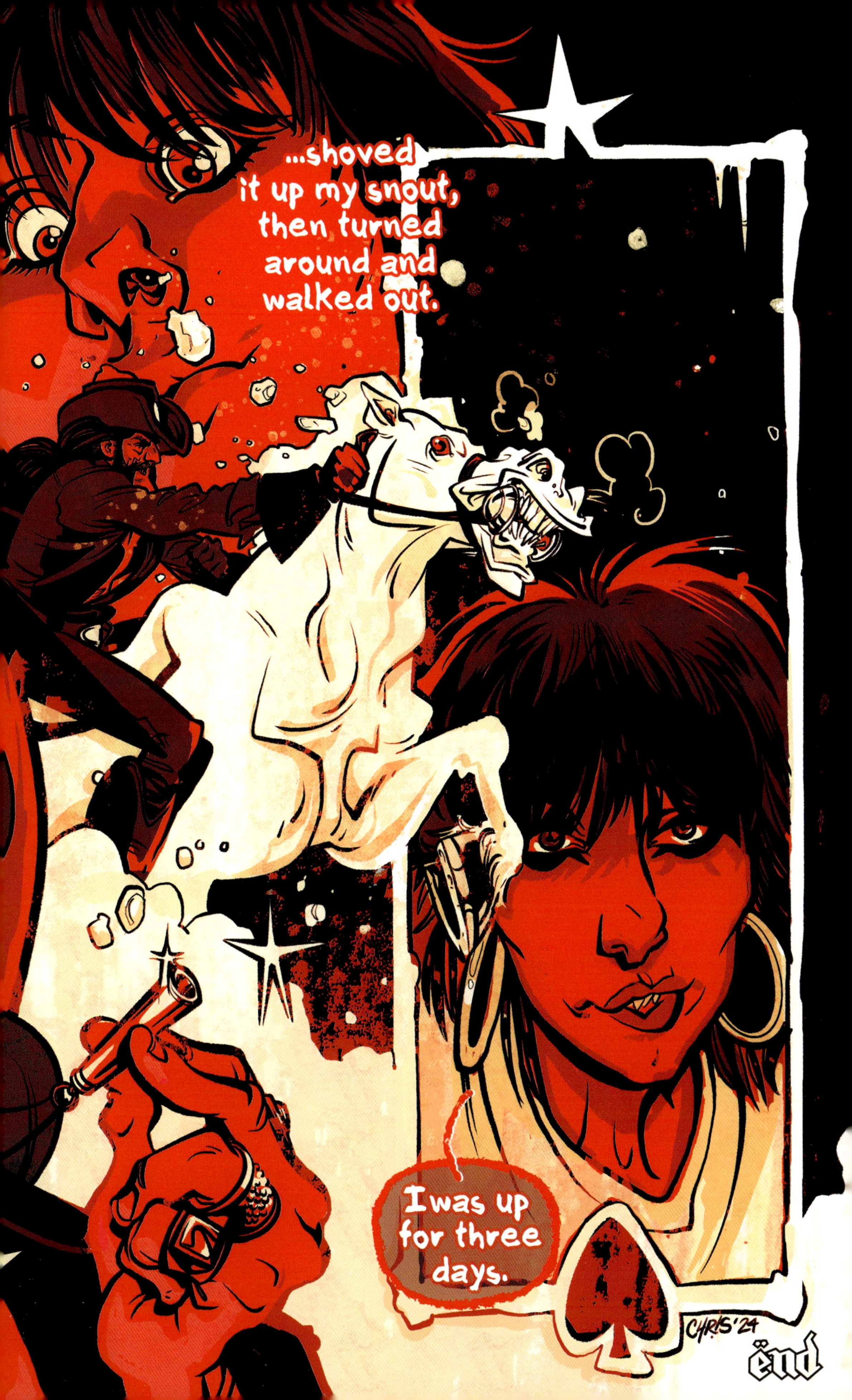
...shoved it up my snout, then turned around and walked out.
I was up for three days.
CHRIS '24
end

"Girlschool would get back from tour, and there'd be all these little postcards sent to us from Lemmy."

FIRST MET
LEMMY
IN
1978

kim mcauliffe

FOUNDER +
LEAD SINGER
GIRLSCHOOL

STORY ILLUSTRATED BY FRED HARPER

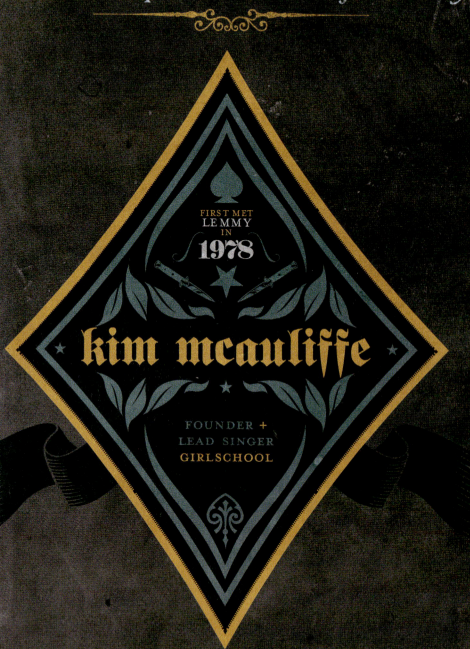

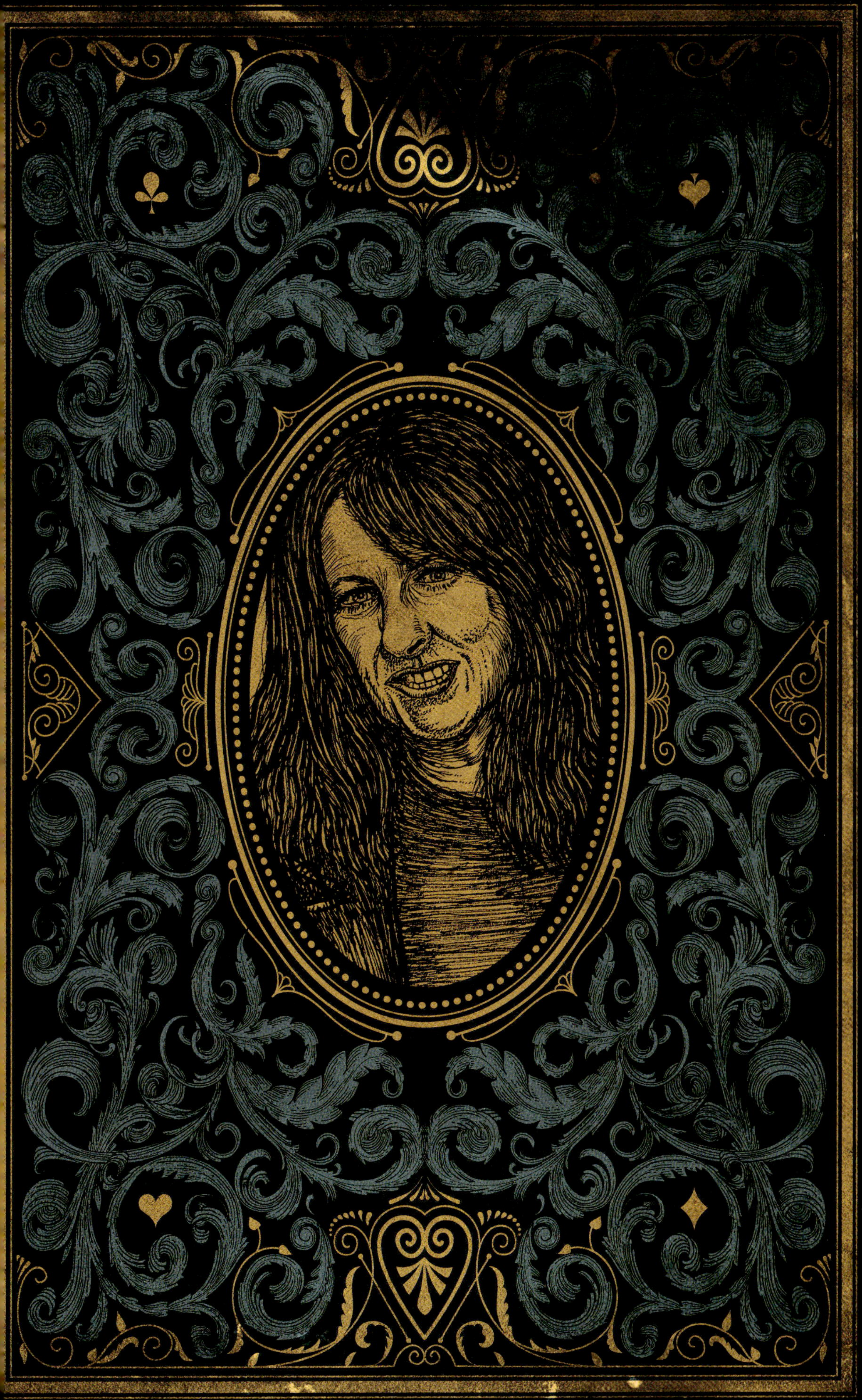

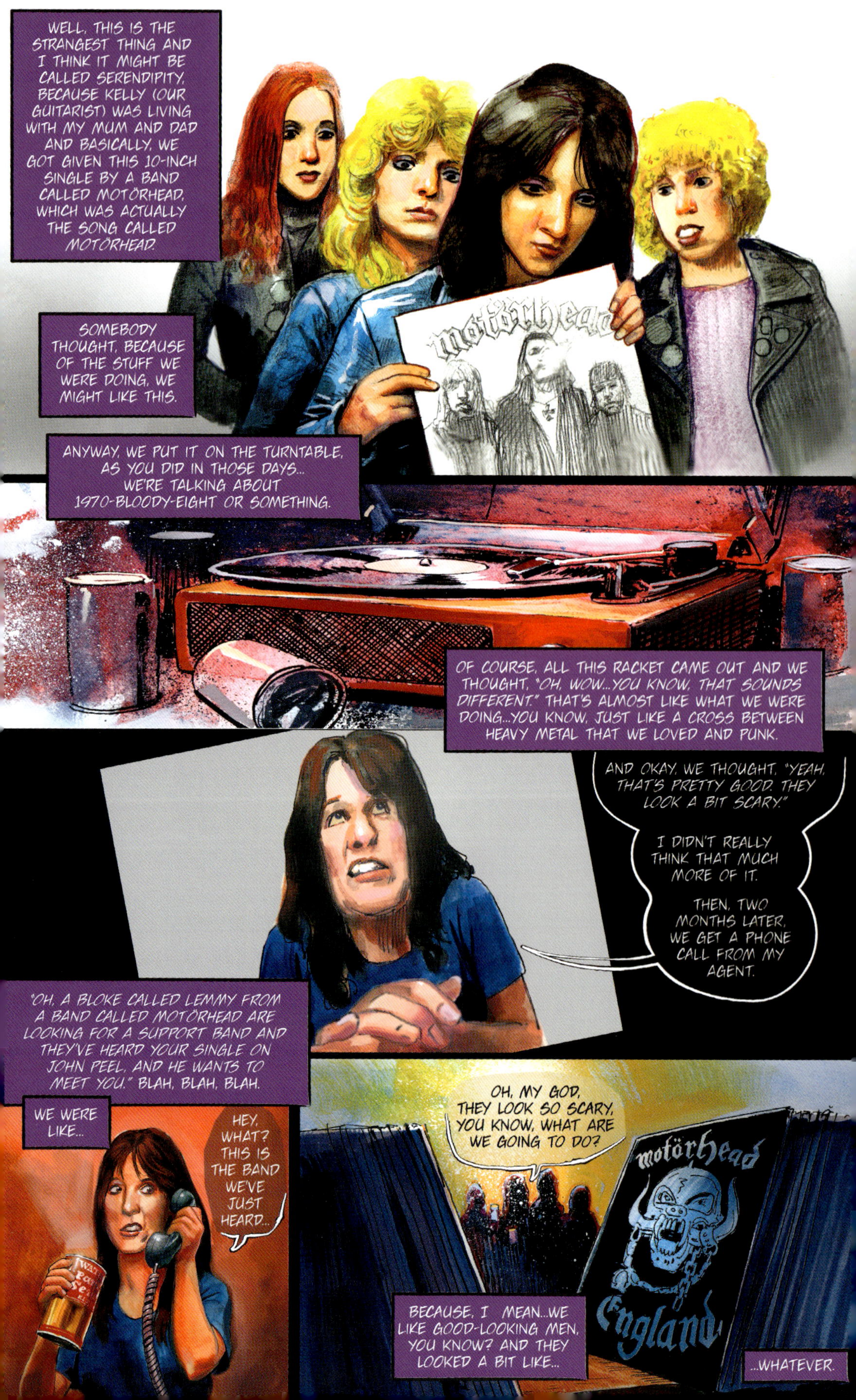
WELL, THIS IS THE STRANGEST THING AND I THINK IT MIGHT BE CALLED SERENDIPITY, BECAUSE KELLY (OUR GUITARIST) WAS LIVING WITH MY MUM AND DAD AND BASICALLY, WE GOT GIVEN THIS 10-INCH SINGLE BY A BAND CALLED MOTÖRHEAD, WHICH WAS ACTUALLY THE SONG CALLED MOTÖRHEAD.
SOMEBODY THOUGHT, BECAUSE OF THE STUFF WE WERE DOING, WE MIGHT LIKE THIS.
motörhead
ANYWAY, WE PUT IT ON THE TURNTABLE, AS YOU DID IN THOSE DAYS... WE'RE TALKING ABOUT 1970-BLOODY-EIGHT OR SOMETHING.
OF COURSE, ALL THIS RACKET CAME OUT AND WE THOUGHT, "OH, WOW...YOU KNOW, THAT SOUNDS DIFFERENT." THAT'S ALMOST LIKE WHAT WE WERE DOING...YOU KNOW, JUST LIKE A CROSS BETWEEN HEAVY METAL THAT WE LOVED AND PUNK.
AND OKAY, WE THOUGHT, "YEAH, THAT'S PRETTY GOOD. THEY LOOK A BIT SCARY."
I DIDN'T REALLY THINK THAT MUCH MORE OF IT.
THEN, TWO MONTHS LATER, WE GET A PHONE CALL FROM MY AGENT.
"OH, A BLOKE CALLED LEMMY FROM A BAND CALLED MOTÖRHEAD ARE LOOKING FOR A SUPPORT BAND AND THEY'VE HEARD YOUR SINGLE ON JOHN PEEL, AND HE WANTS TO MEET YOU." BLAH, BLAH, BLAH.
WE WERE LIKE...
HEY, WHAT? THIS IS THE BAND WE'VE JUST HEARD...
OH, MY GOD, THEY LOOK SO SCARY, YOU KNOW, WHAT ARE WE GOING TO DO?
motörhead
England
BECAUSE, I MEAN...WE LIKE GOOD-LOOKING MEN, YOU KNOW? AND THEY LOOKED A BIT LIKE...
...WHATEVER.

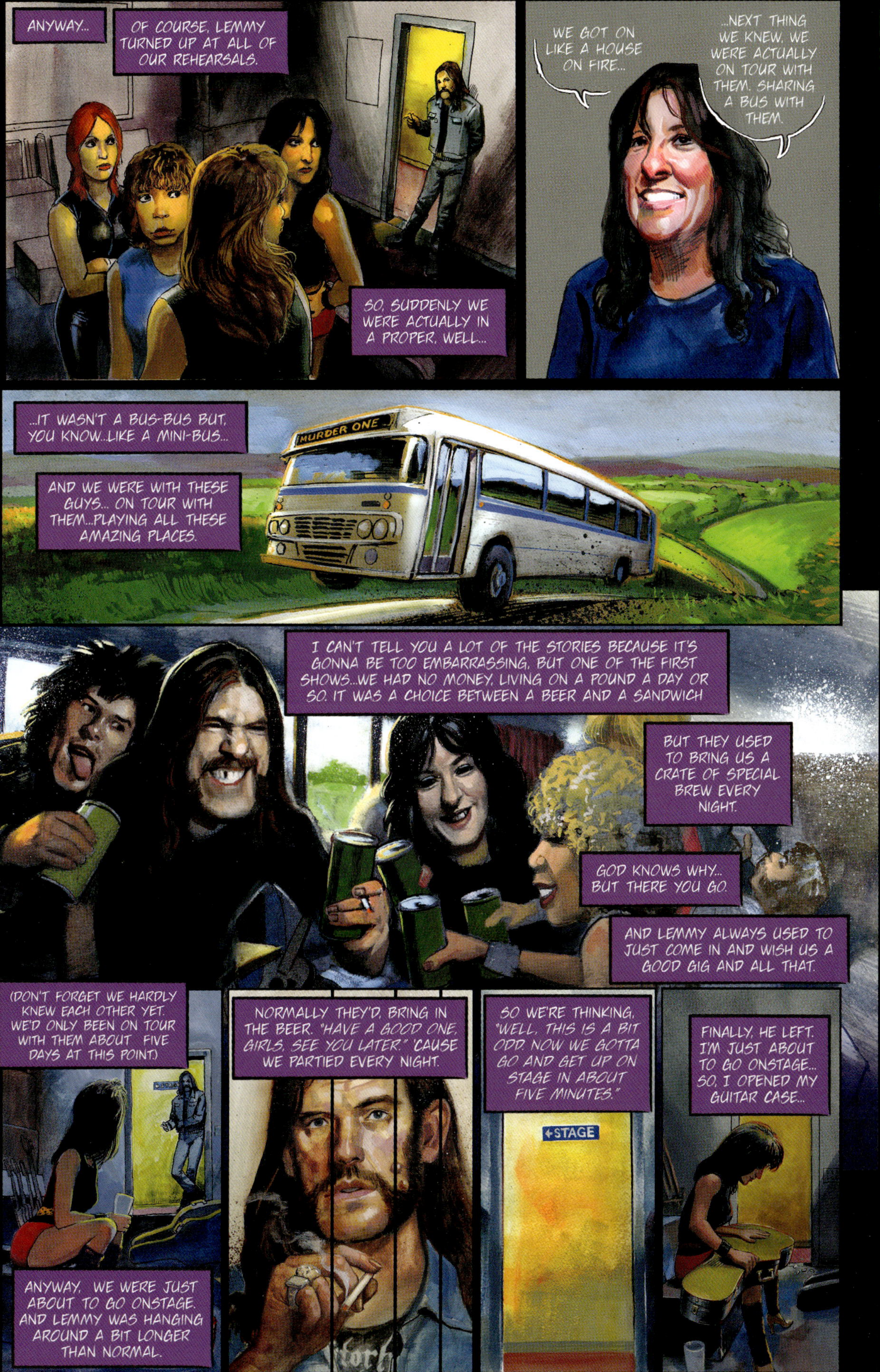
ANYWAY...
OF COURSE, LEMMY TURNED UP AT ALL OF OUR REHEARSALS.
SO, SUDDENLY WE WERE ACTUALLY IN A PROPER, WELL...
WE GOT ON LIKE A HOUSE ON FIRE...
...NEXT THING WE KNEW, WE WERE ACTUALLY ON TOUR WITH THEM, SHARING A BUS WITH THEM.
...IT WASN'T A BUS-BUS BUT, YOU KNOW...LIKE A MINI-BUS...
MURDER ONE
AND WE WERE WITH THESE GUYS... ON TOUR WITH THEM...PLAYING ALL THESE AMAZING PLACES.
I CAN'T TELL YOU A LOT OF THE STORIES BECAUSE IT'S GONNA BE TOO EMBARRASSING, BUT ONE OF THE FIRST SHOWS...WE HAD NO MONEY, LIVING ON A POUND A DAY OR SO. IT WAS A CHOICE BETWEEN A BEER AND A SANDWICH
BUT THEY USED TO BRING US A CRATE OF SPECIAL BREW EVERY NIGHT.
GOD KNOWS WHY... BUT THERE YOU GO.
AND LEMMY ALWAYS USED TO JUST COME IN AND WISH US A GOOD GIG AND ALL THAT.
(DON'T FORGET WE HARDLY KNEW EACH OTHER YET. WE'D ONLY BEEN ON TOUR WITH THEM ABOUT FIVE DAYS AT THIS POINT.)
ANYWAY, WE WERE JUST ABOUT TO GO ONSTAGE. AND LEMMY WAS HANGING AROUND A BIT LONGER THAN NORMAL.
NORMALLY THEY'D, BRING IN THE BEER. "HAVE A GOOD ONE, GIRLS. SEE YOU LATER." 'CAUSE WE PARTIED EVERY NIGHT.
SO WE'RE THINKING, "WELL, THIS IS A BIT ODD. NOW WE GOTTA GO AND GET UP ON STAGE IN ABOUT FIVE MINUTES."
STAGE
FINALLY, HE LEFT. I'M JUST ABOUT TO GO ONSTAGE... SO, I OPENED MY GUITAR CASE...

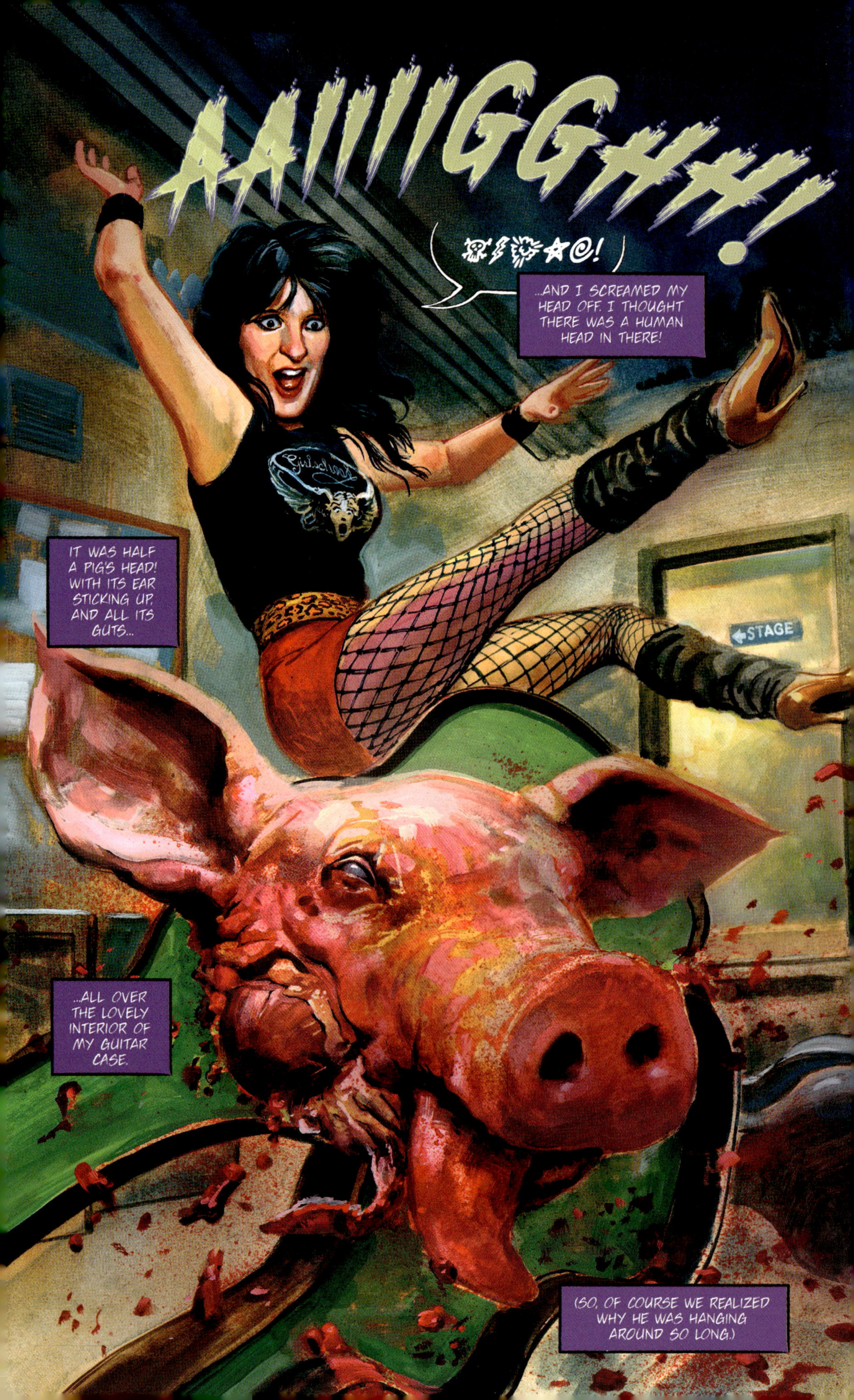
AAIIIIGGHH!
...AND I SCREAMED MY HEAD OFF. I THOUGHT THERE WAS A HUMAN HEAD IN THERE!
IT WAS HALF A PIG'S HEAD! WITH ITS EAR STICKING UP, AND ALL ITS GUTS...
STAGE
...ALL OVER THE LOVELY INTERIOR OF MY GUITAR CASE.
(SO, OF COURSE WE REALIZED WHY HE WAS HANGING AROUND SO LONG.)

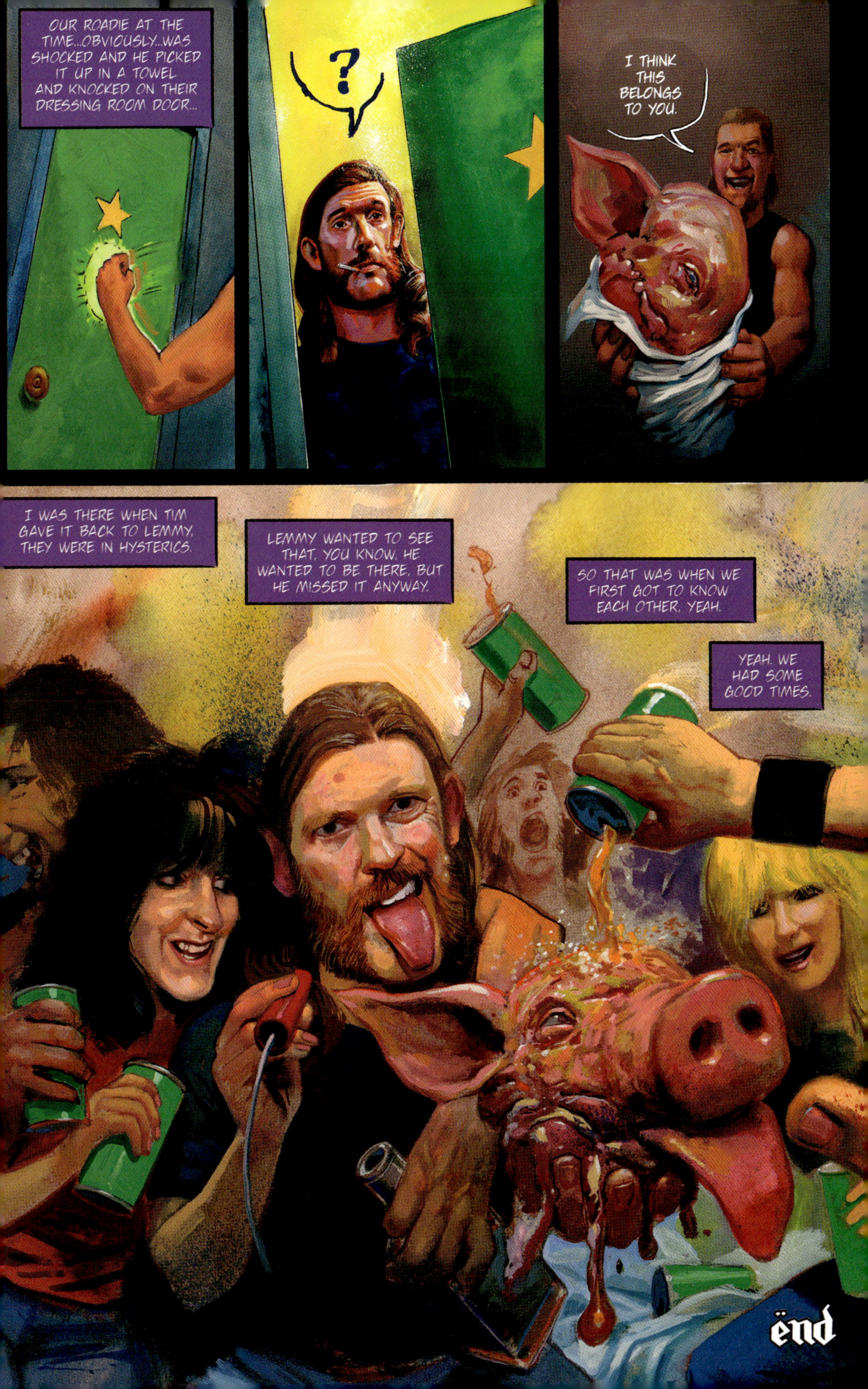
OUR ROADIE AT THE TIME...OBVIOUSLY...WAS SHOCKED AND HE PICKED IT UP IN A TOWEL AND KNOCKED ON THEIR DRESSING ROOM DOOR...
?
I THINK THIS BELONGS TO YOU.
I WAS THERE WHEN TIM GAVE IT BACK TO LEMMY. THEY WERE IN HYSTERICS.
LEMMY WANTED TO SEE THAT, YOU KNOW. HE WANTED TO BE THERE, BUT HE MISSED IT ANYWAY.
SO THAT WAS WHEN WE FIRST GOT TO KNOW EACH OTHER, YEAH.
YEAH. WE HAD SOME GOOD TIMES.
ënd

I never saw him being rude, I never saw him impatient, I never saw him wasted, He was a polite, English gentleman."

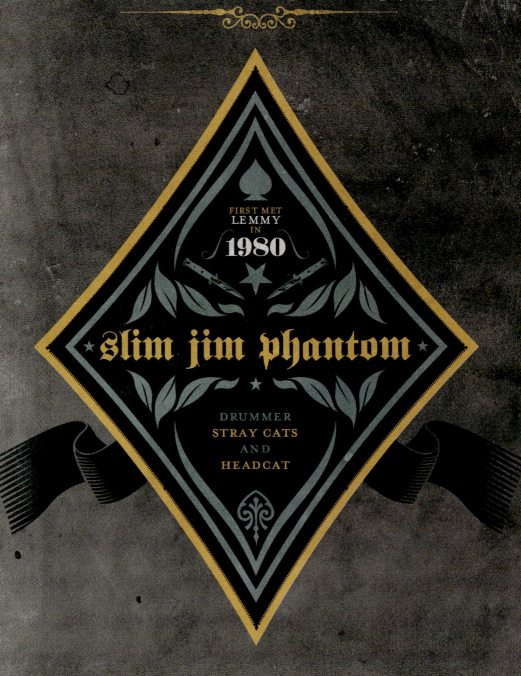

FIRST MET LEMMY IN 1980

slim jim phantom

DRUMMER STRAY CATS AND HEADCAT

STORY ILLUSTRATED BY BOB FINGERMAN

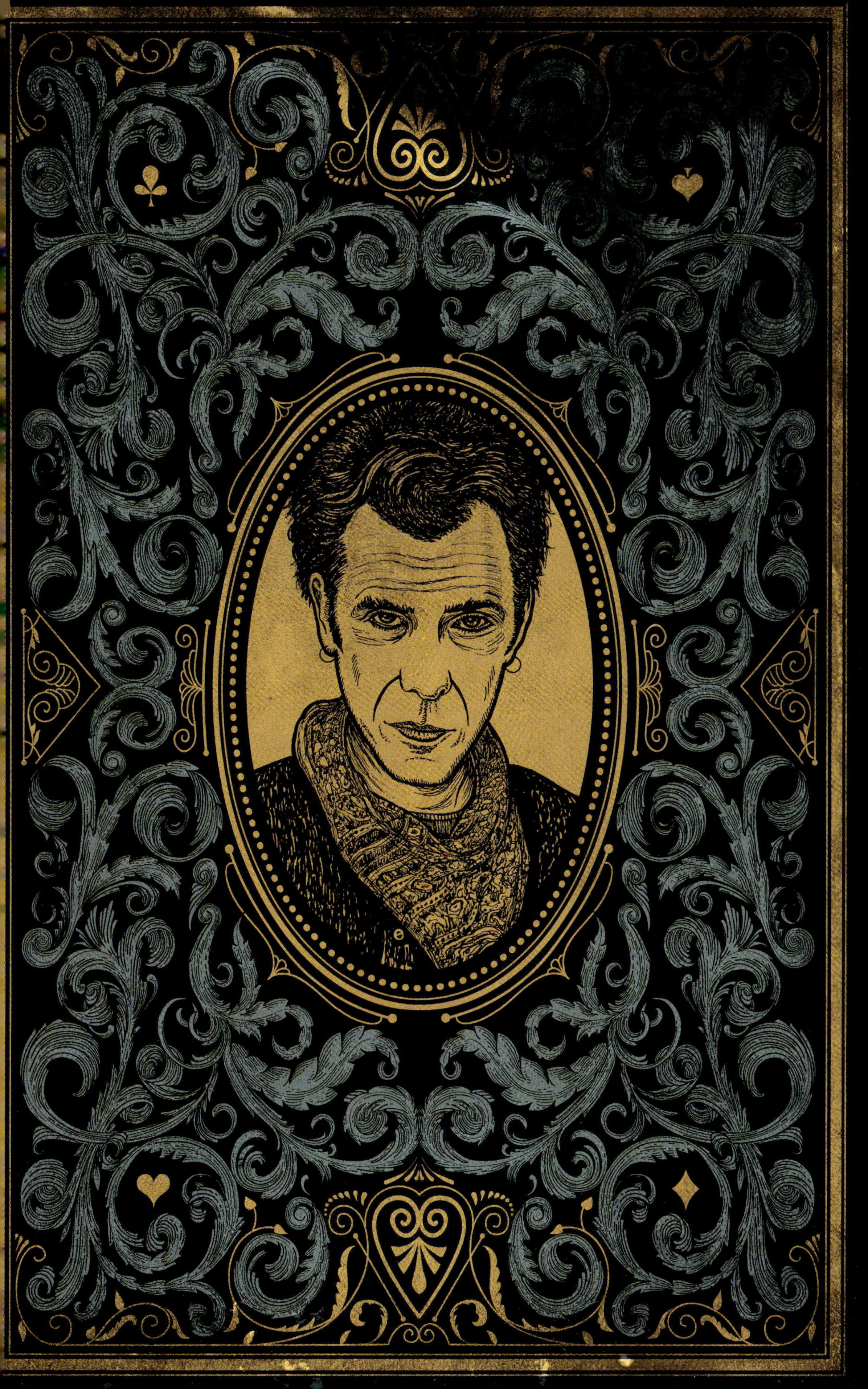

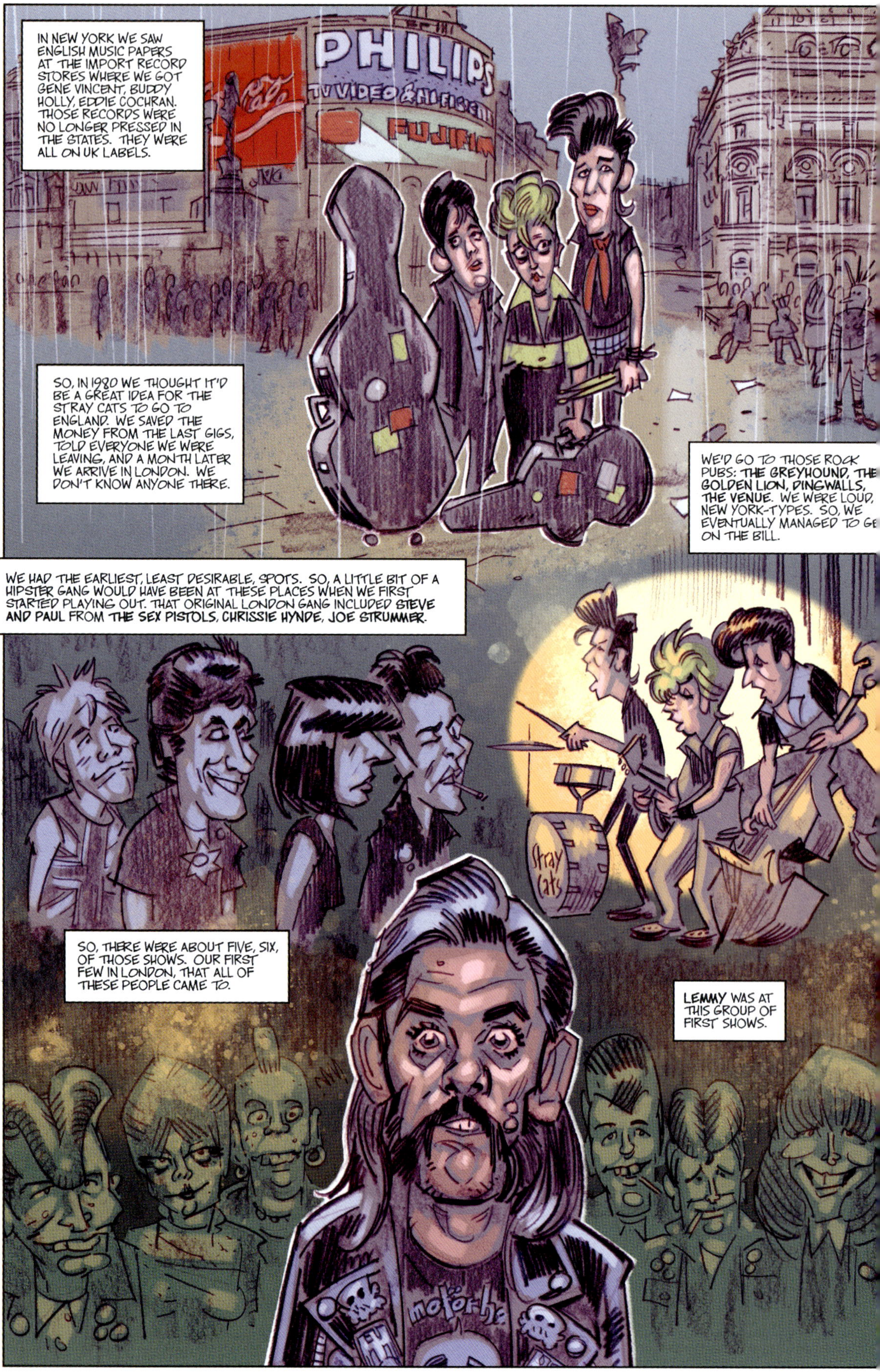
IN NEW YORK WE SAW ENGLISH MUSIC PAPERS AT THE IMPORT RECORD STORES WHERE WE GOT GENE VINCENT, BUDDY HOLLY, EDDIE COCHRAN. THOSE RECORDS WERE NO LONGER PRESSED IN THE STATES. THEY WERE ALL ON UK LABELS.
PHILIPS
SO, IN 1980 WE THOUGHT IT'D BE A GREAT IDEA FOR THE STRAY CATS TO GO TO ENGLAND. WE SAVED THE MONEY FROM THE LAST GIGS, TOLD EVERYONE WE WERE LEAVING, AND A MONTH LATER WE ARRIVE IN LONDON. WE DON'T KNOW ANYONE THERE.
WE'D GO TO THOSE ROCK PUBS: **THE GREYHOUND, THE GOLDEN LION, DINGWALLS, THE VENUE**. WE WERE LOUD, NEW YORK-TYPES. SO, WE EVENTUALLY MANAGED TO GE ON THE BILL.
WE HAD THE EARLIEST, LEAST DESIRABLE, SPOTS. SO, A LITTLE BIT OF A HIPSTER GANG WOULD HAVE BEEN AT THESE PLACES WHEN WE FIRST STARTED PLAYING OUT. THAT ORIGINAL LONDON GANG INCLUDED **STEVE AND PAUL** FROM **THE SEX PISTOLS, CHRISSIE HYNDE, JOE STRUMMER**.
Stray Cats
SO, THERE WERE ABOUT FIVE, SIX, OF THOSE SHOWS. OUR FIRST FEW IN LONDON, THAT ALL OF THESE PEOPLE CAME TO.
LEMMY WAS AT THIS GROUP OF FIRST SHOWS.

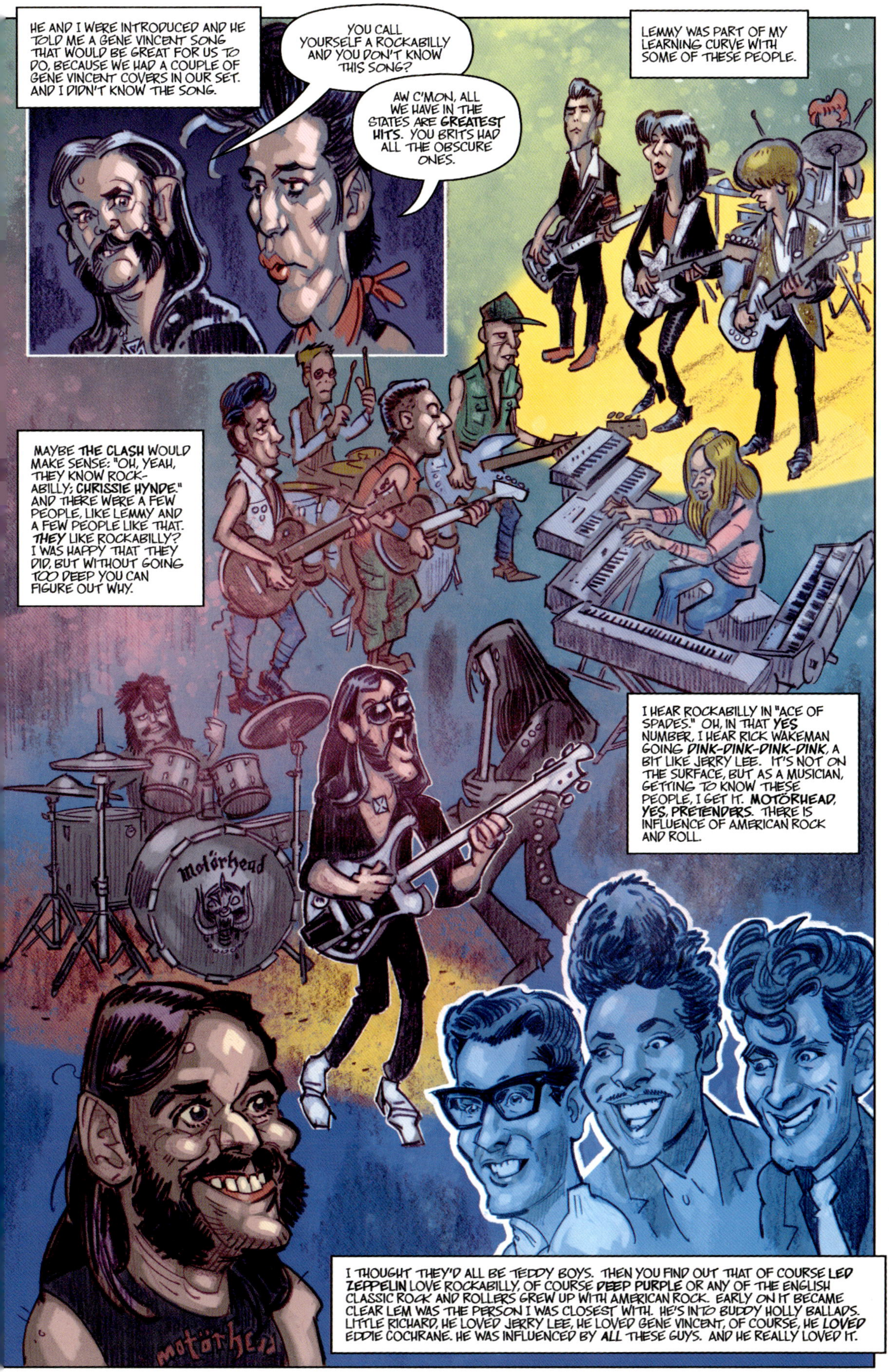
HE AND I WERE INTRODUCED AND HE TOLD ME A GENE VINCENT SONG THAT WOULD BE GREAT FOR US TO DO, BECAUSE WE HAD A COUPLE OF GENE VINCENT COVERS IN OUR SET. AND I DIDN'T KNOW THE SONG.
YOU CALL YOURSELF A ROCKABILLY AND YOU DON'T KNOW THIS SONG?
AW C'MON, ALL WE HAVE IN THE STATES ARE **GREATEST HITS**. YOU BRITS HAD ALL THE OBSCURE ONES.
LEMMY WAS PART OF MY LEARNING CURVE WITH SOME OF THESE PEOPLE.
MAYBE **THE CLASH** WOULD MAKE SENSE: "OH, YEAH, THEY KNOW ROCK-ABILLY; **CHRISSIE HYNDE**." AND THERE WERE A FEW PEOPLE, LIKE LEMMY AND A FEW PEOPLE LIKE THAT. **THEY** LIKE ROCKABILLY? I WAS HAPPY THAT THEY DID, BUT WITHOUT GOING TOO DEEP YOU CAN FIGURE OUT WHY.
I HEAR ROCKABILLY IN "ACE OF SPADES." OH, IN THAT **YES** NUMBER, I HEAR RICK WAKEMAN GOING ***DINK-DINK-DINK-DINK***, A BIT LIKE JERRY LEE. IT'S NOT ON THE SURFACE, BUT AS A MUSICIAN, GETTING TO KNOW THESE PEOPLE, I GET IT. **MOTÖRHEAD, YES, PRETENDERS.** THERE IS INFLUENCE OF AMERICAN ROCK AND ROLL.
Motörhead
I THOUGHT THEY'D ALL BE TEDDY BOYS. THEN YOU FIND OUT THAT OF COURSE **LED ZEPPELIN** LOVE ROCKABILLY, OF COURSE **DEEP PURPLE** OR ANY OF THE ENGLISH CLASSIC ROCK AND ROLLERS GREW UP WITH AMERICAN ROCK. EARLY ON IT BECAME CLEAR LEM WAS THE PERSON I WAS CLOSEST WITH. HE'S INTO BUDDY HOLLY BALLADS. LITTLE RICHARD, HE LOVED JERRY LEE, HE LOVED GENE VINCENT, OF COURSE, HE **LOVED** EDDIE COCHRANE. HE WAS INFLUENCED BY **ALL** THESE GUYS. AND HE REALLY LOVED IT.

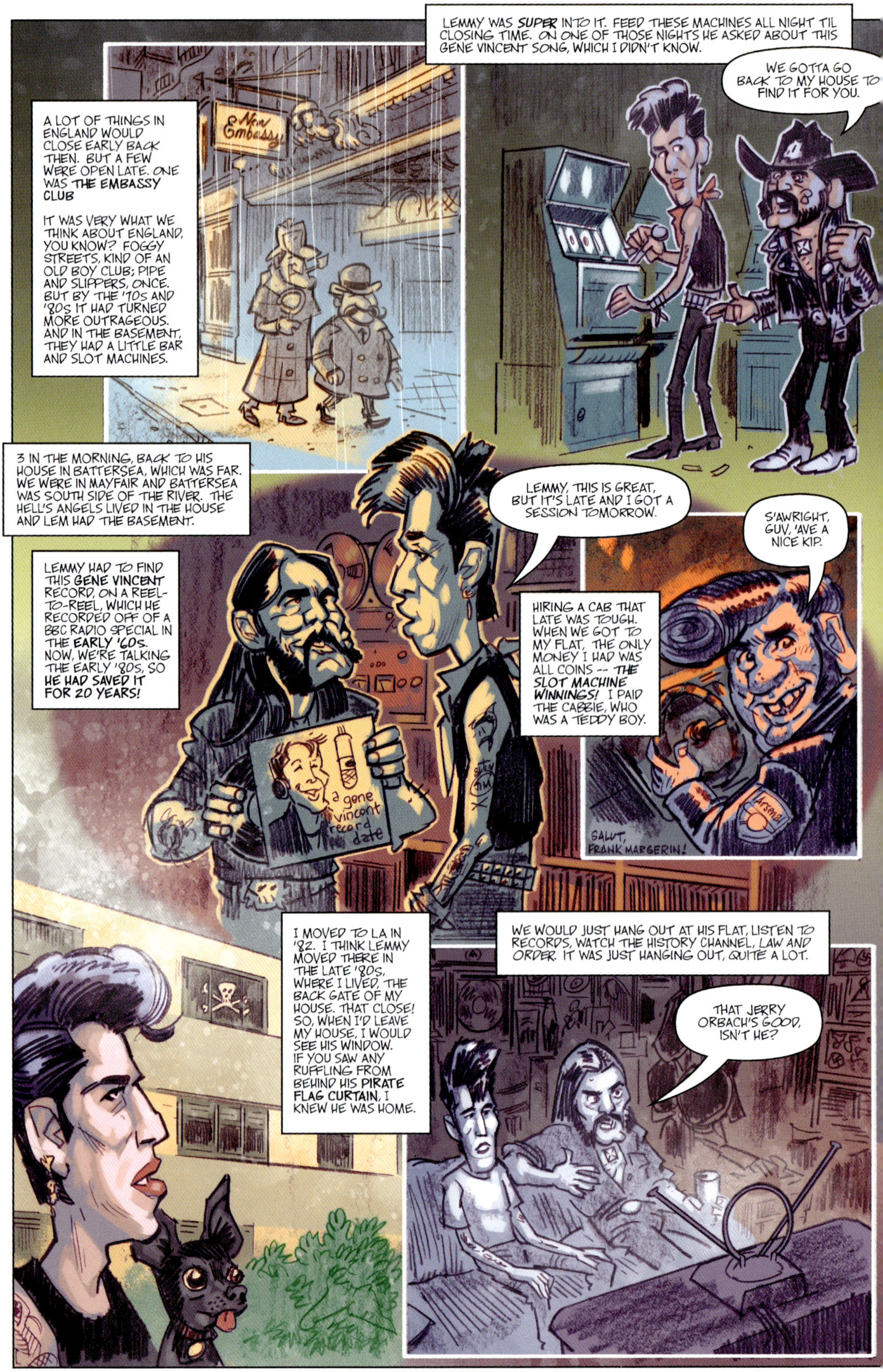
LEMMY WAS SUPER INTO IT. FEED THESE MACHINES ALL NIGHT TIL CLOSING TIME. ON ONE OF THOSE NIGHTS HE ASKED ABOUT THIS GENE VINCENT SONG, WHICH I DIDN'T KNOW.
A LOT OF THINGS IN ENGLAND WOULD CLOSE EARLY BACK THEN. BUT A FEW WERE OPEN LATE. ONE WAS THE EMBASSY CLUB
IT WAS VERY WHAT WE THINK ABOUT ENGLAND, YOU KNOW? FOGGY STREETS, KIND OF AN OLD BOY CLUB; PIPE AND SLIPPERS, ONCE. BUT BY THE '70s AND '80s IT HAD TURNED MORE OUTRAGEOUS. AND IN THE BASEMENT, THEY HAD A LITTLE BAR AND SLOT MACHINES.
New Embassy
WE GOTTA GO BACK TO MY HOUSE TO FIND IT FOR YOU.
3 IN THE MORNING, BACK TO HIS HOUSE IN BATTERSEA, WHICH WAS FAR. WE WERE IN MAYFAIR AND BATTERSEA WAS SOUTH SIDE OF THE RIVER. THE HELL'S ANGELS LIVED IN THE HOUSE AND LEM HAD THE BASEMENT.
LEMMY HAD TO FIND THIS GENE VINCENT RECORD, ON A REEL-TO-REEL, WHICH HE RECORDED OFF OF A BBC RADIO SPECIAL IN THE EARLY '60s. NOW, WE'RE TALKING THE EARLY '80s, SO HE HAD SAVED IT FOR 20 YEARS!
a gene vincent record date
LEMMY, THIS IS GREAT, BUT IT'S LATE AND I GOT A SESSION TOMORROW.
HIRING A CAB THAT LATE WAS TOUGH. WHEN WE GOT TO MY FLAT, THE ONLY MONEY I HAD WAS ALL COINS -- THE SLOT MACHINE WINNINGS! I PAID THE CABBIE, WHO WAS A TEDDY BOY.
S'AWRIGHT, GUV, 'AVE A NICE KIP.
SALUT, FRANK MARGERIN!
I MOVED TO LA IN '82. I THINK LEMMY MOVED THERE IN THE LATE '80s, WHERE I LIVED, THE BACK GATE OF MY HOUSE. THAT CLOSE! SO, WHEN I'D LEAVE MY HOUSE, I WOULD SEE HIS WINDOW. IF YOU SAW ANY RUFFLING FROM BEHIND HIS PIRATE FLAG CURTAIN, I KNEW HE WAS HOME.
WE WOULD JUST HANG OUT AT HIS FLAT, LISTEN TO RECORDS, WATCH THE HISTORY CHANNEL, LAW AND ORDER. IT WAS JUST HANGING OUT, QUITE A LOT.
THAT JERRY ORBACH'S GOOD, ISN'T HE?

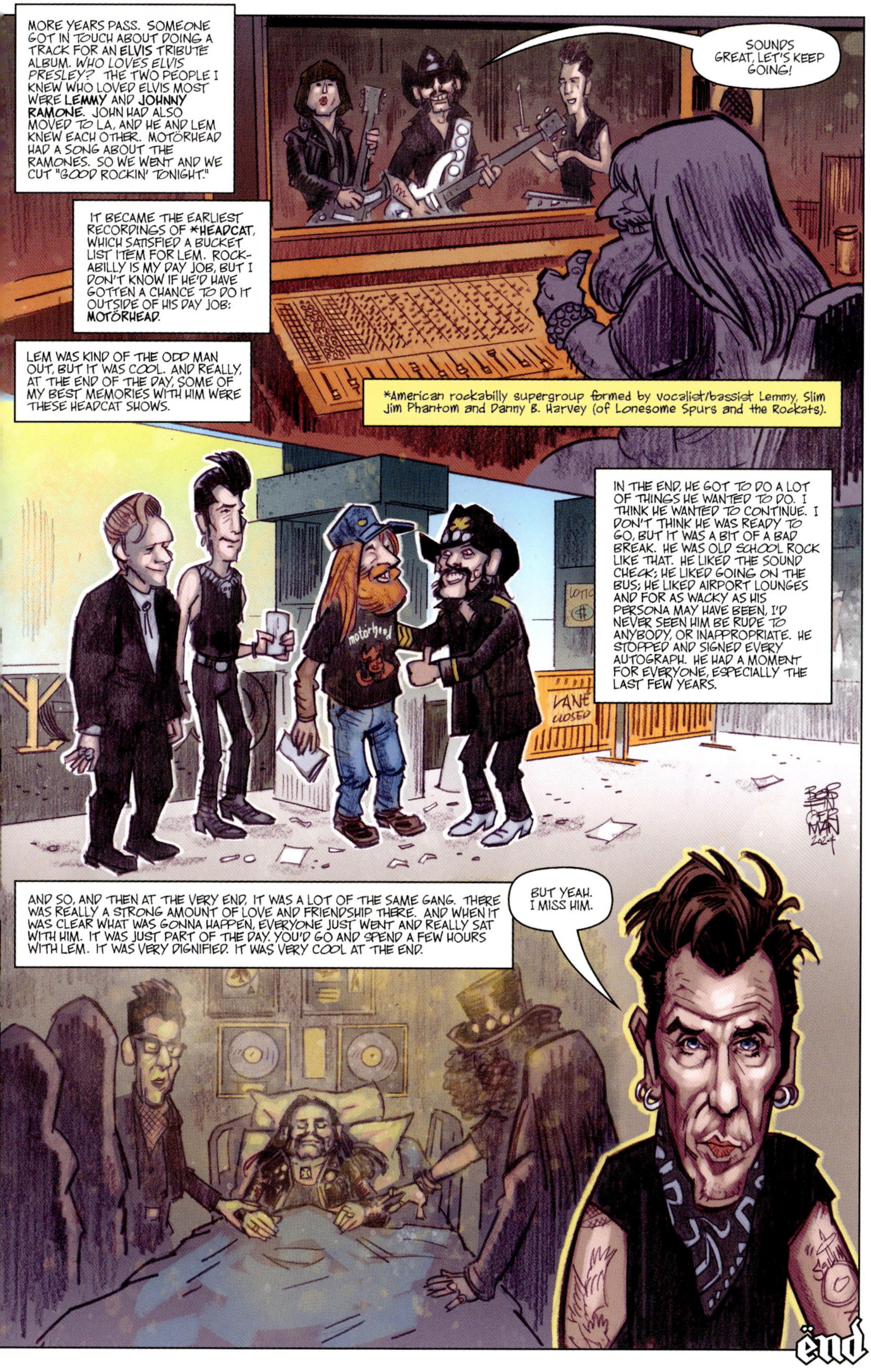
MORE YEARS PASS. SOMEONE GOT IN TOUCH ABOUT DOING A TRACK FOR AN ELVIS TRIBUTE ALBUM. WHO LOVES ELVIS PRESLEY? THE TWO PEOPLE I KNEW WHO LOVED ELVIS MOST WERE LEMMY AND JOHNNY RAMONE. JOHN HAD ALSO MOVED TO LA, AND HE AND LEM KNEW EACH OTHER. MOTÖRHEAD HAD A SONG ABOUT THE RAMONES. SO WE WENT AND WE CUT "GOOD ROCKIN' TONIGHT."
SOUNDS GREAT, LET'S KEEP GOING!
IT BECAME THE EARLIEST RECORDINGS OF *HEADCAT, WHICH SATISFIED A BUCKET LIST ITEM FOR LEM. ROCK-ABILLY IS MY DAY JOB, BUT I DON'T KNOW IF HE'D HAVE GOTTEN A CHANCE TO DO IT OUTSIDE OF HIS DAY JOB: MOTÖRHEAD.
LEM WAS KIND OF THE ODD MAN OUT, BUT IT WAS COOL. AND REALLY, AT THE END OF THE DAY, SOME OF MY BEST MEMORIES WITH HIM WERE THESE HEADCAT SHOWS.
*American rockabilly supergroup formed by vocalist/bassist Lemmy, Slim Jim Phantom and Danny B. Harvey (of Lonesome Spurs and the Rockats).
IN THE END, HE GOT TO DO A LOT OF THINGS HE WANTED TO DO. I THINK HE WANTED TO CONTINUE. I DON'T THINK HE WAS READY TO GO, BUT IT WAS A BIT OF A BAD BREAK. HE WAS OLD SCHOOL ROCK LIKE THAT. HE LIKED THE SOUND CHECK; HE LIKED GOING ON THE BUS; HE LIKED AIRPORT LOUNGES AND FOR AS WACKY AS HIS PERSONA MAY HAVE BEEN, I'D NEVER SEEN HIM BE RUDE TO ANYBODY, OR INAPPROPRIATE. HE STOPPED AND SIGNED EVERY AUTOGRAPH. HE HAD A MOMENT FOR EVERYONE, ESPECIALLY THE LAST FEW YEARS.
motörhead
LANE CLOSED
AND SO, AND THEN AT THE VERY END, IT WAS A LOT OF THE SAME GANG. THERE WAS REALLY A STRONG AMOUNT OF LOVE AND FRIENDSHIP THERE. AND WHEN IT WAS CLEAR WHAT WAS GONNA HAPPEN, EVERYONE JUST WENT AND REALLY SAT WITH HIM. IT WAS JUST PART OF THE DAY. YOU'D GO AND SPEND A FEW HOURS WITH LEM. IT WAS VERY DIGNIFIED. IT WAS VERY COOL AT THE END.
BUT YEAH. I MISS HIM.
ënd

"When I say that Lemmy is the primary reason Metallica exists, it's not some cheap exaggeration."

FIRST MET LEMMY IN 1981

lars ulrich

FOUNDER
METALLICA
PRESIDENT
MOTÖRHEAD
FANCLUB

STORY ILLUSTRATED BY STEVE CHANKS

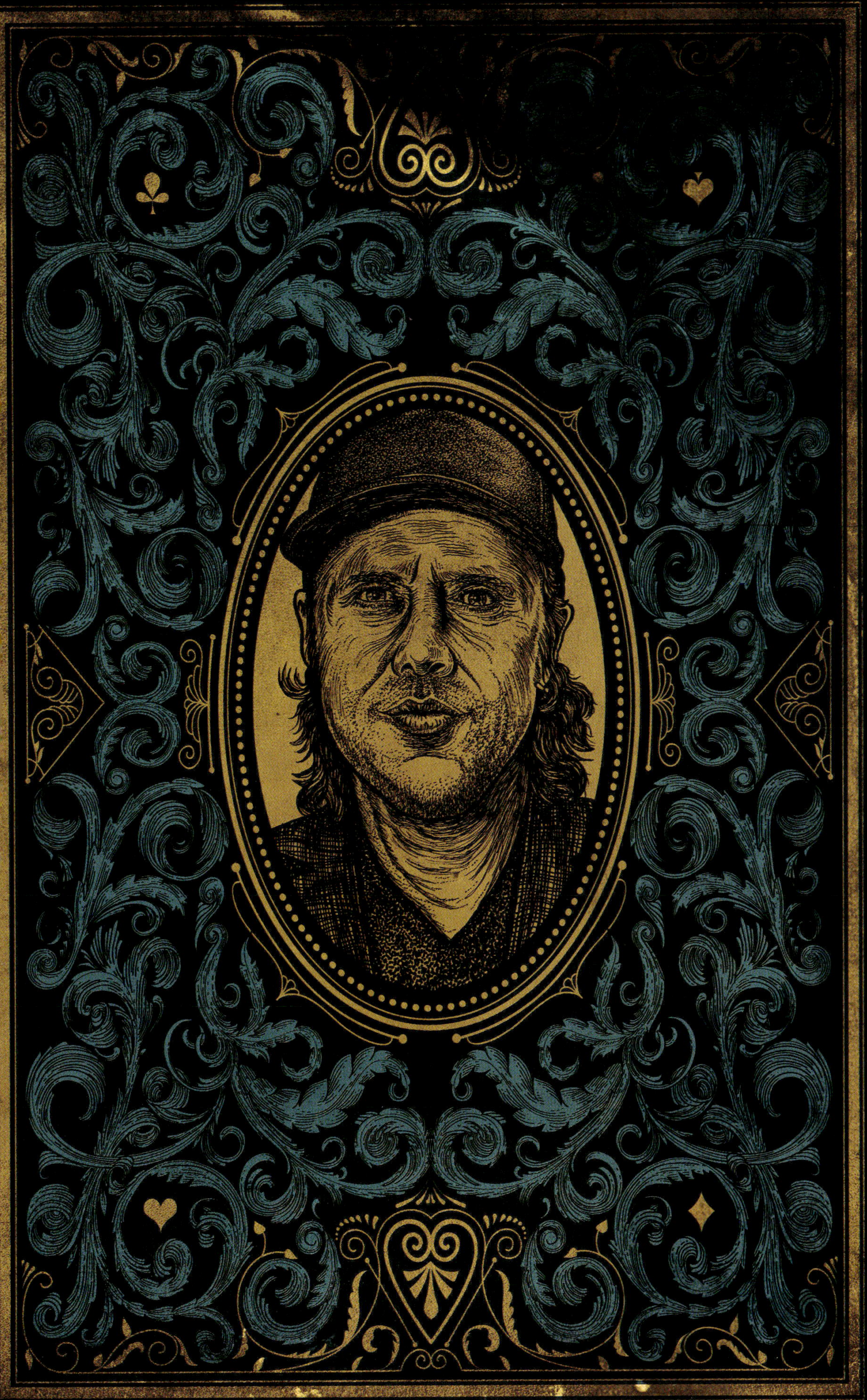

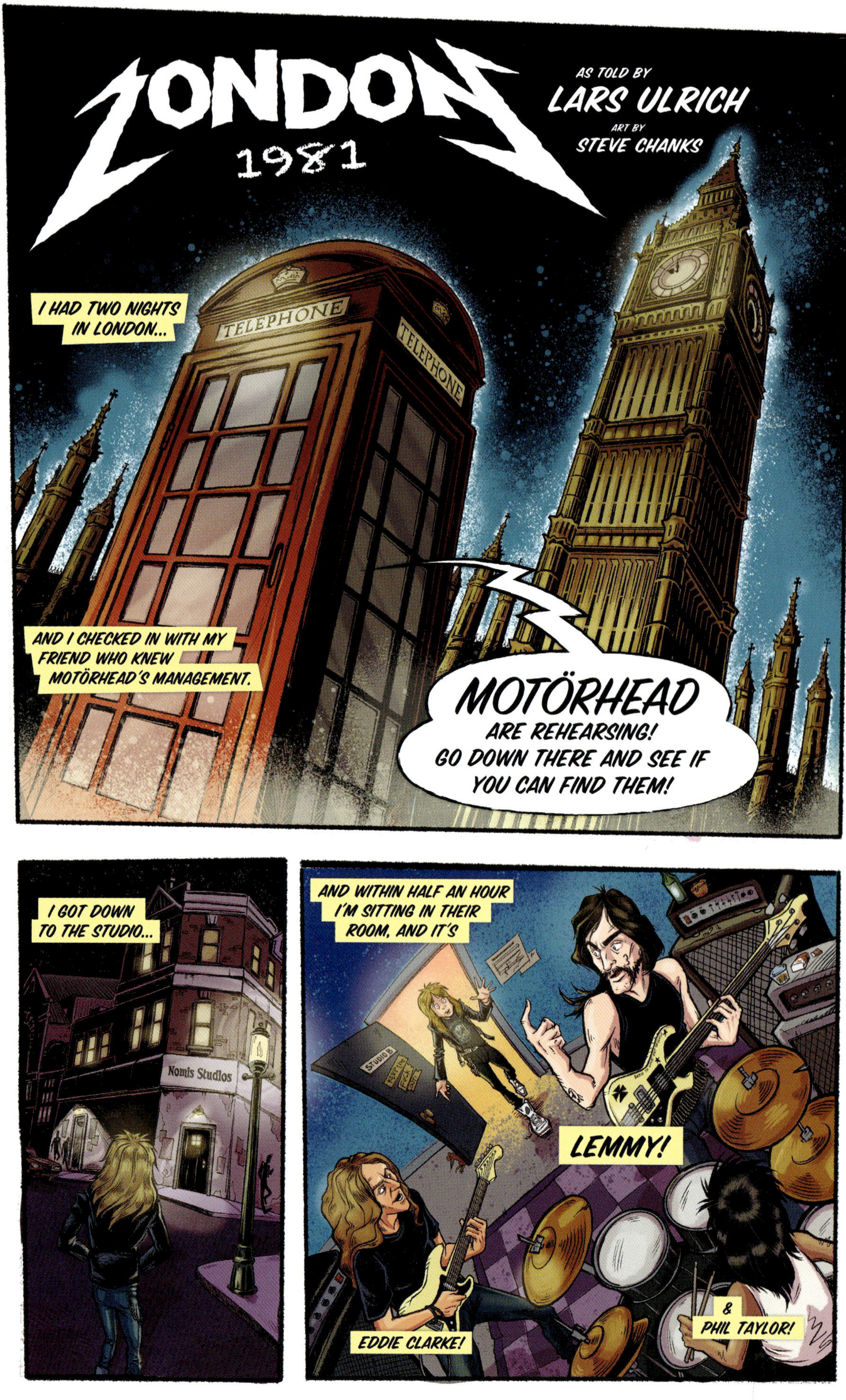
LONDON 1981
AS TOLD BY LARS ULRICH
ART BY STEVE CHANKS
I HAD TWO NIGHTS IN LONDON...
TELEPHONE
TELEPHONE
AND I CHECKED IN WITH MY FRIEND WHO KNEW MOTÖRHEAD'S MANAGEMENT.
MOTÖRHEAD ARE REHEARSING! GO DOWN THERE AND SEE IF YOU CAN FIND THEM!
I GOT DOWN TO THE STUDIO...
Nomis Studios
AND WITHIN HALF AN HOUR I'M SITTING IN THEIR ROOM, AND IT'S
LEMMY!
EDDIE CLARKE!
& PHIL TAYLOR!

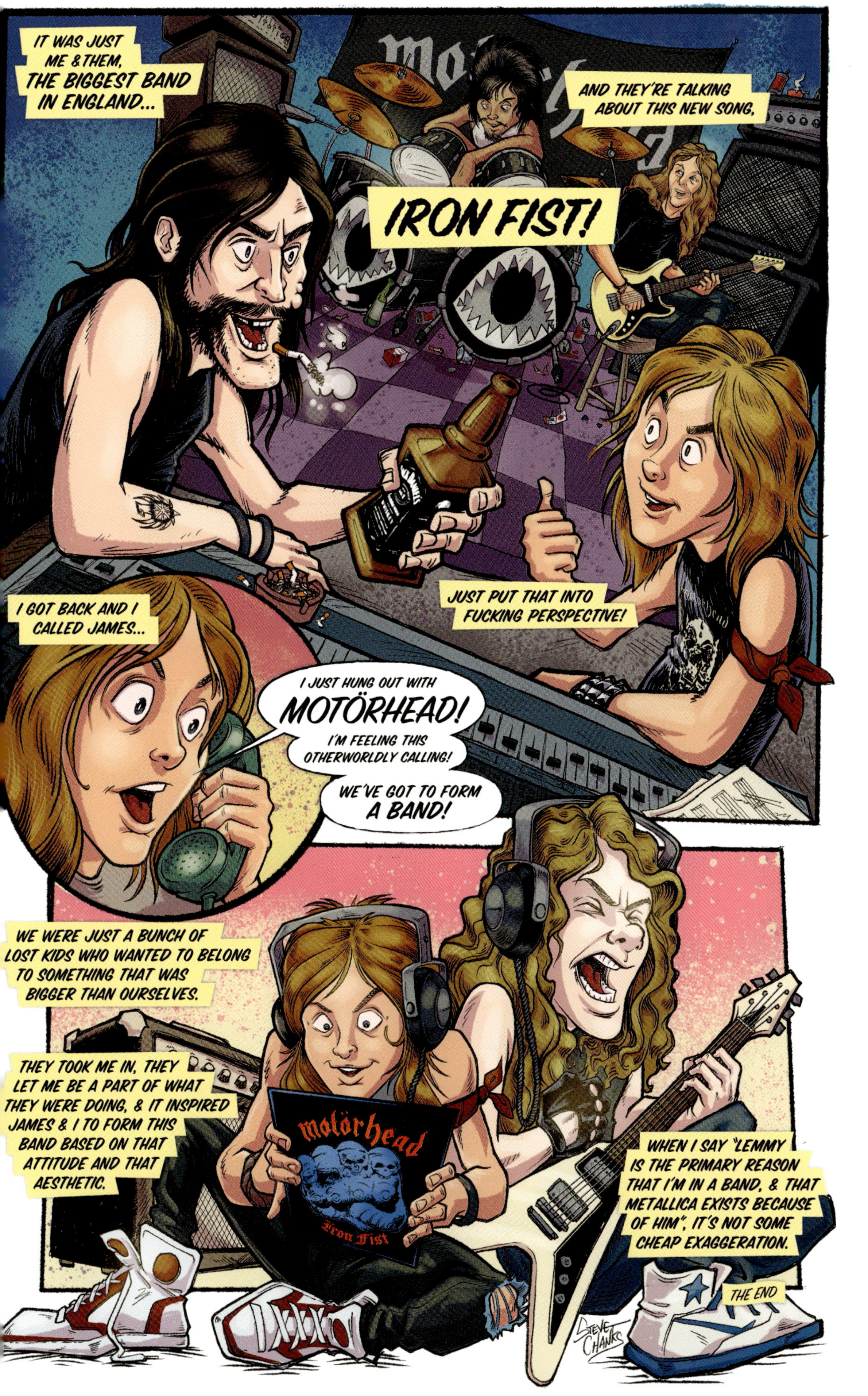
IT WAS JUST ME & THEM, THE BIGGEST BAND IN ENGLAND...
AND THEY'RE TALKING ABOUT THIS NEW SONG,
IRON FIST!
JUST PUT THAT INTO FUCKING PERSPECTIVE!
I GOT BACK AND I CALLED JAMES...
I JUST HUNG OUT WITH MOTÖRHEAD!
I'M FEELING THIS OTHERWORLDLY CALLING!
WE'VE GOT TO FORM A BAND!
WE WERE JUST A BUNCH OF LOST KIDS WHO WANTED TO BELONG TO SOMETHING THAT WAS BIGGER THAN OURSELVES.
THEY TOOK ME IN, THEY LET ME BE A PART OF WHAT THEY WERE DOING, & IT INSPIRED JAMES & I TO FORM THIS BAND BASED ON THAT ATTITUDE AND THAT AESTHETIC.
motörhead
Iron Fist
WHEN I SAY "LEMMY IS THE PRIMARY REASON THAT I'M IN A BAND, & THAT METALLICA EXISTS BECAUSE OF HIM", IT'S NOT SOME CHEAP EXAGGERATION.
THE END
STEVE CHANKS

"Rest in peace Lemmy, a man I saw playing the fruit machines in late night dives."

FIRST MET LEMMY IN 1981

neil gaiman

WRITER
CREATOR
SANDMAN
GOOD OMENS
CORALINE

STORY ILLUSTRATED BY DAVE CHISHOLM

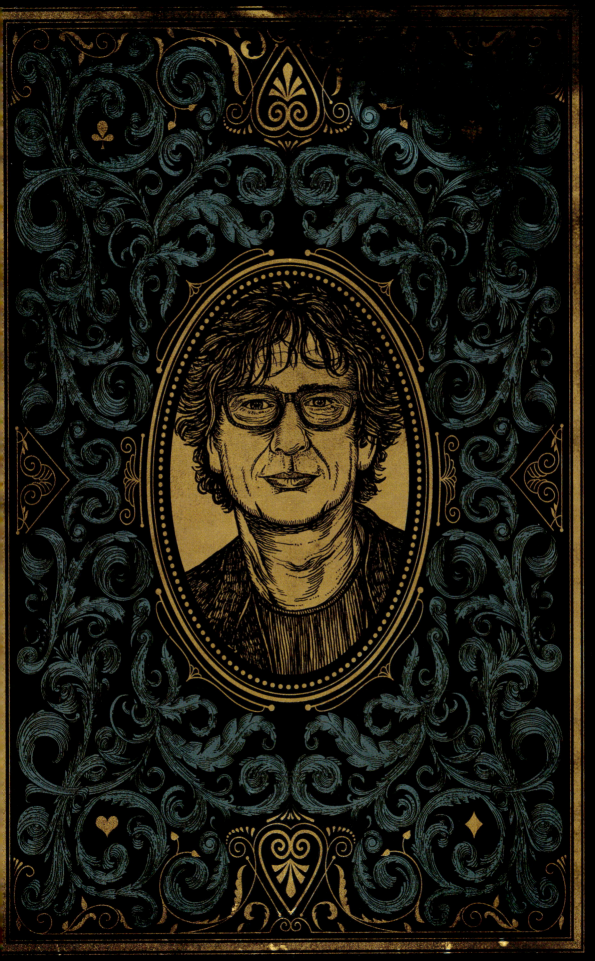

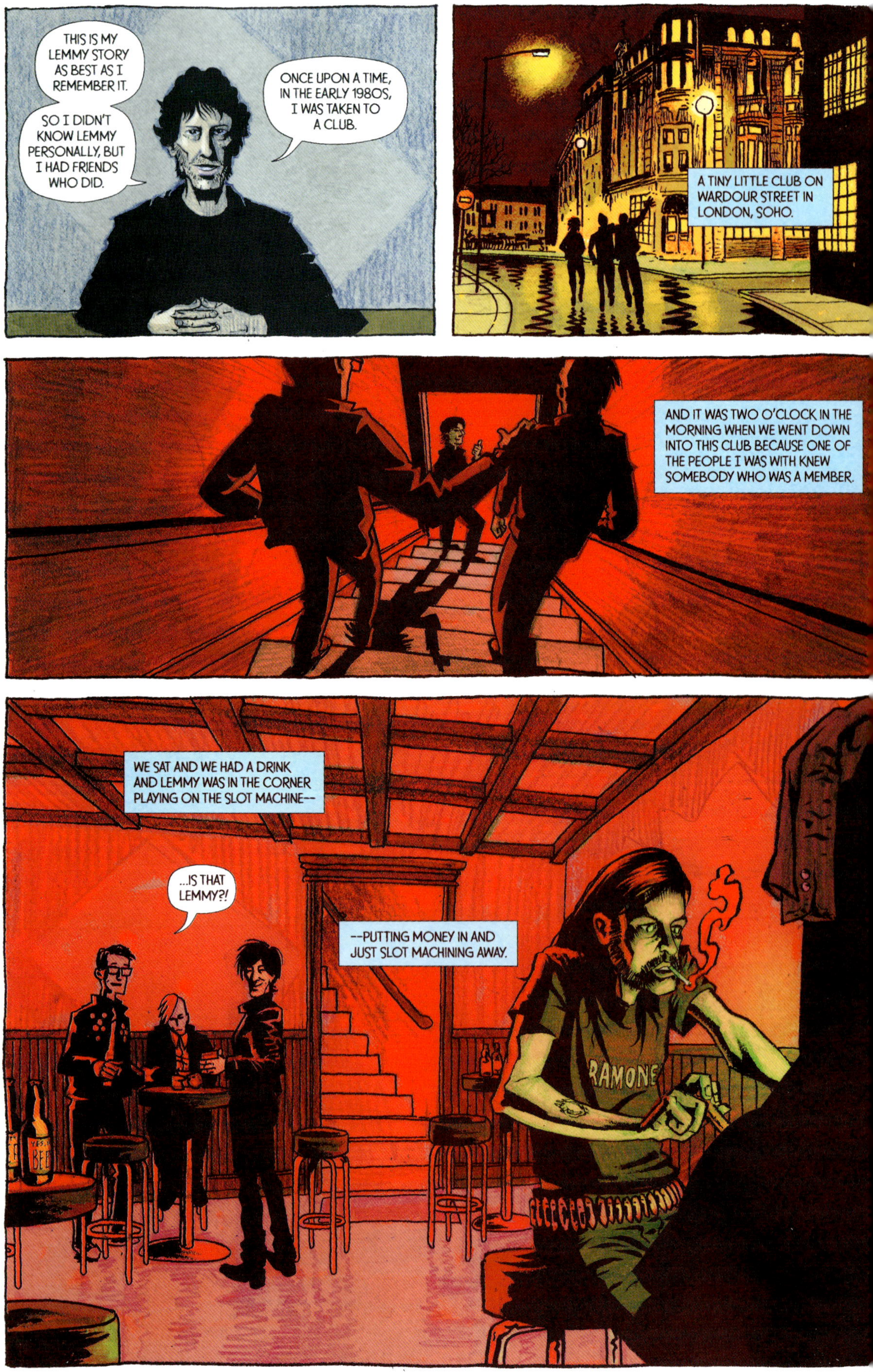

THIS IS MY LEMMY STORY AS BEST AS I REMEMBER IT.
SO I DIDN'T KNOW LEMMY PERSONALLY, BUT I HAD FRIENDS WHO DID.
ONCE UPON A TIME, IN THE EARLY 1980S, I WAS TAKEN TO A CLUB.
A TINY LITTLE CLUB ON WARDOUR STREET IN LONDON, SOHO.
AND IT WAS TWO O'CLOCK IN THE MORNING WHEN WE WENT DOWN INTO THIS CLUB BECAUSE ONE OF THE PEOPLE I WAS WITH KNEW SOMEBODY WHO WAS A MEMBER.
WE SAT AND WE HAD A DRINK AND LEMMY WAS IN THE CORNER PLAYING ON THE SLOT MACHINE--
...IS THAT LEMMY?!
--PUTTING MONEY IN AND JUST SLOT MACHINING AWAY.
RAMONE

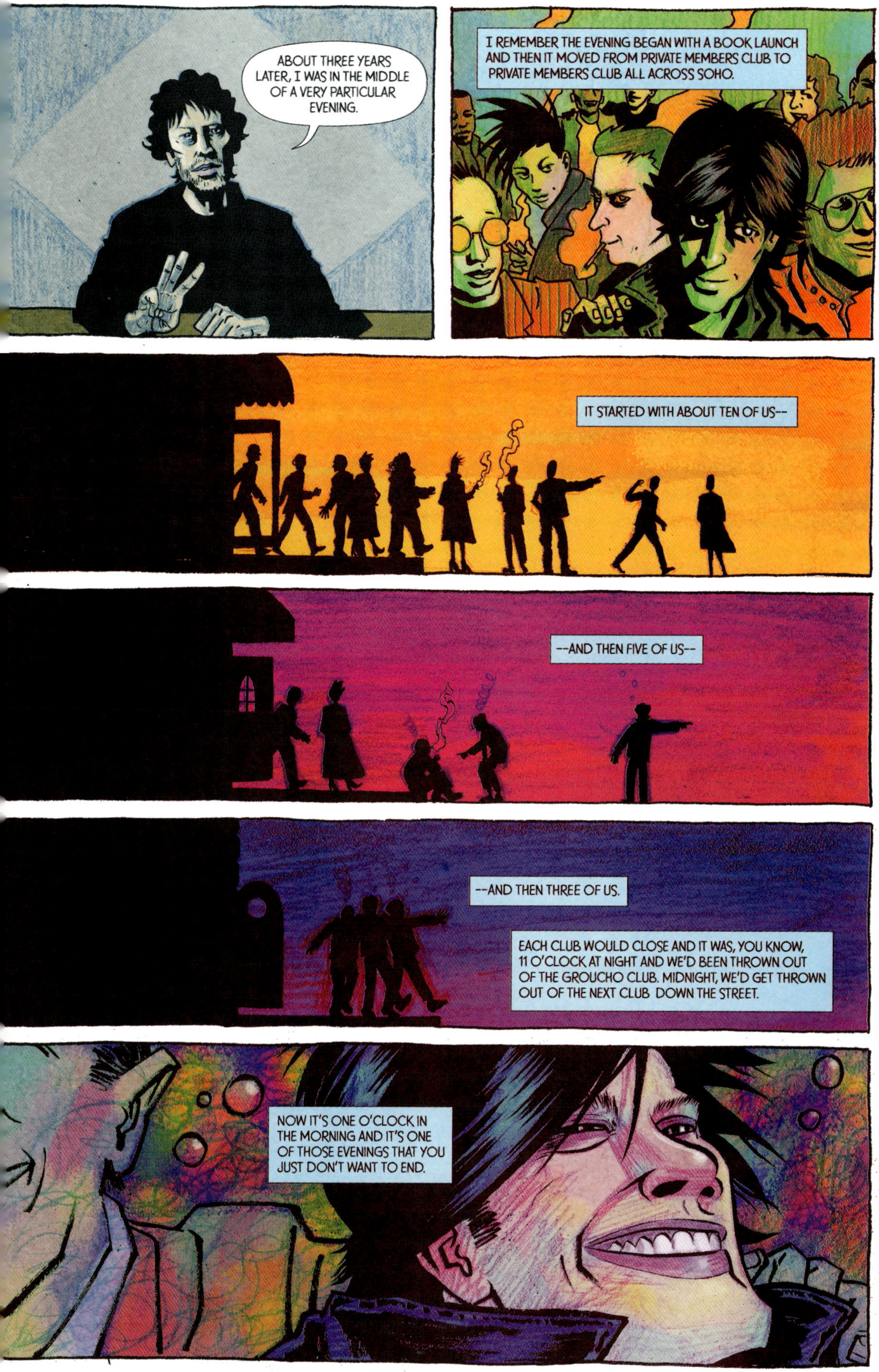
ABOUT THREE YEARS LATER, I WAS IN THE MIDDLE OF A VERY PARTICULAR EVENING.
I REMEMBER THE EVENING BEGAN WITH A BOOK LAUNCH AND THEN IT MOVED FROM PRIVATE MEMBERS CLUB TO PRIVATE MEMBERS CLUB ALL ACROSS SOHO.
IT STARTED WITH ABOUT TEN OF US--
--AND THEN FIVE OF US--
--AND THEN THREE OF US.
EACH CLUB WOULD CLOSE AND IT WAS, YOU KNOW, 11 O'CLOCK AT NIGHT AND WE'D BEEN THROWN OUT OF THE GROUCHO CLUB. MIDNIGHT, WE'D GET THROWN OUT OF THE NEXT CLUB DOWN THE STREET.
NOW IT'S ONE O'CLOCK IN THE MORNING AND IT'S ONE OF THOSE EVENINGS THAT YOU JUST DON'T WANT TO END.

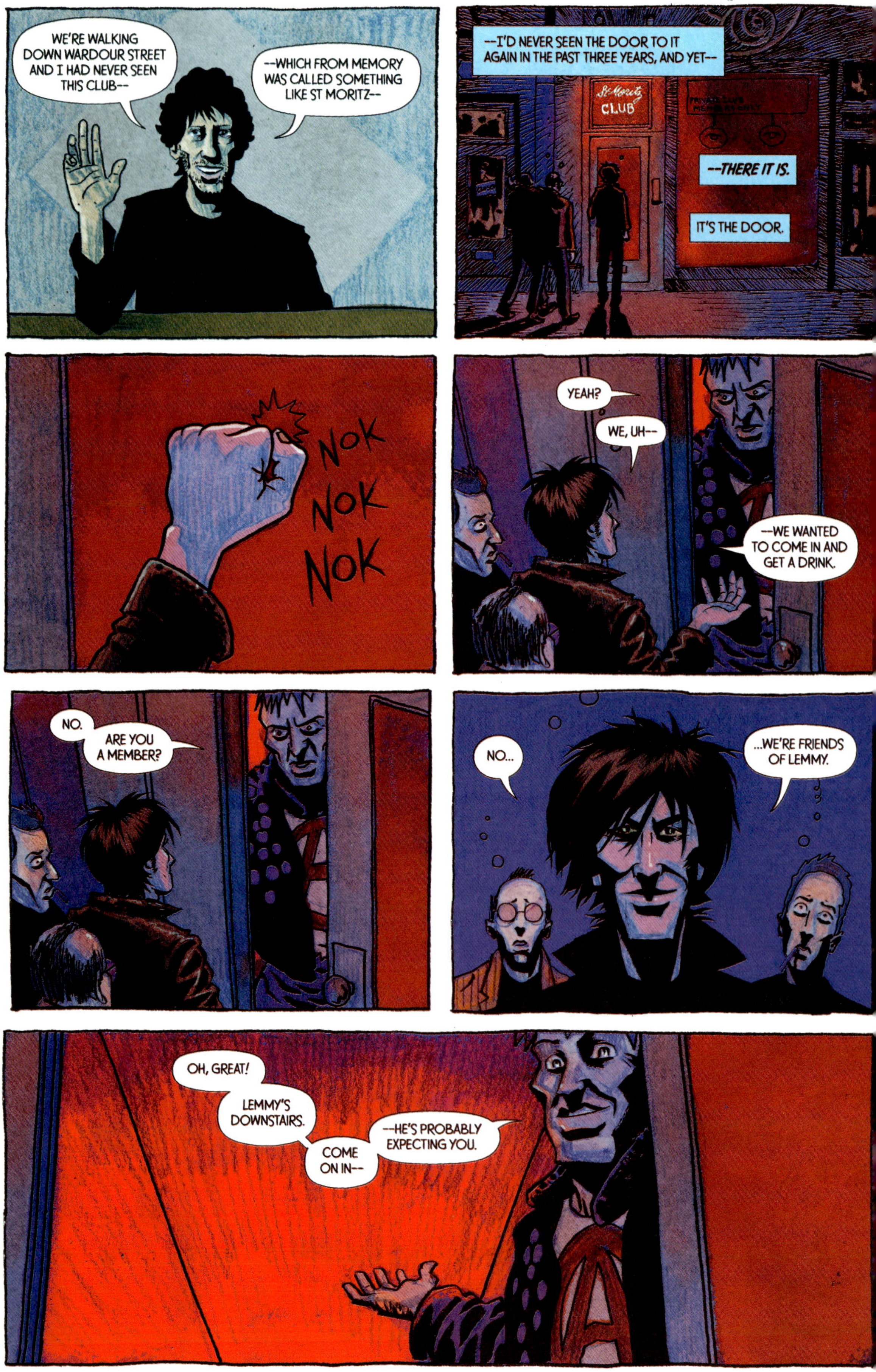
WE'RE WALKING DOWN WARDOUR STREET AND I HAD NEVER SEEN THIS CLUB--
--WHICH FROM MEMORY WAS CALLED SOMETHING LIKE ST MORITZ--
--I'D NEVER SEEN THE DOOR TO IT AGAIN IN THE PAST THREE YEARS, AND YET--
St Moritz CLUB
--THERE IT IS.
IT'S THE DOOR.
NOK
NOK
NOK
YEAH?
WE, UH--
--WE WANTED TO COME IN AND GET A DRINK.
NO.
ARE YOU A MEMBER?
NO...
...WE'RE FRIENDS OF LEMMY.
OH, GREAT!
LEMMY'S DOWNSTAIRS.
COME ON IN--
--HE'S PROBABLY EXPECTING YOU.

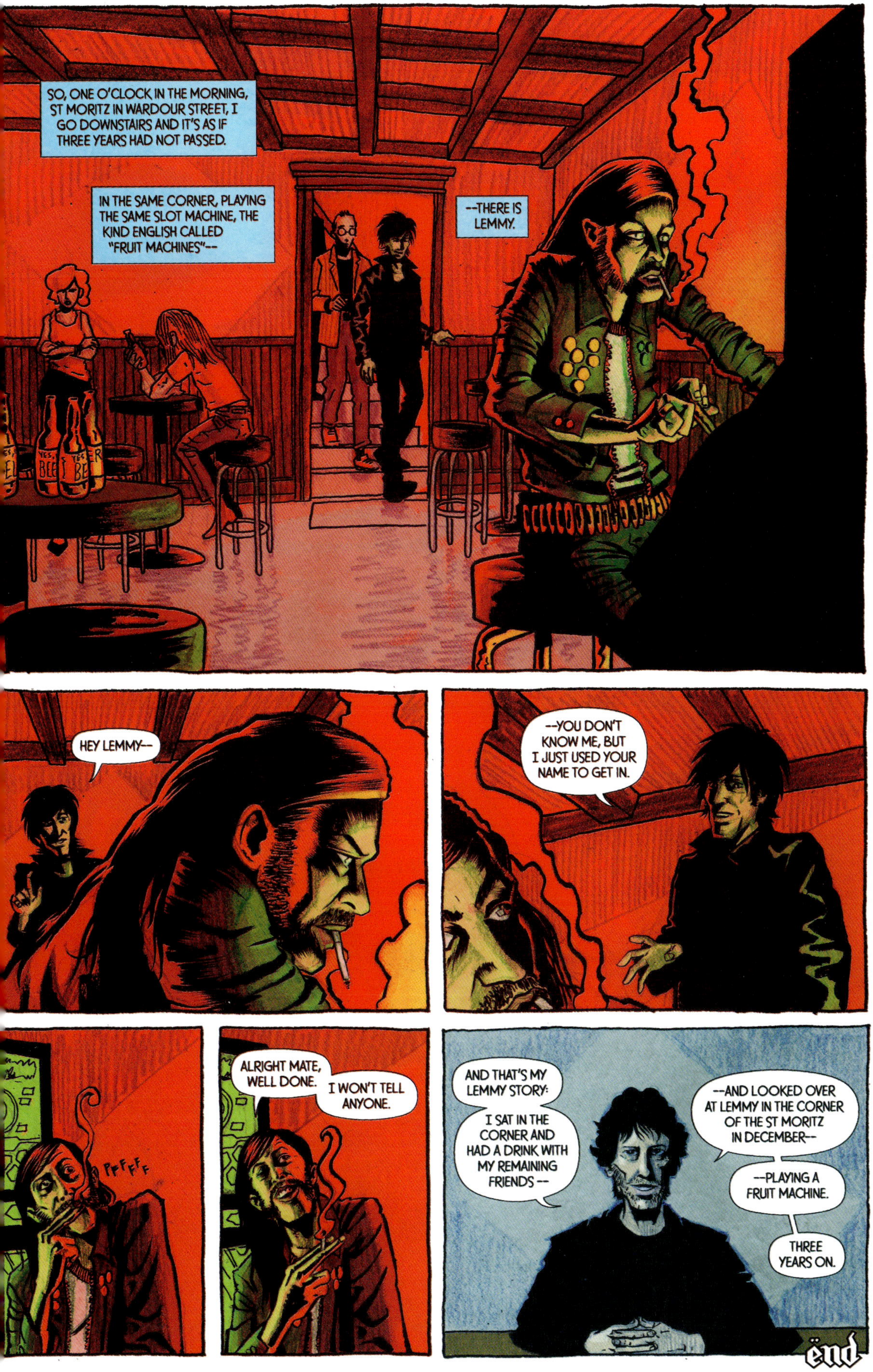
SO, ONE O'CLOCK IN THE MORNING, ST MORITZ IN WARDOUR STREET, I GO DOWNSTAIRS AND IT'S AS IF THREE YEARS HAD NOT PASSED.
IN THE SAME CORNER, PLAYING THE SAME SLOT MACHINE, THE KIND ENGLISH CALLED "FRUIT MACHINES"--
--THERE IS LEMMY.
HEY LEMMY--
--YOU DON'T KNOW ME, BUT I JUST USED YOUR NAME TO GET IN.
PFFFFF
ALRIGHT MATE, WELL DONE.
I WON'T TELL ANYONE.
AND THAT'S MY LEMMY STORY:
I SAT IN THE CORNER AND HAD A DRINK WITH MY REMAINING FRIENDS --
--AND LOOKED OVER AT LEMMY IN THE CORNER OF THE ST MORITZ IN DECEMBER--
--PLAYING A FRUIT MACHINE.
THREE YEARS ON.
end

"If Lemmy had not stepped in, no doubt, Twisted Sister would have been bottled off the stage."

FIRST MET
LEMMY
IN
1982

dee snider

OUTSPOKEN
FRONTMAN
TWISTED
SISTER

STORY ILLUSTRATED BY JAYJAY JACKSON

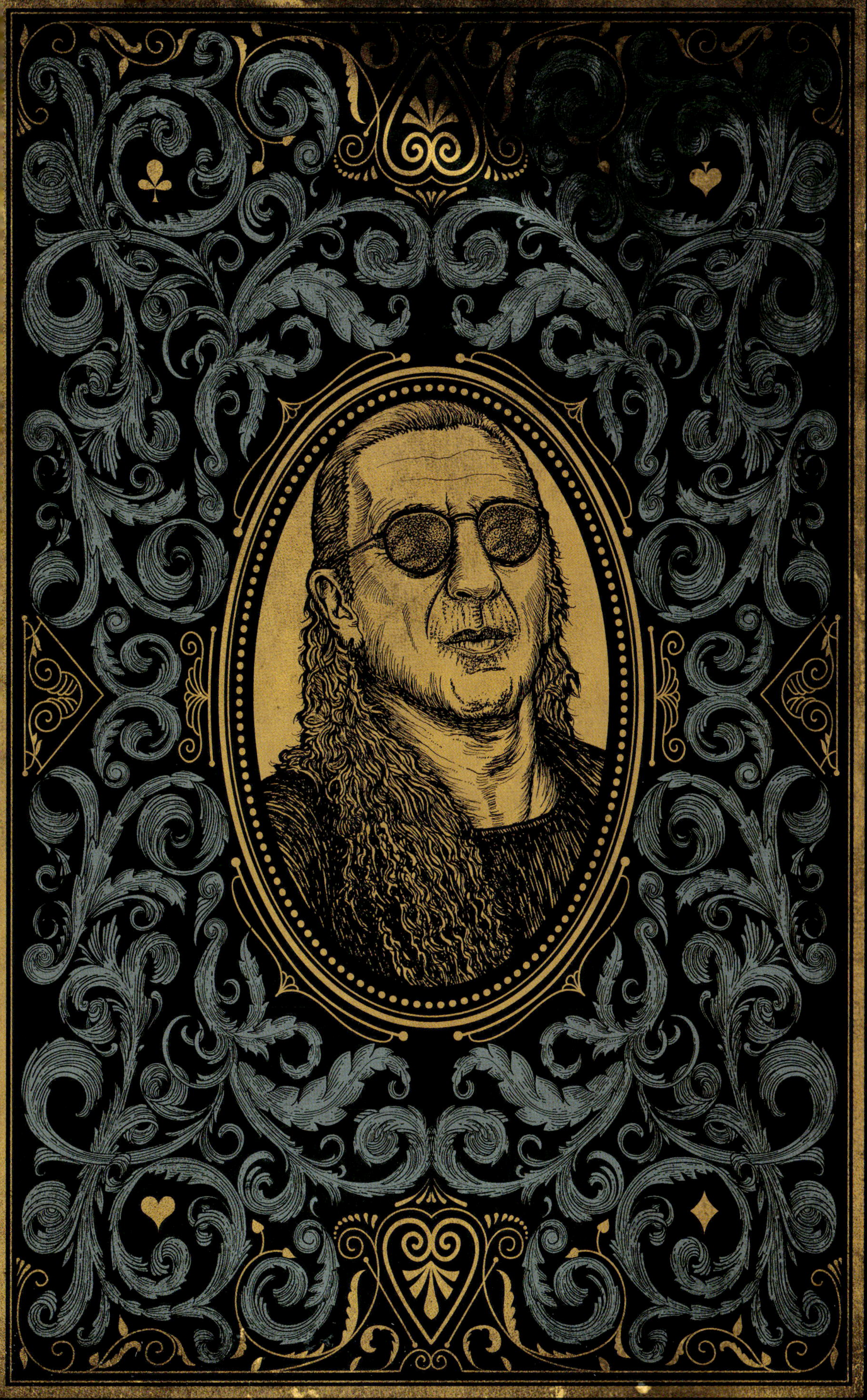

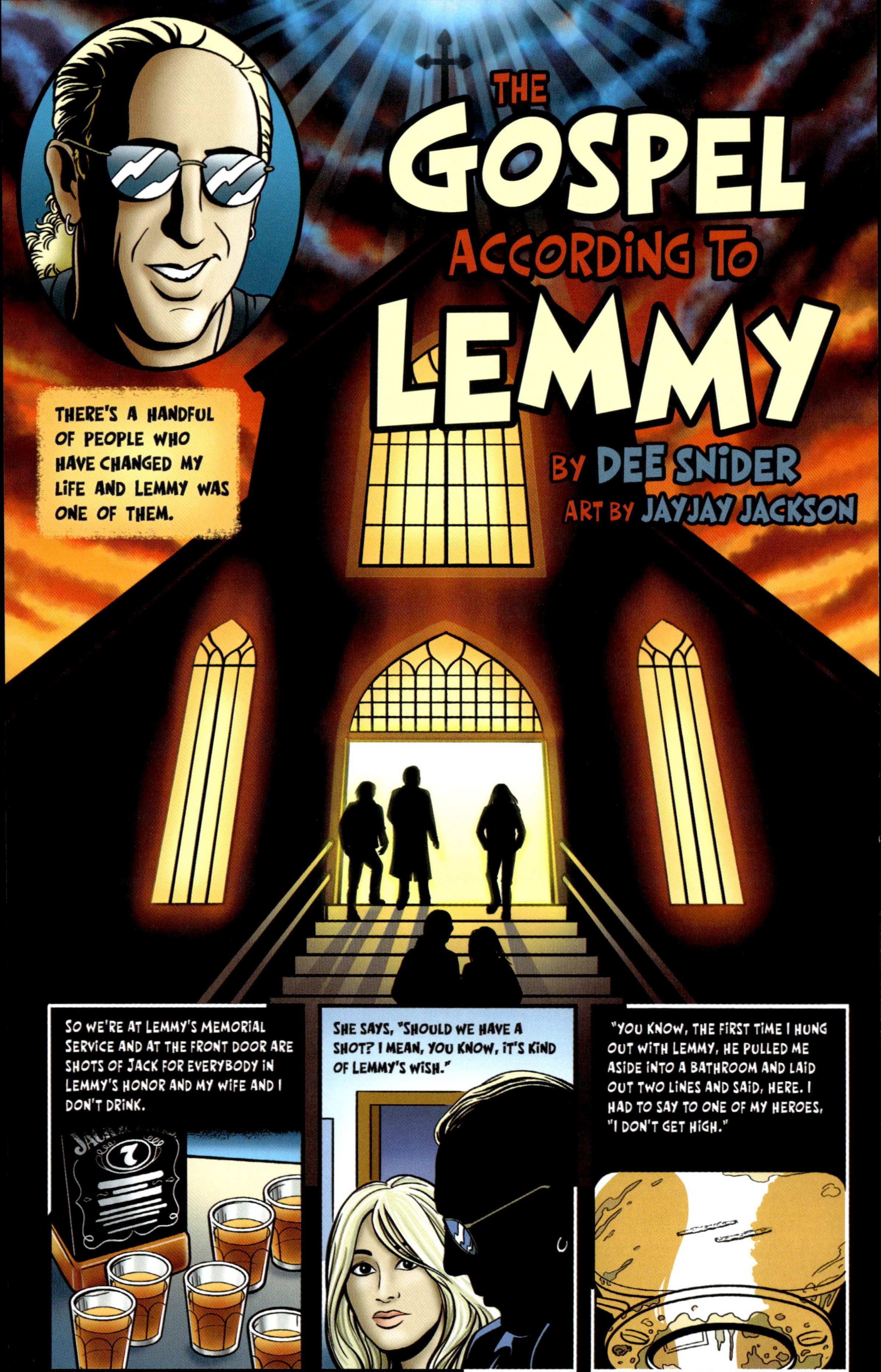
THE GOSPEL ACCORDING TO LEMMY
BY DEE SNIDER
ART BY JAYJAY JACKSON
THERE'S A HANDFUL OF PEOPLE WHO HAVE CHANGED MY LIFE AND LEMMY WAS ONE OF THEM.
SO WE'RE AT LEMMY'S MEMORIAL SERVICE AND AT THE FRONT DOOR ARE SHOTS OF JACK FOR EVERYBODY IN LEMMY'S HONOR AND MY WIFE AND I DON'T DRINK.
SHE SAYS, "SHOULD WE HAVE A SHOT? I MEAN, YOU KNOW, IT'S KIND OF LEMMY'S WISH."
"YOU KNOW, THE FIRST TIME I HUNG OUT WITH LEMMY, HE PULLED ME ASIDE INTO A BATHROOM AND LAID OUT TWO LINES AND SAID, HERE. I HAD TO SAY TO ONE OF MY HEROES, "I DON'T GET HIGH."

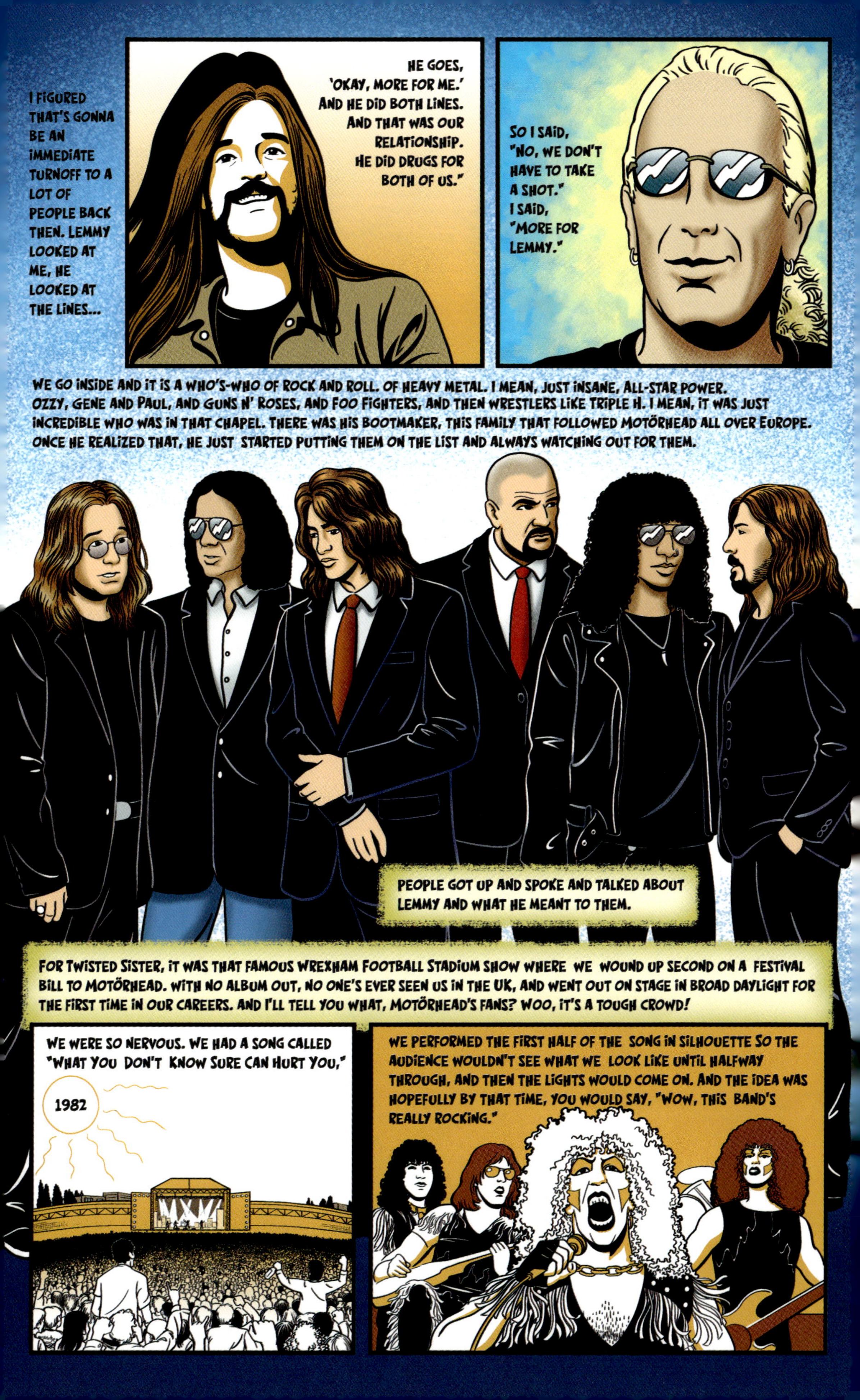
I FIGURED THAT'S GONNA BE AN IMMEDIATE TURNOFF TO A LOT OF PEOPLE BACK THEN. LEMMY LOOKED AT ME, HE LOOKED AT THE LINES...
HE GOES, 'OKAY, MORE FOR ME.' AND HE DID BOTH LINES. AND THAT WAS OUR RELATIONSHIP. HE DID DRUGS FOR BOTH OF US."
SO I SAID, "NO, WE DON'T HAVE TO TAKE A SHOT." I SAID, "MORE FOR LEMMY."
WE GO INSIDE AND IT IS A WHO'S-WHO OF ROCK AND ROLL. OF HEAVY METAL. I MEAN, JUST INSANE, ALL-STAR POWER. OZZY, GENE AND PAUL, AND GUNS N' ROSES, AND FOO FIGHTERS, AND THEN WRESTLERS LIKE TRIPLE H. I MEAN, IT WAS JUST INCREDIBLE WHO WAS IN THAT CHAPEL. THERE WAS HIS BOOTMAKER, THIS FAMILY THAT FOLLOWED MOTÖRHEAD ALL OVER EUROPE. ONCE HE REALIZED THAT, HE JUST STARTED PUTTING THEM ON THE LIST AND ALWAYS WATCHING OUT FOR THEM.
PEOPLE GOT UP AND SPOKE AND TALKED ABOUT LEMMY AND WHAT HE MEANT TO THEM.
FOR TWISTED SISTER, IT WAS THAT FAMOUS WREXHAM FOOTBALL STADIUM SHOW WHERE WE WOUND UP SECOND ON A FESTIVAL BILL TO MOTÖRHEAD. WITH NO ALBUM OUT, NO ONE'S EVER SEEN US IN THE UK, AND WENT OUT ON STAGE IN BROAD DAYLIGHT FOR THE FIRST TIME IN OUR CAREERS. AND I'LL TELL YOU WHAT, MOTÖRHEAD'S FANS? WOO, IT'S A TOUGH CROWD!
WE WERE SO NERVOUS. WE HAD A SONG CALLED "WHAT YOU DON'T KNOW SURE CAN HURT YOU,"
1982
WE PERFORMED THE FIRST HALF OF THE SONG IN SILHOUETTE SO THE AUDIENCE WOULDN'T SEE WHAT WE LOOK LIKE UNTIL HALFWAY THROUGH, AND THEN THE LIGHTS WOULD COME ON. AND THE IDEA WAS HOPEFULLY BY THAT TIME, YOU WOULD SAY, "WOW, THIS BAND'S REALLY ROCKING."

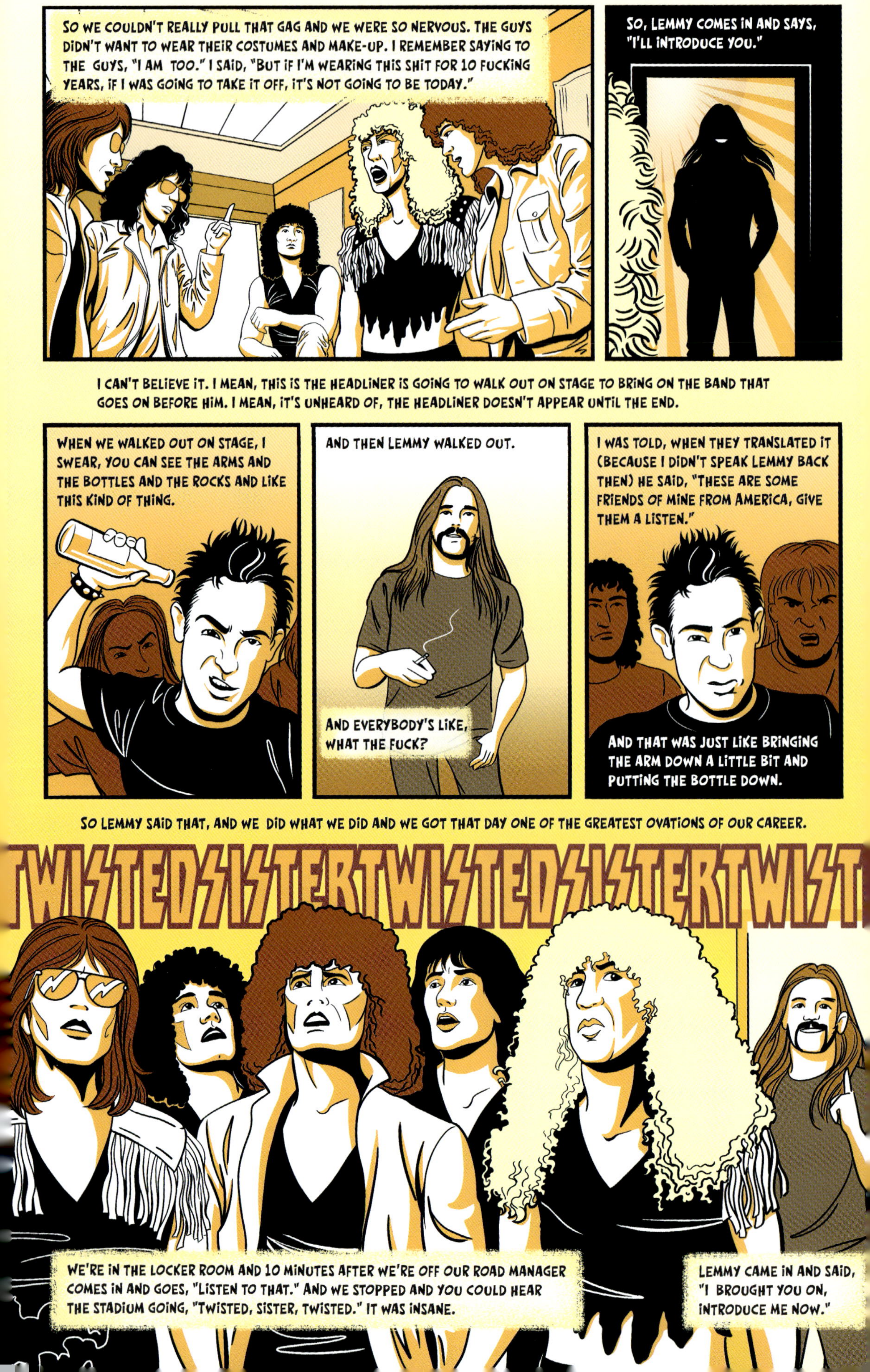
SO WE COULDN'T REALLY PULL THAT GAG AND WE WERE SO NERVOUS. THE GUYS DIDN'T WANT TO WEAR THEIR COSTUMES AND MAKE-UP. I REMEMBER SAYING TO THE GUYS, "I AM TOO." I SAID, "BUT IF I'M WEARING THIS SHIT FOR 10 FUCKING YEARS, IF I WAS GOING TO TAKE IT OFF, IT'S NOT GOING TO BE TODAY."
SO, LEMMY COMES IN AND SAYS, "I'LL INTRODUCE YOU."
I CAN'T BELIEVE IT. I MEAN, THIS IS THE HEADLINER IS GOING TO WALK OUT ON STAGE TO BRING ON THE BAND THAT GOES ON BEFORE HIM. I MEAN, IT'S UNHEARD OF, THE HEADLINER DOESN'T APPEAR UNTIL THE END.
WHEN WE WALKED OUT ON STAGE, I SWEAR, YOU CAN SEE THE ARMS AND THE BOTTLES AND THE ROCKS AND LIKE THIS KIND OF THING.
AND THEN LEMMY WALKED OUT.
AND EVERYBODY'S LIKE, WHAT THE FUCK?
I WAS TOLD, WHEN THEY TRANSLATED IT (BECAUSE I DIDN'T SPEAK LEMMY BACK THEN) HE SAID, "THESE ARE SOME FRIENDS OF MINE FROM AMERICA, GIVE THEM A LISTEN."
AND THAT WAS JUST LIKE BRINGING THE ARM DOWN A LITTLE BIT AND PUTTING THE BOTTLE DOWN.
SO LEMMY SAID THAT, AND WE DID WHAT WE DID AND WE GOT THAT DAY ONE OF THE GREATEST OVATIONS OF OUR CAREER.
TWISTEDSISTERTWISTEDSISTERTWIST
WE'RE IN THE LOCKER ROOM AND 10 MINUTES AFTER WE'RE OFF OUR ROAD MANAGER COMES IN AND GOES, "LISTEN TO THAT." AND WE STOPPED AND YOU COULD HEAR THE STADIUM GOING, "TWISTED, SISTER, TWISTED." IT WAS INSANE.
LEMMY CAME IN AND SAID, "I BROUGHT YOU ON, INTRODUCE ME NOW."

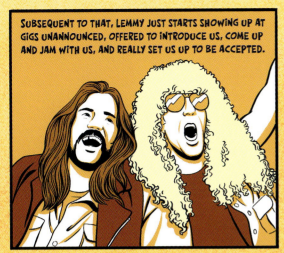
SUBSEQUENT TO THAT, LEMMY JUST STARTS SHOWING UP AT GIGS UNANNOUNCED, OFFERED TO INTRODUCE US, COME UP AND JAM WITH US, AND REALLY SET US UP TO BE ACCEPTED.

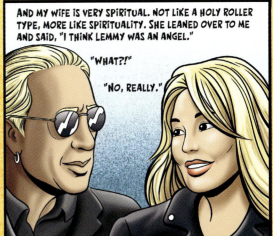
AND MY WIFE IS VERY SPIRITUAL. NOT LIKE A HOLY ROLLER TYPE, MORE LIKE SPIRITUALITY. SHE LEANED OVER TO ME AND SAID, "I THINK LEMMY WAS AN ANGEL."

"WHAT?!"

"NO, REALLY."

"THEY SAY THAT GOD PUTS ANGELS ON EARTH TO GUIDE US ON OUR WAY, TO HELP US ALONG. YOU LISTEN AND EVERYBODY'S STORY IS HOW LEMMY WAS SUDDENLY THERE FOR THEM AT A TIME THAT THEY NEEDED HIM TO BE. ALL THESE PEOPLE, HE HAS BEEN THERE FOR" SHE SAYS, "THIS IS WHAT THE ANGELS THAT ARE SENT DOWN TO EARTH ARE HERE TO DO, TO HELP US ALONG OUR WAY."

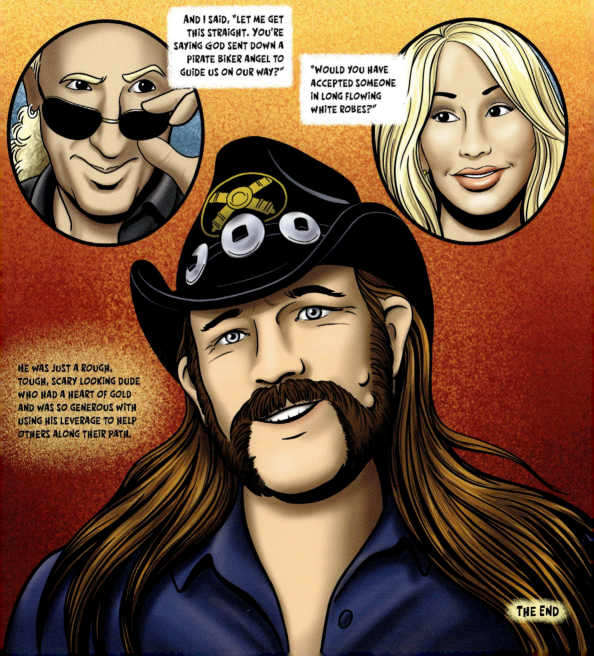

AND I SAID, "LET ME GET THIS STRAIGHT. YOU'RE SAYING GOD SENT DOWN A PIRATE BIKER ANGEL TO GUIDE US ON OUR WAY?"

"WOULD YOU HAVE ACCEPTED SOMEONE IN LONG FLOWING WHITE ROBES?"

HE WAS JUST A ROUGH, TOUGH, SCARY LOOKING DUDE WHO HAD A HEART OF GOLD AND WAS SO GENEROUS WITH USING HIS LEVERAGE TO HELP OTHERS ALONG THEIR PATH.

THE END

"Lemmy is one of the greatest pillars of what Rock & Roll is to me. Just one really sweet motherfucker."

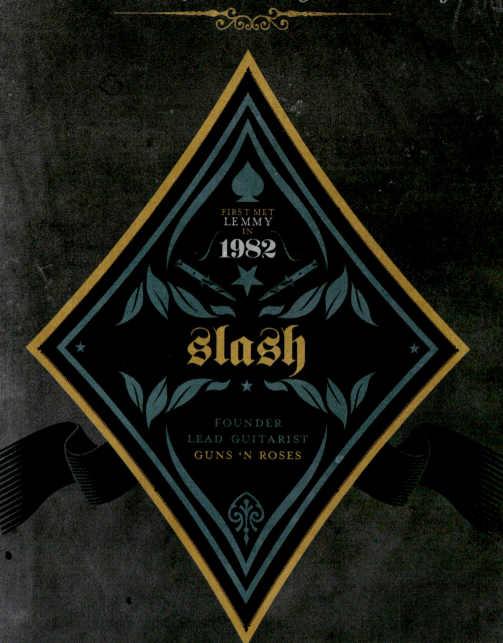

FIRST MET LEMMY IN 1982

slash

FOUNDER
LEAD GUITARIST
GUNS 'N ROSES

STORY ILLUSTRATED BY FELIPE SOBREIRO

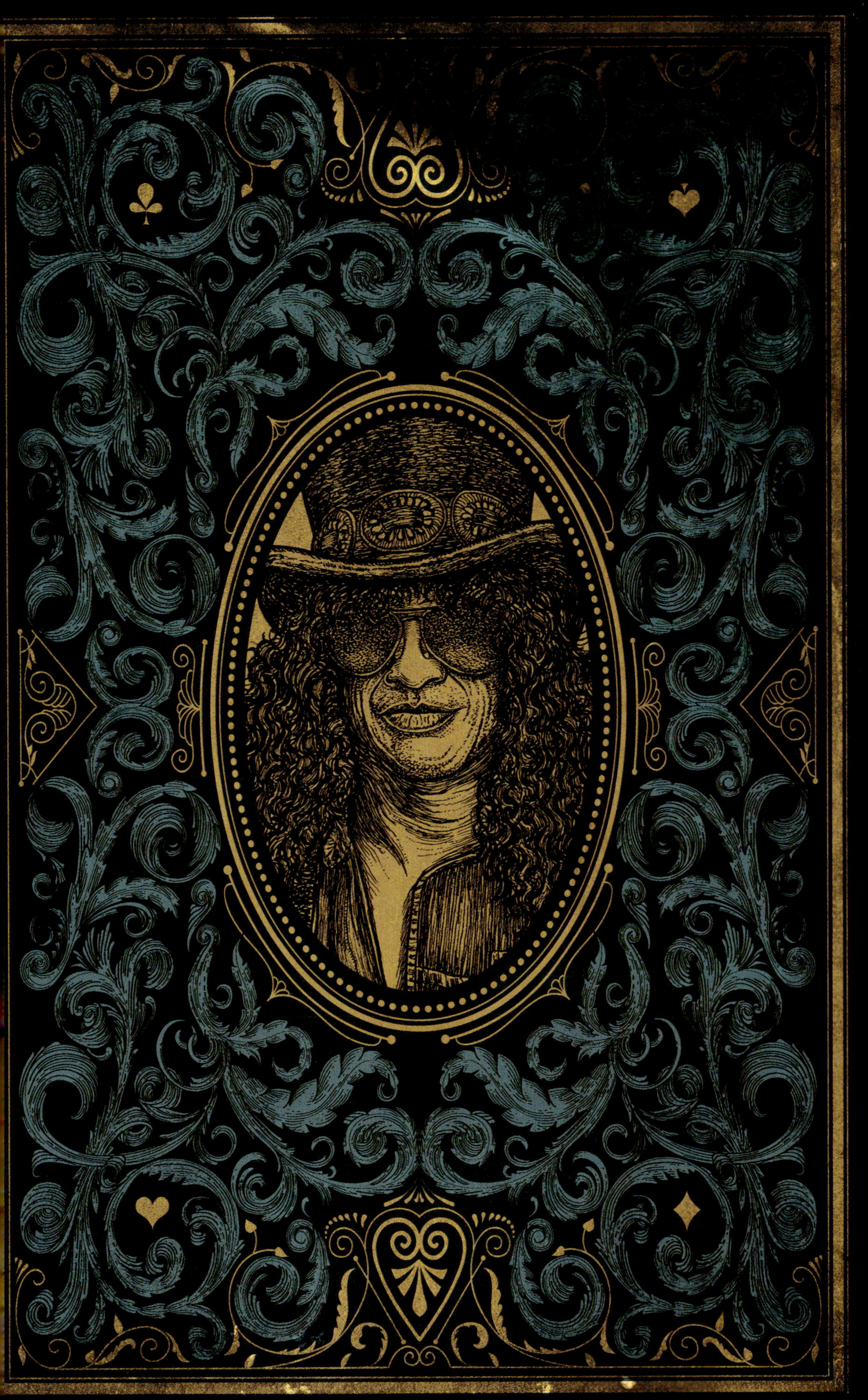

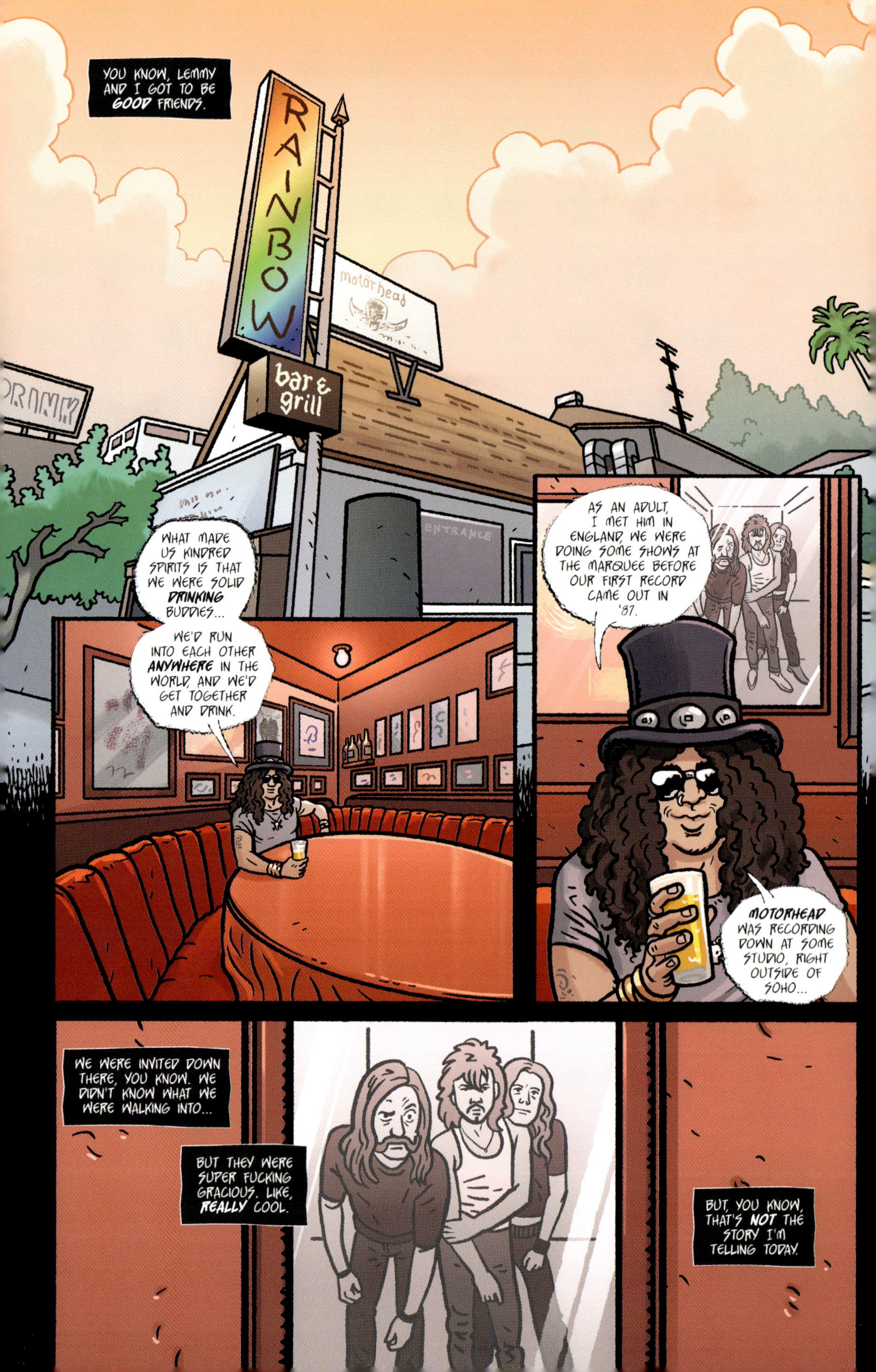

YOU KNOW, LEMMY AND I GOT TO BE GOOD FRIENDS.
RAINBOW
bar & grill
motörhead
ENTRANCE
WHAT MADE US KINDRED SPIRITS IS THAT WE WERE SOLID DRINKING BUDDIES...
WE'D RUN INTO EACH OTHER ANYWHERE IN THE WORLD, AND WE'D GET TOGETHER AND DRINK.
AS AN ADULT, I MET HIM IN ENGLAND. WE WERE DOING SOME SHOWS AT THE MARQUEE BEFORE OUR FIRST RECORD CAME OUT IN '87.
MOTORHEAD WAS RECORDING DOWN AT SOME STUDIO, RIGHT OUTSIDE OF SOHO...
WE WERE INVITED DOWN THERE, YOU KNOW. WE DIDN'T KNOW WHAT WE WERE WALKING INTO...
BUT THEY WERE SUPER FUCKING GRACIOUS. LIKE, REALLY COOL.
BUT, YOU KNOW, THAT'S NOT THE STORY I'M TELLING TODAY.

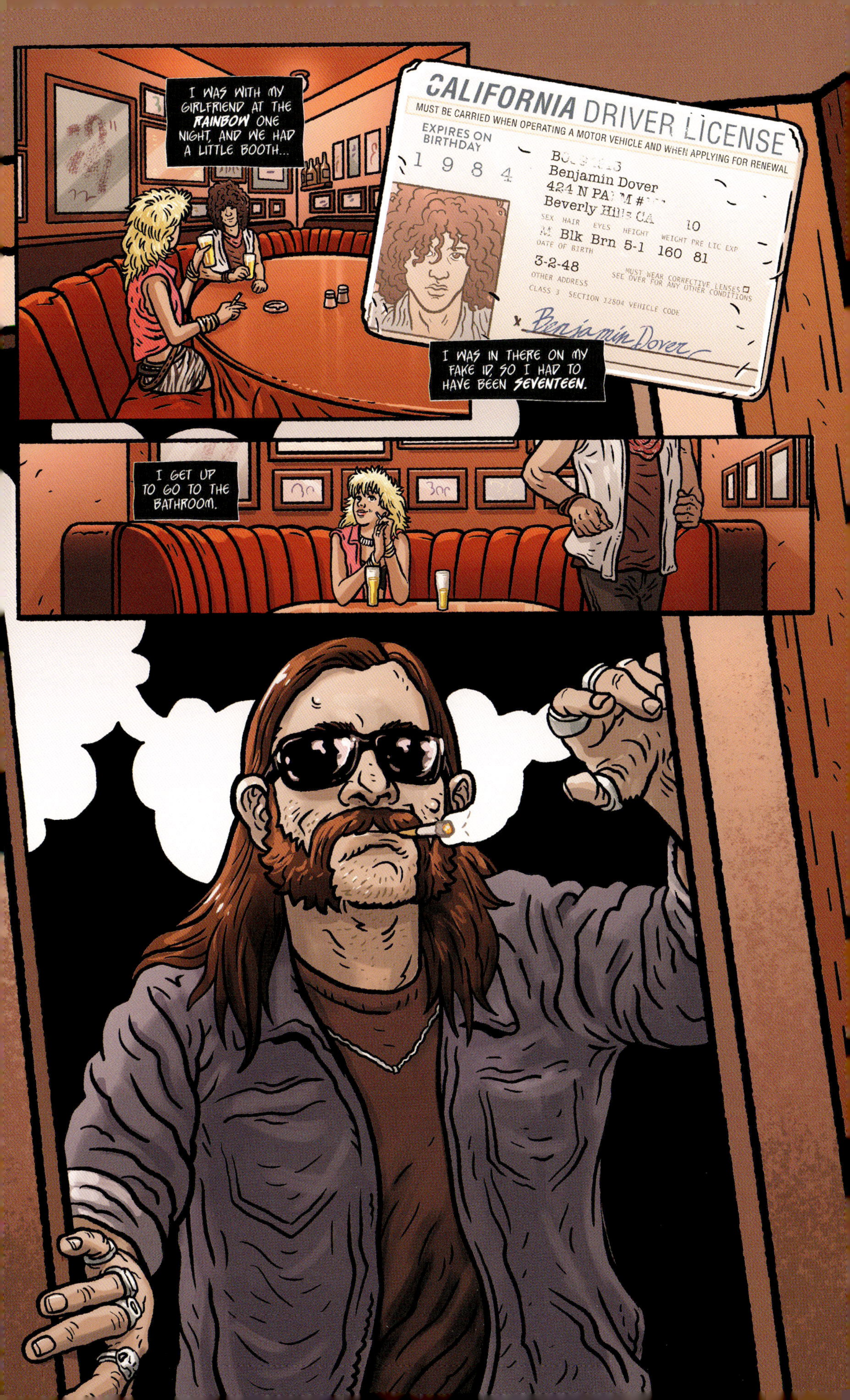

I WAS WITH MY GIRLFRIEND AT THE RAINBOW ONE NIGHT, AND WE HAD A LITTLE BOOTH...
CALIFORNIA DRIVER LICENSE
MUST BE CARRIED WHEN OPERATING A MOTOR VEHICLE AND WHEN APPLYING FOR RENEWAL
EXPIRES ON BIRTHDAY
1984
Benjamin Dover
SEX HAIR EYES HEIGHT WEIGHT PRE LIC EXP
Blk Brn 5-1 160 81
DATE OF BIRTH
3-2-48
OTHER ADDRESS
MUST WEAR CORRECTIVE LENSES
SEE OVER FOR ANY OTHER CONDITIONS
CLASS 3 SECTION 12804 VEHICLE CODE
Benjamin Dover
I WAS IN THERE ON MY FAKE ID, SO I HAD TO HAVE BEEN SEVENTEEN.
I GET UP TO GO TO THE BATHROOM.

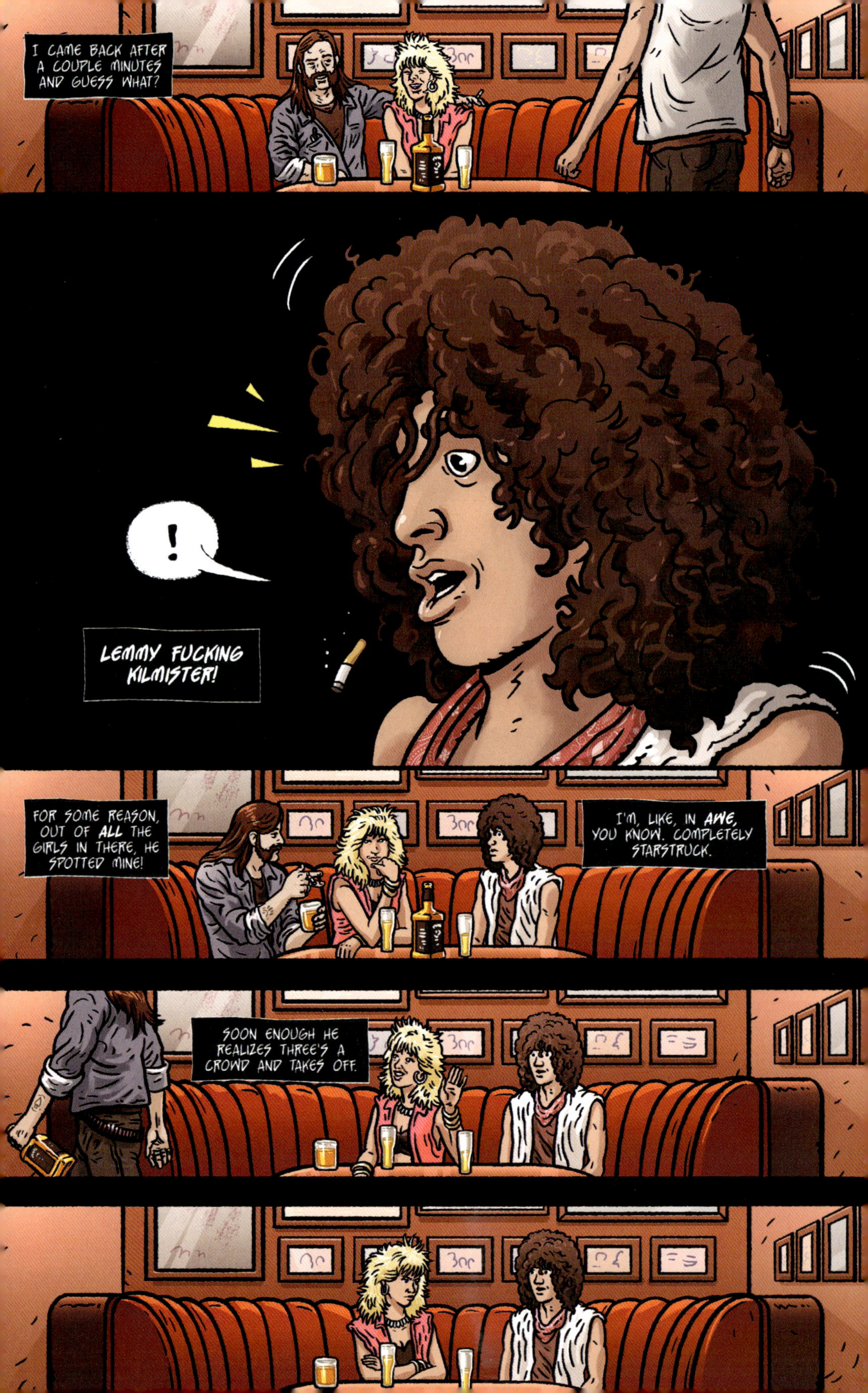
I CAME BACK AFTER A COUPLE MINUTES AND GUESS WHAT?
!
LEMMY FUCKING KILMISTER!
FOR SOME REASON, OUT OF ALL THE GIRLS IN THERE, HE SPOTTED MINE!
I'M, LIKE, IN AWE, YOU KNOW. COMPLETELY STARSTRUCK.
SOON ENOUGH HE REALIZES THREE'S A CROWD AND TAKES OFF.

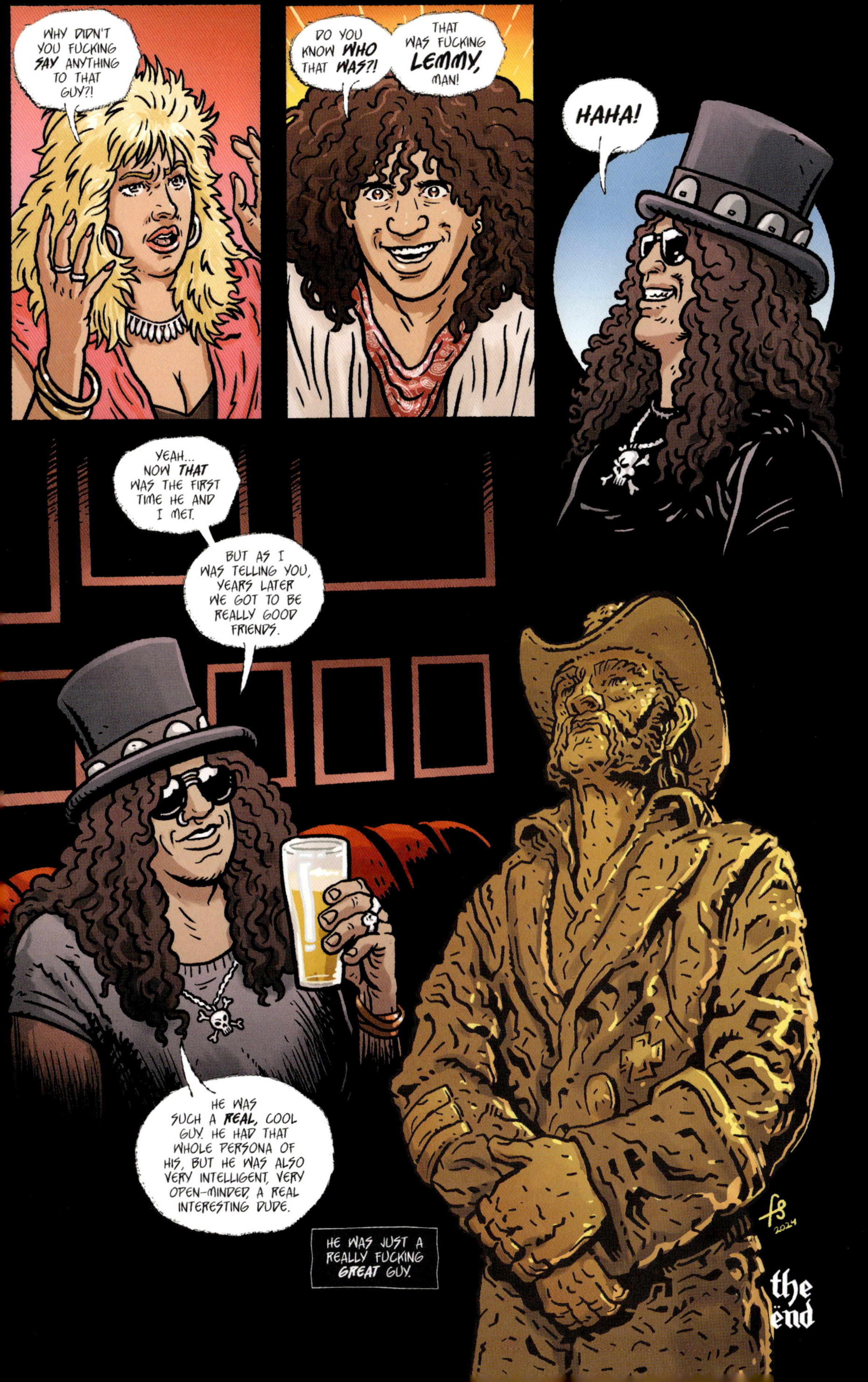
WHY DIDN'T YOU FUCKING SAY ANYTHING TO THAT GUY?!
DO YOU KNOW WHO THAT WAS?!
THAT WAS FUCKING LEMMY, MAN!
HAHA!
YEAH... NOW THAT WAS THE FIRST TIME HE AND I MET.
BUT AS I WAS TELLING YOU, YEARS LATER WE GOT TO BE REALLY GOOD FRIENDS.
HE WAS SUCH A REAL, COOL GUY. HE HAD THAT WHOLE PERSONA OF HIS, BUT HE WAS ALSO VERY INTELLIGENT, VERY OPEN-MINDED, A REAL INTERESTING DUDE.
HE WAS JUST A REALLY FUCKING GREAT GUY.
2024
the ënd

"Lemmy was the living embodiment of treating people with respect. His manners were quite impeccable."

FIRST MET LEMMY IN 1982

steffan chirazi

MOTÖRHEAD
CREATIVE
WRITER
FRIEND

STORY ILLUSTRATED BY GIDEON KENDALL

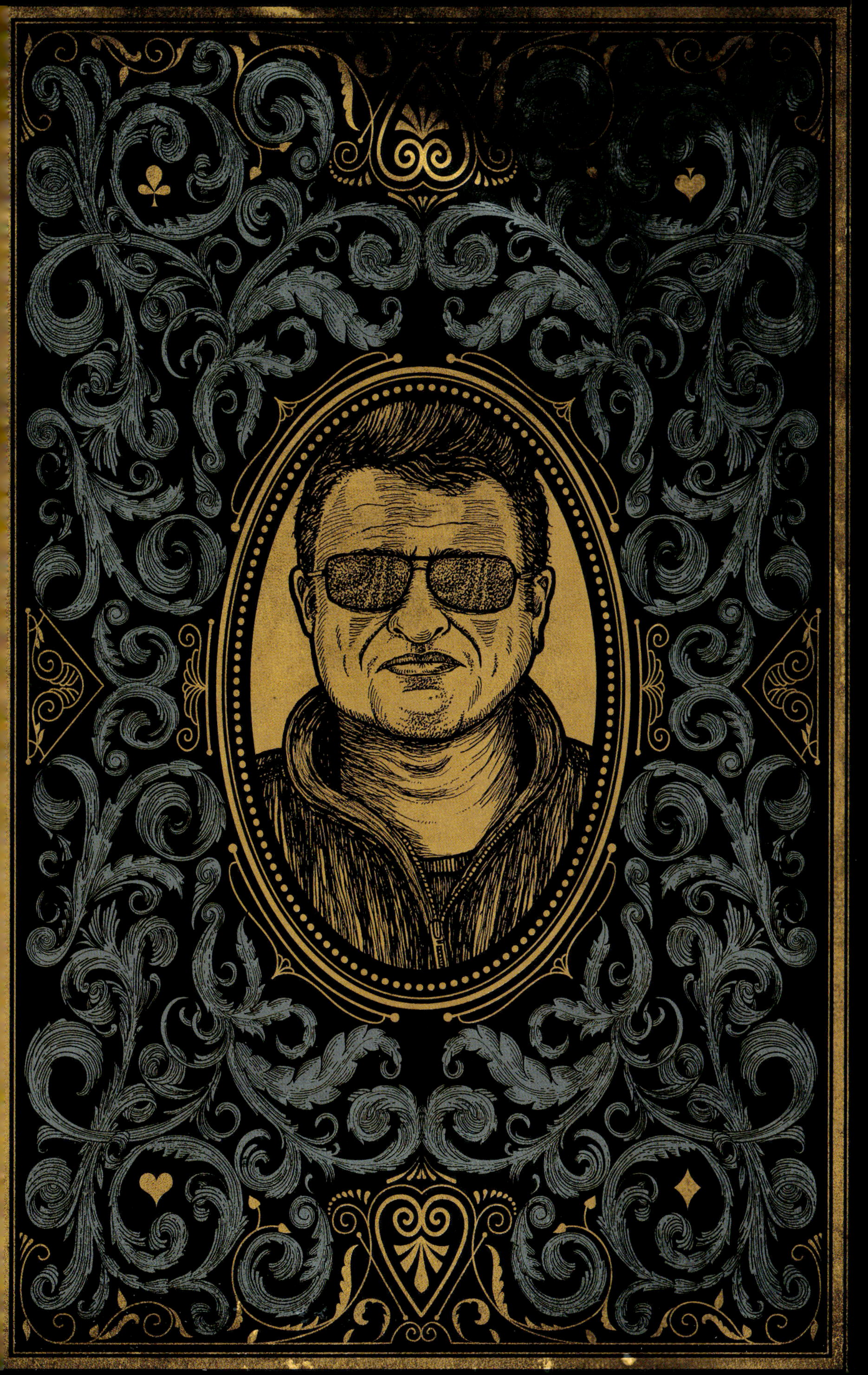

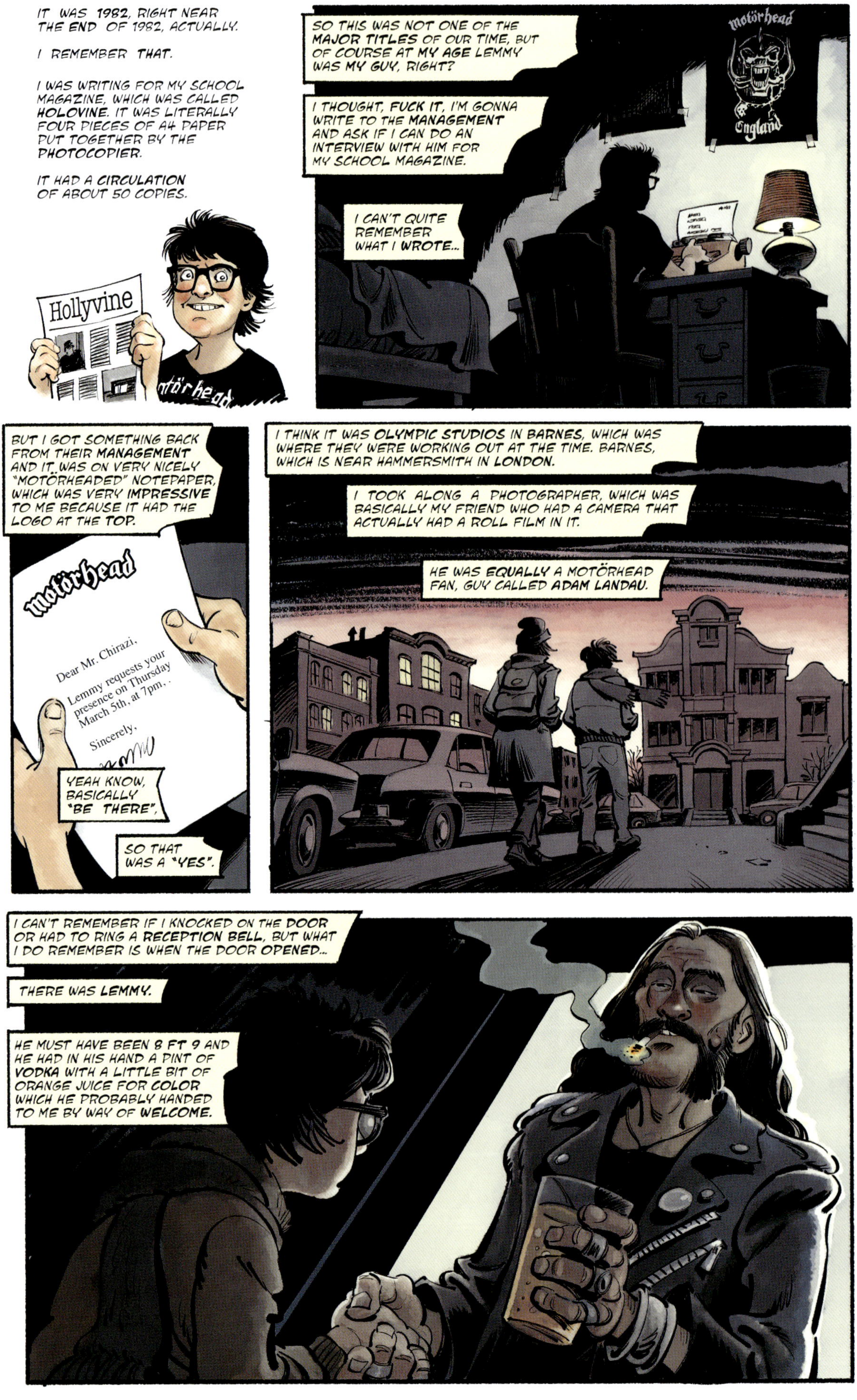
IT WAS 1982, RIGHT NEAR THE END OF 1982, ACTUALLY.
I REMEMBER THAT.
I WAS WRITING FOR MY SCHOOL MAGAZINE, WHICH WAS CALLED HOLOVINE. IT WAS LITERALLY FOUR PIECES OF A4 PAPER PUT TOGETHER BY THE PHOTOCOPIER.
IT HAD A CIRCULATION OF ABOUT 50 COPIES.
Hollyvine
motörhead
SO THIS WAS NOT ONE OF THE MAJOR TITLES OF OUR TIME, BUT OF COURSE AT MY AGE LEMMY WAS MY GUY, RIGHT?
I THOUGHT, FUCK IT, I'M GONNA WRITE TO THE MANAGEMENT AND ASK IF I CAN DO AN INTERVIEW WITH HIM FOR MY SCHOOL MAGAZINE.
motörhead
England
I CAN'T QUITE REMEMBER WHAT I WROTE...
BUT I GOT SOMETHING BACK FROM THEIR MANAGEMENT AND IT WAS ON VERY NICELY "MOTÖRHEADED" NOTEPAPER, WHICH WAS VERY IMPRESSIVE TO ME BECAUSE IT HAD THE LOGO AT THE TOP.
motörhead
Dear Mr. Chirazi,
Lemmy requests your presence on Thursday March 5th, at 7pm.,
Sincerely,
YEAH KNOW, BASICALLY "BE THERE",
SO THAT WAS A "YES".
I THINK IT WAS OLYMPIC STUDIOS IN BARNES, WHICH WAS WHERE THEY WERE WORKING OUT AT THE TIME. BARNES, WHICH IS NEAR HAMMERSMITH IN LONDON.
I TOOK ALONG A PHOTOGRAPHER, WHICH WAS BASICALLY MY FRIEND WHO HAD A CAMERA THAT ACTUALLY HAD A ROLL FILM IN IT.
HE WAS EQUALLY A MOTÖRHEAD FAN, GUY CALLED ADAM LANDAU.
I CAN'T REMEMBER IF I KNOCKED ON THE DOOR OR HAD TO RING A RECEPTION BELL, BUT WHAT I DO REMEMBER IS WHEN THE DOOR OPENED...
THERE WAS LEMMY.
HE MUST HAVE BEEN 8 FT 9 AND HE HAD IN HIS HAND A PINT OF VODKA WITH A LITTLE BIT OF ORANGE JUICE FOR COLOR WHICH HE PROBABLY HANDED TO ME BY WAY OF WELCOME.

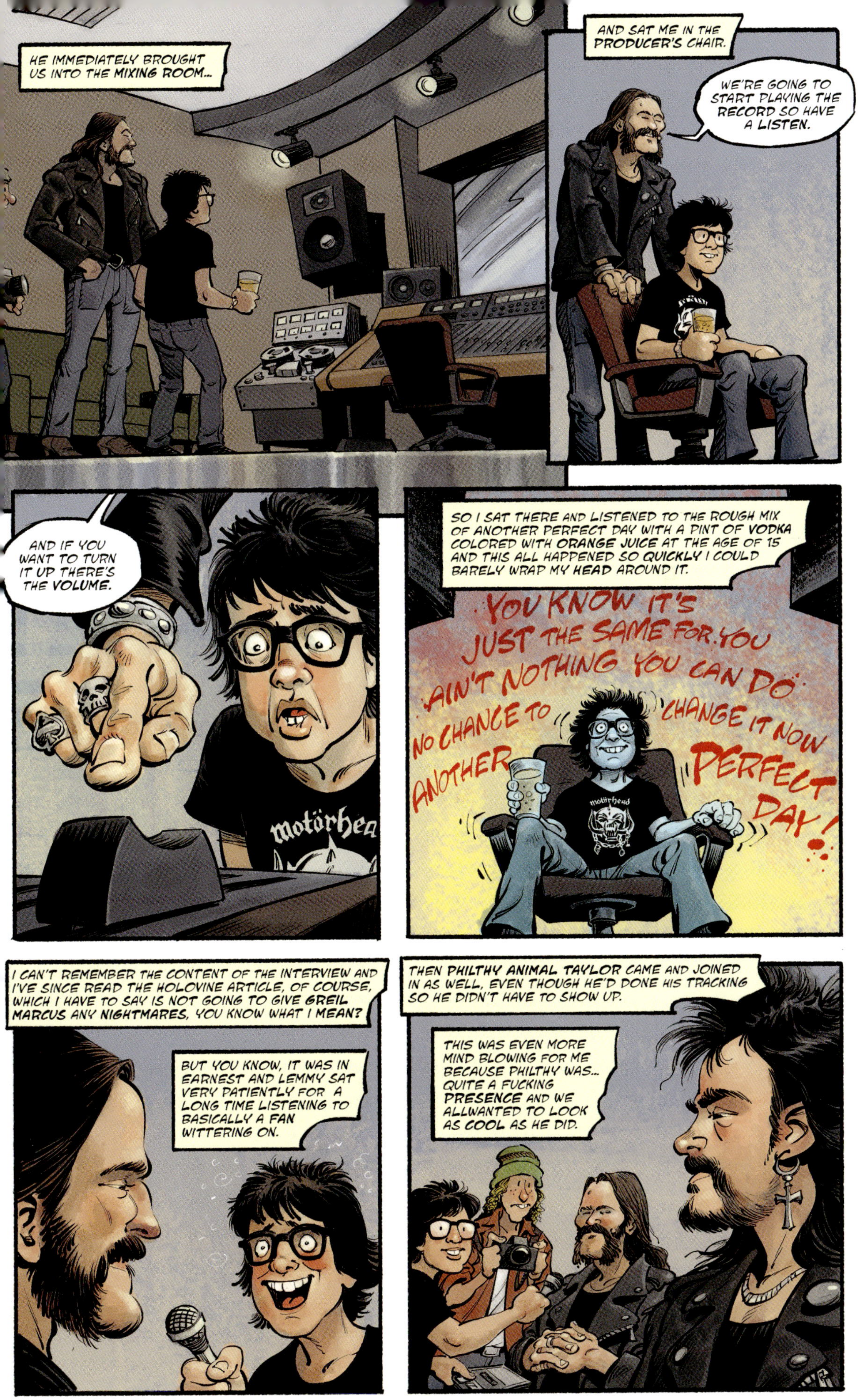
HE IMMEDIATELY BROUGHT US INTO THE MIXING ROOM...
AND SAT ME IN THE PRODUCER'S CHAIR.
WE'RE GOING TO START PLAYING THE RECORD SO HAVE A LISTEN.
AND IF YOU WANT TO TURN IT UP THERE'S THE VOLUME.
motörhea
SO I SAT THERE AND LISTENED TO THE ROUGH MIX OF ANOTHER PERFECT DAY WITH A PINT OF VODKA COLORED WITH ORANGE JUICE AT THE AGE OF 15 AND THIS ALL HAPPENED SO QUICKLY I COULD BARELY WRAP MY HEAD AROUND IT.
YOU KNOW IT'S JUST THE SAME FOR YOU AIN'T NOTHING YOU CAN DO NO CHANCE TO CHANGE IT NOW ANOTHER PERFECT DAY!
motörhead
I CAN'T REMEMBER THE CONTENT OF THE INTERVIEW AND I'VE SINCE READ THE HOLOVINE ARTICLE, OF COURSE, WHICH I HAVE TO SAY IS NOT GOING TO GIVE GREIL MARCUS ANY NIGHTMARES, YOU KNOW WHAT I MEAN?
BUT YOU KNOW, IT WAS IN EARNEST AND LEMMY SAT VERY PATIENTLY FOR A LONG TIME LISTENING TO BASICALLY A FAN WITTERING ON.
THEN PHILTHY ANIMAL TAYLOR CAME AND JOINED IN AS WELL, EVEN THOUGH HE'D DONE HIS TRACKING SO HE DIDN'T HAVE TO SHOW UP.
THIS WAS EVEN MORE MIND BLOWING FOR ME BECAUSE PHILTHY WAS... QUITE A FUCKING PRESENCE AND WE ALLWANTED TO LOOK AS COOL AS HE DID.

SO THEY ENDED UP HANGING OUT WITH US FOR THE BETTER PART OF 3 HOURS. AS I REMEMBER, IT WAS QUITE SOME TIME.

I CRACKED THAT JOKE ABOUT *ROLLING STONE*... THEY TREATED US LIKE WE WERE ROLLING STONE AND WEREN'T.

I REMEMBER GETTING A RIDE HOME FROM MY FRIEND ADAM'S PARENTS, WHO CAME TO PICK US UP AND I LITERALLY SPRINTED INTO MY PARENT'S FLAT AND I MADE THEM LISTEN TO THE INTERVIEW. SO THAT WAS THE FIRST TIME I MET LEMMY AND THAT WAS THE BEGINNING OF MANY.

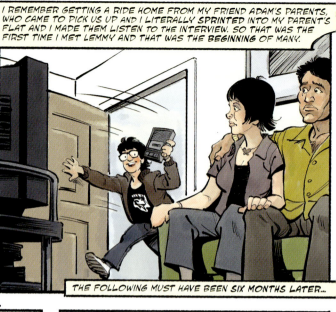

THE FOLLOWING MUST HAVE BEEN SIX MONTHS LATER...

IMBUED BY THE *CONFIDENCE* OF HAVING HAD MY HERO ENTERTAIN ME FOR AN EVENING, (I MANAGED TO) BULLSHIT MY WAY INTO AN INTERNSHIP AT *SOUNDS* MUSIC PAPER.

IT WAS REALLY EXCITING.

"WHAT DO YOU WANT TO DO A STORY ON?"

GARY BUSHELL

"I WANT TO DO A STORY ON MOTÖRHEAD'S NEW ALBUM, *ANOTHER PERFECT DAY*, BECAUSE IT SEEMS LIKE EVERYONE HATES IT."

"I THINK IT'S ABSOLUTELY BRILLIANT."

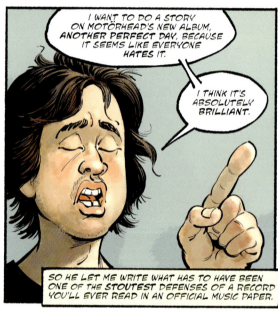

SO HE LET ME WRITE WHAT HAS TO HAVE BEEN ONE OF THE *STOUTEST* DEFENSES OF A RECORD YOU'LL EVER READ IN AN OFFICIAL MUSIC PAPER.

AND THEY PRINTED IT, HALF PAGE OF IT, AND SO, I SAW LEMMY AT A FESTIVAL IN DUBLIN THAT SUMMER AND WAS GIVEN THE *HALLOWED* BACKSTAGE PASS FOR THE FIRST TIME IN MY LIFE, ACTUALLY,

WAS THE FIRST BACKSTAGE PASS I EVER GOT TO THAT FESTIVAL.

HE CAME UP TO ME AND GAVE ME THE BIGGEST HUG, WHICH MEANT THAT MY NOSE ENDED UP IN HIS ARMPIT.

IT'S A *SMELL* I CAN REMEMBER TO THIS DAY.

IT'S A *CURIOUS* SMELL I CAN TELL YOU.

MANY LIVES LIVED IN THAT ARMPIT, I'M SURE.

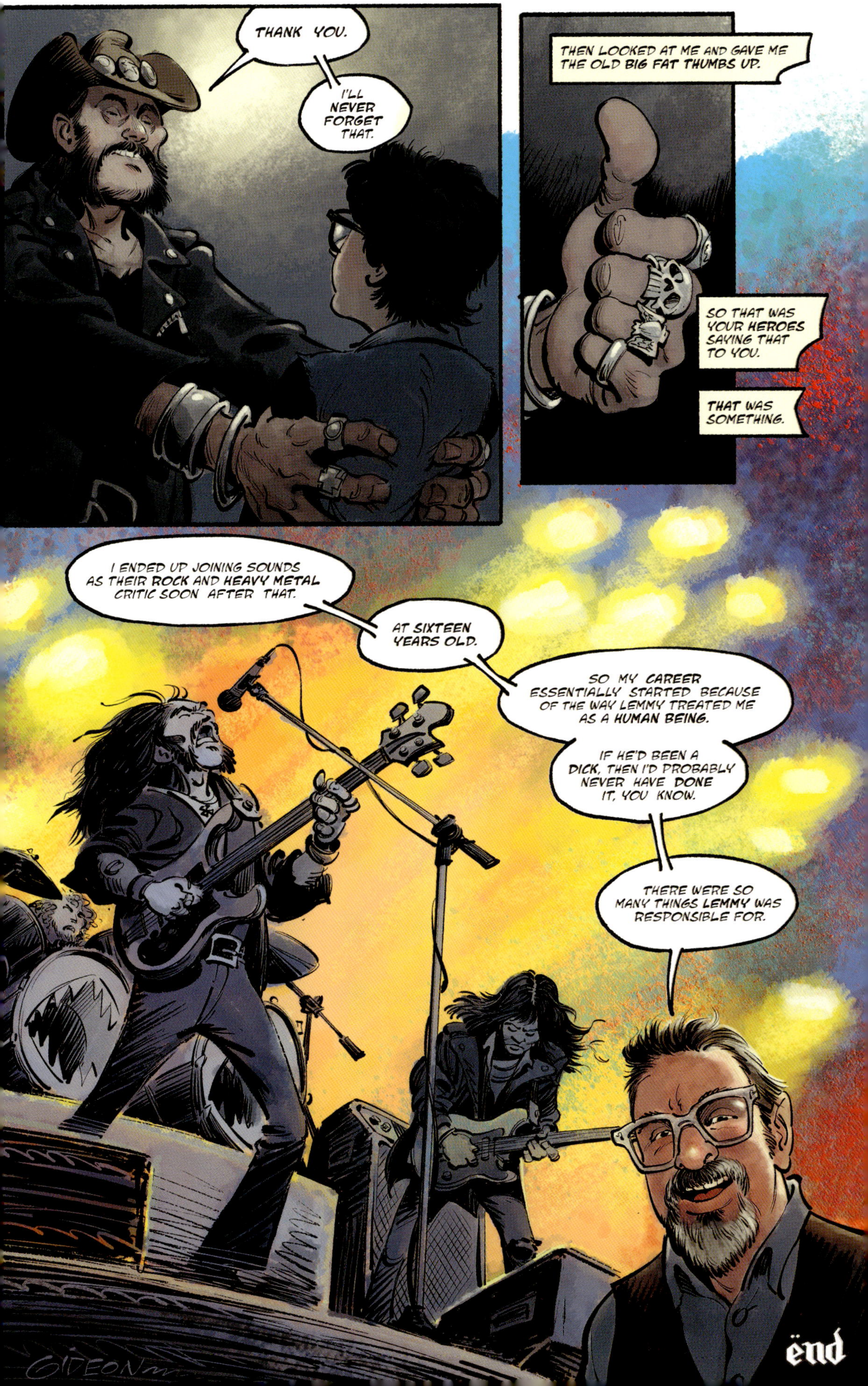
THANK YOU.
I'LL NEVER FORGET THAT.
THEN LOOKED AT ME AND GAVE ME THE OLD BIG FAT THUMBS UP.
SO THAT WAS YOUR HEROES SAYING THAT TO YOU.
THAT WAS SOMETHING.
I ENDED UP JOINING SOUNDS AS THEIR ROCK AND HEAVY METAL CRITIC SOON AFTER THAT.
AT SIXTEEN YEARS OLD.
SO MY CAREER ESSENTIALLY STARTED BECAUSE OF THE WAY LEMMY TREATED ME AS A HUMAN BEING.
IF HE'D BEEN A DICK, THEN I'D PROBABLY NEVER HAVE DONE IT, YOU KNOW.
THERE WERE SO MANY THINGS LEMMY WAS RESPONSIBLE FOR.
GIDEON
ënd

"I love you Lemmy, my big brother.
The man who changed the face of Rock & Roll forever."

FIRST MET
LEMMY
IN
1984

lita ford

ROCK & ROLL
GODDESS +
LEAD GUITARIST
THE
RUNAWAYS

STORY ILLUSTRATED BY RON JOSEPH

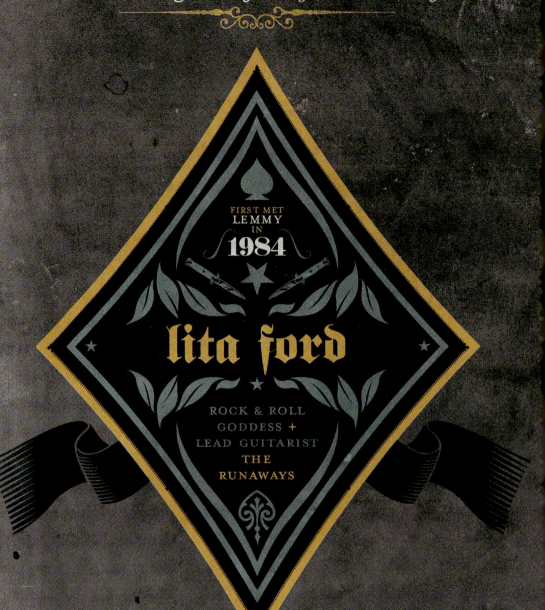

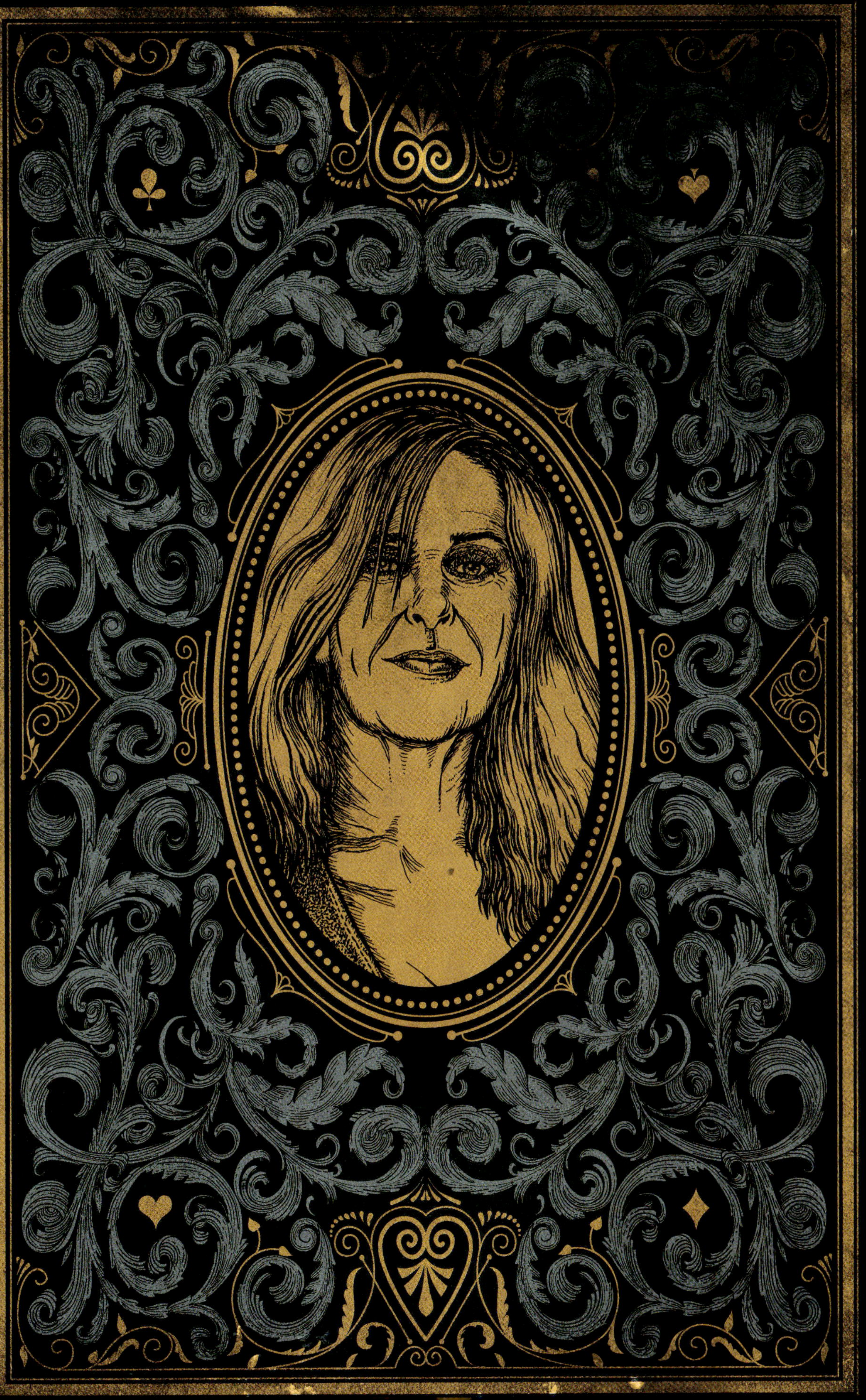

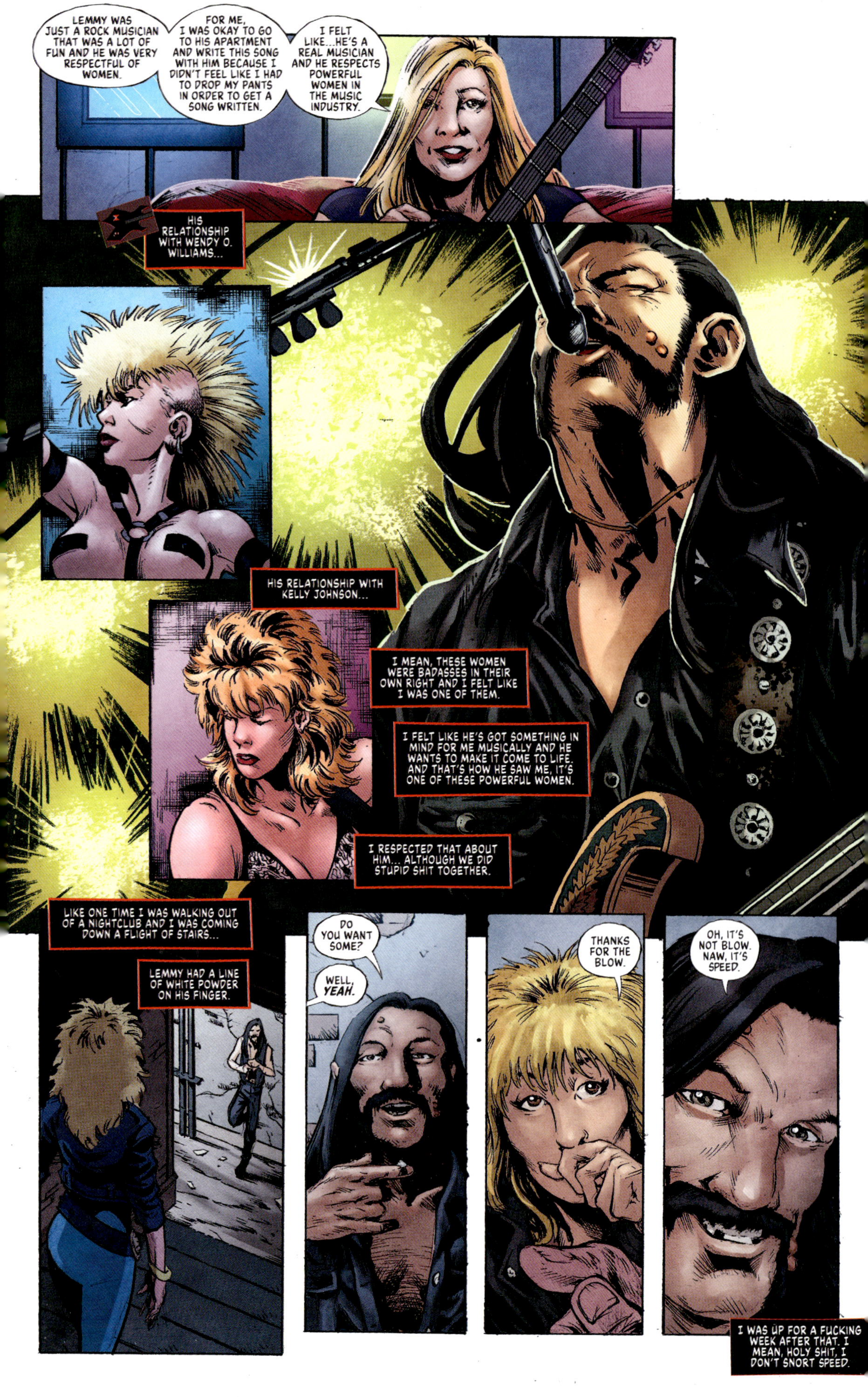
LEMMY WAS JUST A ROCK MUSICIAN THAT WAS A LOT OF FUN AND HE WAS VERY RESPECTFUL OF WOMEN.
FOR ME, I WAS OKAY TO GO TO HIS APARTMENT AND WRITE THIS SONG WITH HIM BECAUSE I DIDN'T FEEL LIKE I HAD TO DROP MY PANTS IN ORDER TO GET A SONG WRITTEN.
I FELT LIKE...HE'S A REAL MUSICIAN AND HE RESPECTS POWERFUL WOMEN IN THE MUSIC INDUSTRY.
HIS RELATIONSHIP WITH WENDY O. WILLIAMS...
HIS RELATIONSHIP WITH KELLY JOHNSON...
I MEAN, THESE WOMEN WERE BADASSES IN THEIR OWN RIGHT AND I FELT LIKE I WAS ONE OF THEM.
I FELT LIKE HE'S GOT SOMETHING IN MIND FOR ME MUSICALLY AND HE WANTS TO MAKE IT COME TO LIFE. AND THAT'S HOW HE SAW ME, IT'S ONE OF THESE POWERFUL WOMEN.
I RESPECTED THAT ABOUT HIM... ALTHOUGH WE DID STUPID SHIT TOGETHER.
LIKE ONE TIME I WAS WALKING OUT OF A NIGHTCLUB AND I WAS COMING DOWN A FLIGHT OF STAIRS...
LEMMY HAD A LINE OF WHITE POWDER ON HIS FINGER.
DO YOU WANT SOME?
WELL, *YEAH.*
THANKS FOR THE BLOW.
OH, IT'S NOT BLOW. NAW, IT'S SPEED.
I WAS UP FOR A FUCKING WEEK AFTER THAT. I MEAN, HOLY SHIT, I DON'T SNORT SPEED.

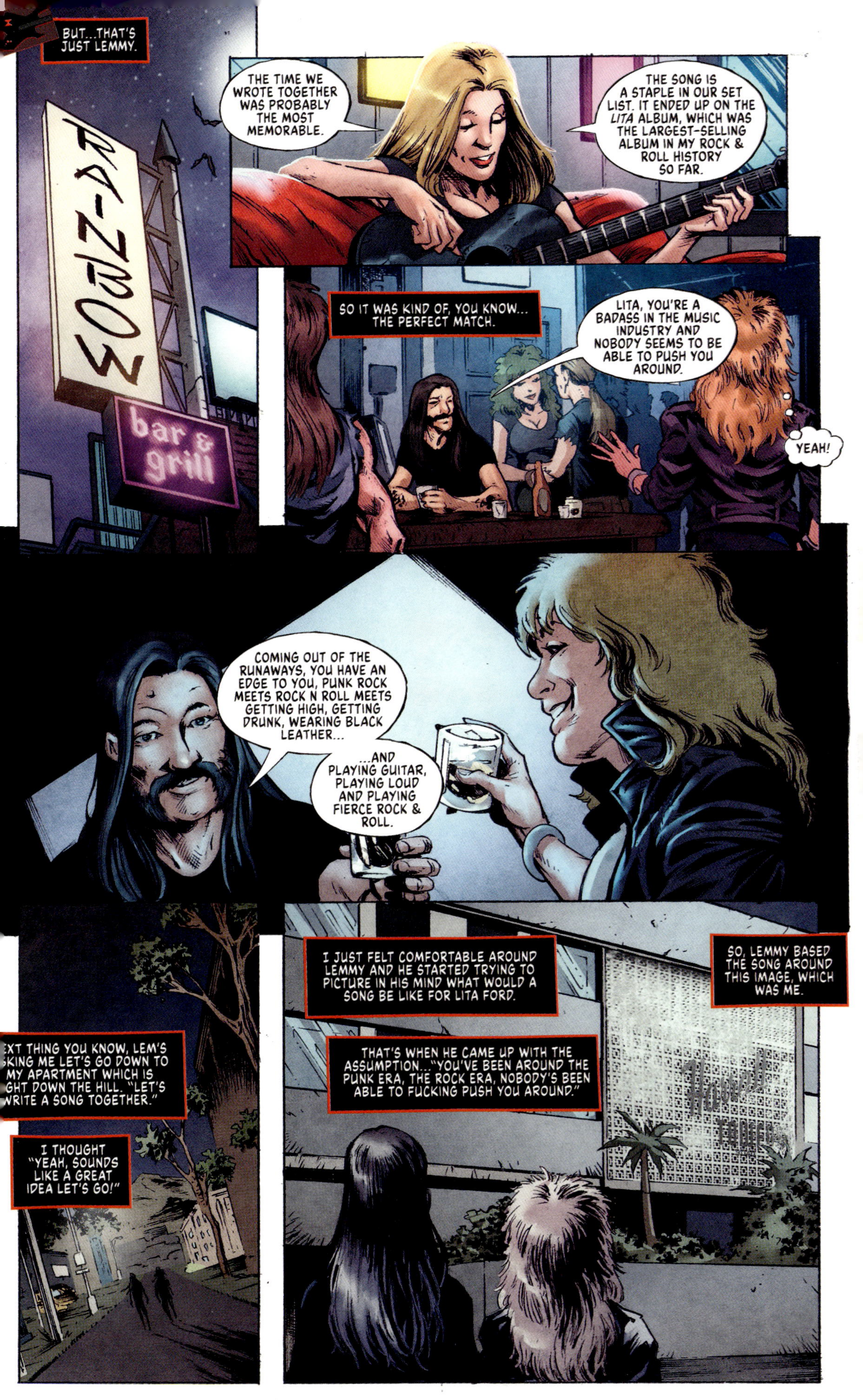

BUT...THAT'S JUST LEMMY.
THE TIME WE WROTE TOGETHER WAS PROBABLY THE MOST MEMORABLE.
THE SONG IS A STAPLE IN OUR SET LIST. IT ENDED UP ON THE *LITA* ALBUM, WHICH WAS THE LARGEST-SELLING ALBUM IN MY ROCK & ROLL HISTORY SO FAR.
bar & grill
SO IT WAS KIND OF, YOU KNOW... THE PERFECT MATCH.
LITA, YOU'RE A BADASS IN THE MUSIC INDUSTRY AND NOBODY SEEMS TO BE ABLE TO PUSH YOU AROUND.
YEAH!
COMING OUT OF THE RUNAWAYS, YOU HAVE AN EDGE TO YOU, PUNK ROCK MEETS ROCK N ROLL MEETS GETTING HIGH, GETTING DRUNK, WEARING BLACK LEATHER...
...AND PLAYING GUITAR, PLAYING LOUD AND PLAYING FIERCE ROCK & ROLL.
XT THING YOU KNOW, LEM'S KING ME LET'S GO DOWN TO MY APARTMENT WHICH IS GHT DOWN THE HILL. "LET'S WRITE A SONG TOGETHER."
I THOUGHT "YEAH, SOUNDS LIKE A GREAT IDEA LET'S GO!"
I JUST FELT COMFORTABLE AROUND LEMMY AND HE STARTED TRYING TO PICTURE IN HIS MIND WHAT WOULD A SONG BE LIKE FOR LITA FORD.
SO, LEMMY BASED THE SONG AROUND THIS IMAGE, WHICH WAS ME.
THAT'S WHEN HE CAME UP WITH THE ASSUMPTION..."YOU'VE BEEN AROUND THE PUNK ERA, THE ROCK ERA, NOBODY'S BEEN ABLE TO FUCKING PUSH YOU AROUND."

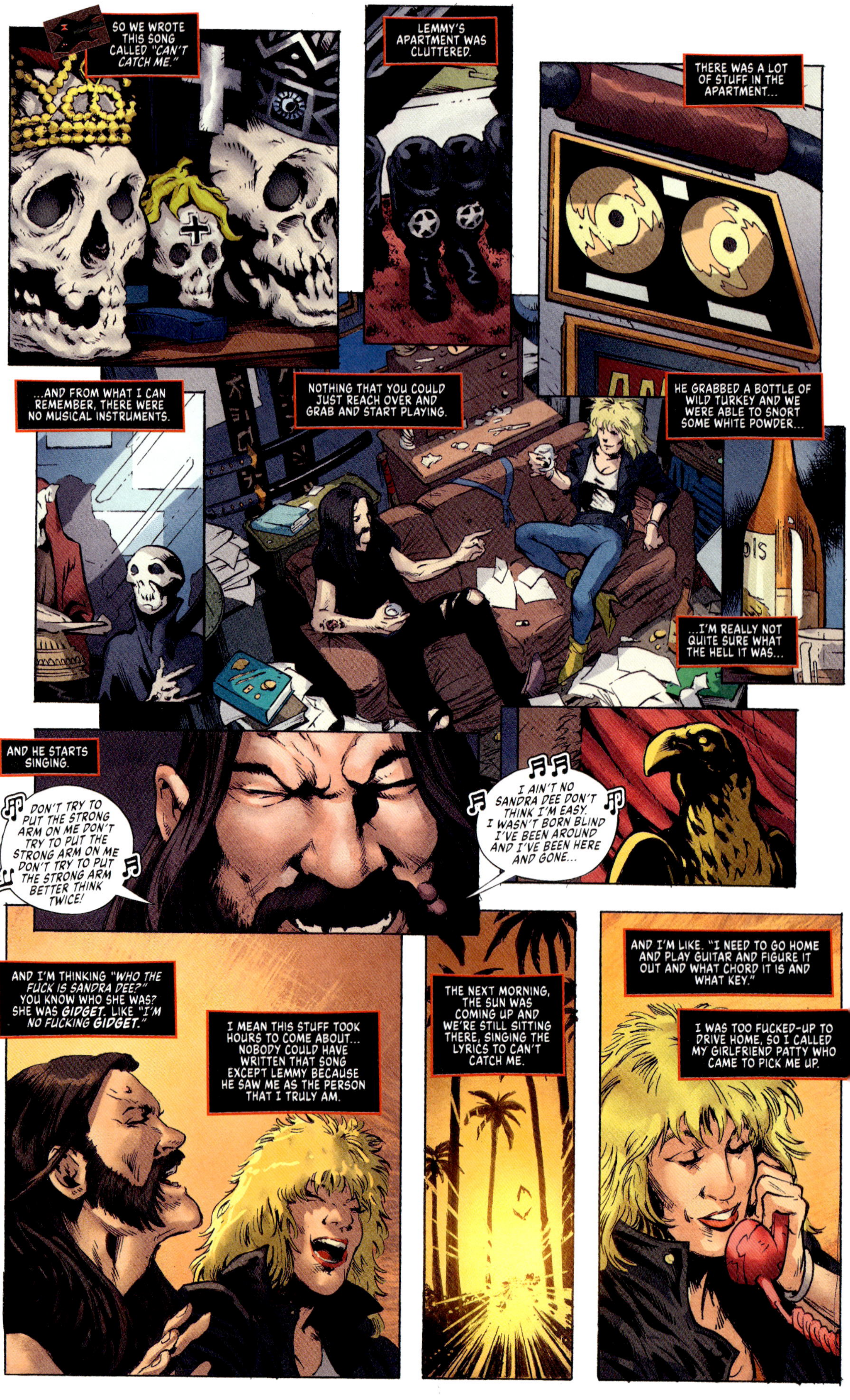
SO WE WROTE THIS SONG CALLED "CAN'T CATCH ME."
LEMMY'S APARTMENT WAS CLUTTERED.
THERE WAS A LOT OF STUFF IN THE APARTMENT...
...AND FROM WHAT I CAN REMEMBER, THERE WERE NO MUSICAL INSTRUMENTS.
NOTHING THAT YOU COULD JUST REACH OVER AND GRAB AND START PLAYING.
HE GRABBED A BOTTLE OF WILD TURKEY AND WE WERE ABLE TO SNORT SOME WHITE POWDER...
...I'M REALLY NOT QUITE SURE WHAT THE HELL IT WAS...
AND HE STARTS SINGING.
DON'T TRY TO PUT THE STRONG ARM ON ME DON'T TRY TO PUT THE STRONG ARM ON ME DON'T TRY TO PUT THE STRONG ARM BETTER THINK TWICE!
I AIN'T NO SANDRA DEE DON'T THINK I'M EASY. I WASN'T BORN BLIND I'VE BEEN AROUND AND I'VE BEEN HERE AND GONE...
AND I'M THINKING "WHO THE FUCK IS SANDRA DEE?" YOU KNOW WHO SHE WAS? SHE WAS GIDGET. LIKE "I'M NO FUCKING GIDGET."
I MEAN THIS STUFF TOOK HOURS TO COME ABOUT... NOBODY COULD HAVE WRITTEN THAT SONG EXCEPT LEMMY BECAUSE HE SAW ME AS THE PERSON THAT I TRULY AM.
THE NEXT MORNING, THE SUN WAS COMING UP AND WE'RE STILL SITTING THERE, SINGING THE LYRICS TO CAN'T CATCH ME.
AND I'M LIKE. "I NEED TO GO HOME AND PLAY GUITAR AND FIGURE IT OUT AND WHAT CHORD IT IS AND WHAT KEY."
I WAS TOO FUCKED-UP TO DRIVE HOME, SO I CALLED MY GIRLFRIEND PATTY WHO CAME TO PICK ME UP.

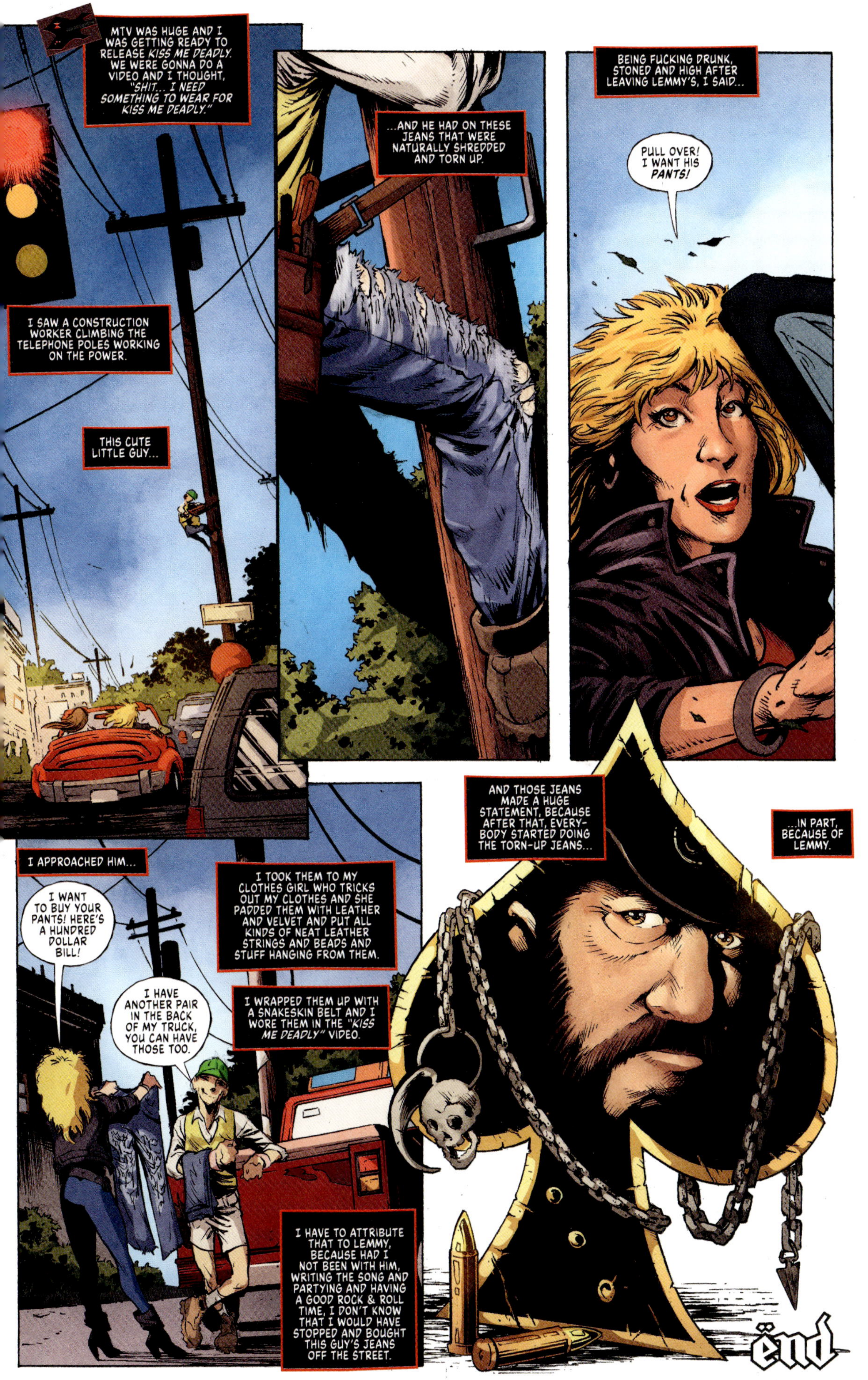
MTV WAS HUGE AND I WAS GETTING READY TO RELEASE *KISS ME DEADLY*. WE WERE GONNA DO A VIDEO AND I THOUGHT, *"SHIT... I NEED SOMETHING TO WEAR FOR KISS ME DEADLY."*
I SAW A CONSTRUCTION WORKER CLIMBING THE TELEPHONE POLES WORKING ON THE POWER.
THIS CUTE LITTLE GUY...
...AND HE HAD ON THESE JEANS THAT WERE NATURALLY SHREDDED AND TORN UP.
BEING FUCKING DRUNK, STONED AND HIGH AFTER LEAVING LEMMY'S, I SAID...
PULL OVER! I WANT HIS *PANTS!*
I APPROACHED HIM...
I WANT TO BUY YOUR PANTS! HERE'S A HUNDRED DOLLAR BILL!
I HAVE ANOTHER PAIR IN THE BACK OF MY TRUCK, YOU CAN HAVE THOSE TOO.
I TOOK THEM TO MY CLOTHES GIRL WHO TRICKS OUT MY CLOTHES AND SHE PADDED THEM WITH LEATHER AND VELVET AND PUT ALL KINDS OF NEAT LEATHER STRINGS AND BEADS AND STUFF HANGING FROM THEM.
I WRAPPED THEM UP WITH A SNAKESKIN BELT AND I WORE THEM IN THE *"KISS ME DEADLY"* VIDEO.
I HAVE TO ATTRIBUTE THAT TO LEMMY, BECAUSE HAD I NOT BEEN WITH HIM, WRITING THE SONG AND PARTYING AND HAVING A GOOD ROCK & ROLL TIME, I DON'T KNOW THAT I WOULD HAVE STOPPED AND BOUGHT THIS GUY'S JEANS OFF THE STREET.
AND THOSE JEANS MADE A HUGE STATEMENT, BECAUSE AFTER THAT, EVERY-BODY STARTED DOING THE TORN-UP JEANS...
...IN PART, BECAUSE OF LEMMY.
ënd

"A lot of people are acknowledging what us rockers knew all along – Motörhead is the best and Lemmy is God."

FIRST MET LEMMY IN 1986

riki rachtman

OWNER THE CATHOUSE
HOST HEADBANGER'S BALL

STORY ILLUSTRATED BY STEVE KURTH

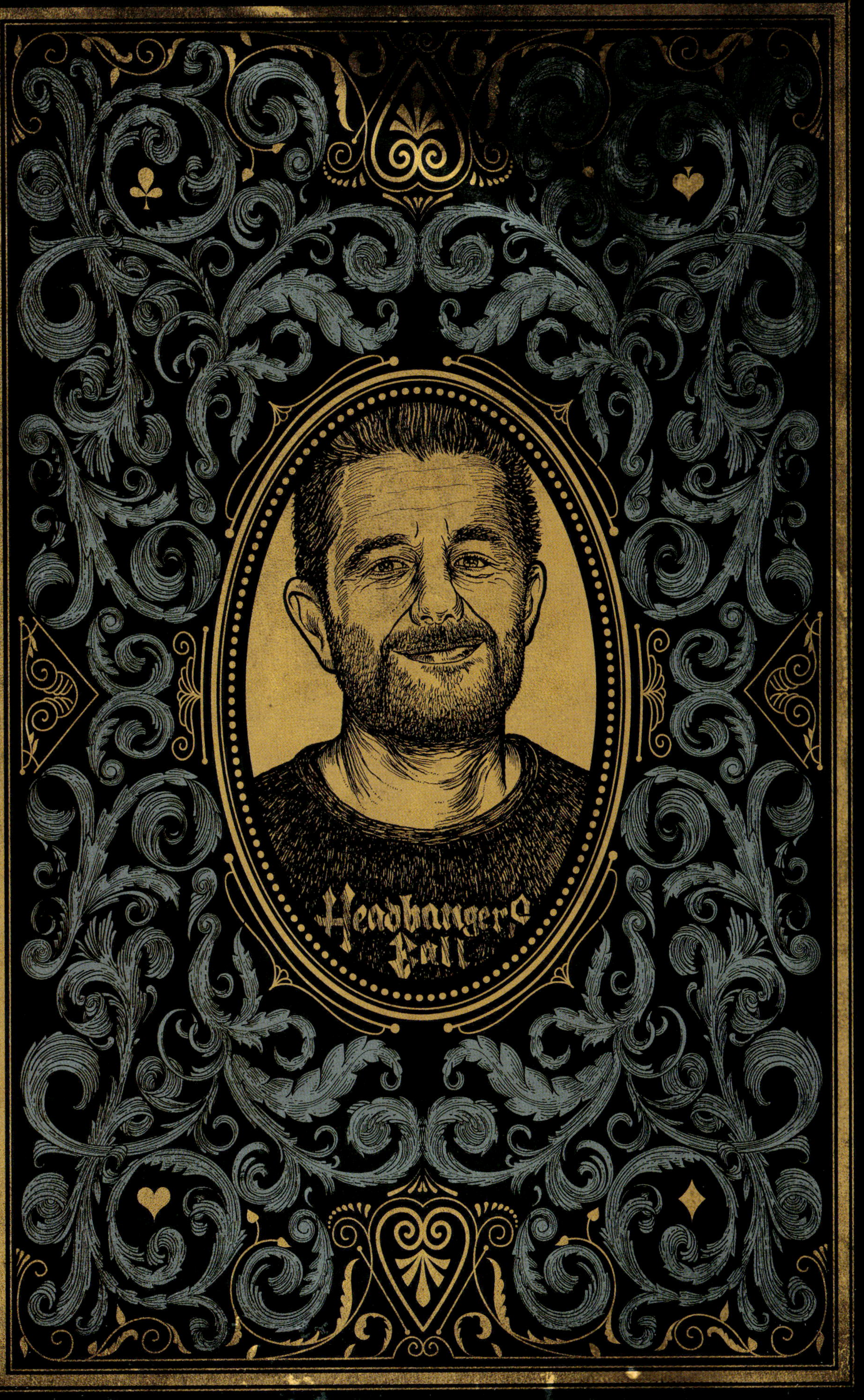
Headbangers
Ball

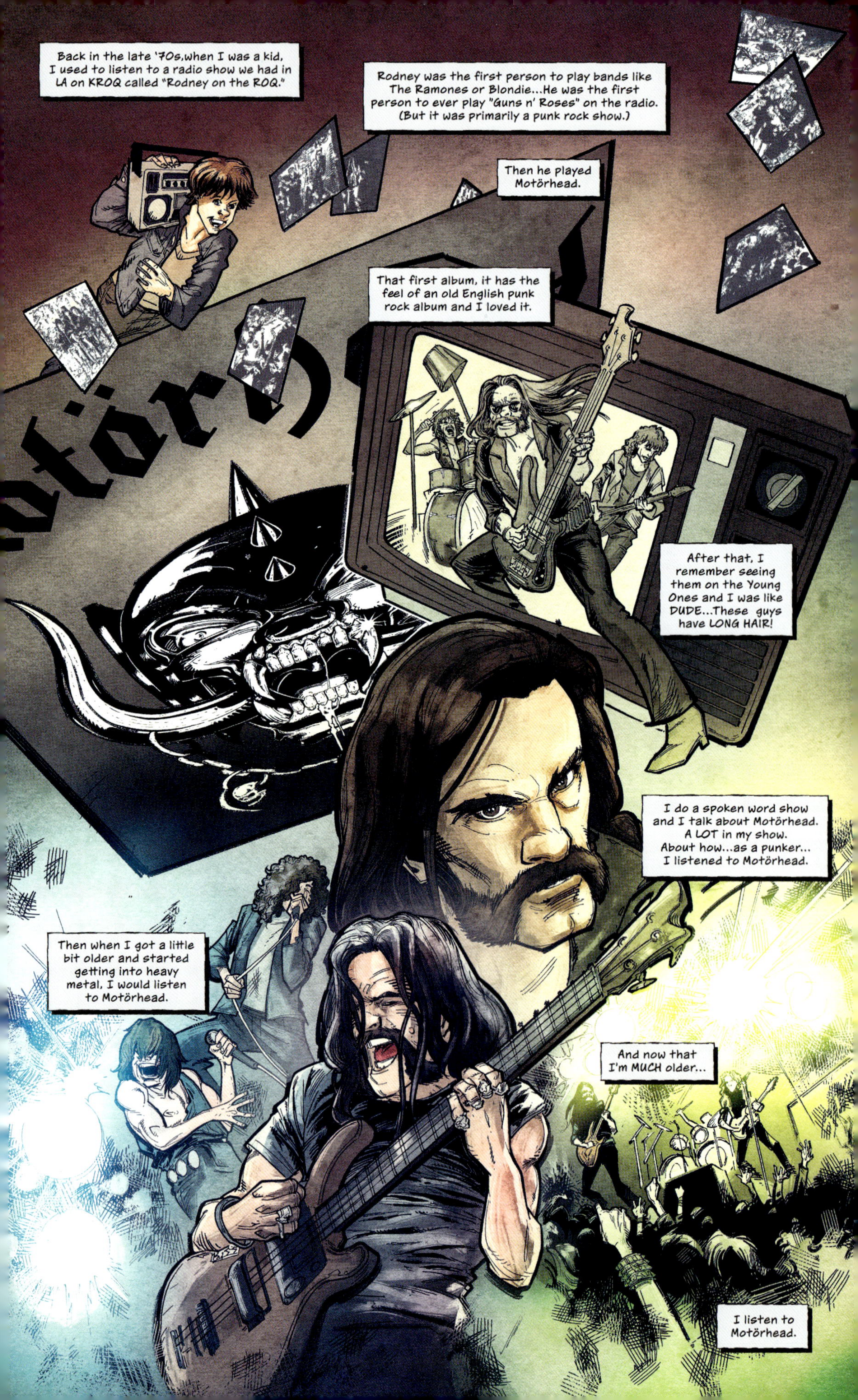

Back in the late '70s, when I was a kid, I used to listen to a radio show we had in LA on KROQ called "Rodney on the ROQ."
Rodney was the first person to play bands like The Ramones or Blondie...He was the first person to ever play "Guns n' Roses" on the radio. (But it was primarily a punk rock show.)
Then he played Motörhead.
That first album, it has the feel of an old English punk rock album and I loved it.
After that, I remember seeing them on the Young Ones and I was like DUDE...These guys have LONG HAIR!
I do a spoken word show and I talk about Motörhead. A LOT in my show. About how...as a punker... I listened to Motörhead.
Then when I got a little bit older and started getting into heavy metal, I would listen to Motörhead.
And now that I'm MUCH older...
I listen to Motörhead.

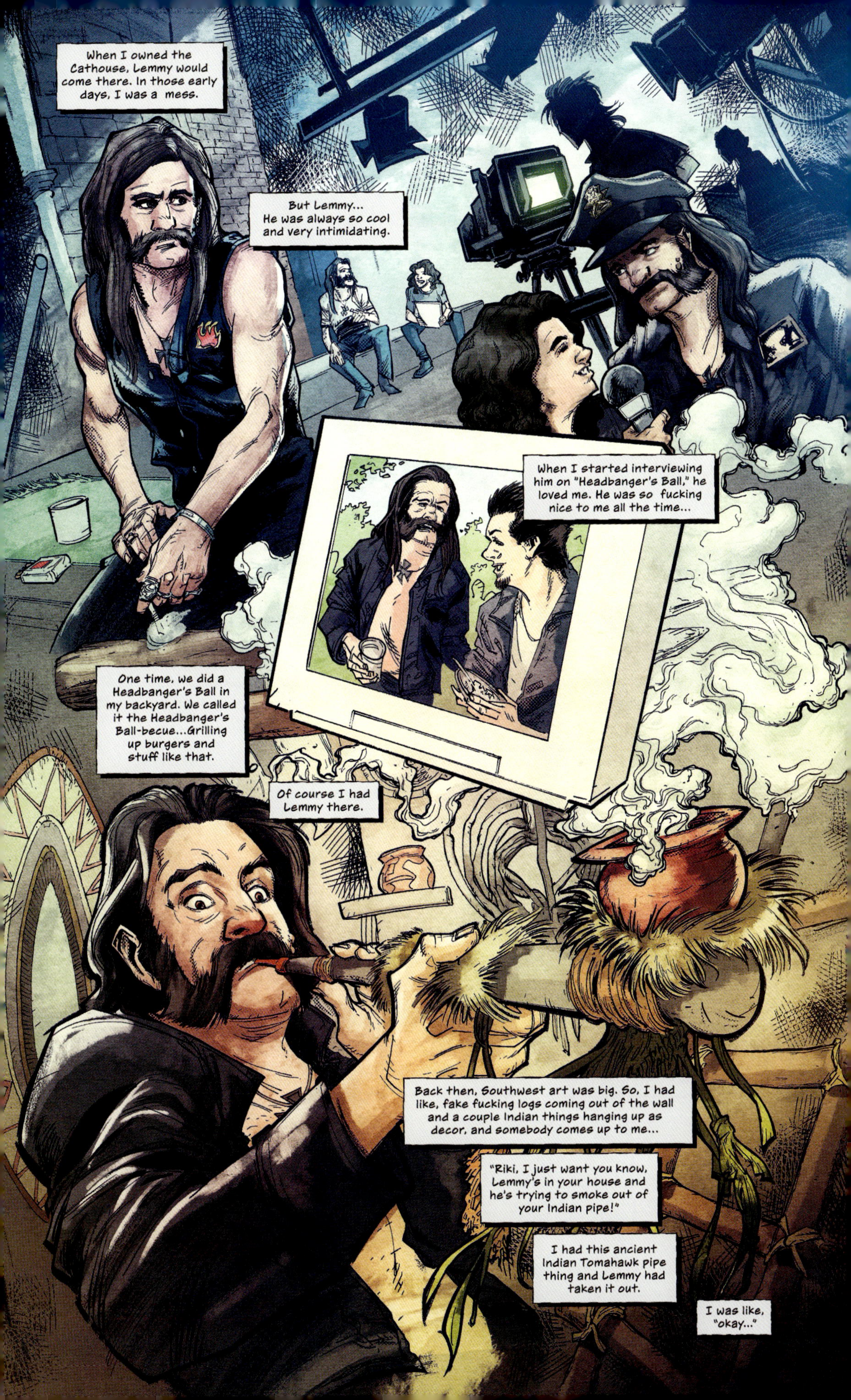

When I owned the Cathouse, Lemmy would come there. In those early days, I was a mess.
But Lemmy... He was always so cool and very intimidating.
When I started interviewing him on "Headbanger's Ball," he loved me. He was so fucking nice to me all the time...
One time, we did a Headbanger's Ball in my backyard. We called it the Headbanger's Ball-becue...Grilling up burgers and stuff like that.
Of course I had Lemmy there.
Back then, Southwest art was big. So, I had like, fake fucking logs coming out of the wall and a couple Indian things hanging up as decor, and somebody comes up to me...
"Riki, I just want you know, Lemmy's in your house and he's trying to smoke out of your Indian pipe!"
I had this ancient Indian Tomahawk pipe thing and Lemmy had taken it out.
I was like, "okay..."

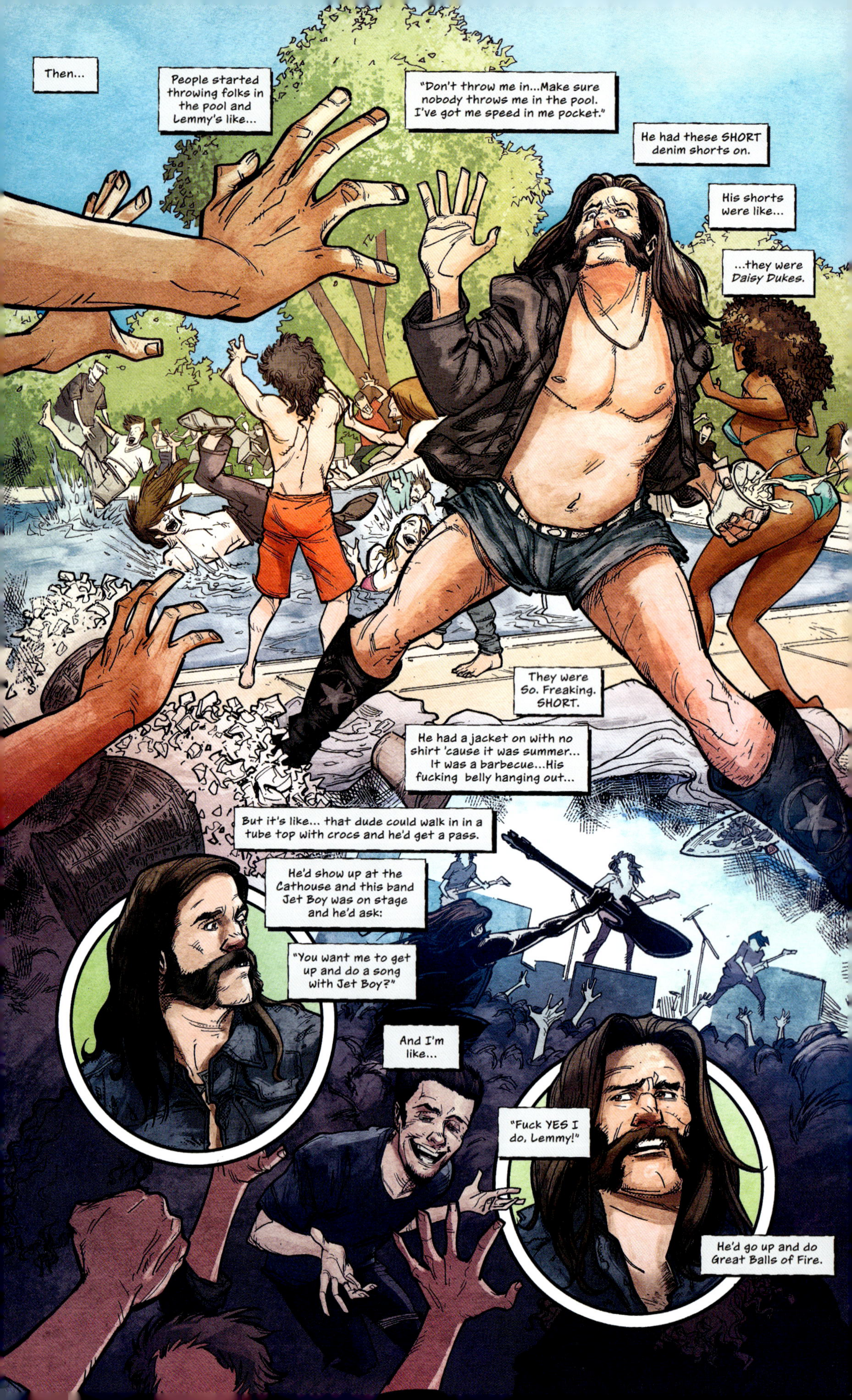
Then...
People started throwing folks in the pool and Lemmy's like...
"Don't throw me in...Make sure nobody throws me in the pool. I've got me speed in me pocket."
He had these SHORT denim shorts on.
His shorts were like...
...they were Daisy Dukes.
They were So. Freaking. SHORT.
He had a jacket on with no shirt 'cause it was summer... It was a barbecue...His fucking belly hanging out...
But it's like... that dude could walk in in a tube top with crocs and he'd get a pass.
He'd show up at the Cathouse and this band Jet Boy was on stage and he'd ask:
"You want me to get up and do a song with Jet Boy?"
And I'm like...
"Fuck YES I do, Lemmy!"
He'd go up and do Great Balls of Fire.

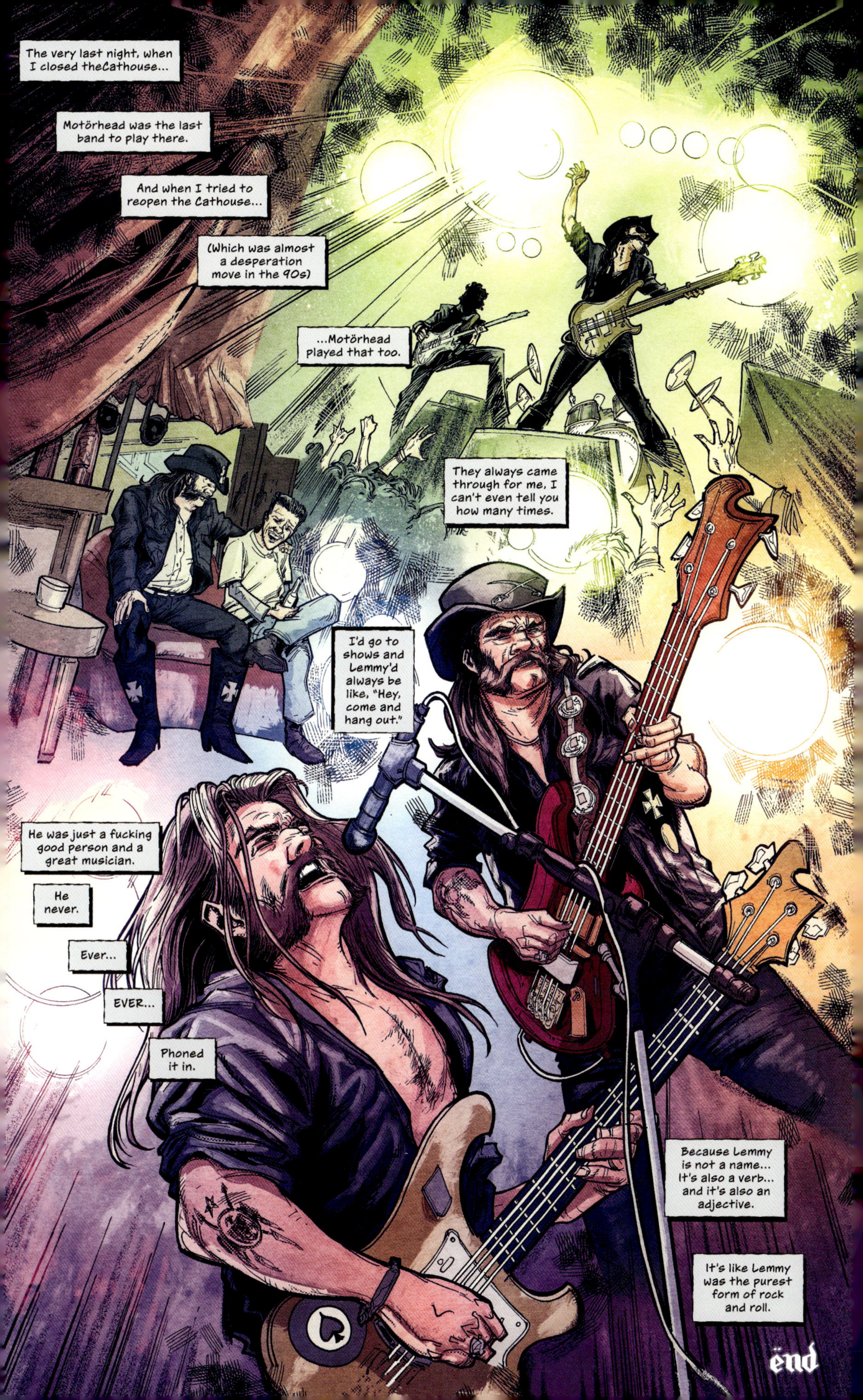
The very last night, when I closed theCathouse...
Motörhead was the last band to play there.
And when I tried to reopen the Cathouse...
(Which was almost a desperation move in the 90s)
...Motörhead played that too.
They always came through for me, I can't even tell you how many times.
I'd go to shows and Lemmy'd always be like, "Hey, come and hang out."
He was just a fucking good person and a great musician.
He never.
Ever...
EVER...
Phoned it in.
Because Lemmy is not a name... It's also a verb... and it's also an adjective.
It's like Lemmy was the purest form of rock and roll.
ënd

"Lemmy was more blunt and honest than anyone I've ever talked to in my life. Bless his gnarly soul."

FIRST MET LEMMY IN 1987

penelope spheeris

DIRECTOR
WAYNE'S WORLD + DECLINE OF WESTERN CIVILIZATION

STORY ILLUSTRATED BY SHANE PATRICK WHITE

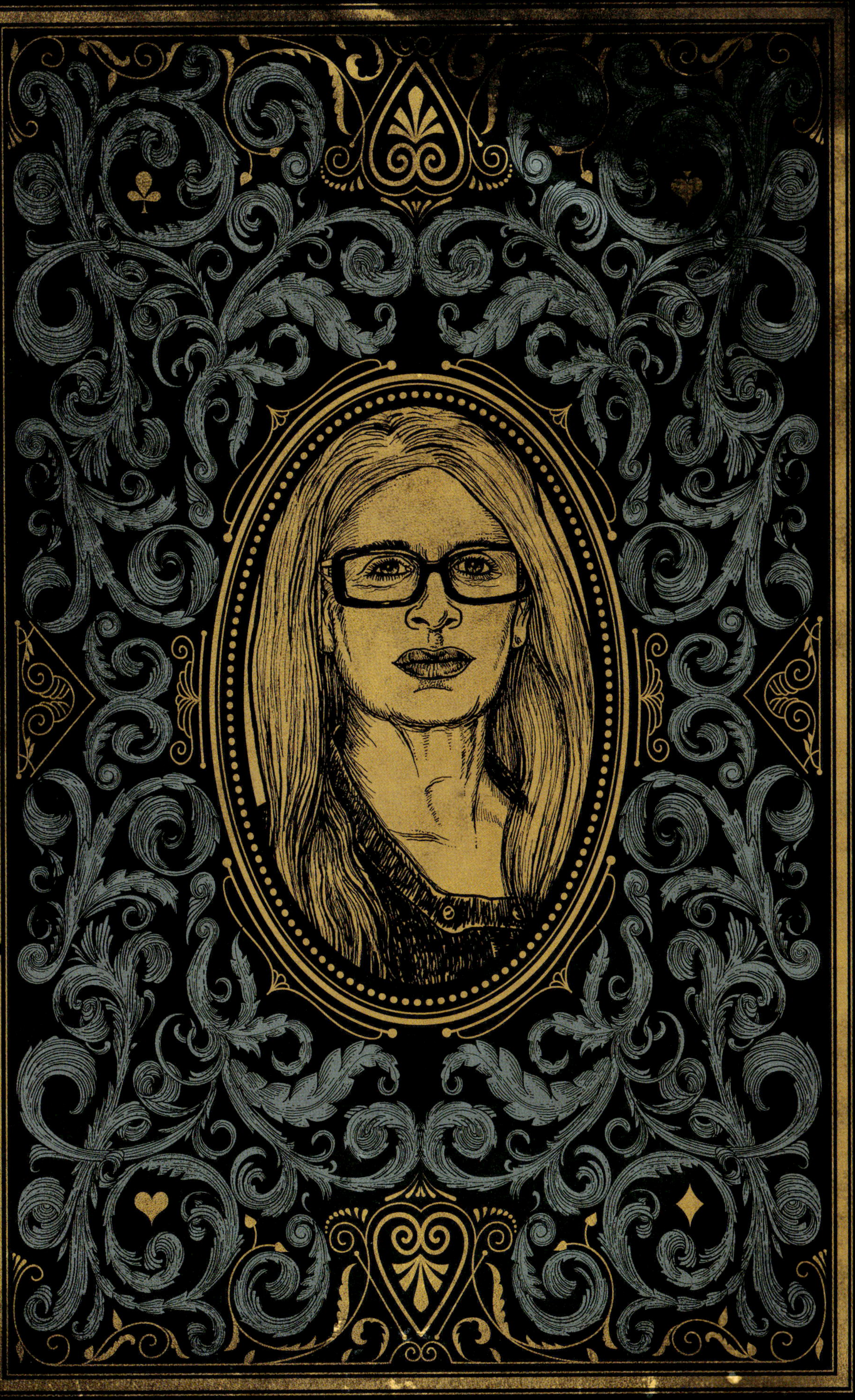

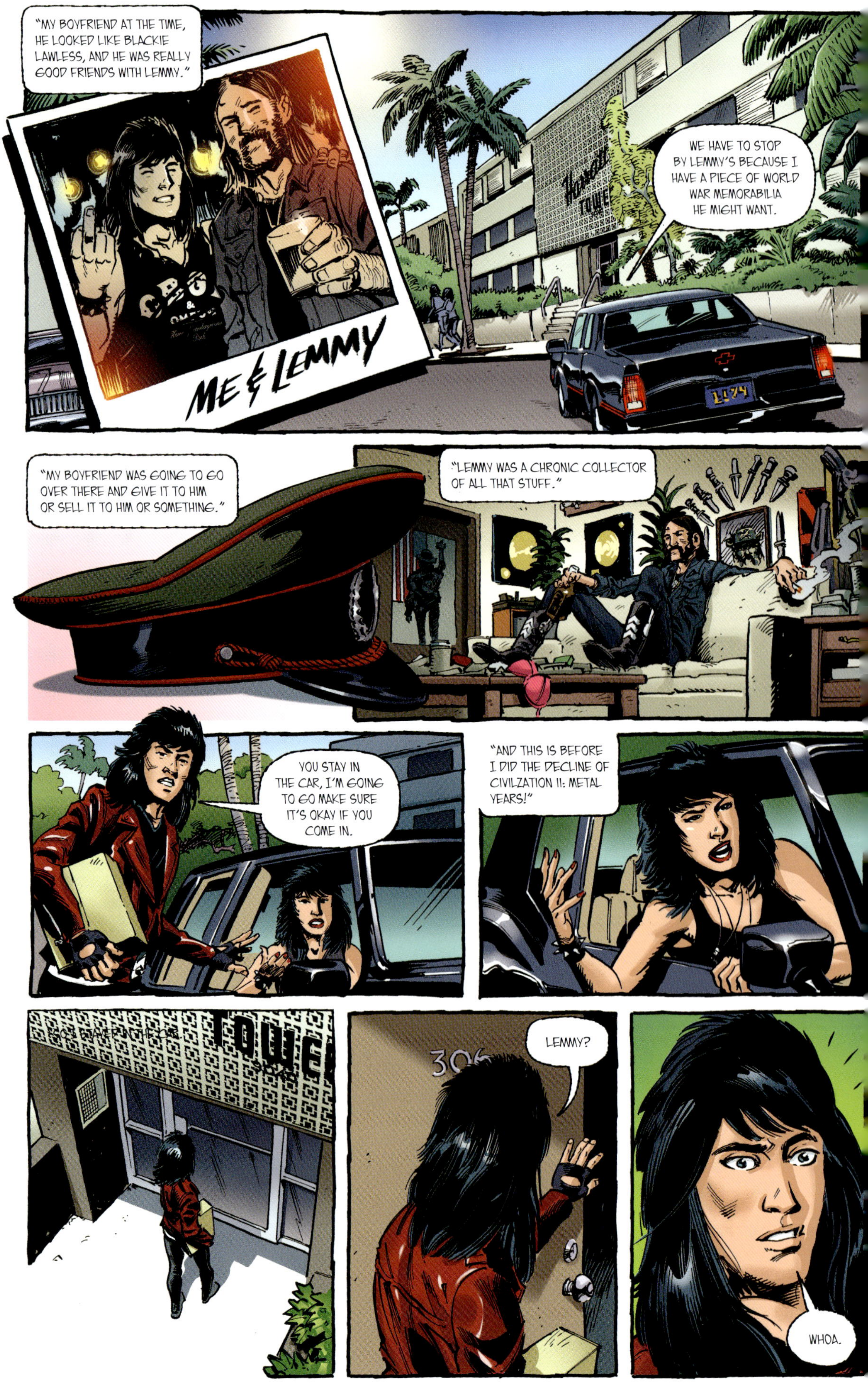
"MY BOYFRIEND AT THE TIME, HE LOOKED LIKE BLACKIE LAWLESS, AND HE WAS REALLY GOOD FRIENDS WITH LEMMY."
ME & LEMMY
WE HAVE TO STOP BY LEMMY'S BECAUSE I HAVE A PIECE OF WORLD WAR MEMORABILIA HE MIGHT WANT.
"MY BOYFRIEND WAS GOING TO GO OVER THERE AND GIVE IT TO HIM OR SELL IT TO HIM OR SOMETHING."
"LEMMY WAS A CHRONIC COLLECTOR OF ALL THAT STUFF."
YOU STAY IN THE CAR, I'M GOING TO GO MAKE SURE IT'S OKAY IF YOU COME IN.
"AND THIS IS BEFORE I DID THE DECLINE OF CIVILZATION II: METAL YEARS!"
LEMMY?
WHOA.

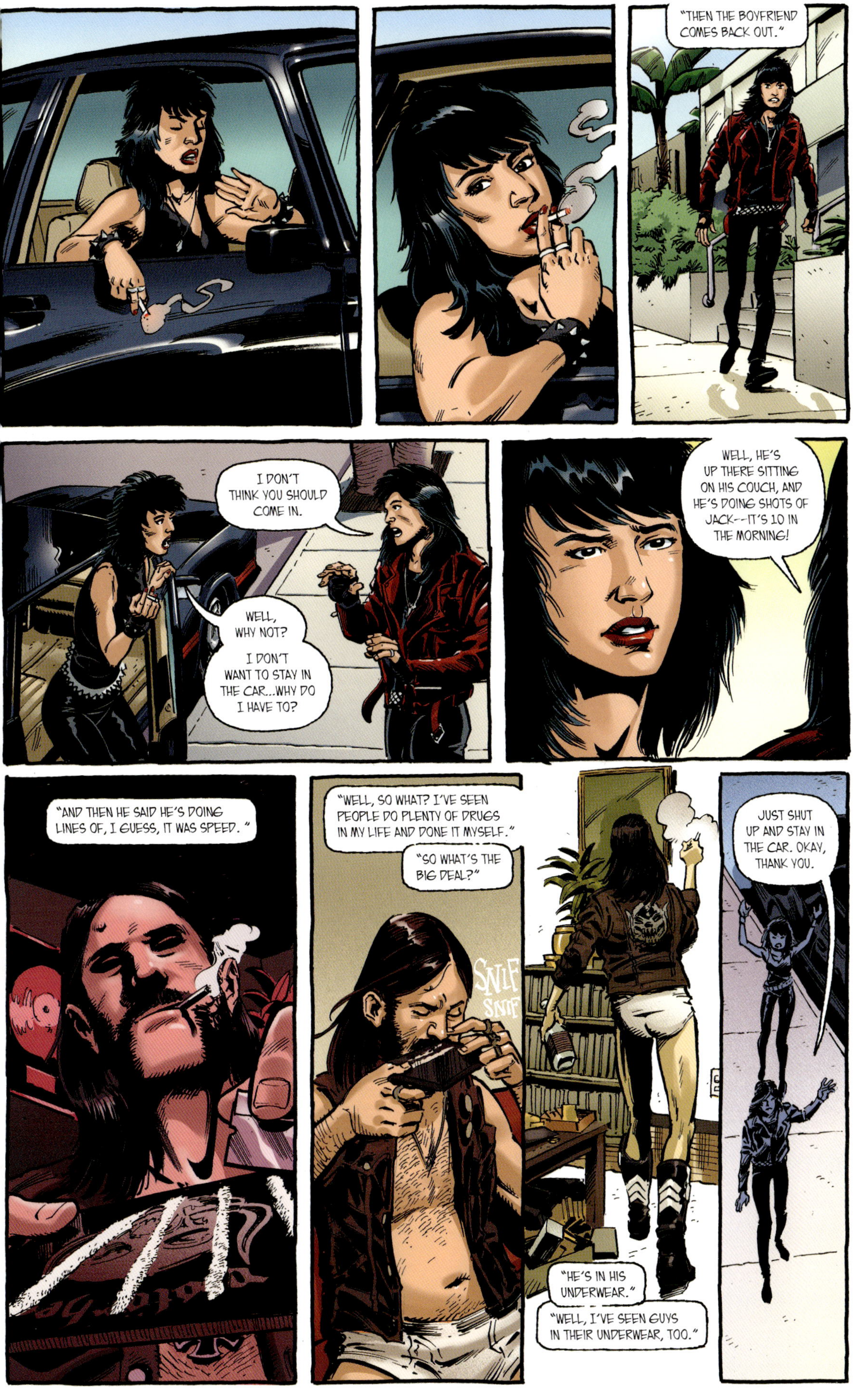
"THEN THE BOYFRIEND COMES BACK OUT."
I DON'T THINK YOU SHOULD COME IN.
WELL, WHY NOT?
I DON'T WANT TO STAY IN THE CAR...WHY DO I HAVE TO?
WELL, HE'S UP THERE SITTING ON HIS COUCH, AND HE'S DOING SHOTS OF JACK--IT'S 10 IN THE MORNING!
"AND THEN HE SAID HE'S DOING LINES OF, I GUESS, IT WAS SPEED."
"WELL, SO WHAT? I'VE SEEN PEOPLE DO PLENTY OF DRUGS IN MY LIFE AND DONE IT MYSELF."
"SO WHAT'S THE BIG DEAL?"
SNIF
SNIF
"HE'S IN HIS UNDERWEAR."
"WELL, I'VE SEEN GUYS IN THEIR UNDERWEAR, TOO."
JUST SHUT UP AND STAY IN THE CAR. OKAY, THANK YOU.

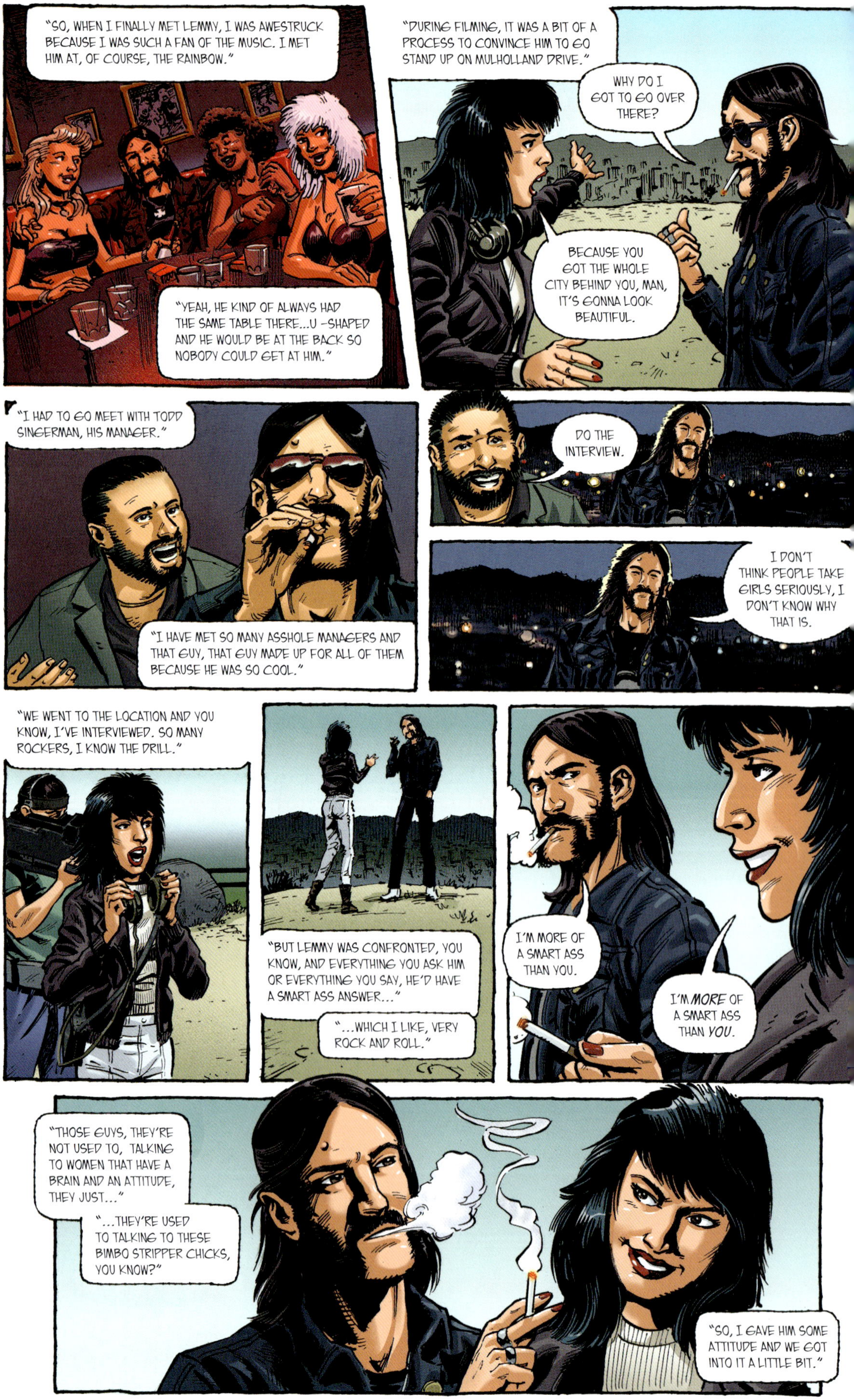
"SO, WHEN I FINALLY MET LEMMY, I WAS AWESTRUCK BECAUSE I WAS SUCH A FAN OF THE MUSIC. I MET HIM AT, OF COURSE, THE RAINBOW."
"YEAH, HE KIND OF ALWAYS HAD THE SAME TABLE THERE...U -SHAPED AND HE WOULD BE AT THE BACK SO NOBODY COULD GET AT HIM."
"DURING FILMING, IT WAS A BIT OF A PROCESS TO CONVINCE HIM TO GO STAND UP ON MULHOLLAND DRIVE."
WHY DO I GOT TO GO OVER THERE?
BECAUSE YOU GOT THE WHOLE CITY BEHIND YOU, MAN, IT'S GONNA LOOK BEAUTIFUL.
"I HAD TO GO MEET WITH TODD SINGERMAN, HIS MANAGER."
"I HAVE MET SO MANY ASSHOLE MANAGERS AND THAT GUY, THAT GUY MADE UP FOR ALL OF THEM BECAUSE HE WAS SO COOL."
DO THE INTERVIEW.
I DON'T THINK PEOPLE TAKE GIRLS SERIOUSLY, I DON'T KNOW WHY THAT IS.
"WE WENT TO THE LOCATION AND YOU KNOW, I'VE INTERVIEWED. SO MANY ROCKERS, I KNOW THE DRILL."
"BUT LEMMY WAS CONFRONTED, YOU KNOW, AND EVERYTHING YOU ASK HIM OR EVERYTHING YOU SAY, HE'D HAVE A SMART ASS ANSWER..."
"...WHICH I LIKE, VERY ROCK AND ROLL."
I'M MORE OF A SMART ASS THAN YOU.
I'M *MORE* OF A SMART ASS THAN *YOU*.
"THOSE GUYS, THEY'RE NOT USED TO, TALKING TO WOMEN THAT HAVE A BRAIN AND AN ATTITUDE, THEY JUST..."
"...THEY'RE USED TO TALKING TO THESE BIMBO STRIPPER CHICKS, YOU KNOW?"
"SO, I GAVE HIM SOME ATTITUDE AND WE GOT INTO IT A LITTLE BIT."

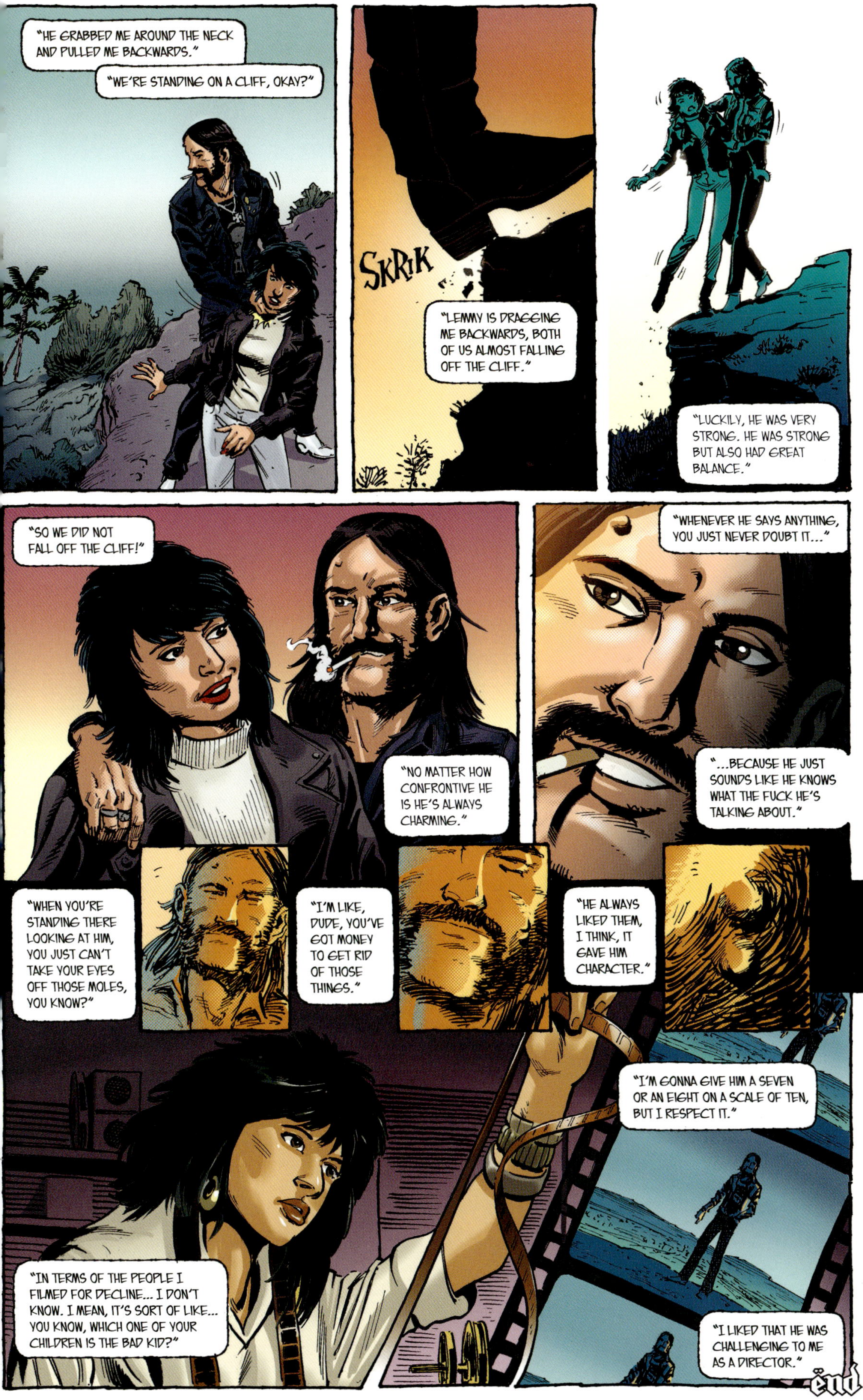
"HE GRABBED ME AROUND THE NECK AND PULLED ME BACKWARDS."
"WE'RE STANDING ON A CLIFF, OKAY?"
SKRIK
"LEMMY IS DRAGGING ME BACKWARDS, BOTH OF US ALMOST FALLING OFF THE CLIFF."
"LUCKILY, HE WAS VERY STRONG. HE WAS STRONG BUT ALSO HAD GREAT BALANCE."
"SO WE DID NOT FALL OFF THE CLIFF!"
"NO MATTER HOW CONFRONTIVE HE IS HE'S ALWAYS CHARMING."
"WHENEVER HE SAYS ANYTHING, YOU JUST NEVER DOUBT IT..."
"...BECAUSE HE JUST SOUNDS LIKE HE KNOWS WHAT THE FUCK HE'S TALKING ABOUT."
"WHEN YOU'RE STANDING THERE LOOKING AT HIM, YOU JUST CAN'T TAKE YOUR EYES OFF THOSE MOLES, YOU KNOW?"
"I'M LIKE, DUDE, YOU'VE GOT MONEY TO GET RID OF THOSE THINGS."
"HE ALWAYS LIKED THEM, I THINK, IT GAVE HIM CHARACTER."
"I'M GONNA GIVE HIM A SEVEN OR AN EIGHT ON A SCALE OF TEN, BUT I RESPECT IT."
"IN TERMS OF THE PEOPLE I FILMED FOR DECLINE... I DON'T KNOW. I MEAN, IT'S SORT OF LIKE... YOU KNOW, WHICH ONE OF YOUR CHILDREN IS THE BAD KID?"
"I LIKED THAT HE WAS CHALLENGING TO ME AS A DIRECTOR."
ënd

"When Lemmy sang live, you could actually hear him over the actual stage monitors!"

FIRST MET LEMMY IN 1987

dave navarro

FOUNDER
GUITARIST
JANE'S ADDICTION
HOST
INKMASTERS

STORY ILLUSTRATED BY JIM MAHFOOD

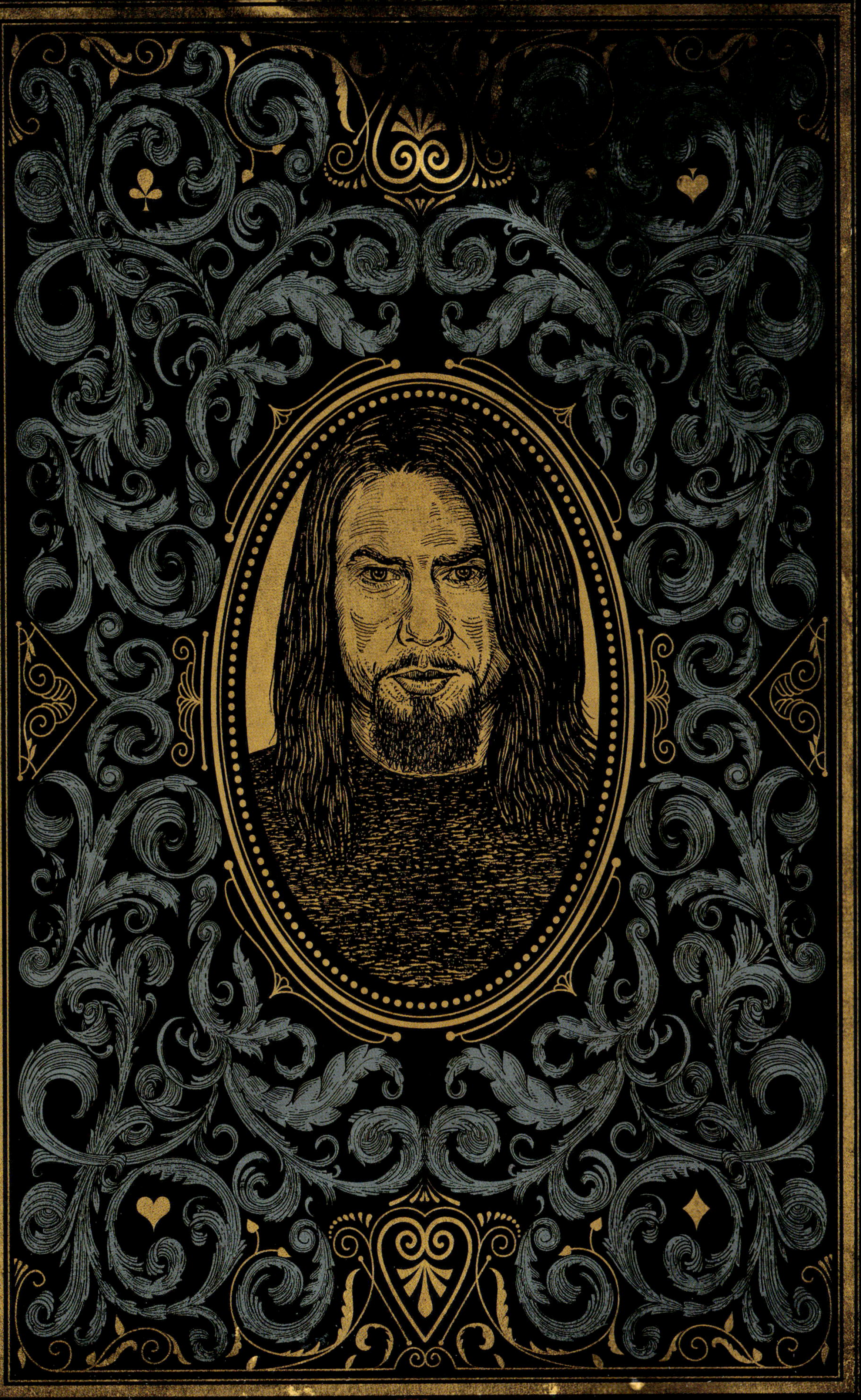

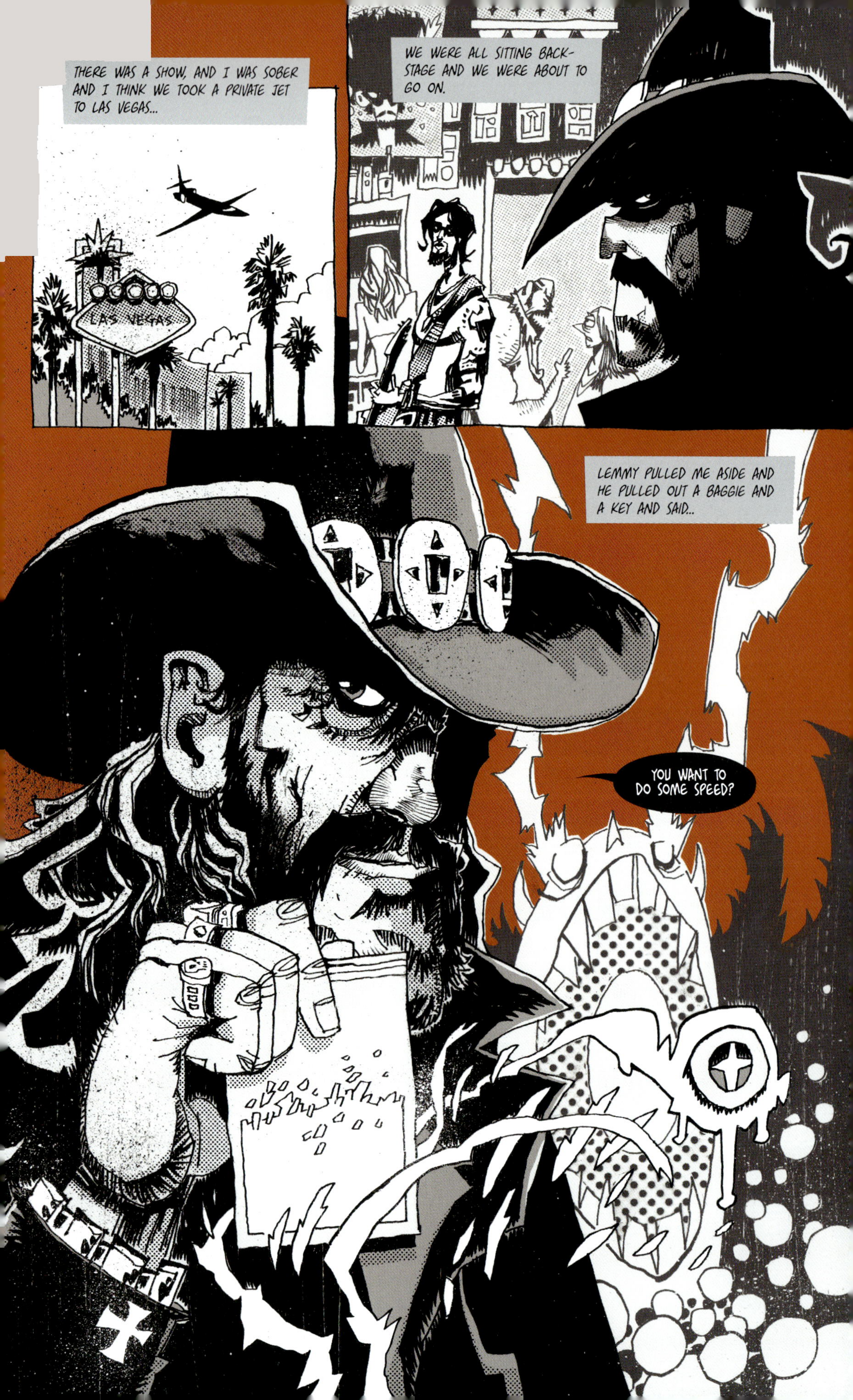
THERE WAS A SHOW, AND I WAS SOBER AND I THINK WE TOOK A PRIVATE JET TO LAS VEGAS...
LAS VEGAS
WE WERE ALL SITTING BACK-STAGE AND WE WERE ABOUT TO GO ON.
LEMMY PULLED ME ASIDE AND HE PULLED OUT A BAGGIE AND A KEY AND SAID...
YOU WANT TO DO SOME SPEED?

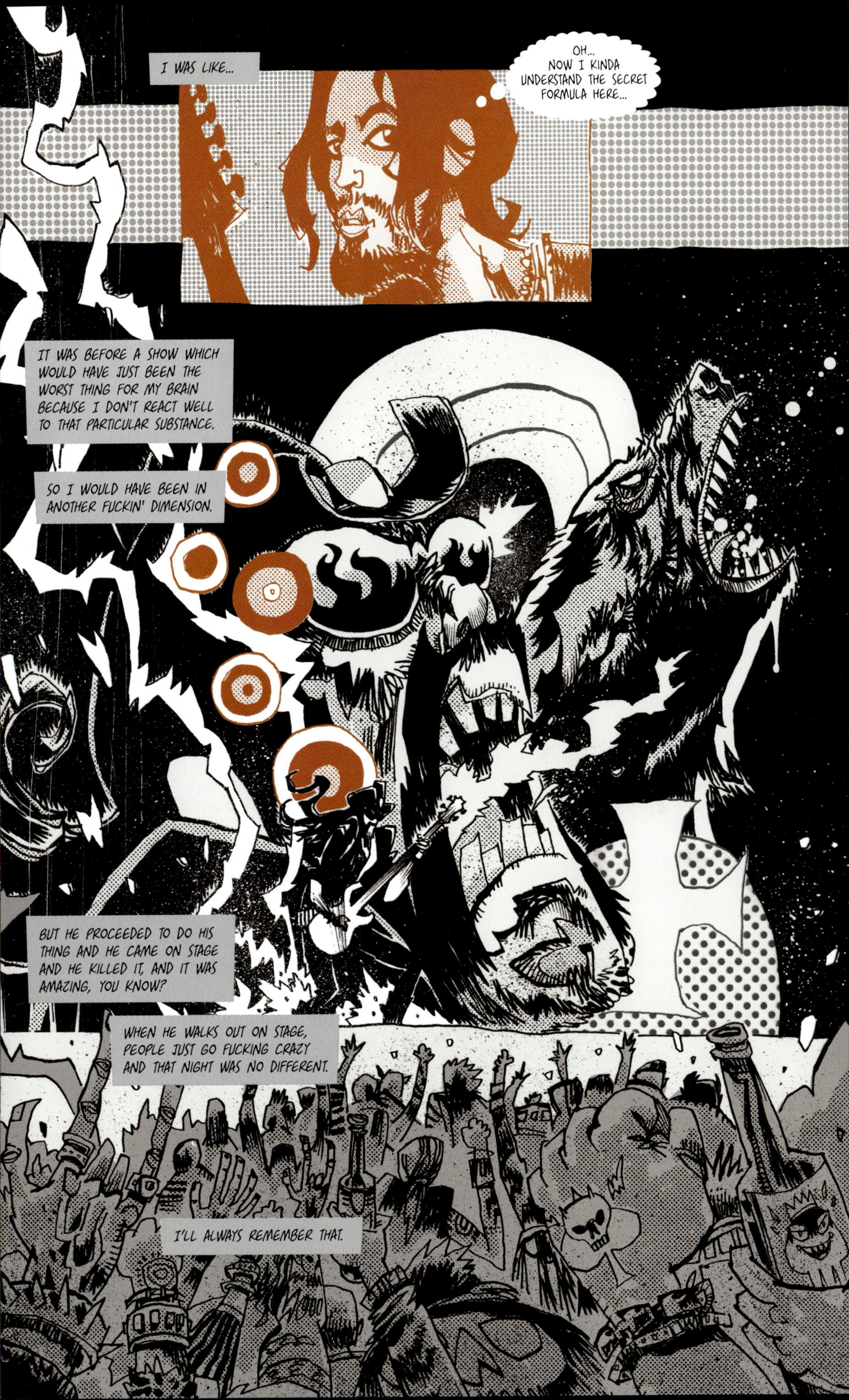
I WAS LIKE...
OH... NOW I KINDA UNDERSTAND THE SECRET FORMULA HERE...
IT WAS BEFORE A SHOW WHICH WOULD HAVE JUST BEEN THE WORST THING FOR MY BRAIN BECAUSE I DON'T REACT WELL TO THAT PARTICULAR SUBSTANCE.
SO I WOULD HAVE BEEN IN ANOTHER FUCKIN' DIMENSION.
BUT HE PROCEEDED TO DO HIS THING AND HE CAME ON STAGE AND HE KILLED IT, AND IT WAS AMAZING, YOU KNOW?
WHEN HE WALKS OUT ON STAGE, PEOPLE JUST GO FUCKING CRAZY AND THAT NIGHT WAS NO DIFFERENT.
I'LL ALWAYS REMEMBER THAT.

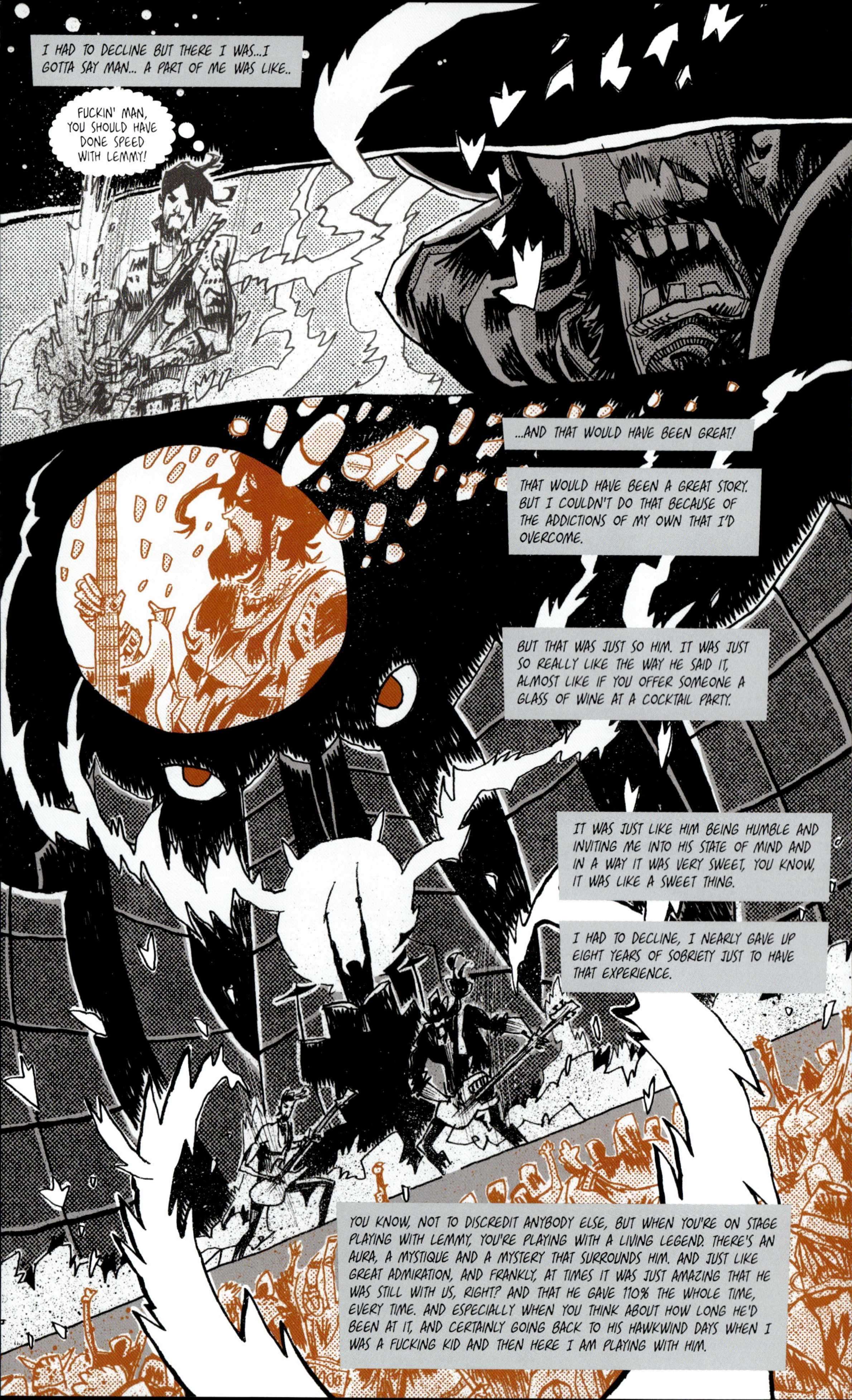
I HAD TO DECLINE BUT THERE I WAS...I GOTTA SAY MAN... A PART OF ME WAS LIKE..
FUCKIN' MAN, YOU SHOULD HAVE DONE SPEED WITH LEMMY!
...AND THAT WOULD HAVE BEEN GREAT!
THAT WOULD HAVE BEEN A GREAT STORY. BUT I COULDN'T DO THAT BECAUSE OF THE ADDICTIONS OF MY OWN THAT I'D OVERCOME.
BUT THAT WAS JUST SO HIM. IT WAS JUST SO REALLY LIKE THE WAY HE SAID IT, ALMOST LIKE IF YOU OFFER SOMEONE A GLASS OF WINE AT A COCKTAIL PARTY.
IT WAS JUST LIKE HIM BEING HUMBLE AND INVITING ME INTO HIS STATE OF MIND AND IN A WAY IT WAS VERY SWEET, YOU KNOW, IT WAS LIKE A SWEET THING.
I HAD TO DECLINE, I NEARLY GAVE UP EIGHT YEARS OF SOBRIETY JUST TO HAVE THAT EXPERIENCE.
YOU KNOW, NOT TO DISCREDIT ANYBODY ELSE, BUT WHEN YOU'RE ON STAGE PLAYING WITH LEMMY, YOU'RE PLAYING WITH A LIVING LEGEND. THERE'S AN AURA, A MYSTIQUE AND A MYSTERY THAT SURROUNDS HIM. AND JUST LIKE GREAT ADMIRATION, AND FRANKLY, AT TIMES IT WAS JUST AMAZING THAT HE WAS STILL WITH US, RIGHT? AND THAT HE GAVE 110% THE WHOLE TIME, EVERY TIME. AND ESPECIALLY WHEN YOU THINK ABOUT HOW LONG HE'D BEEN AT IT, AND CERTAINLY GOING BACK TO HIS HAWKWIND DAYS WHEN I WAS A FUCKING KID AND THEN HERE I AM PLAYING WITH HIM.

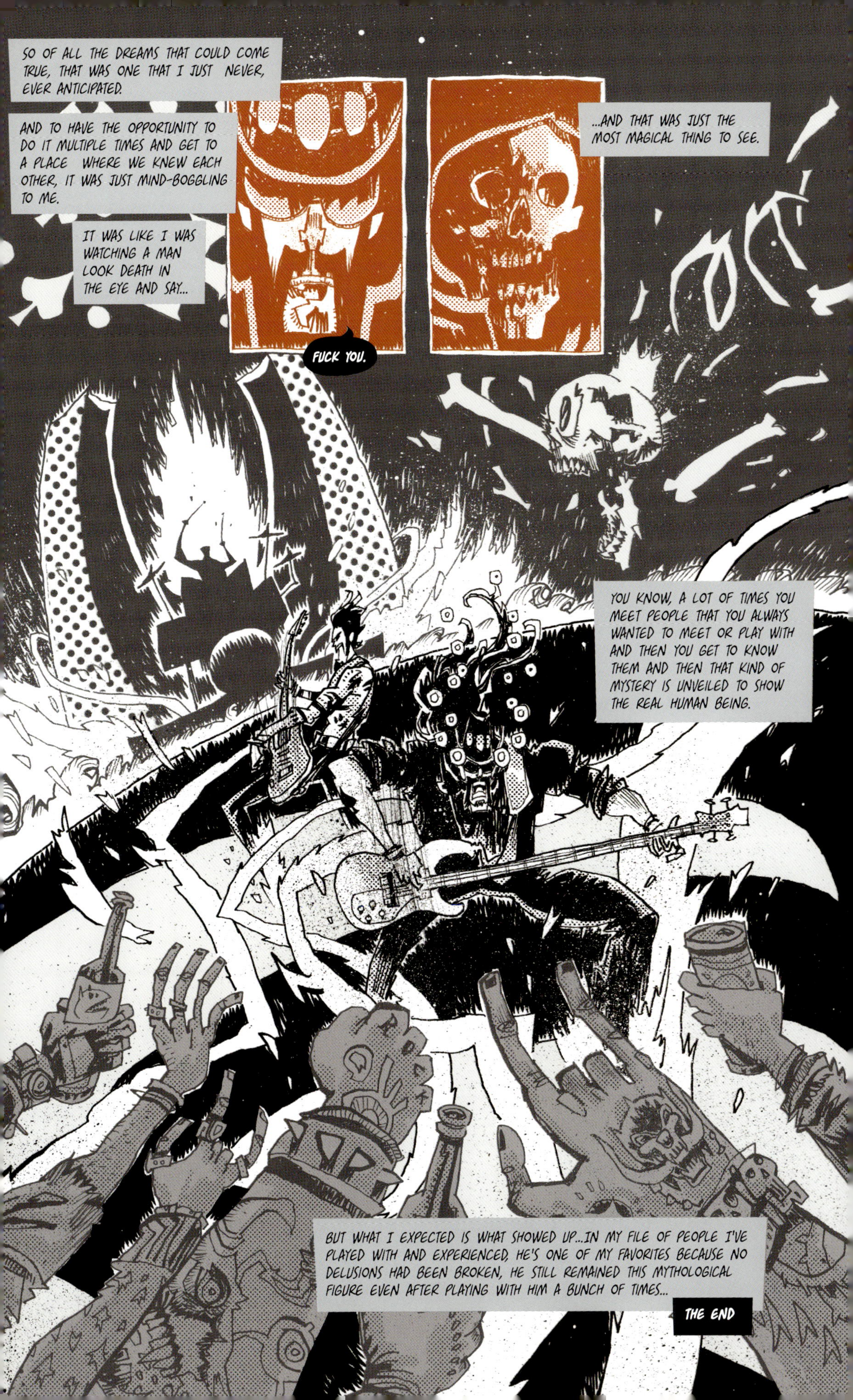
SO OF ALL THE DREAMS THAT COULD COME TRUE, THAT WAS ONE THAT I JUST NEVER, EVER ANTICIPATED.
AND TO HAVE THE OPPORTUNITY TO DO IT MULTIPLE TIMES AND GET TO A PLACE WHERE WE KNEW EACH OTHER, IT WAS JUST MIND-BOGGLING TO ME.
IT WAS LIKE I WAS WATCHING A MAN LOOK DEATH IN THE EYE AND SAY...
FUCK YOU.
...AND THAT WAS JUST THE MOST MAGICAL THING TO SEE.
YOU KNOW, A LOT OF TIMES YOU MEET PEOPLE THAT YOU ALWAYS WANTED TO MEET OR PLAY WITH AND THEN YOU GET TO KNOW THEM AND THEN THAT KIND OF MYSTERY IS UNVEILED TO SHOW THE REAL HUMAN BEING.
BUT WHAT I EXPECTED IS WHAT SHOWED UP...IN MY FILE OF PEOPLE I'VE PLAYED WITH AND EXPERIENCED, HE'S ONE OF MY FAVORITES BECAUSE NO DELUSIONS HAD BEEN BROKEN, HE STILL REMAINED THIS MYTHOLOGICAL FIGURE EVEN AFTER PLAYING WITH HIM A BUNCH OF TIMES...
THE END

"Lemmy wouldn't want anyone mourning his death. He'd want people happy, celebrating his life."

FIRST MET LEMMY IN 1989

mikkey dee

DRUMMER
MOTÖRHEAD
KING DIAMOND
SCORPIONS

STORY ILLUSTRATED BY LUKE MCGARRY

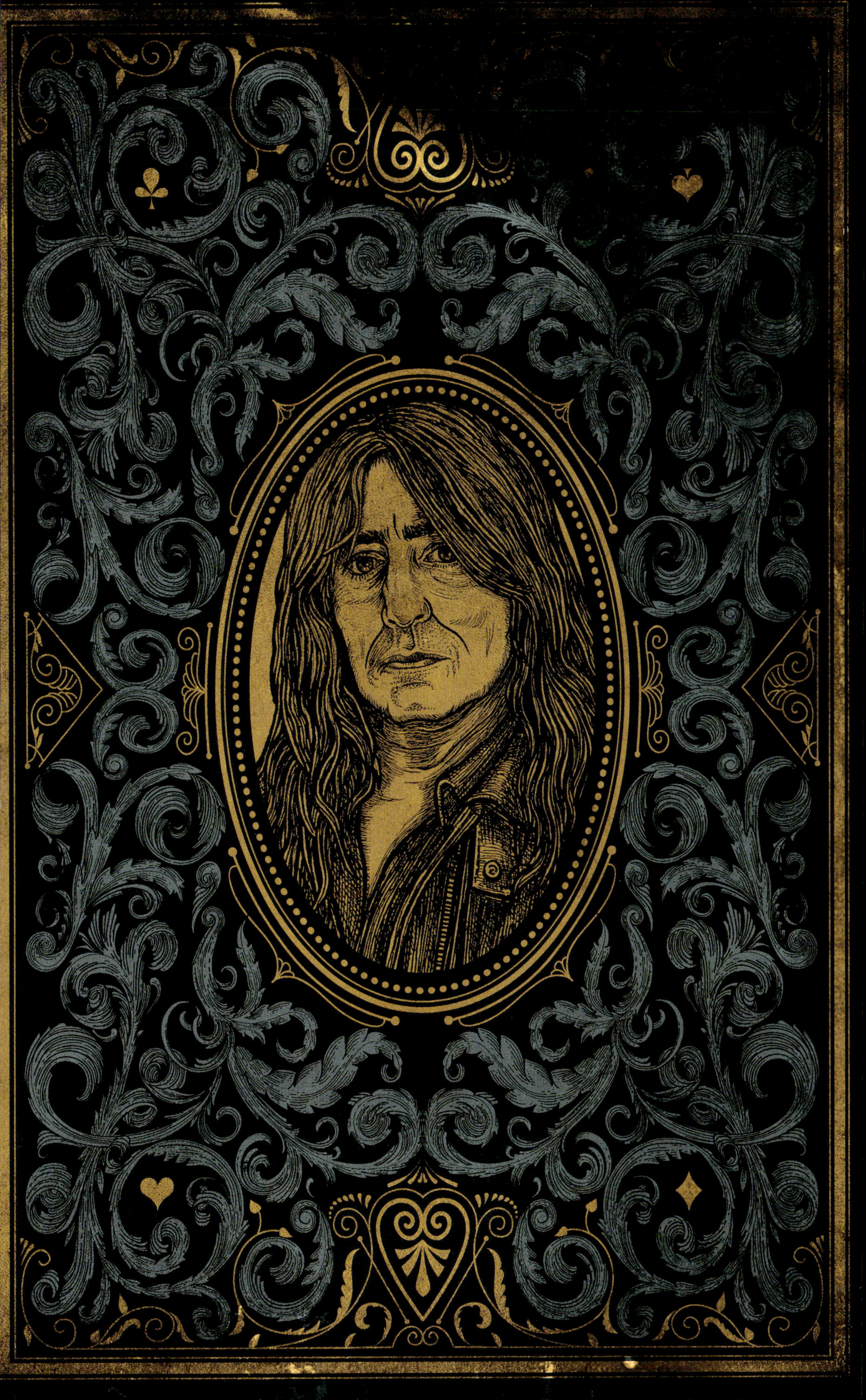

mikkey dee

ILLUSTRATED BY
LUKE McGARRY

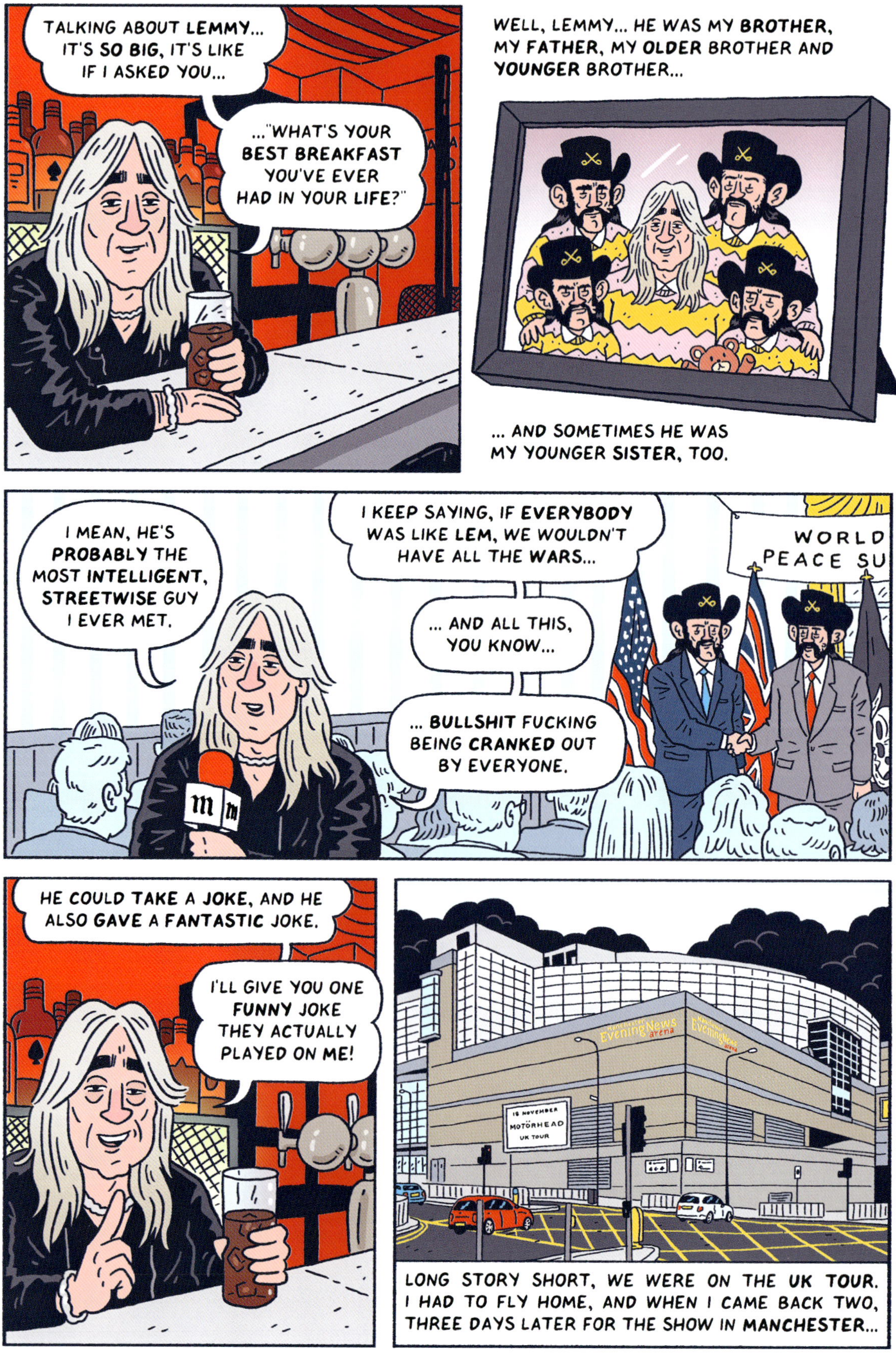

TALKING ABOUT LEMMY... IT'S SO BIG, IT'S LIKE IF I ASKED YOU...
..."WHAT'S YOUR BEST BREAKFAST YOU'VE EVER HAD IN YOUR LIFE?"
WELL, LEMMY... HE WAS MY BROTHER, MY FATHER, MY OLDER BROTHER AND YOUNGER BROTHER...
... AND SOMETIMES HE WAS MY YOUNGER SISTER, TOO.
I MEAN, HE'S PROBABLY THE MOST INTELLIGENT, STREETWISE GUY I EVER MET.
I KEEP SAYING, IF EVERYBODY WAS LIKE LEM, WE WOULDN'T HAVE ALL THE WARS...
... AND ALL THIS, YOU KNOW...
... BULLSHIT FUCKING BEING CRANKED OUT BY EVERYONE.
WORLD PEACE SU
HE COULD TAKE A JOKE, AND HE ALSO GAVE A FANTASTIC JOKE.
I'LL GIVE YOU ONE FUNNY JOKE THEY ACTUALLY PLAYED ON ME!
18 NOVEMBER
MOTÖRHEAD
UK TOUR
LONG STORY SHORT, WE WERE ON THE UK TOUR. I HAD TO FLY HOME, AND WHEN I CAME BACK TWO, THREE DAYS LATER FOR THE SHOW IN MANCHESTER...

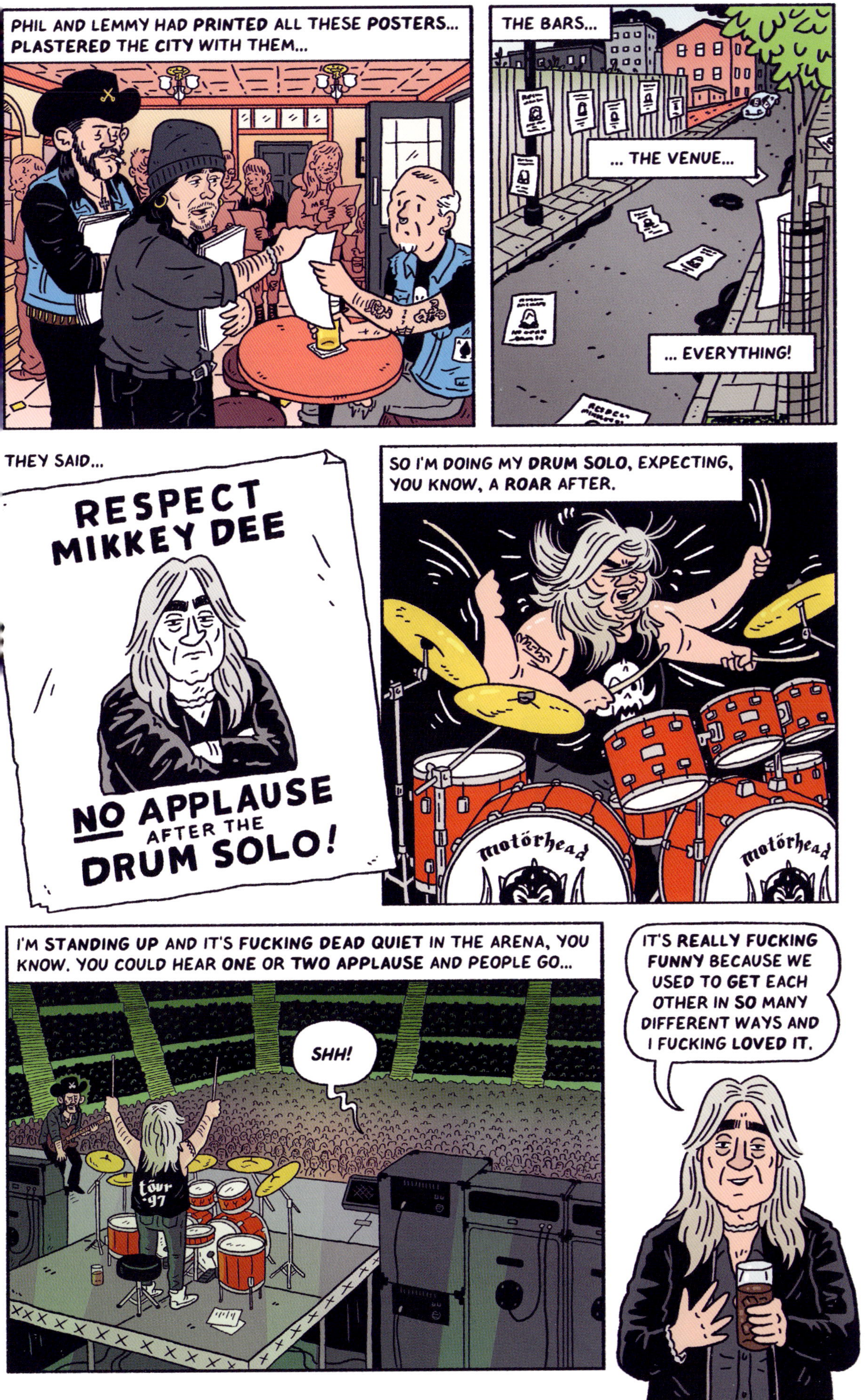
PHIL AND LEMMY HAD PRINTED ALL THESE POSTERS... PLASTERED THE CITY WITH THEM...
THE BARS...
... THE VENUE...
... EVERYTHING!
THEY SAID...
RESPECT MIKKEY DEE
NO APPLAUSE AFTER THE DRUM SOLO!
SO I'M DOING MY DRUM SOLO, EXPECTING, YOU KNOW, A ROAR AFTER.
motörhead
motörhead
I'M STANDING UP AND IT'S FUCKING DEAD QUIET IN THE ARENA, YOU KNOW. YOU COULD HEAR ONE OR TWO APPLAUSE AND PEOPLE GO...
SHH!
tour '97
IT'S REALLY FUCKING FUNNY BECAUSE WE USED TO GET EACH OTHER IN SO MANY DIFFERENT WAYS AND I FUCKING LOVED IT.

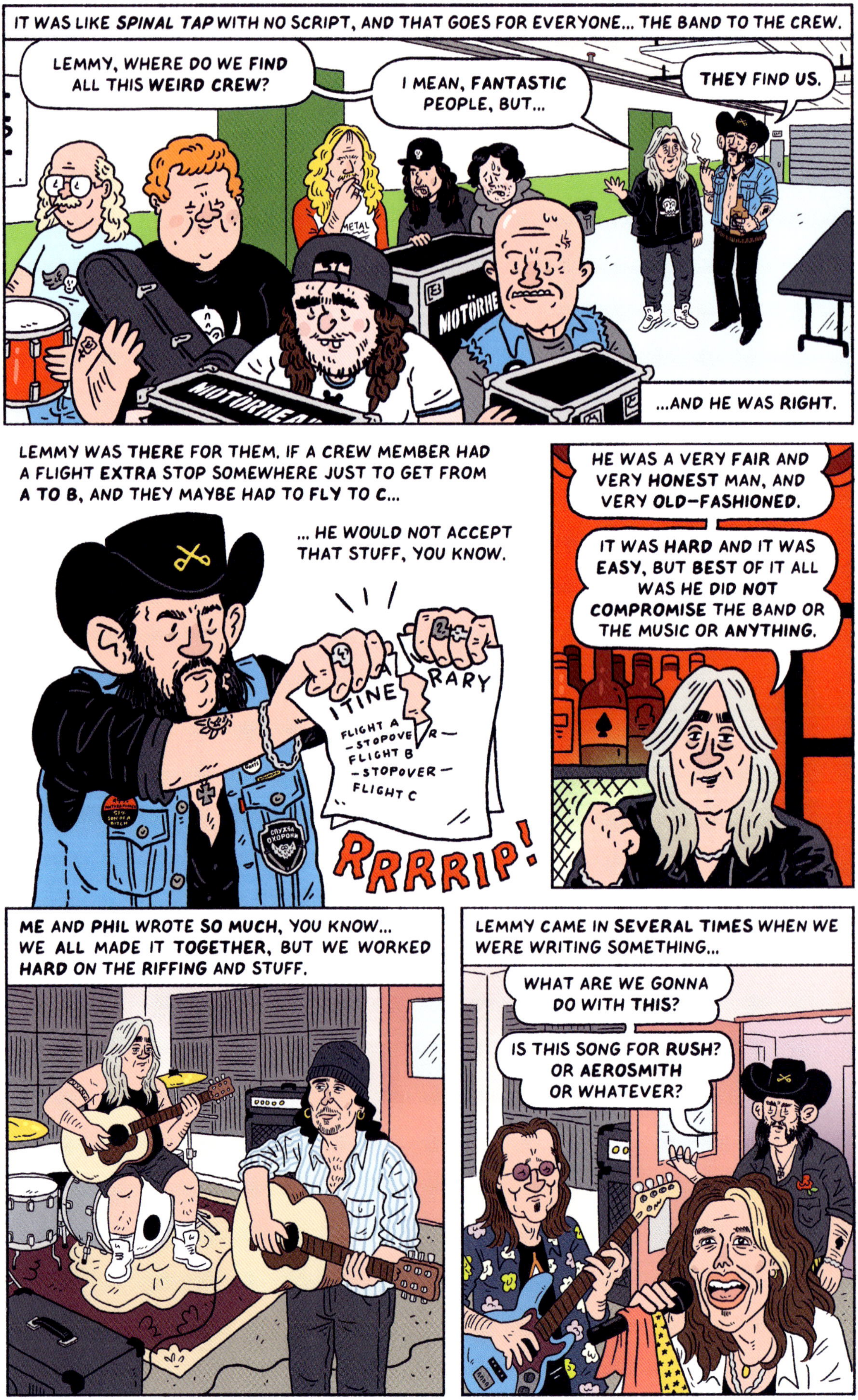
IT WAS LIKE SPINAL TAP WITH NO SCRIPT, AND THAT GOES FOR EVERYONE... THE BAND TO THE CREW.
LEMMY, WHERE DO WE FIND ALL THIS WEIRD CREW?
I MEAN, FANTASTIC PEOPLE, BUT...
THEY FIND US.
METAL
MOTÖRHE
...AND HE WAS RIGHT.
LEMMY WAS THERE FOR THEM. IF A CREW MEMBER HAD A FLIGHT EXTRA STOP SOMEWHERE JUST TO GET FROM A TO B, AND THEY MAYBE HAD TO FLY TO C...
... HE WOULD NOT ACCEPT THAT STUFF, YOU KNOW.
ITINERARY
FLIGHT A
-STOPOVER-
FLIGHT B
-STOPOVER-
FLIGHT C
RRRRIP!
HE WAS A VERY FAIR AND VERY HONEST MAN, AND VERY OLD-FASHIONED.
IT WAS HARD AND IT WAS EASY, BUT BEST OF IT ALL WAS HE DID NOT COMPROMISE THE BAND OR THE MUSIC OR ANYTHING.
ME AND PHIL WROTE SO MUCH, YOU KNOW... WE ALL MADE IT TOGETHER, BUT WE WORKED HARD ON THE RIFFING AND STUFF.
LEMMY CAME IN SEVERAL TIMES WHEN WE WERE WRITING SOMETHING...
WHAT ARE WE GONNA DO WITH THIS?
IS THIS SONG FOR RUSH? OR AEROSMITH OR WHATEVER?

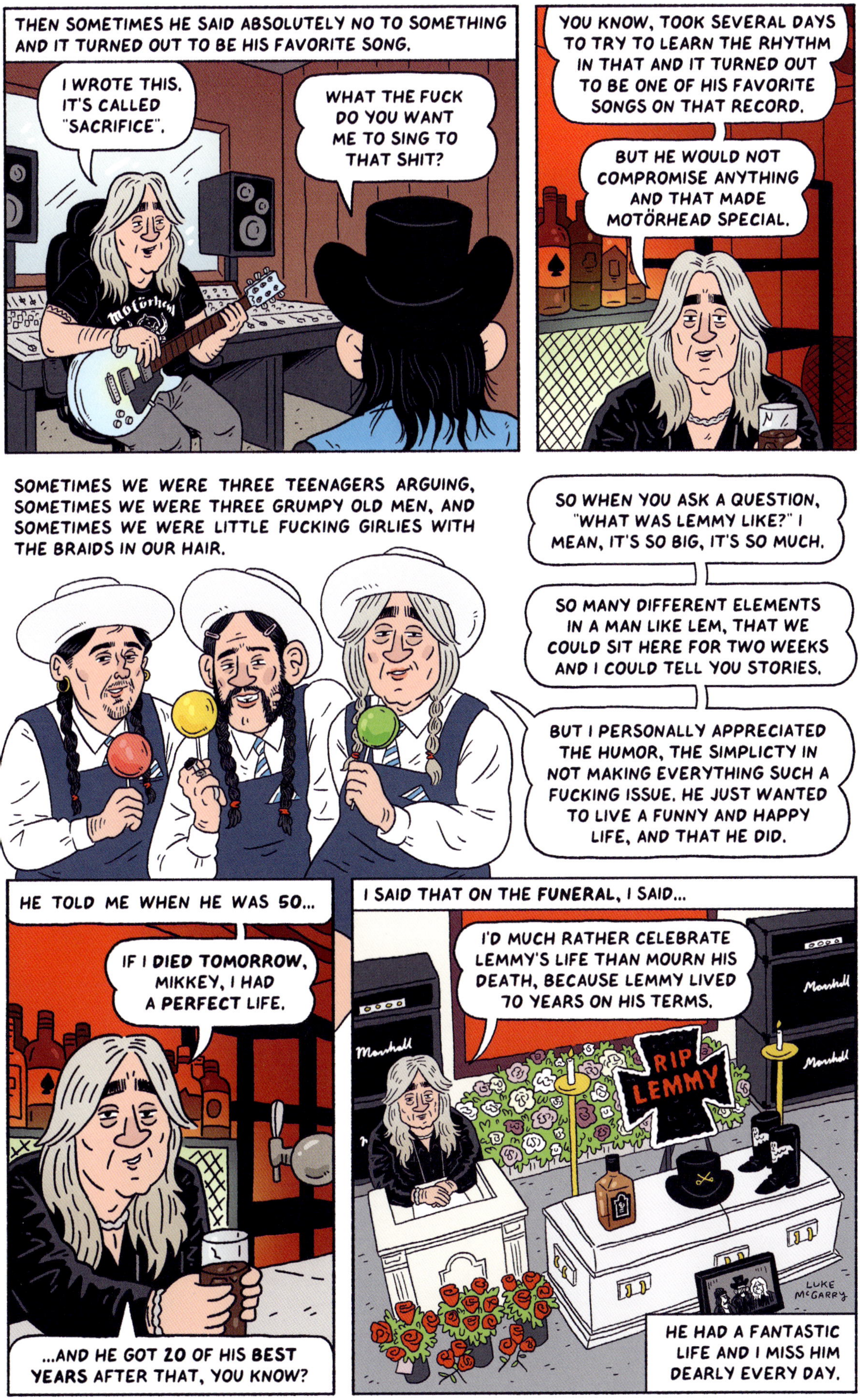
THEN SOMETIMES HE SAID ABSOLUTELY NO TO SOMETHING AND IT TURNED OUT TO BE HIS FAVORITE SONG.
I WROTE THIS. IT'S CALLED "SACRIFICE".
WHAT THE FUCK DO YOU WANT ME TO SING TO THAT SHIT?
YOU KNOW, TOOK SEVERAL DAYS TO TRY TO LEARN THE RHYTHM IN THAT AND IT TURNED OUT TO BE ONE OF HIS FAVORITE SONGS ON THAT RECORD.
BUT HE WOULD NOT COMPROMISE ANYTHING AND THAT MADE MOTÖRHEAD SPECIAL.
SOMETIMES WE WERE THREE TEENAGERS ARGUING, SOMETIMES WE WERE THREE GRUMPY OLD MEN, AND SOMETIMES WE WERE LITTLE FUCKING GIRLIES WITH THE BRAIDS IN OUR HAIR.
SO WHEN YOU ASK A QUESTION, "WHAT WAS LEMMY LIKE?" I MEAN, IT'S SO BIG, IT'S SO MUCH.
SO MANY DIFFERENT ELEMENTS IN A MAN LIKE LEM, THAT WE COULD SIT HERE FOR TWO WEEKS AND I COULD TELL YOU STORIES.
BUT I PERSONALLY APPRECIATED THE HUMOR, THE SIMPLICTY IN NOT MAKING EVERYTHING SUCH A FUCKING ISSUE. HE JUST WANTED TO LIVE A FUNNY AND HAPPY LIFE, AND THAT HE DID.
HE TOLD ME WHEN HE WAS 50...
IF I DIED TOMORROW, MIKKEY, I HAD A PERFECT LIFE.
...AND HE GOT 20 OF HIS BEST YEARS AFTER THAT, YOU KNOW?
I SAID THAT ON THE FUNERAL, I SAID...
I'D MUCH RATHER CELEBRATE LEMMY'S LIFE THAN MOURN HIS DEATH, BECAUSE LEMMY LIVED 70 YEARS ON HIS TERMS.
Marshall
RIP LEMMY
LUKE McGARRY
HE HAD A FANTASTIC LIFE AND I MISS HIM DEARLY EVERY DAY.

"Lemmy had the most agressive bass tone ever. As a kid, I was like 'Is that even a guitar!?'"

FIRST MET LEMMY IN 1989

chuck billy

FOUNDER + FRONTMAN TESTAMENT

STORY ILLUSTRATED BY RYAN DUNLAVEY

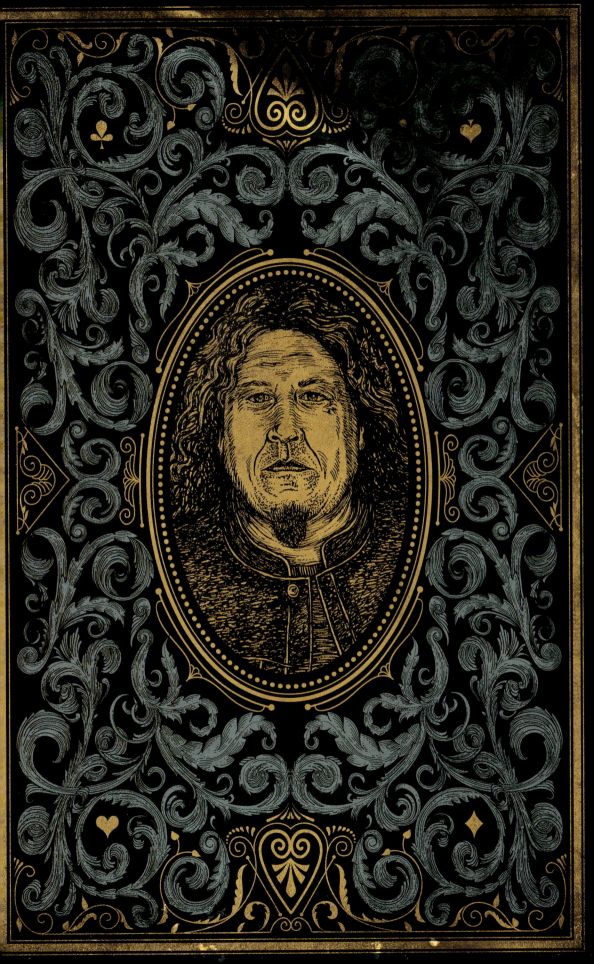

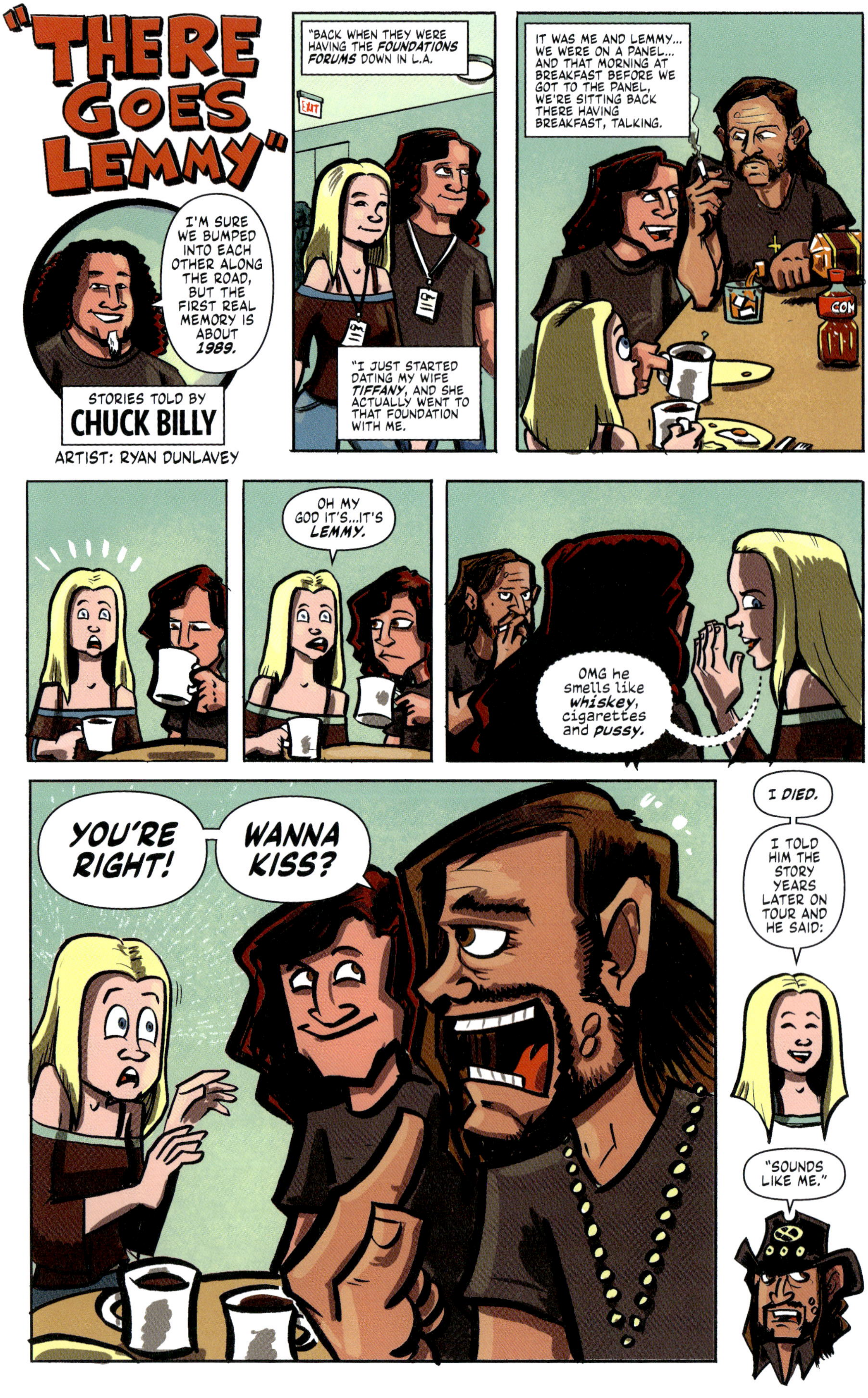
"THERE GOES LEMMY"
I'M SURE WE BUMPED INTO EACH OTHER ALONG THE ROAD, BUT THE FIRST REAL MEMORY IS ABOUT *1989.*
STORIES TOLD BY
CHUCK BILLY
ARTIST: RYAN DUNLAVEY
"BACK WHEN THEY WERE HAVING THE *FOUNDATIONS FORUMS* DOWN IN L.A.
EXIT
"I JUST STARTED DATING MY WIFE *TIFFANY*, AND SHE ACTUALLY WENT TO THAT FOUNDATION WITH ME.
IT WAS ME AND LEMMY... WE WERE ON A PANEL... AND THAT MORNING AT BREAKFAST BEFORE WE GOT TO THE PANEL, WE'RE SITTING BACK THERE HAVING BREAKFAST, TALKING.
OH MY GOD IT'S...IT'S *LEMMY.*
OMG he smells like *whiskey*, cigarettes and *pussy.*
YOU'RE RIGHT!
WANNA KISS?
I *DIED.*
I TOLD HIM THE STORY YEARS LATER ON TOUR AND HE SAID:
"SOUNDS LIKE ME."

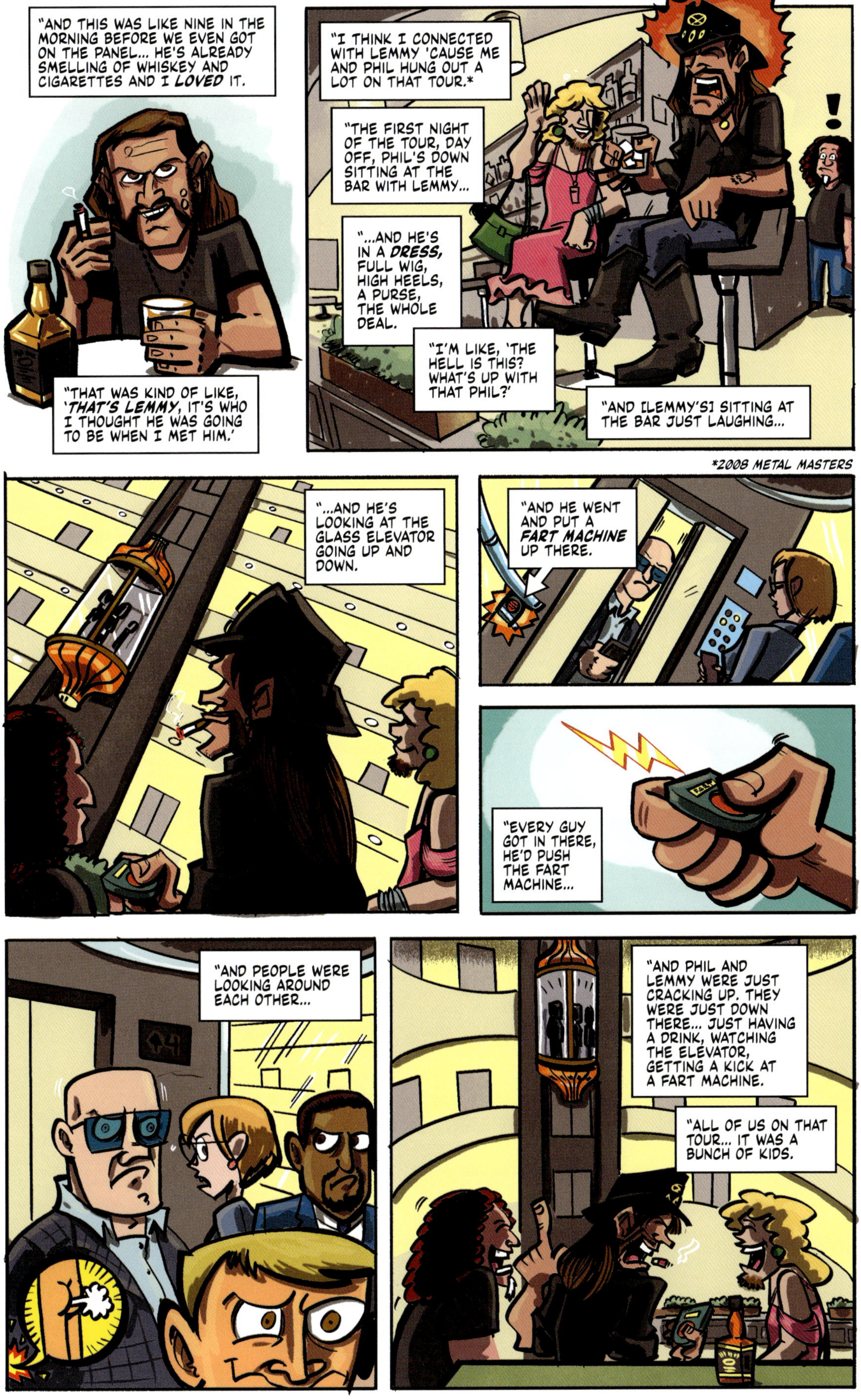
"AND THIS WAS LIKE NINE IN THE MORNING BEFORE WE EVEN GOT ON THE PANEL... HE'S ALREADY SMELLING OF WHISKEY AND CIGARETTES AND I LOVED IT.
"THAT WAS KIND OF LIKE, 'THAT'S LEMMY, IT'S WHO I THOUGHT HE WAS GOING TO BE WHEN I MET HIM.'
"I THINK I CONNECTED WITH LEMMY 'CAUSE ME AND PHIL HUNG OUT A LOT ON THAT TOUR.*
"THE FIRST NIGHT OF THE TOUR, DAY OFF, PHIL'S DOWN SITTING AT THE BAR WITH LEMMY...
"...AND HE'S IN A DRESS, FULL WIG, HIGH HEELS, A PURSE, THE WHOLE DEAL.
"I'M LIKE, 'THE HELL IS THIS? WHAT'S UP WITH THAT PHIL?'
"AND [LEMMY'S] SITTING AT THE BAR JUST LAUGHING...
*2008 METAL MASTERS
"...AND HE'S LOOKING AT THE GLASS ELEVATOR GOING UP AND DOWN.
"AND HE WENT AND PUT A FART MACHINE UP THERE.
"EVERY GUY GOT IN THERE, HE'D PUSH THE FART MACHINE...
"AND PEOPLE WERE LOOKING AROUND EACH OTHER...
"AND PHIL AND LEMMY WERE JUST CRACKING UP. THEY WERE JUST DOWN THERE... JUST HAVING A DRINK, WATCHING THE ELEVATOR, GETTING A KICK AT A FART MACHINE.
"ALL OF US ON THAT TOUR... IT WAS A BUNCH OF KIDS.

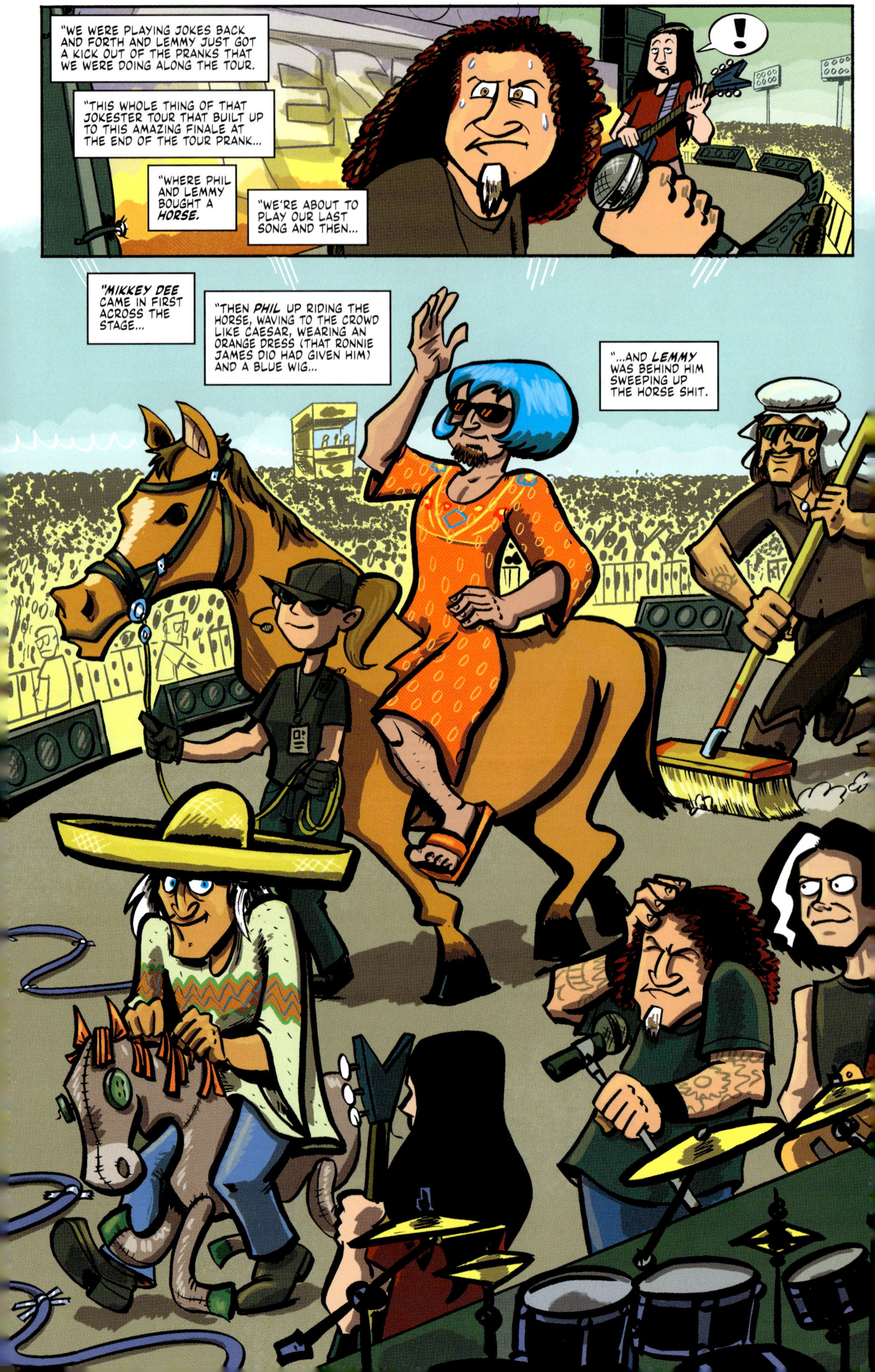
"WE WERE PLAYING JOKES BACK AND FORTH AND LEMMY JUST GOT A KICK OUT OF THE PRANKS THAT WE WERE DOING ALONG THE TOUR.
"THIS WHOLE THING OF THAT JOKESTER TOUR THAT BUILT UP TO THIS AMAZING FINALE AT THE END OF THE TOUR PRANK...
"WHERE PHIL AND LEMMY BOUGHT A HORSE.
"WE'RE ABOUT TO PLAY OUR LAST SONG AND THEN...
!
"MIKKEY DEE CAME IN FIRST ACROSS THE STAGE...
"THEN PHIL UP RIDING THE HORSE, WAVING TO THE CROWD LIKE CAESAR, WEARING AN ORANGE DRESS (THAT RONNIE JAMES DIO HAD GIVEN HIM) AND A BLUE WIG...
"...AND LEMMY WAS BEHIND HIM SWEEPING UP THE HORSE SHIT.

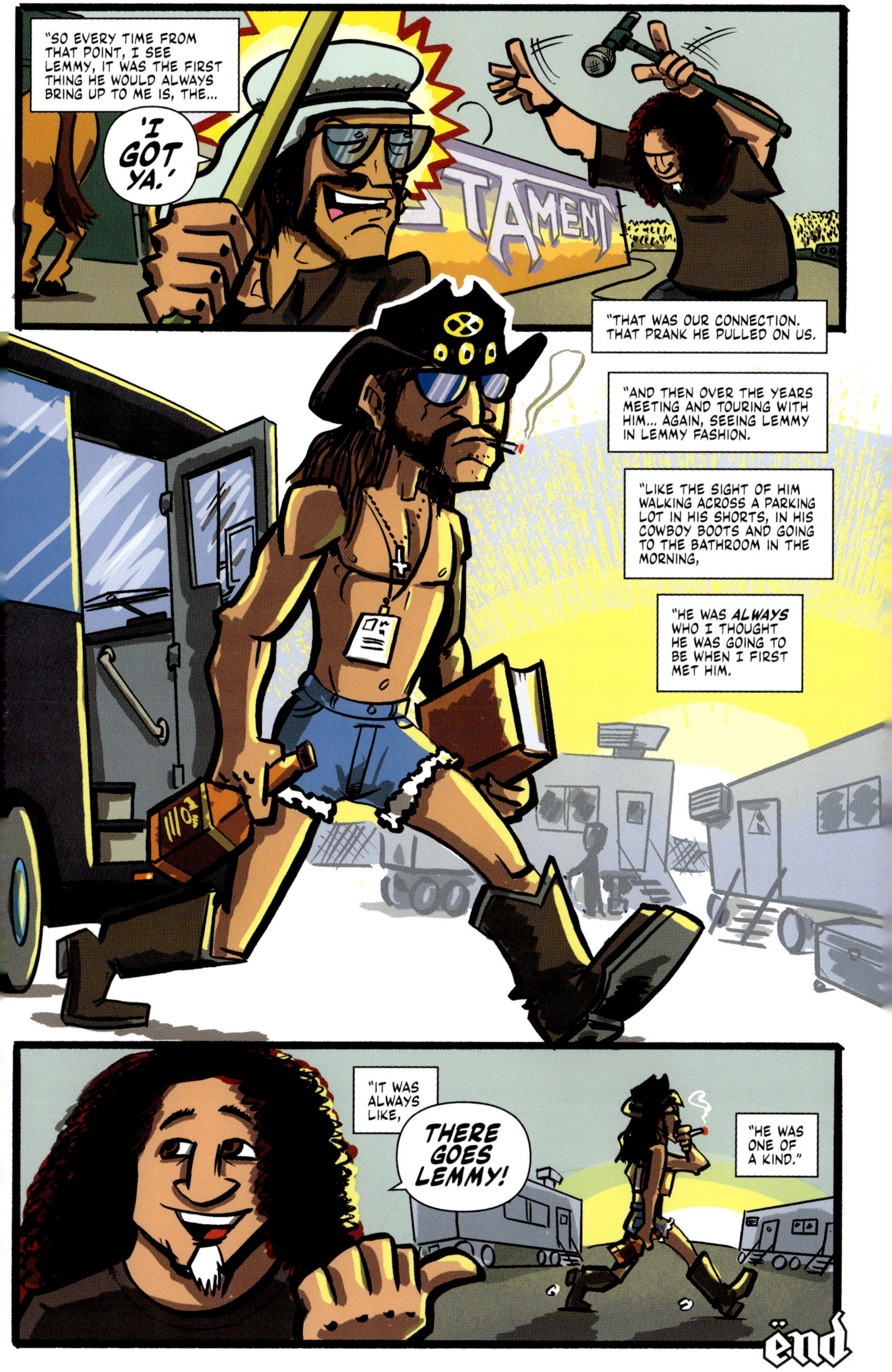
"SO EVERY TIME FROM THAT POINT, I SEE LEMMY, IT WAS THE FIRST THING HE WOULD ALWAYS BRING UP TO ME IS, THE...
'I GOT YA.'
STAMENT
"THAT WAS OUR CONNECTION. THAT PRANK HE PULLED ON US.
"AND THEN OVER THE YEARS MEETING AND TOURING WITH HIM... AGAIN, SEEING LEMMY IN LEMMY FASHION.
"LIKE THE SIGHT OF HIM WALKING ACROSS A PARKING LOT IN HIS SHORTS, IN HIS COWBOY BOOTS AND GOING TO THE BATHROOM IN THE MORNING,
"HE WAS *ALWAYS* WHO I THOUGHT HE WAS GOING TO BE WHEN I FIRST MET HIM.
"IT WAS ALWAYS LIKE,
THERE GOES LEMMY!
"HE WAS ONE OF A KIND."
ënd

"Lemmy was a fixture at the Rainbow. He'd been playing video games there since I was a little kid."

FIRST MET
LEMMY
IN
1990

mikeal maglieri jr

OWNER
THE RAINBOW
BAR & GRILL +
WHISKY
A GO-GO

STORY ILLUSTRATED BY KOREN SHADMI

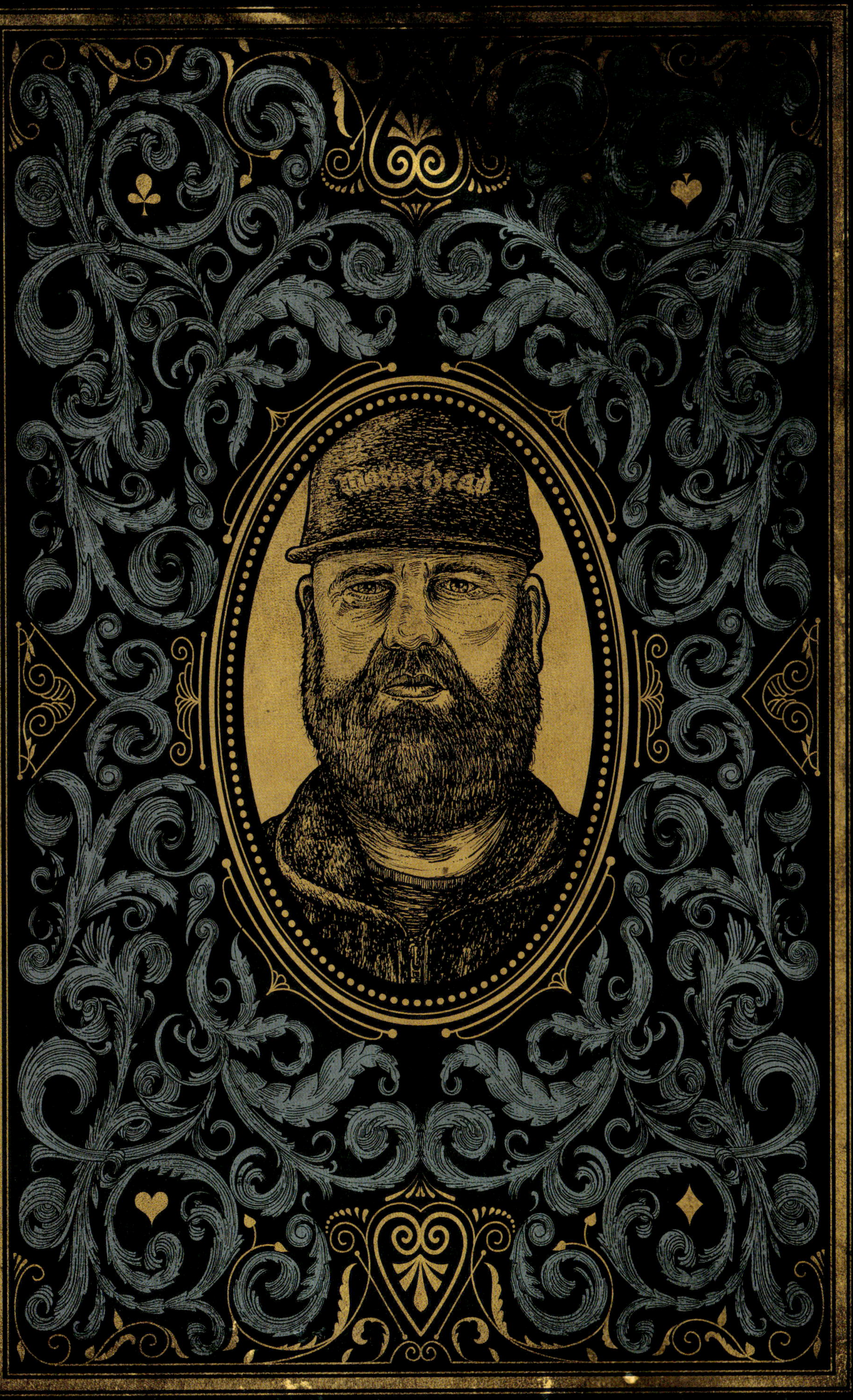

MY FAMILY WAS CLOSE WITH LEMMY WHEN I WAS BORN, SO SINCE I WAS A VERY LITTLE KID I'VE KNOWN LEMMY AND GROWN UP WITH LEMMY, AND YOU KNOW HE LIVED A BLOCK FROM THE RAINBOW FOR MOST OF HIS ADULT LIFE.
WHEN I WAS A KID AT LIKE 12 TO 15 YEARS OLD, LEMMY DIDN'T KNOW ANYTHING ABOUT TECH AND TVS AND STUFF LIKE THAT, AND HE WOULD GO ON TOUR IN JAPAN AND PICK UP A BUNCH OF JAPANESE FORMAT VIDEOS,
プレデター
PREDATOR
HE'D COME BACK AND TODD WOULD CALL ME.
LEMMY'S GOT ALL THESE TAPES... HE CAN'T PLAY THEM.
SO I'D GO OVER THERE AND I TRY TO FIGURE IT OUT AND SOMETIMES I'D HAVE TO FIND THE PLAYER FOR THEM...
I WAS YOUNG AND HE WOULD JUST LAY THERE LIKE A MODEL ON THE COUCH WITH JUST HIS UNDERWEAR ON AND SMOKING A JOINT THE WHOLE TIME AS I'M TRYING TO LIKE EXPLAIN THIS THING.
IT'S THE 80S AND I'M TRYING TO HOOK UP LIKE CONNECTORS WITH DIFFERENT PLAYERS AND FINALLY, I FOUND THEM A THING WHERE YOU CAN SWITCH FROM LIKE PLAYER TO PLAYER TO PLAYER.
IT WAS THIS ONGOING THING THAT WENT ON WITH US FOREVER. BECAUSE HE LOVED THESE WEIRD MOVIES. BUT EVERY TIME I WAS THERE, HE'D BE IN HIS UNDERWEAR, JUST SMOKING A JOINT IN THE SAME POSITION.

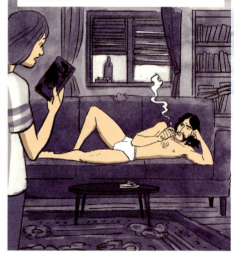

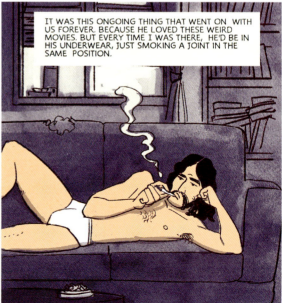

WITH THE MACHINES AT THE RAINBOW, THERE WAS A COMPETITION THAT WENT ON FOR YEARS AND YEARS BETWEEN US, 'CAUSE HE WOULD SIT AND PLAY THESE GAMES FOR HOURS.
WE BOTH GOT REALLY GOOD AT ALL THESE GAMES, IT WAS JUST A THING WHERE WE'D GO BACK AND FORTH ON WHO HAD THE HIGH SCORES.
HE'D GET PISSED AND HAVE AN HOUR LONG RANT
YOU BEAT ME ON HOLLY-WOOD WORD QUIZ!
THERE WAS ONE CONSISTENT GAME HE PLAYED AND BEFORE HE PASSED, WE TOOK THAT GAME OVER TO HIS HOUSE SO HE COULD PLAY IT AND I SWITCHED IT OUT WITH ANOTHER ONE THAT HE WOULD ALSO PLAY THAT WAS ON THE INSIDE BAR.
THAT MACHINE IS IN STORAGE NOW WITH ALL HIS STUFF.
TODD SAID THE OTHER NIGHT:
OH, YOU WANT ME TO BRING IT BACK?
NO, IT'S PROBABLY SAFER WHERE IT IS AND JUST LET IT BE WITH ALL HIS OTHER STUFF.
ESSENTIALLY, WE WANT A ROCK AND ROLL MUSEUM IN HOLLYWOOD, NOT IN CLEVELAND, WHERE WE CAN SHOWCASE LEMMY'S LIFE AND HIS COOL STUFF. ALL THESE CUSTOM BOOTS, AND JACKETS, AND IN THE MIDST OF THAT IS THAT MACHINE.
RAINBOW
bar & grill
WITH LEMMY AND THE RAINBOW, IT'S LIKE IT'S HIS HOME AND, PEOPLE ARE COMING TO TO RESPECT HIM LIKE HE'S STILL HERE. PEOPLE FEEL LIKE THEY'RE WITH LEMMY WHEN THEY'RE HERE, YOU KNOW?
ënd

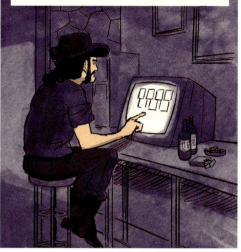

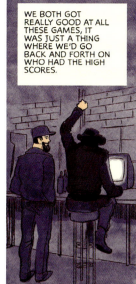

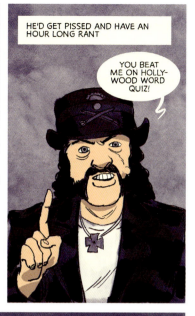

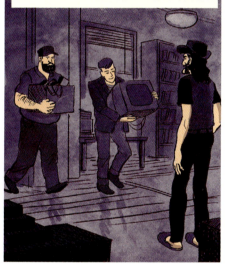

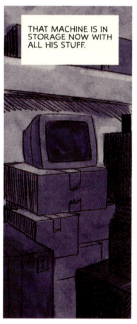

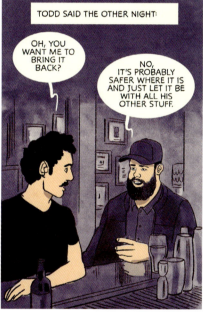

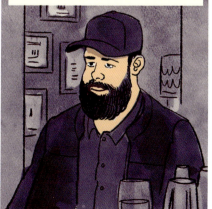

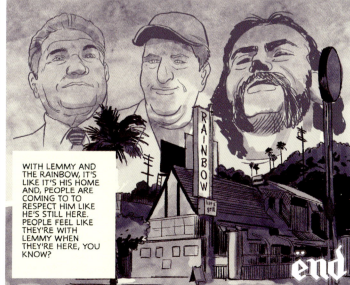

"Lemmy is literally the last true rock star. His legacy will last forever."

FIRST MET LEMMY IN 1991

todd singerman

MANAGER
MOTÖRHEAD +
LEMMY
KILMISTER

STORY ILLUSTRATED BY
JEFF MCCLELLAND + JEFF MCCOMSEY

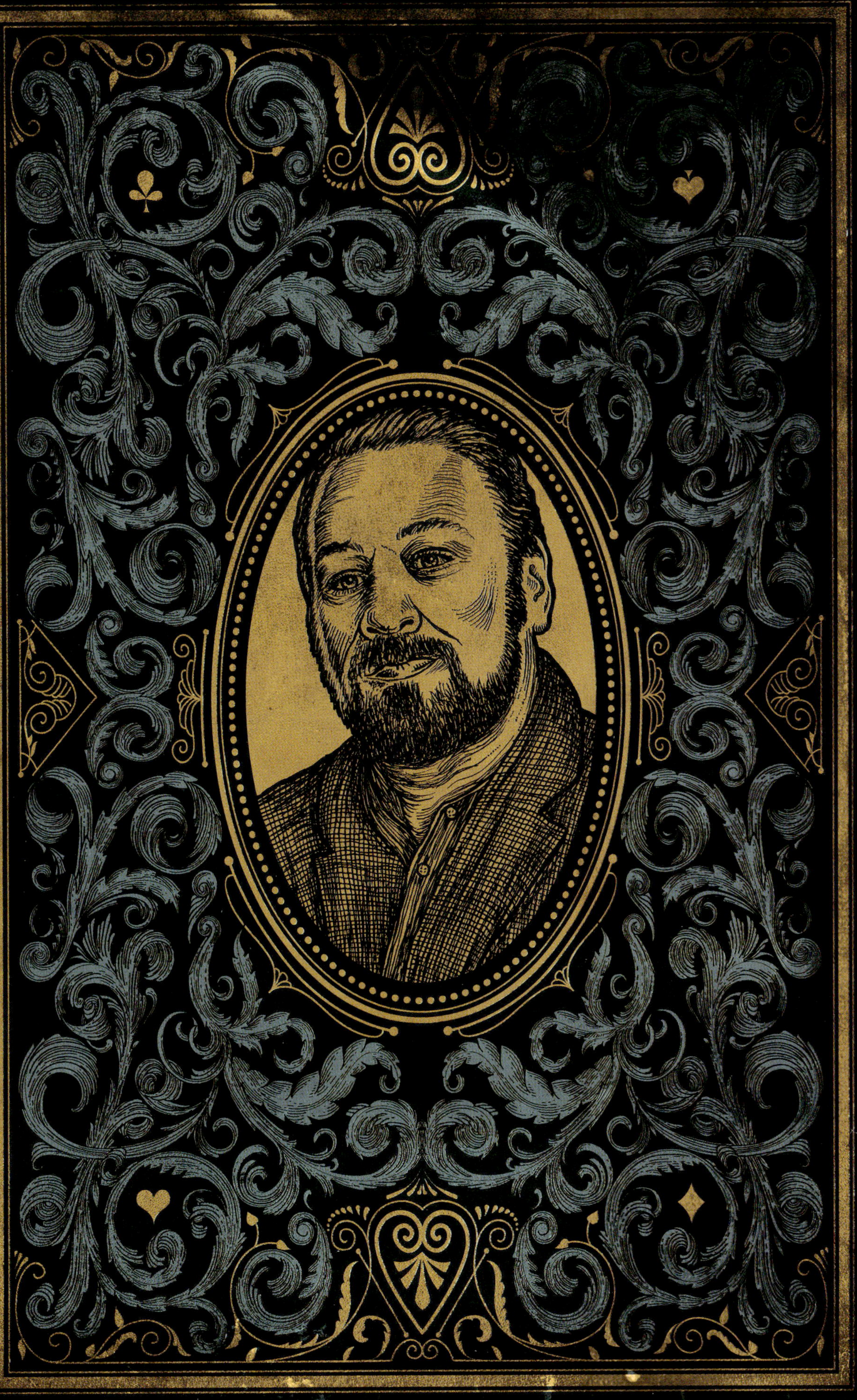

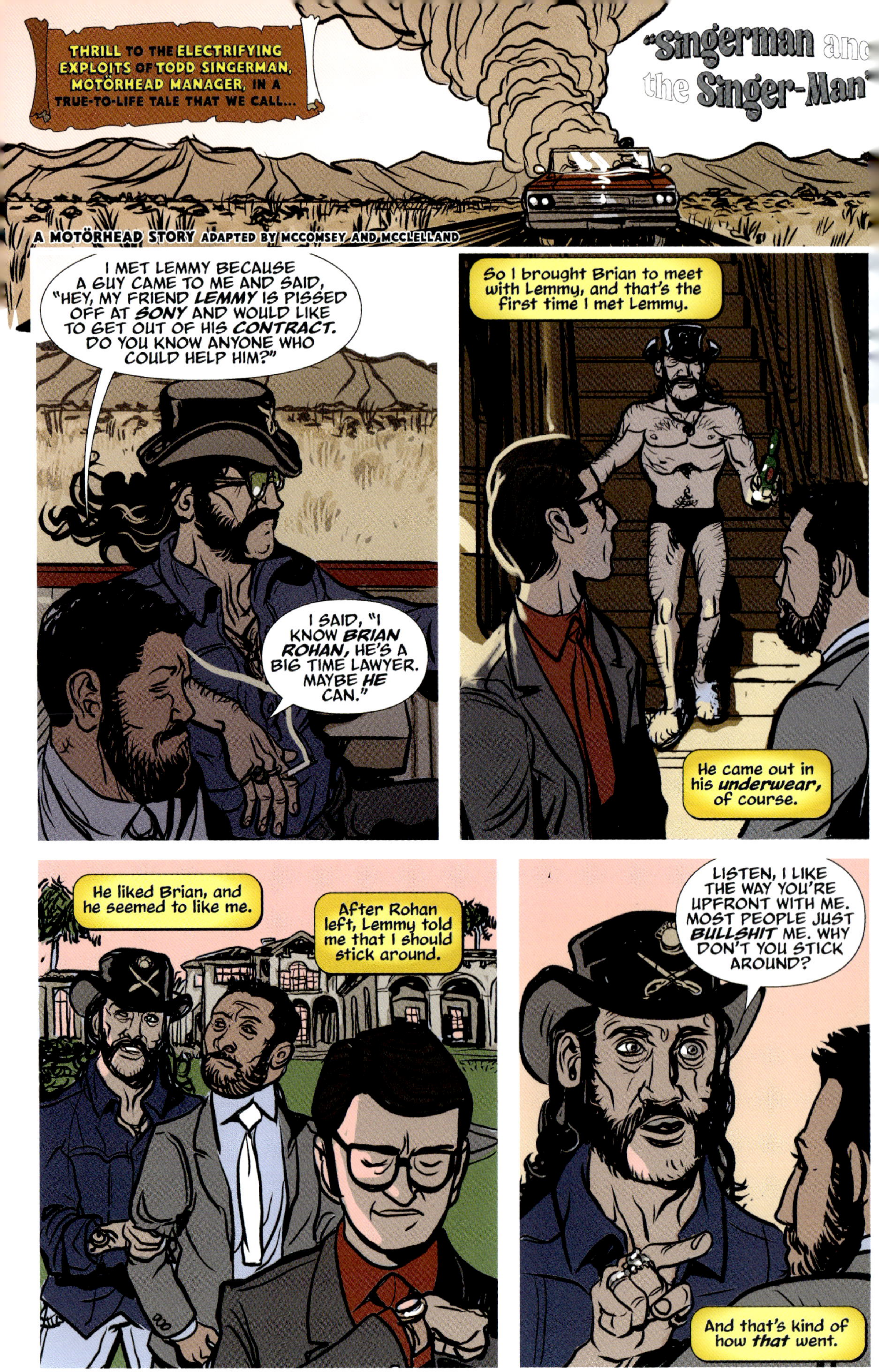
THRILL TO THE ELECTRIFYING EXPLOITS OF TODD SINGERMAN, MOTÖRHEAD MANAGER, IN A TRUE-TO-LIFE TALE THAT WE CALL...
"Singerman and the Singer-Man"
A MOTÖRHEAD STORY ADAPTED BY MCCONSEY AND MCCLELLAND
I MET LEMMY BECAUSE A GUY CAME TO ME AND SAID, "HEY, MY FRIEND LEMMY IS PISSED OFF AT SONY AND WOULD LIKE TO GET OUT OF HIS CONTRACT. DO YOU KNOW ANYONE WHO COULD HELP HIM?"
I SAID, "I KNOW BRIAN ROHAN, HE'S A BIG TIME LAWYER. MAYBE HE CAN."
So I brought Brian to meet with Lemmy, and that's the first time I met Lemmy.
He came out in his underwear, of course.
He liked Brian, and he seemed to like me.
After Rohan left, Lemmy told me that I should stick around.
LISTEN, I LIKE THE WAY YOU'RE UPFRONT WITH ME. MOST PEOPLE JUST BULLSHIT ME. WHY DON'T YOU STICK AROUND?
And that's kind of how that went.

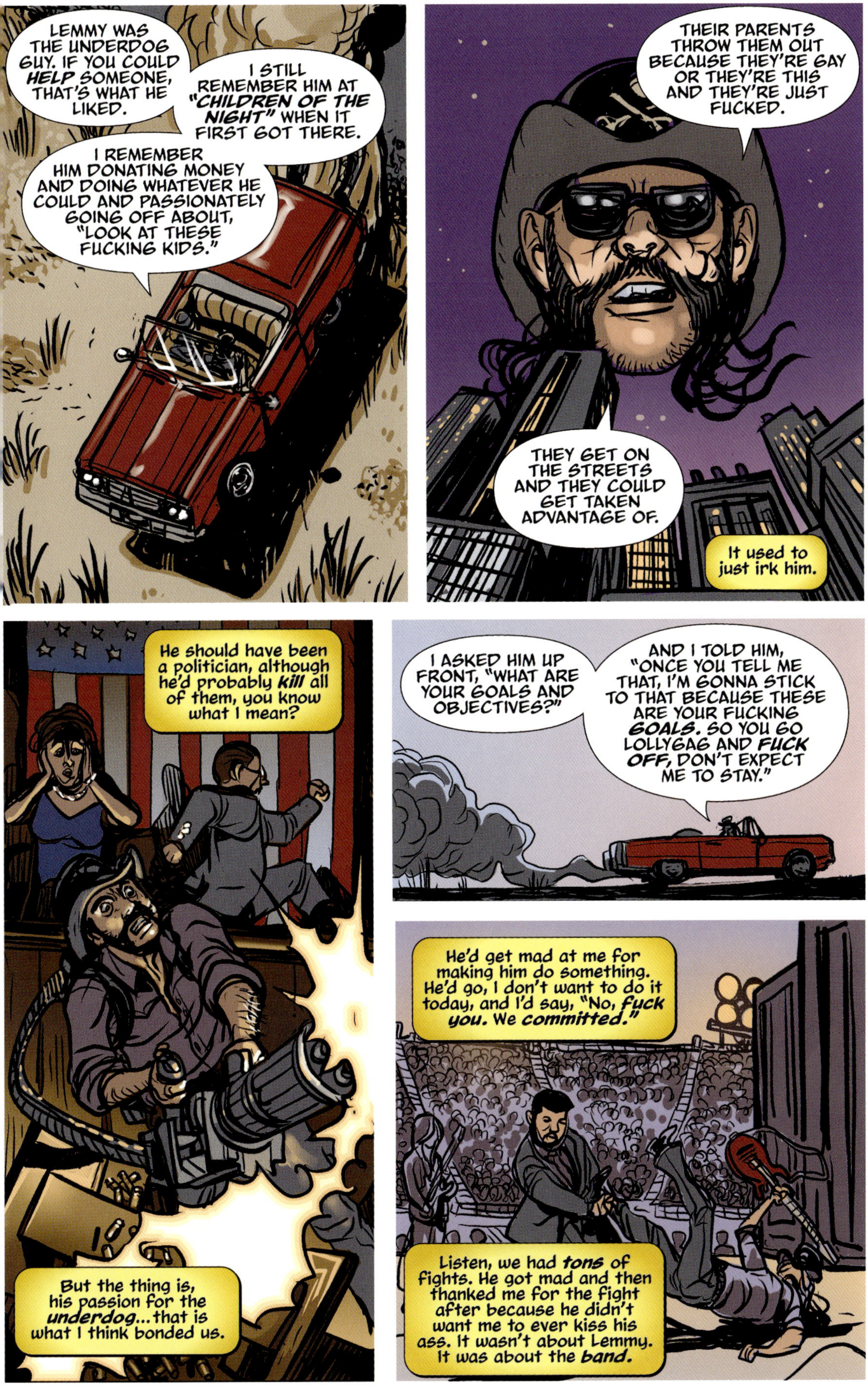
LEMMY WAS THE UNDERDOG GUY. IF YOU COULD **HELP** SOMEONE, THAT'S WHAT HE LIKED.
I STILL REMEMBER HIM AT ***"CHILDREN OF THE NIGHT"*** WHEN IT FIRST GOT THERE.
I REMEMBER HIM DONATING MONEY AND DOING WHATEVER HE COULD AND PASSIONATELY GOING OFF ABOUT, "LOOK AT THESE FUCKING KIDS."
THEIR PARENTS THROW THEM OUT BECAUSE THEY'RE GAY OR THEY'RE THIS AND THEY'RE JUST FUCKED.
THEY GET ON THE STREETS AND THEY COULD GET TAKEN ADVANTAGE OF.
It used to just irk him.
He should have been a politician, although he'd probably ***kill*** all of them, you know what I mean?
But the thing is, his passion for the ***underdog***...that is what I think bonded us.
I ASKED HIM UP FRONT, "WHAT ARE YOUR GOALS AND OBJECTIVES?"
AND I TOLD HIM, "ONCE YOU TELL ME THAT, I'M GONNA STICK TO THAT BECAUSE THESE ARE YOUR FUCKING ***GOALS.*** SO YOU GO LOLLYGAG AND ***FUCK OFF,*** DON'T EXPECT ME TO STAY."
He'd get mad at me for making him do something. He'd go, I don't want to do it today, and I'd say, "No, ***fuck you.*** We ***committed.***"
Listen, we had ***tons*** of fights. He got mad and then thanked me for the fight after because he didn't want me to ever kiss his ass. It wasn't about Lemmy. It was about the ***band.***

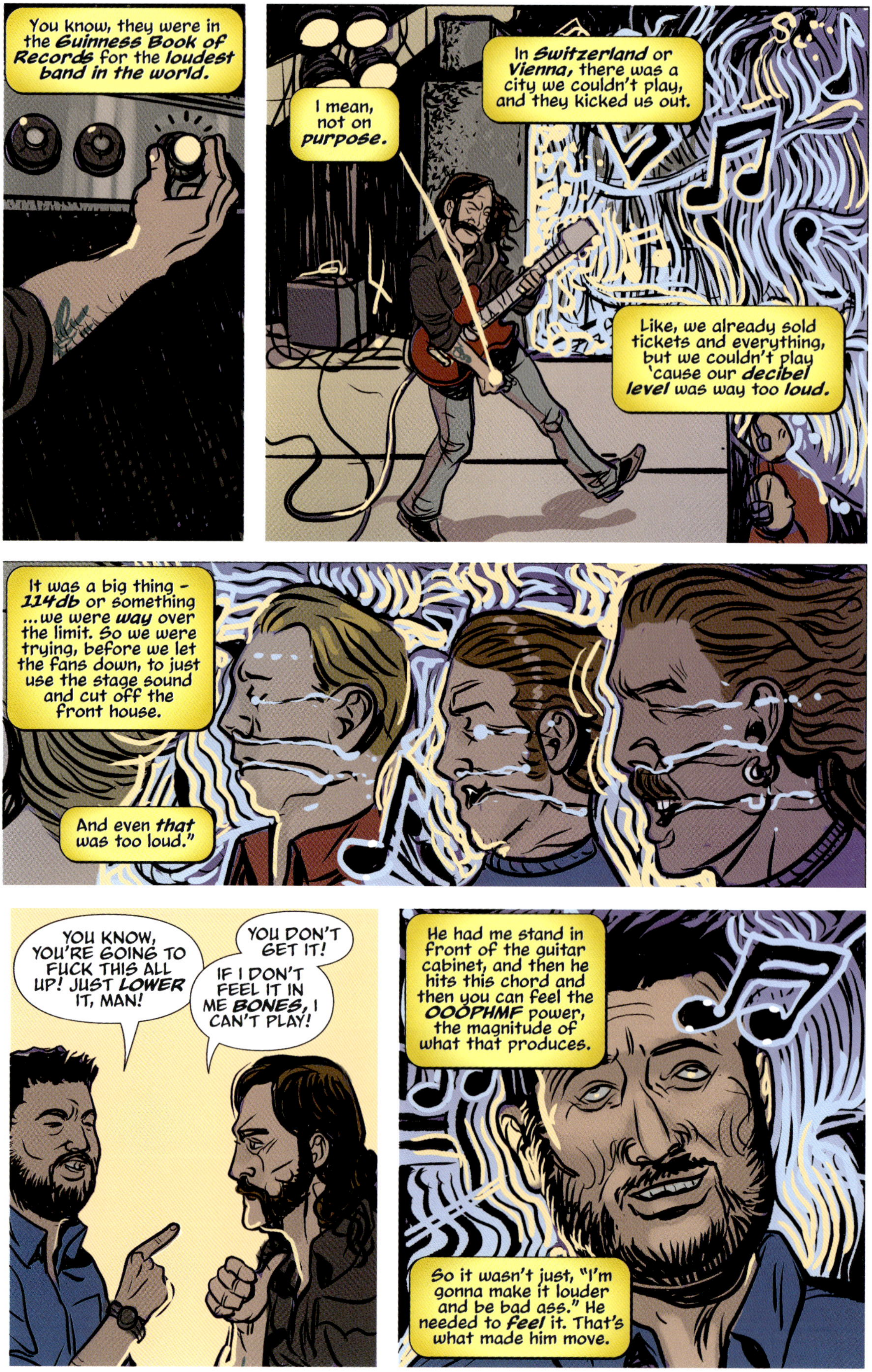
You know, they were in the Guinness Book of Records for the loudest band in the world.
I mean, not on purpose.
In Switzerland or Vienna, there was a city we couldn't play, and they kicked us out.
Like, we already sold tickets and everything, but we couldn't play 'cause our decibel level was way too loud.
It was a big thing - 114db or something ...we were way over the limit. So we were trying, before we let the fans down, to just use the stage sound and cut off the front house.
And even that was too loud."
YOU KNOW, YOU'RE GOING TO FUCK THIS ALL UP! JUST LOWER IT, MAN!
YOU DON'T GET IT!
IF I DON'T FEEL IT IN ME BONES, I CAN'T PLAY!
He had me stand in front of the guitar cabinet, and then he hits this chord and then you can feel the OOOPHMF power, the magnitude of what that produces.
So it wasn't just, "I'm gonna make it louder and be bad ass." He needed to feel it. That's what made him move.

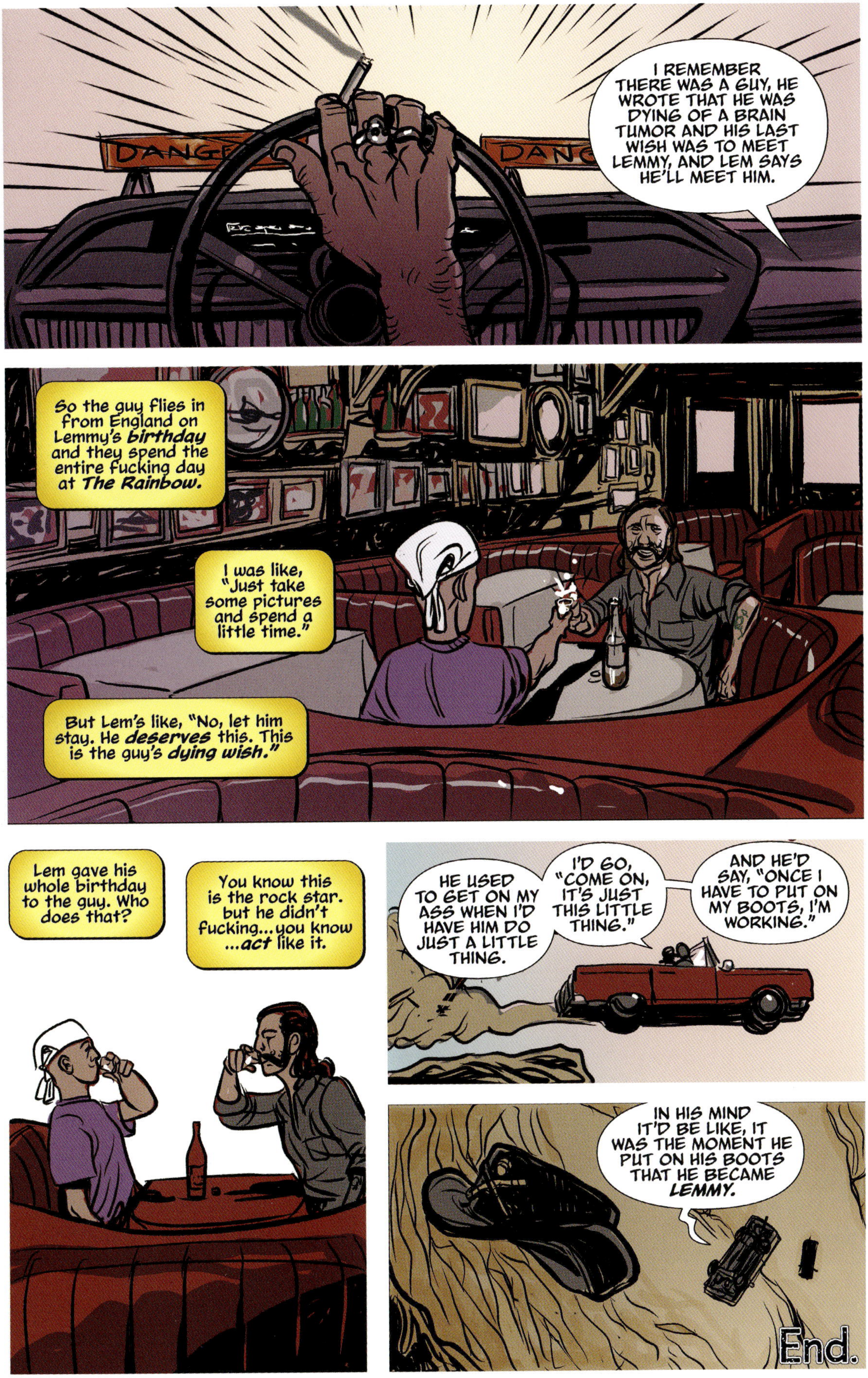
DANGE
DANG
I REMEMBER THERE WAS A GUY, HE WROTE THAT HE WAS DYING OF A BRAIN TUMOR AND HIS LAST WISH WAS TO MEET LEMMY, AND LEM SAYS HE'LL MEET HIM.
So the guy flies in from England on Lemmy's *birthday* and they spend the entire fucking day at *The Rainbow.*
I was like, "Just take some pictures and spend a little time."
But Lem's like, "No, let him stay. He *deserves* this. This is the guy's *dying wish.*"
Lem gave his whole birthday to the guy. Who does that?
You know this is the rock star. but he didn't fucking...you know ...*act* like it.
HE USED TO GET ON MY ASS WHEN I'D HAVE HIM DO JUST A LITTLE THING.
I'D GO, "COME ON, IT'S JUST THIS LITTLE THING."
AND HE'D SAY, "ONCE I HAVE TO PUT ON MY BOOTS, I'M WORKING."
IN HIS MIND IT'D BE LIKE, IT WAS THE MOMENT HE PUT ON HIS BOOTS THAT HE BECAME ***LEMMY.***
End.

"He went out the way he wanted...
playing Rock & Roll every goddamn night."

FIRST MET
LEMMY
IN
1995

lars frederiksen

GUITARIST
SINGER
RANCID

STORY ILLUSTRATED BY WES HARGIS

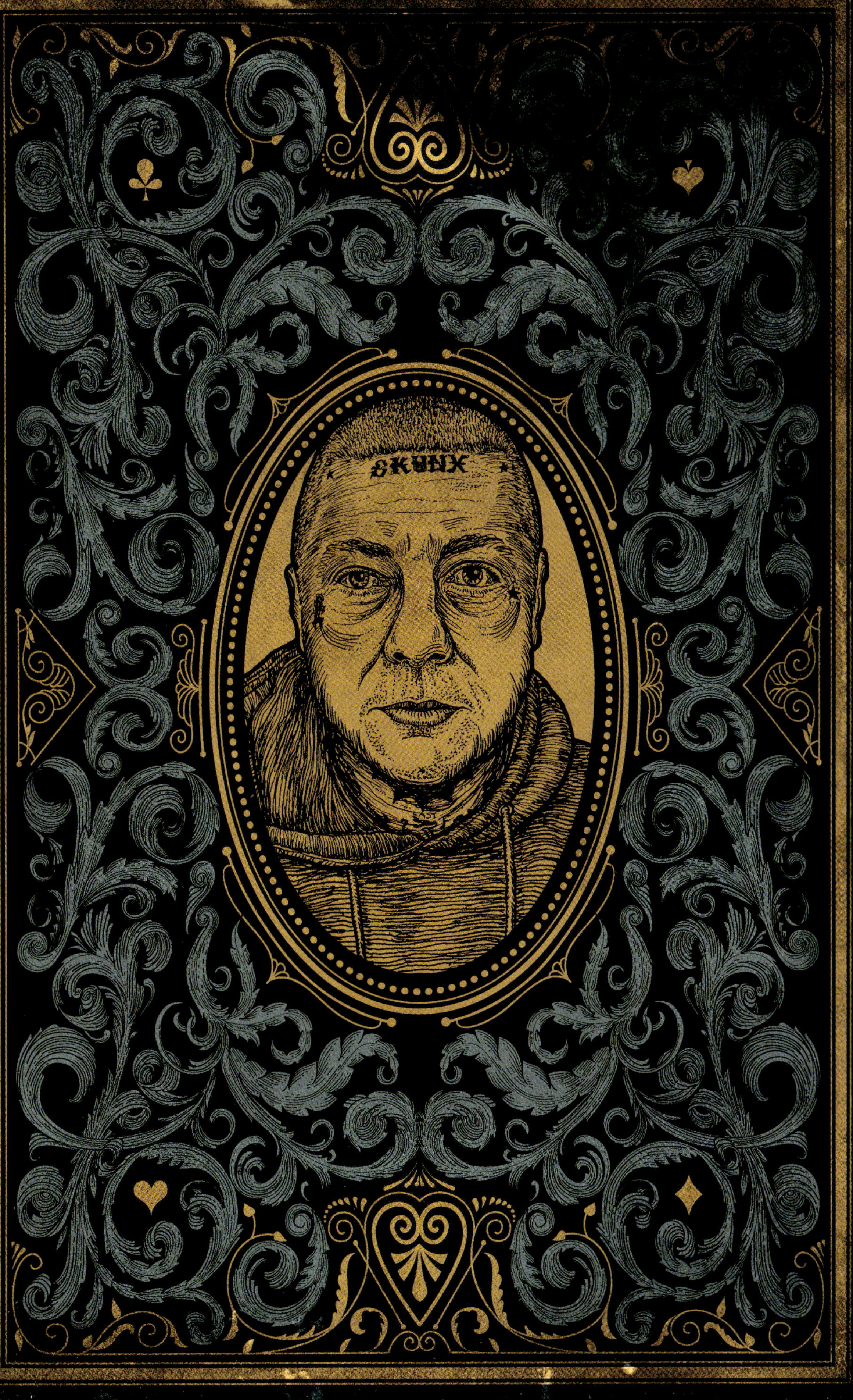
SKUNX

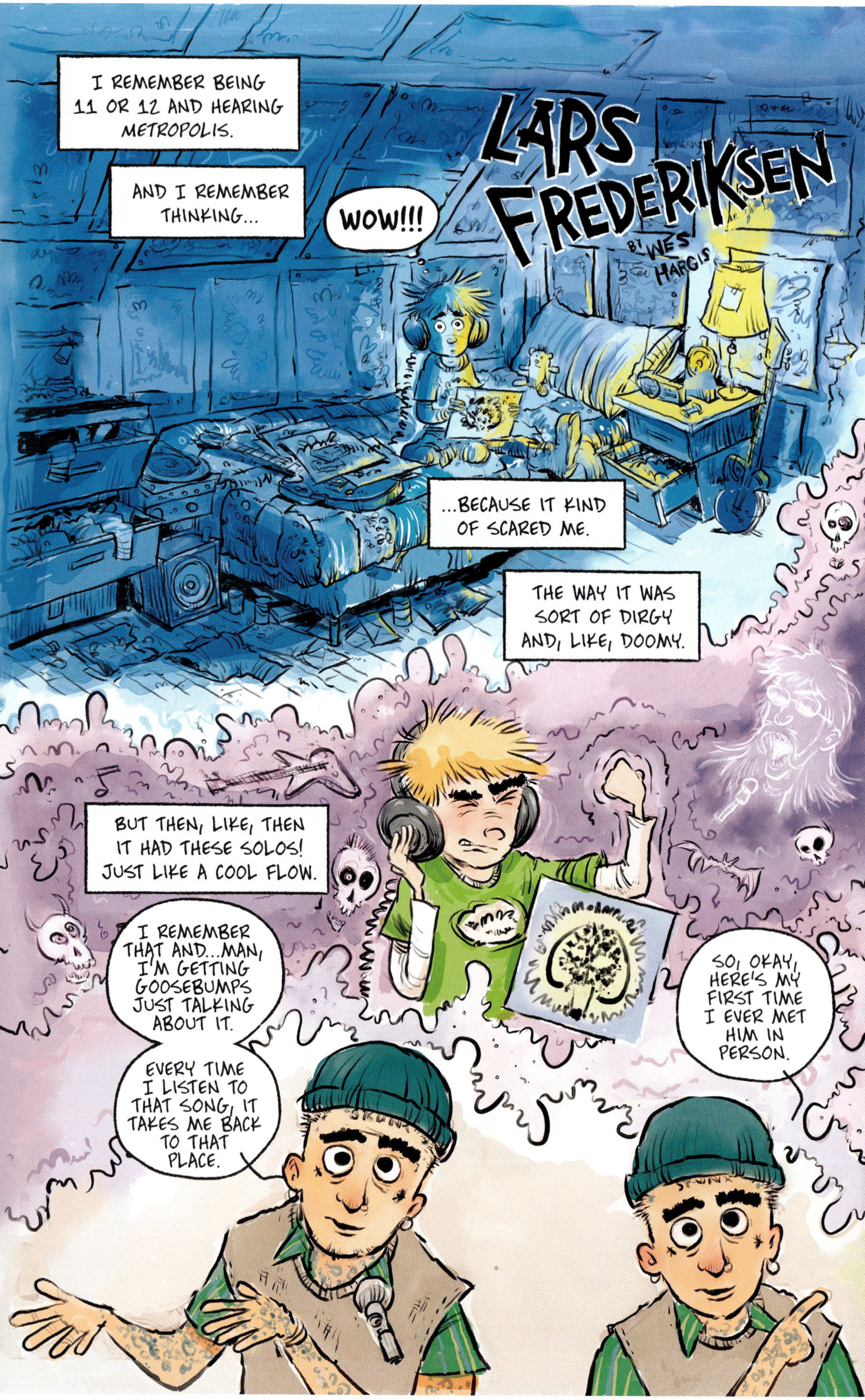
LARS FREDERIKSEN
BY WES HARGIS
I REMEMBER BEING 11 OR 12 AND HEARING METROPOLIS.
AND I REMEMBER THINKING...
WOW!!!
...BECAUSE IT KIND OF SCARED ME.
THE WAY IT WAS SORT OF DIRGY AND, LIKE, DOOMY.
BUT THEN, LIKE, THEN IT HAD THESE SOLOS! JUST LIKE A COOL FLOW.
I REMEMBER THAT AND...MAN, I'M GETTING GOOSEBUMPS JUST TALKING ABOUT IT.
EVERY TIME I LISTEN TO THAT SONG, IT TAKES ME BACK TO THAT PLACE.
SO, OKAY, HERE'S MY FIRST TIME I EVER MET HIM IN PERSON.

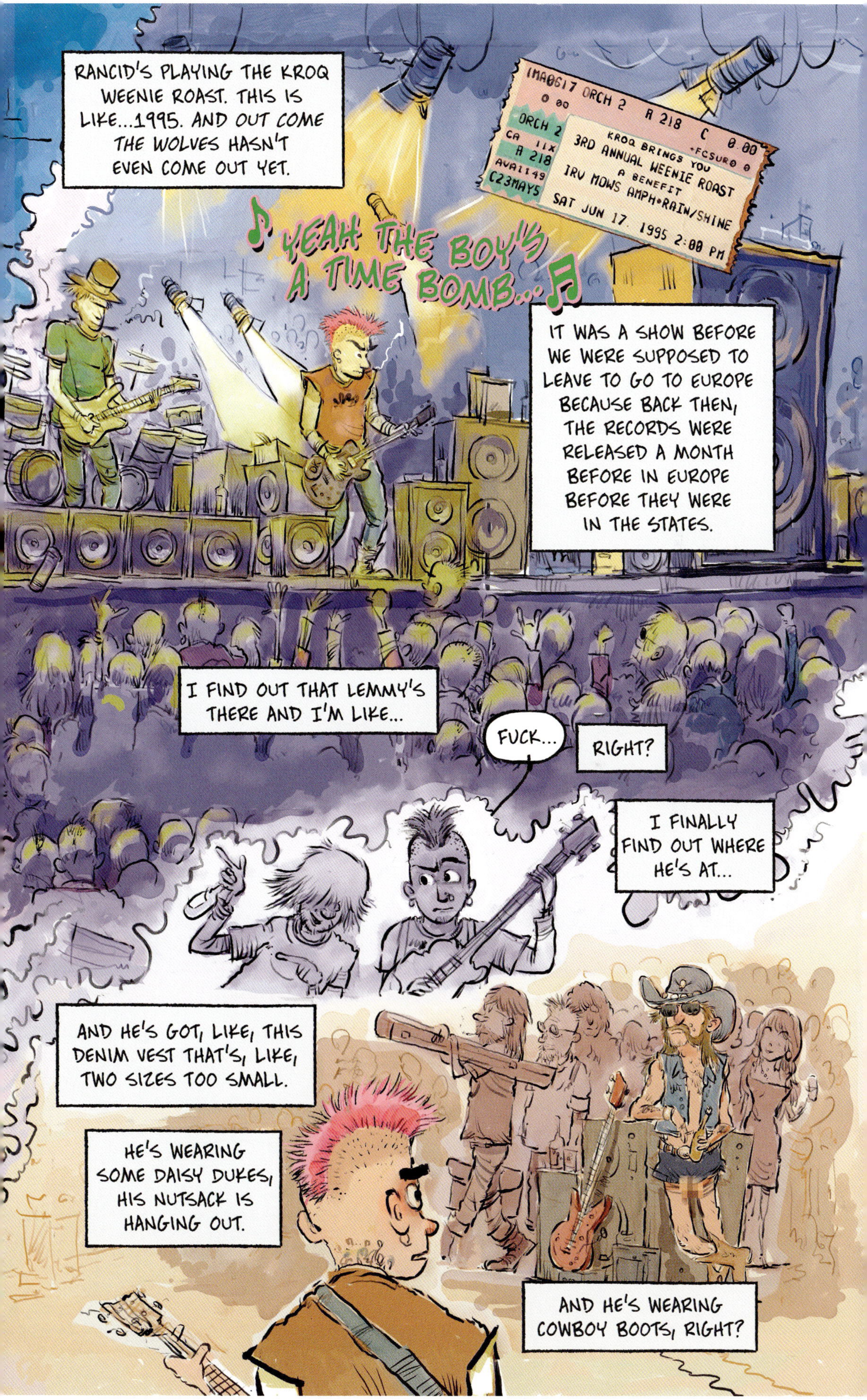
RANCID'S PLAYING THE KROQ WEENIE ROAST. THIS IS LIKE...1995. AND OUT COME THE WOLVES HASN'T EVEN COME OUT YET.
ORCH 2 A 218 C 0.00
KROQ BRINGS YOU 3RD ANNUAL WEENIE ROAST A BENEFIT
IRV MDWS AMPH•RAIN/SHINE
SAT JUN 17, 1995 2:00 PM
YEAH THE BOY'S A TIME BOMB...
IT WAS A SHOW BEFORE WE WERE SUPPOSED TO LEAVE TO GO TO EUROPE BECAUSE BACK THEN, THE RECORDS WERE RELEASED A MONTH BEFORE IN EUROPE BEFORE THEY WERE IN THE STATES.
I FIND OUT THAT LEMMY'S THERE AND I'M LIKE...
FUCK...
RIGHT?
I FINALLY FIND OUT WHERE HE'S AT...
AND HE'S GOT, LIKE, THIS DENIM VEST THAT'S, LIKE, TWO SIZES TOO SMALL.
HE'S WEARING SOME DAISY DUKES, HIS NUTSACK IS HANGING OUT.
AND HE'S WEARING COWBOY BOOTS, RIGHT?

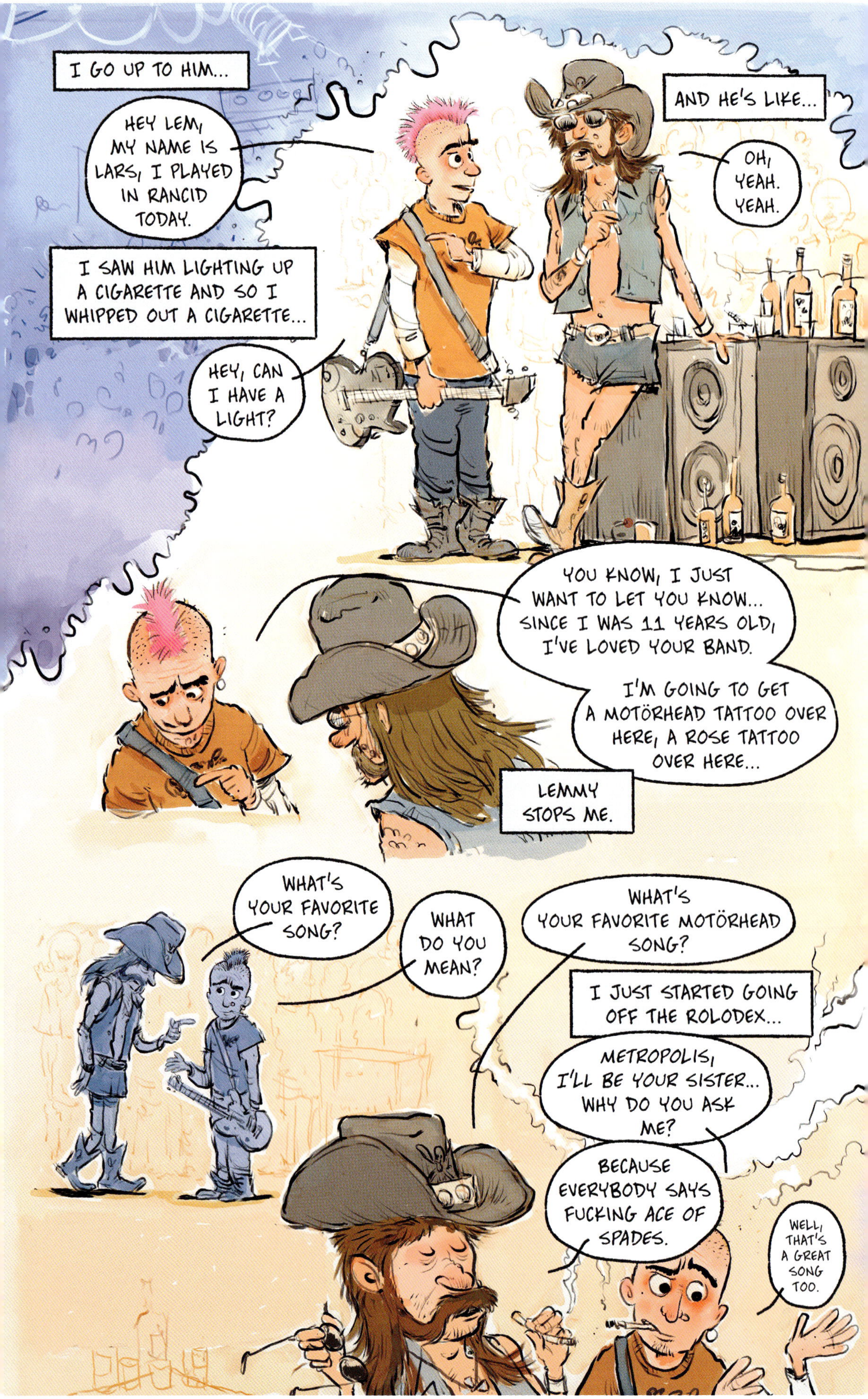
I GO UP TO HIM...
HEY LEM, MY NAME IS LARS, I PLAYED IN RANCID TODAY.
AND HE'S LIKE...
OH, YEAH. YEAH.
I SAW HIM LIGHTING UP A CIGARETTE AND SO I WHIPPED OUT A CIGARETTE...
HEY, CAN I HAVE A LIGHT?
YOU KNOW, I JUST WANT TO LET YOU KNOW... SINCE I WAS 11 YEARS OLD, I'VE LOVED YOUR BAND.
I'M GOING TO GET A MOTÖRHEAD TATTOO OVER HERE, A ROSE TATTOO OVER HERE...
LEMMY STOPS ME.
WHAT'S YOUR FAVORITE SONG?
WHAT DO YOU MEAN?
WHAT'S YOUR FAVORITE MOTÖRHEAD SONG?
I JUST STARTED GOING OFF THE ROLODEX...
METROPOLIS, I'LL BE YOUR SISTER... WHY DO YOU ASK ME?
BECAUSE EVERYBODY SAYS FUCKING ACE OF SPADES.
WELL, THAT'S A GREAT SONG TOO.

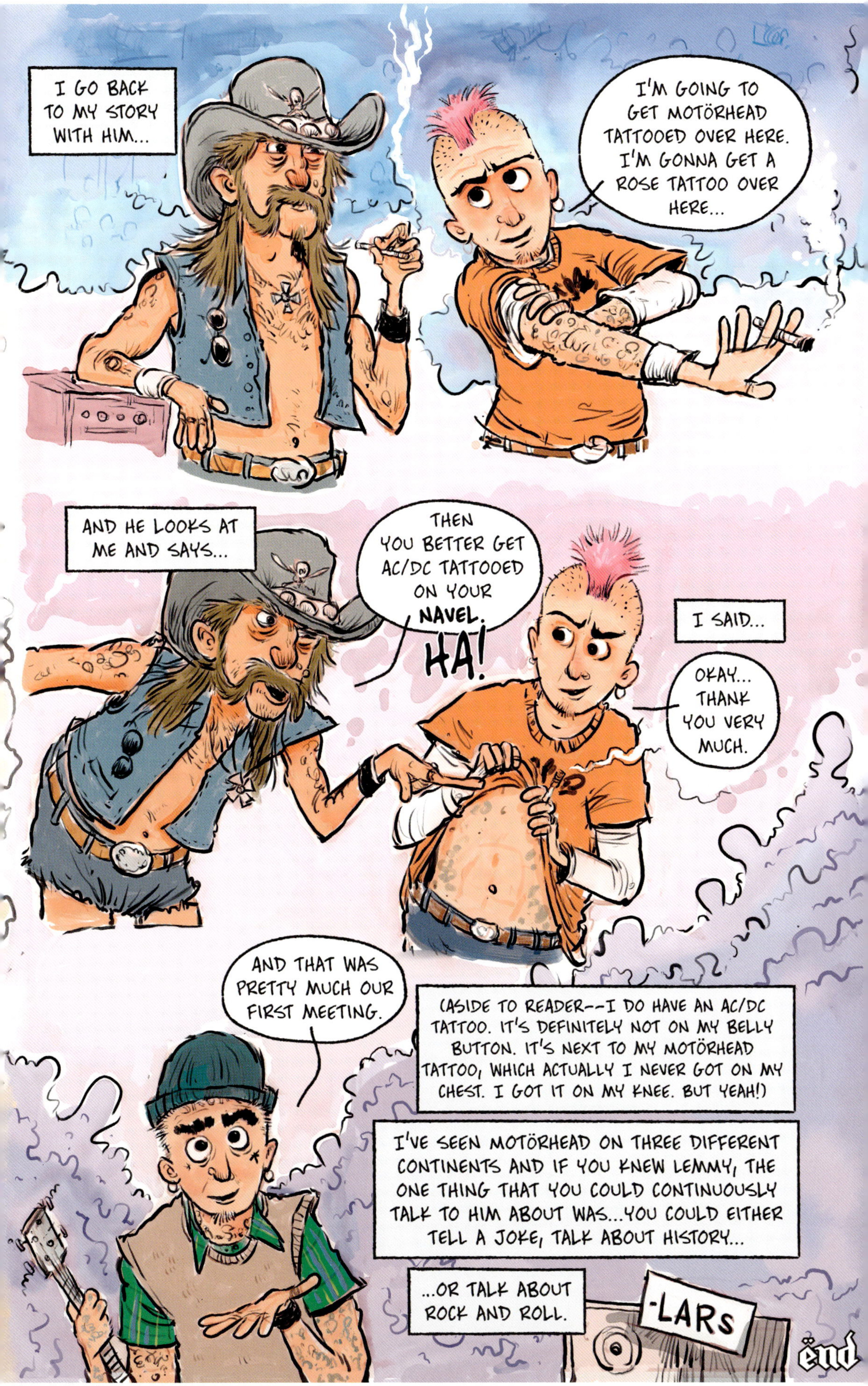
I GO BACK TO MY STORY WITH HIM...
I'M GOING TO GET MOTÖRHEAD TATTOOED OVER HERE. I'M GONNA GET A ROSE TATTOO OVER HERE...
AND HE LOOKS AT ME AND SAYS...
THEN YOU BETTER GET AC/DC TATTOOED ON YOUR **NAVEL.** HA!
I SAID...
OKAY... THANK YOU VERY MUCH.
AND THAT WAS PRETTY MUCH OUR FIRST MEETING.
(ASIDE TO READER--I DO HAVE AN AC/DC TATTOO. IT'S DEFINITELY NOT ON MY BELLY BUTTON. IT'S NEXT TO MY MOTÖRHEAD TATTOO, WHICH ACTUALLY I NEVER GOT ON MY CHEST. I GOT IT ON MY KNEE. BUT YEAH!)
I'VE SEEN MOTÖRHEAD ON THREE DIFFERENT CONTINENTS AND IF YOU KNEW LEMMY, THE ONE THING THAT YOU COULD CONTINUOUSLY TALK TO HIM ABOUT WAS...YOU COULD EITHER TELL A JOKE, TALK ABOUT HISTORY...
...OR TALK ABOUT ROCK AND ROLL.
-LARS
ënd

"Lemmy carved a most frightening, though beautifully iconic figure. An Apocolyptic Whiskey Cowboy Christ."

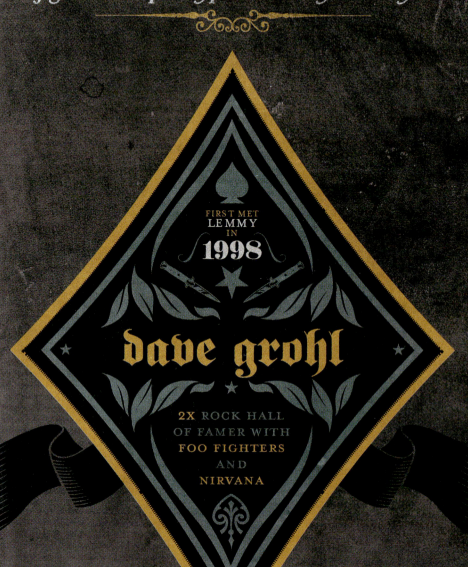

FIRST MET LEMMY IN 1998

dave grohl

2X ROCK HALL OF FAMER WITH FOO FIGHTERS AND NIRVANA

STORY ILLUSTRATED BY BRENT ENGSTROM

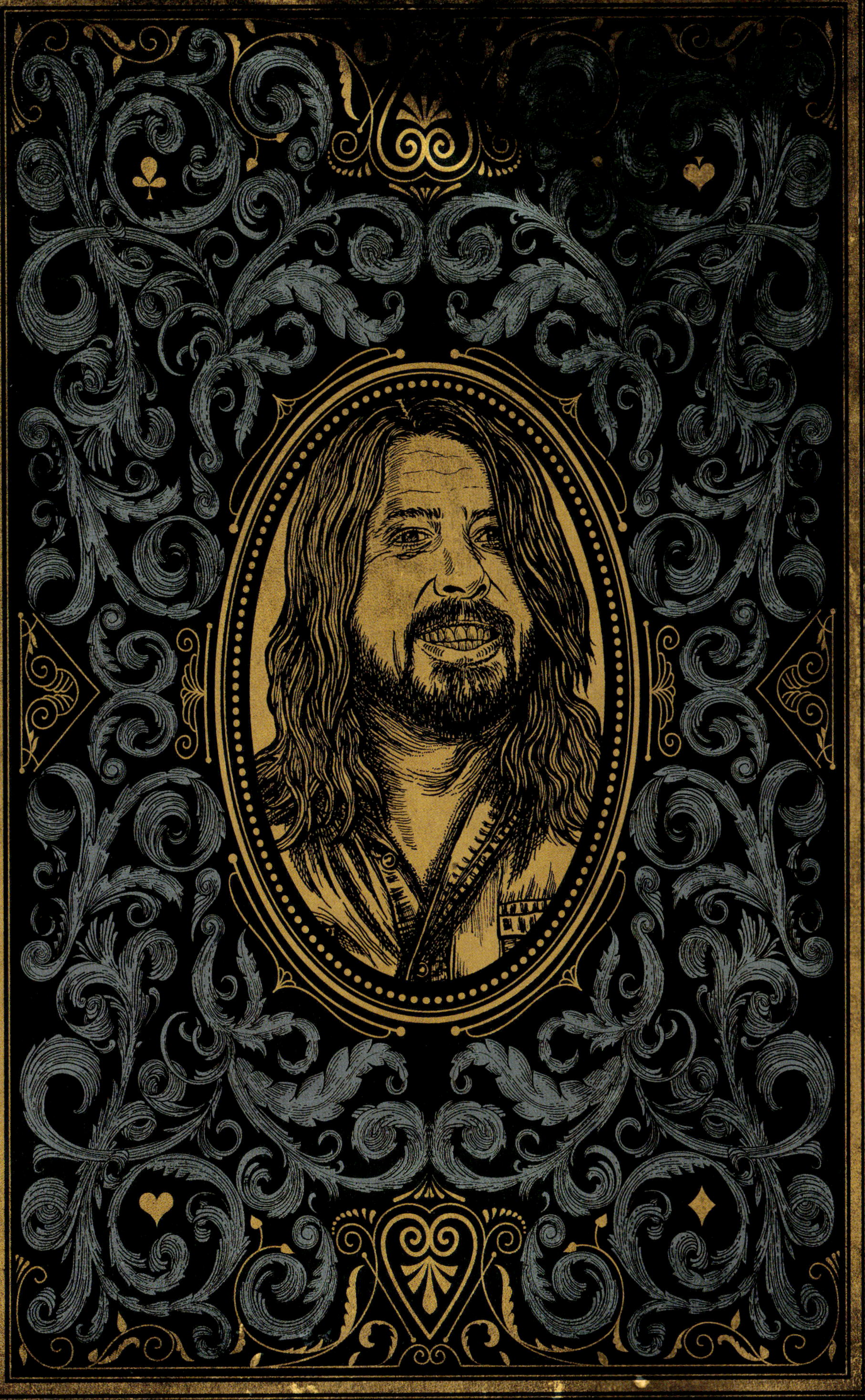

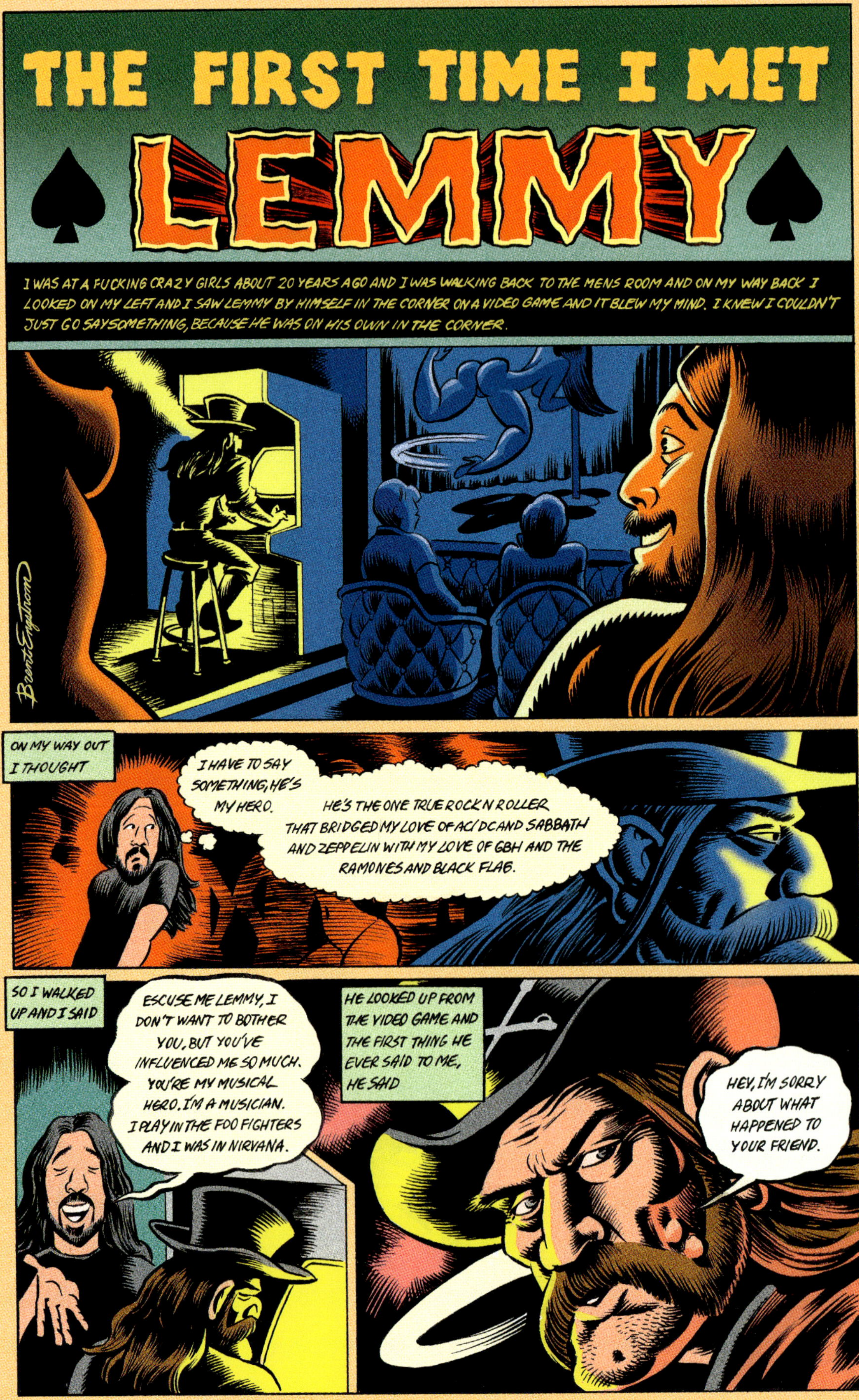
THE FIRST TIME I MET
LEMMY
I WAS AT A FUCKING CRAZY GIRLS ABOUT 20 YEARS AGO AND I WAS WALKING BACK TO THE MENS ROOM AND ON MY WAY BACK I LOOKED ON MY LEFT AND I SAW LEMMY BY HIMSELF IN THE CORNER ON A VIDEO GAME AND IT BLEW MY MIND. I KNEW I COULDN'T JUST GO SAYSOMETHING, BECAUSE HE WAS ON HIS OWN IN THE CORNER.
ON MY WAY OUT I THOUGHT
I HAVE TO SAY SOMETHING, HE'S MY HERO. HE'S THE ONE TRUE ROCK N ROLLER THAT BRIDGED MY LOVE OF AC/DC AND SABBATH AND ZEPPELIN WITH MY LOVE OF GBH AND THE RAMONES AND BLACK FLAG.
SO I WALKED UP AND I SAID
ESCUSE ME LEMMY, I DON'T WANT TO BOTHER YOU, BUT YOU'VE INFLUENCED ME SO MUCH. YOU'RE MY MUSICAL HERO. I'M A MUSICIAN. I PLAY IN THE FOO FIGHTERS AND I WAS IN NIRVANA.
HE LOOKED UP FROM THE VIDEO GAME AND THE FIRST THING HE EVER SAID TO ME, HE SAID
HEY, I'M SORRY ABOUT WHAT HAPPENED TO YOUR FRIEND.

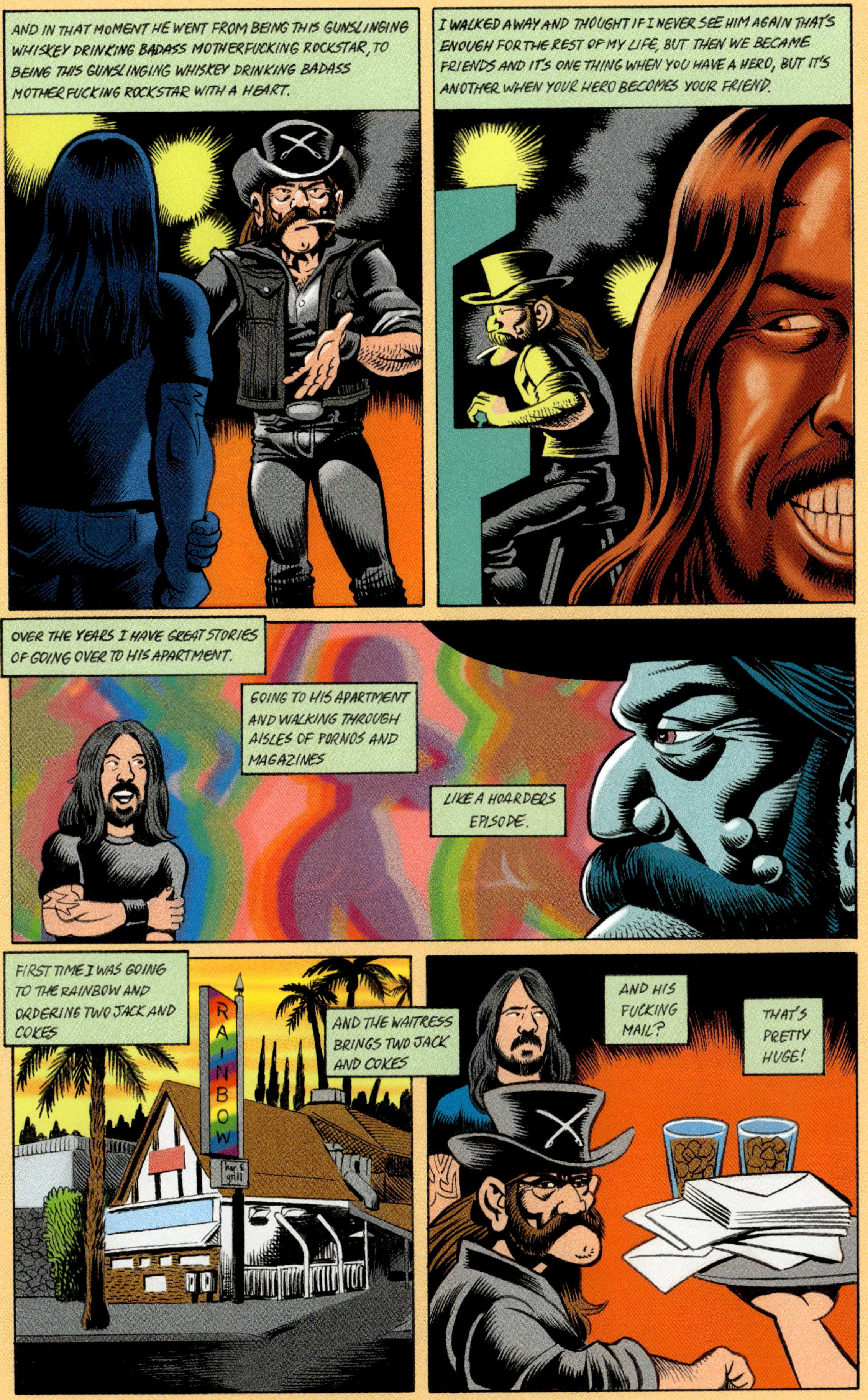
AND IN THAT MOMENT HE WENT FROM BEING THIS GUNSLINGING WHISKEY DRINKING BADASS MOTHERFUCKING ROCKSTAR, TO BEING THIS GUNSLINGING WHISKEY DRINKING BADASS MOTHERFUCKING ROCKSTAR WITH A HEART.
I WALKED AWAY AND THOUGHT IF I NEVER SEE HIM AGAIN THAT'S ENOUGH FOR THE REST OF MY LIFE, BUT THEN WE BECAME FRIENDS AND IT'S ONE THING WHEN YOU HAVE A HERO, BUT IT'S ANOTHER WHEN YOUR HERO BECOMES YOUR FRIEND.
OVER THE YEARS I HAVE GREAT STORIES OF GOING OVER TO HIS APARTMENT.
GOING TO HIS APARTMENT AND WALKING THROUGH AISLES OF PORNOS AND MAGAZINES
LIKE A HOARDERS EPISODE.
FIRST TIME I WAS GOING TO THE RAINBOW AND ORDERING TWO JACK AND COKES
RAINBOW
bar & grill
AND THE WAITRESS BRINGS TWO JACK AND COKES
AND HIS FUCKING MAIL?
THAT'S PRETTY HUGE!

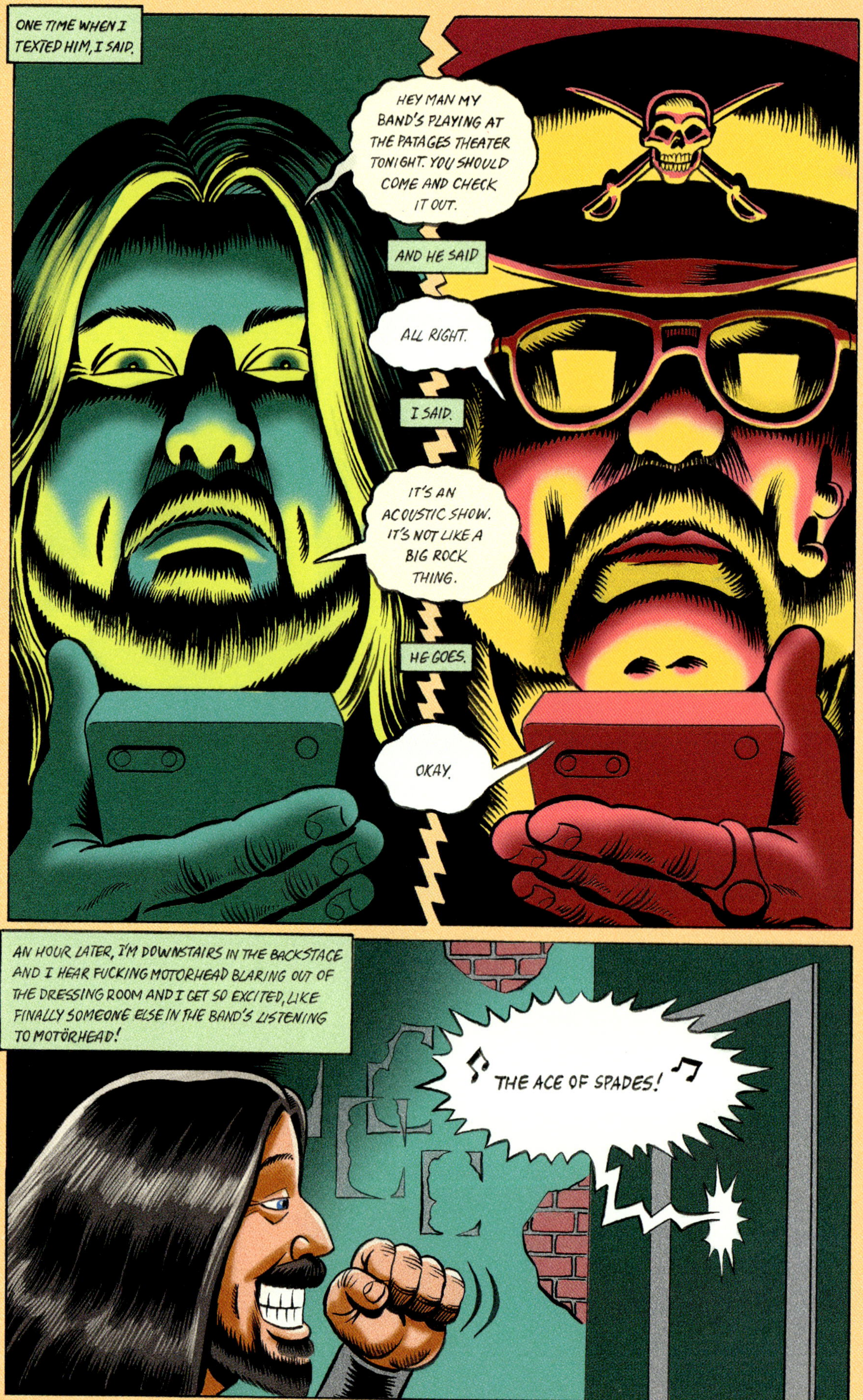
ONE TIME WHEN I TEXTED HIM, I SAID.
HEY MAN MY BAND'S PLAYING AT THE PATAGES THEATER TONIGHT. YOU SHOULD COME AND CHECK IT OUT.
AND HE SAID
ALL RIGHT.
I SAID.
IT'S AN ACOUSTIC SHOW. IT'S NOT LIKE A BIG ROCK THING.
HE GOES.
OKAY.
AN HOUR LATER, I'M DOWNSTAIRS IN THE BACKSTAGE AND I HEAR FUCKING MOTORHEAD BLARING OUT OF THE DRESSING ROOM AND I GET SO EXCITED, LIKE FINALLY SOMEONE ELSE IN THE BAND'S LISTENING TO MOTÖRHEAD!
THE ACE OF SPADES!

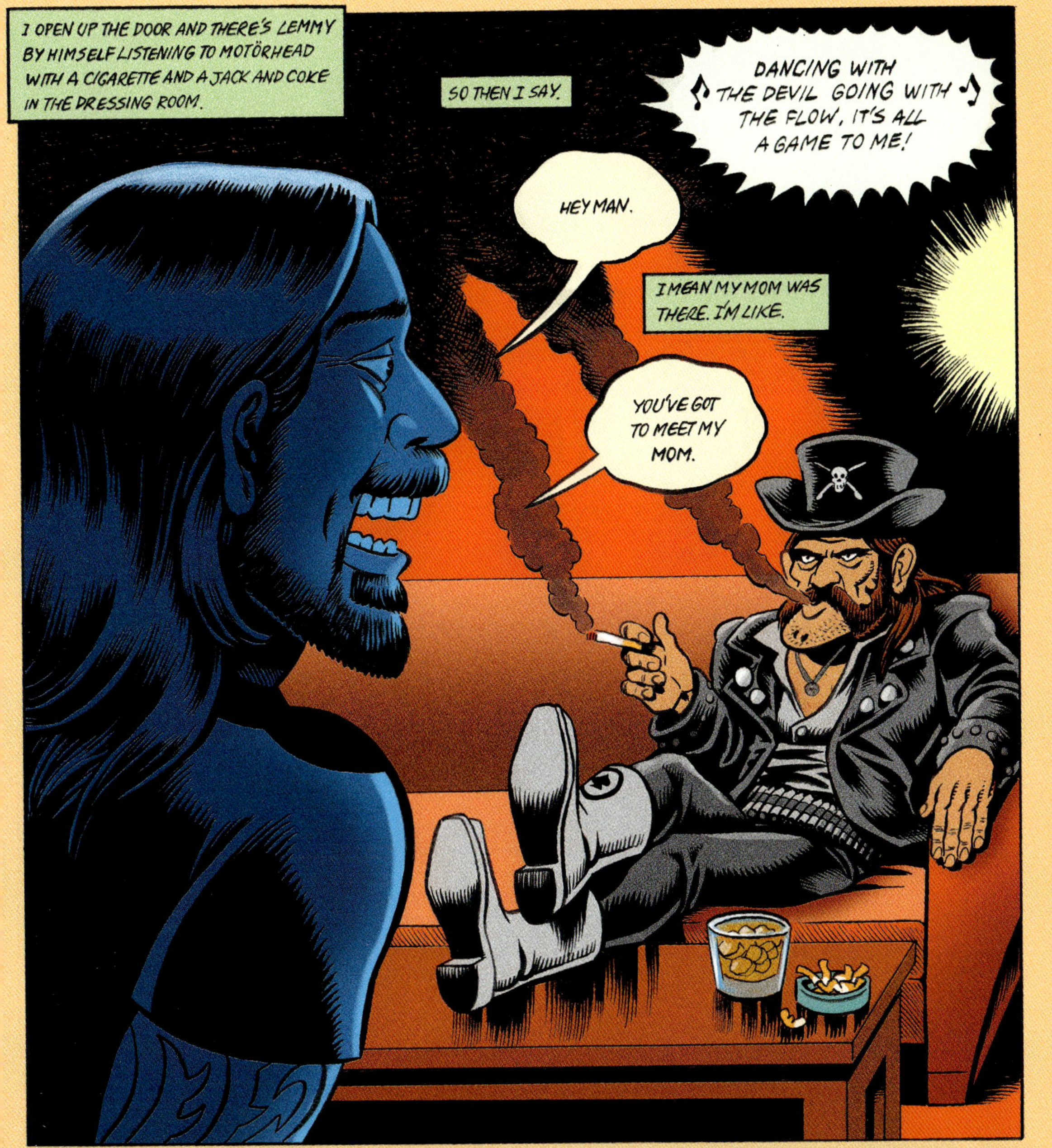
I OPEN UP THE DOOR AND THERE'S LEMMY BY HIMSELF LISTENING TO MOTÖRHEAD WITH A CIGARETTE AND A JACK AND COKE IN THE DRESSING ROOM.
SO THEN I SAY.
DANCING WITH THE DEVIL GOING WITH THE FLOW, IT'S ALL A GAME TO ME!
HEY MAN.
I MEAN MY MOM WAS THERE. I'M LIKE.
YOU'VE GOT TO MEET MY MOM.

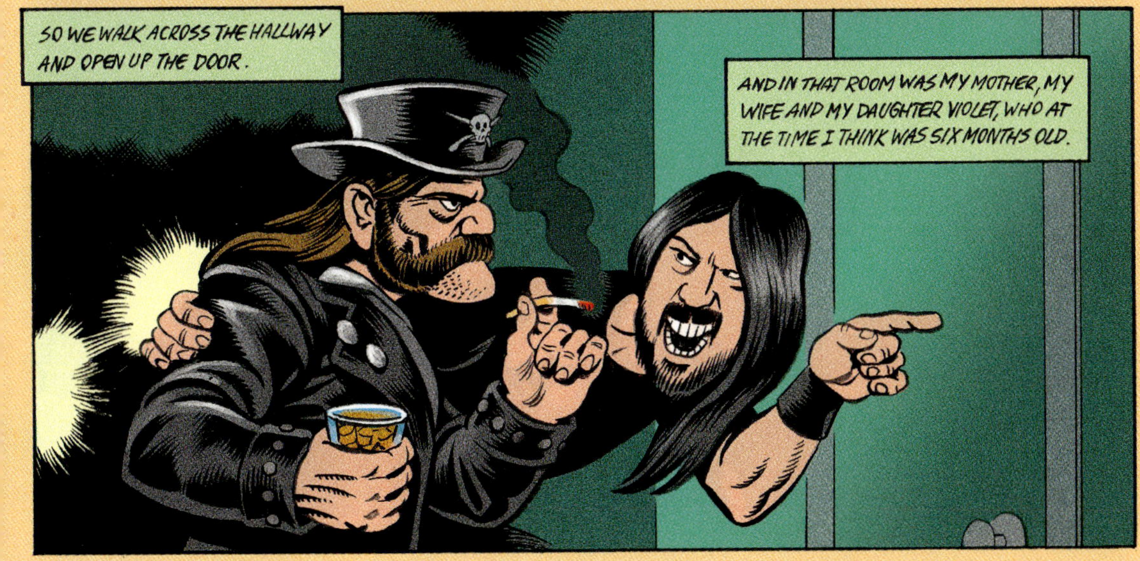
SO WE WALK ACROSS THE HALLWAY AND OPEN UP THE DOOR.
AND IN THAT ROOM WAS MY MOTHER, MY WIFE AND MY DAUGHTER VIOLET, WHO AT THE TIME I THINK WAS SIX MONTHS OLD.

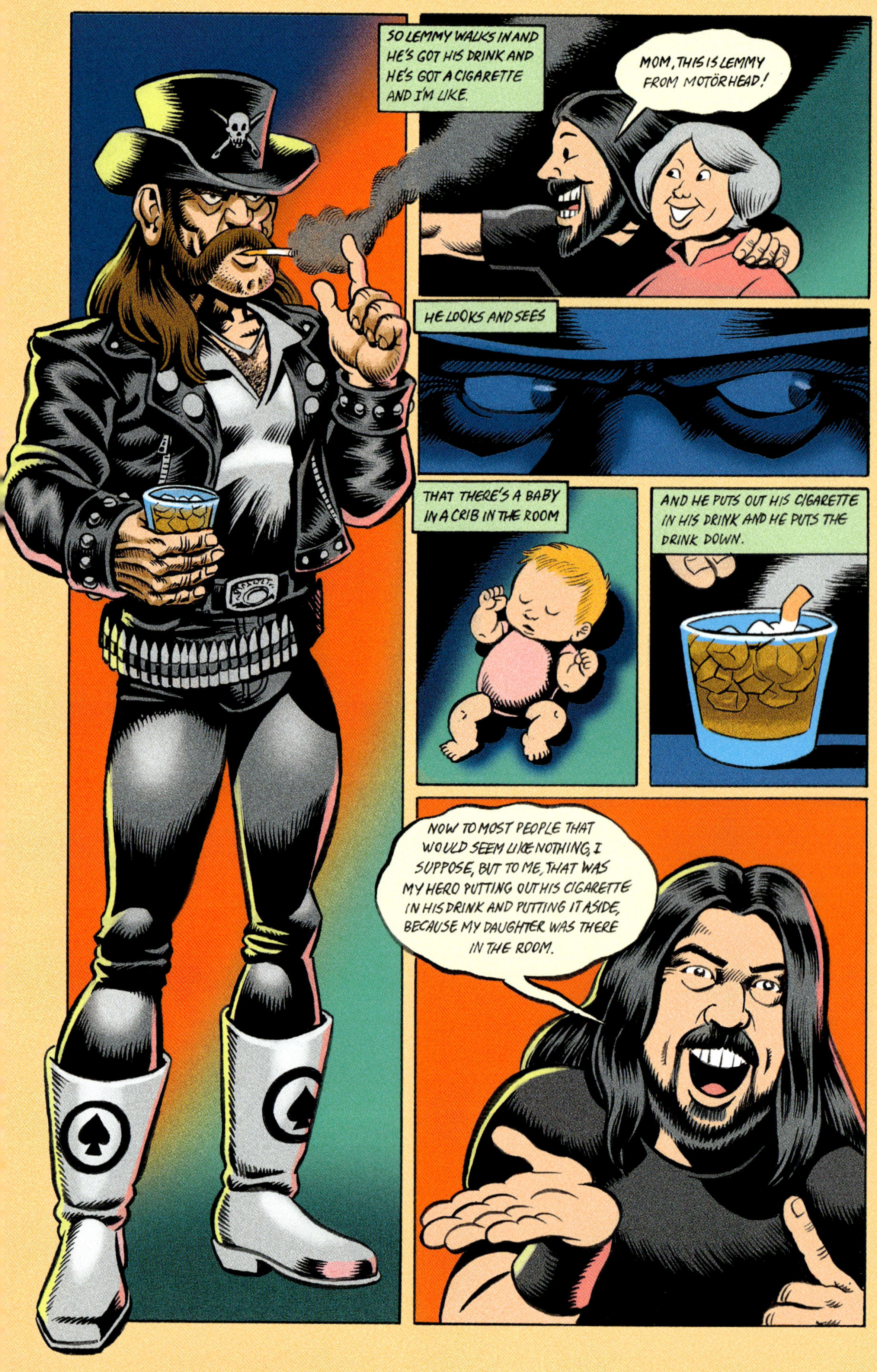
SO LEMMY WALKS IN AND HE'S GOT HIS DRINK AND HE'S GOT A CIGARETTE AND I'M LIKE.
MOM, THIS IS LEMMY FROM MOTÖRHEAD!
HE LOOKS AND SEES
THAT THERE'S A BABY IN A CRIB IN THE ROOM
AND HE PUTS OUT HIS CIGARETTE IN HIS DRINK AND HE PUTS THE DRINK DOWN.
NOW TO MOST PEOPLE THAT WOULD SEEM LIKE NOTHING, I SUPPOSE, BUT TO ME, THAT WAS MY HERO PUTTING OUT HIS CIGARETTE IN HIS DRINK AND PUTTING IT ASIDE, BECAUSE MY DAUGHTER WAS THERE IN THE ROOM.

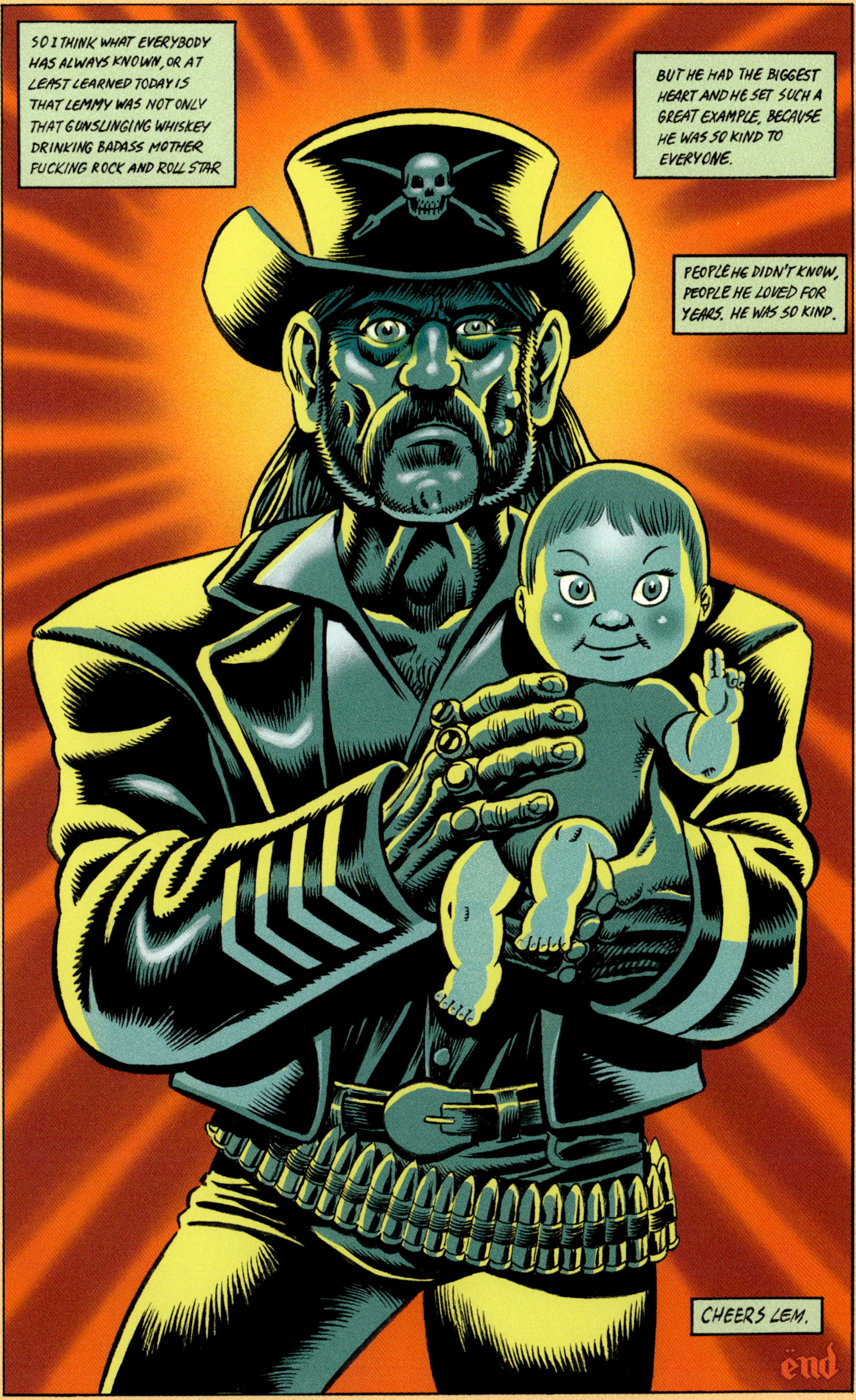
SO I THINK WHAT EVERYBODY HAS ALWAYS KNOWN, OR AT LEAST LEARNED TODAY IS THAT LEMMY WAS NOT ONLY THAT GUNSLINGING WHISKEY DRINKING BADASS MOTHER FUCKING ROCK AND ROLL STAR
BUT HE HAD THE BIGGEST HEART AND HE SET SUCH A GREAT EXAMPLE, BECAUSE HE WAS SO KIND TO EVERYONE.
PEOPLE HE DIDN'T KNOW, PEOPLE HE LOVED FOR YEARS. HE WAS SO KIND.
CHEERS LEM.
ënd

"Lemmy gave me the greatest gifts of all-time, which was his sound and his friendship."

FIRST MET LEMMY IN **2001**

triple h

WRESTLER + CHIEF CREATIVE OFFICER WWE

STORY ILLUSTRATED BY ERIK RODRIGUEZ

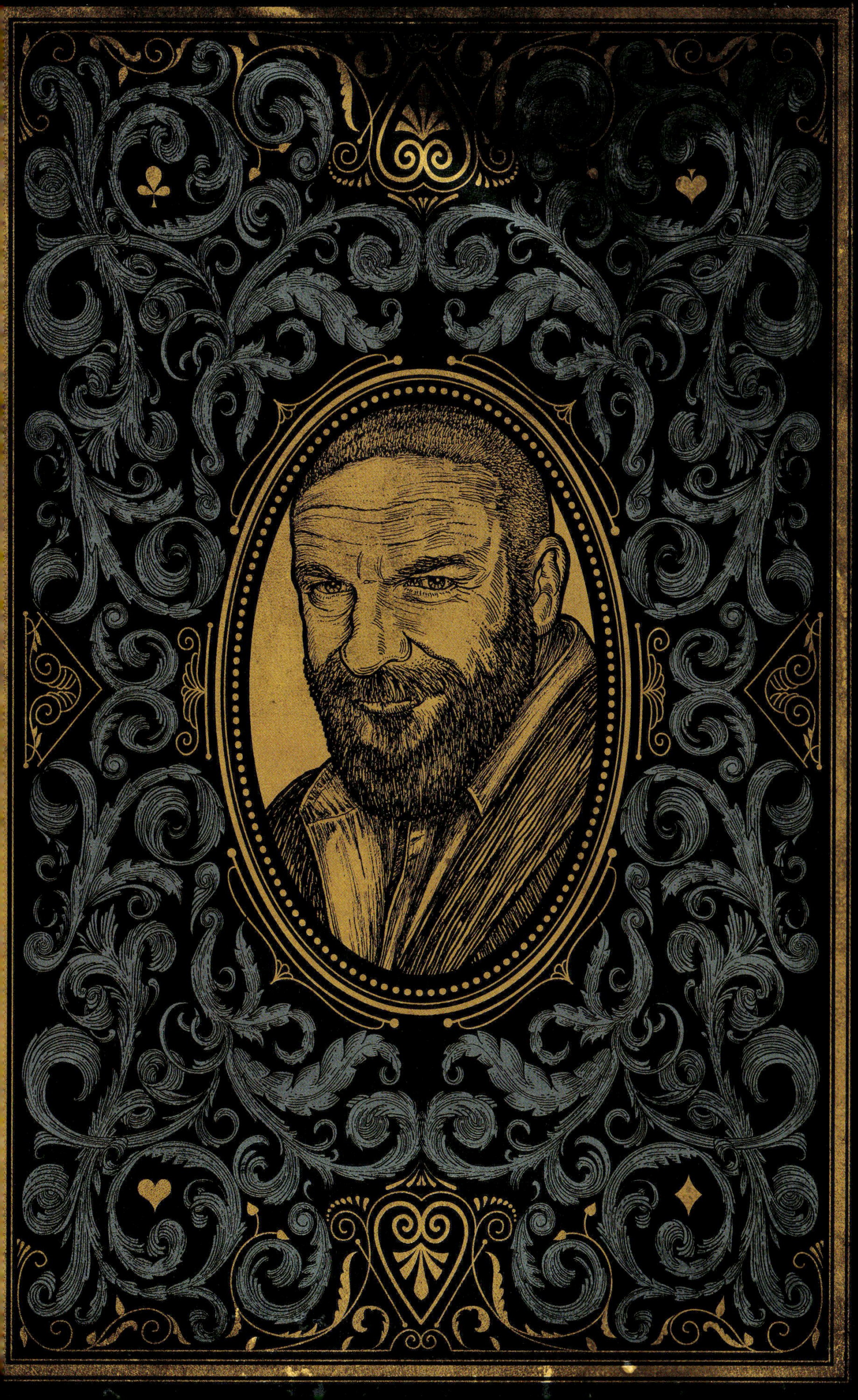

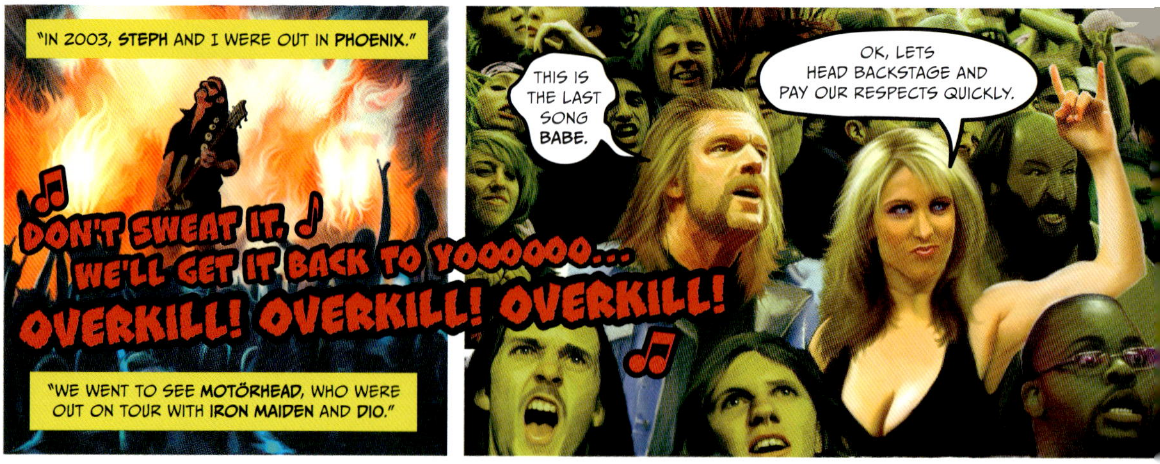
"IN 2003, STEPH AND I WERE OUT IN PHOENIX."
DON'T SWEAT IT, WE'LL GET IT BACK TO YOOOOOO... OVERKILL! OVERKILL! OVERKILL!
"WE WENT TO SEE MOTÖRHEAD, WHO WERE OUT ON TOUR WITH IRON MAIDEN AND DIO."
THIS IS THE LAST SONG BABE.
OK, LETS HEAD BACKSTAGE AND PAY OUR RESPECTS QUICKLY.

THE GAME ALWAYS KNOCKS TWICE

STORY BY PAUL "TRIPLE H" LEVESQUE ♠ ART BY ERIK RODRIGUEZ

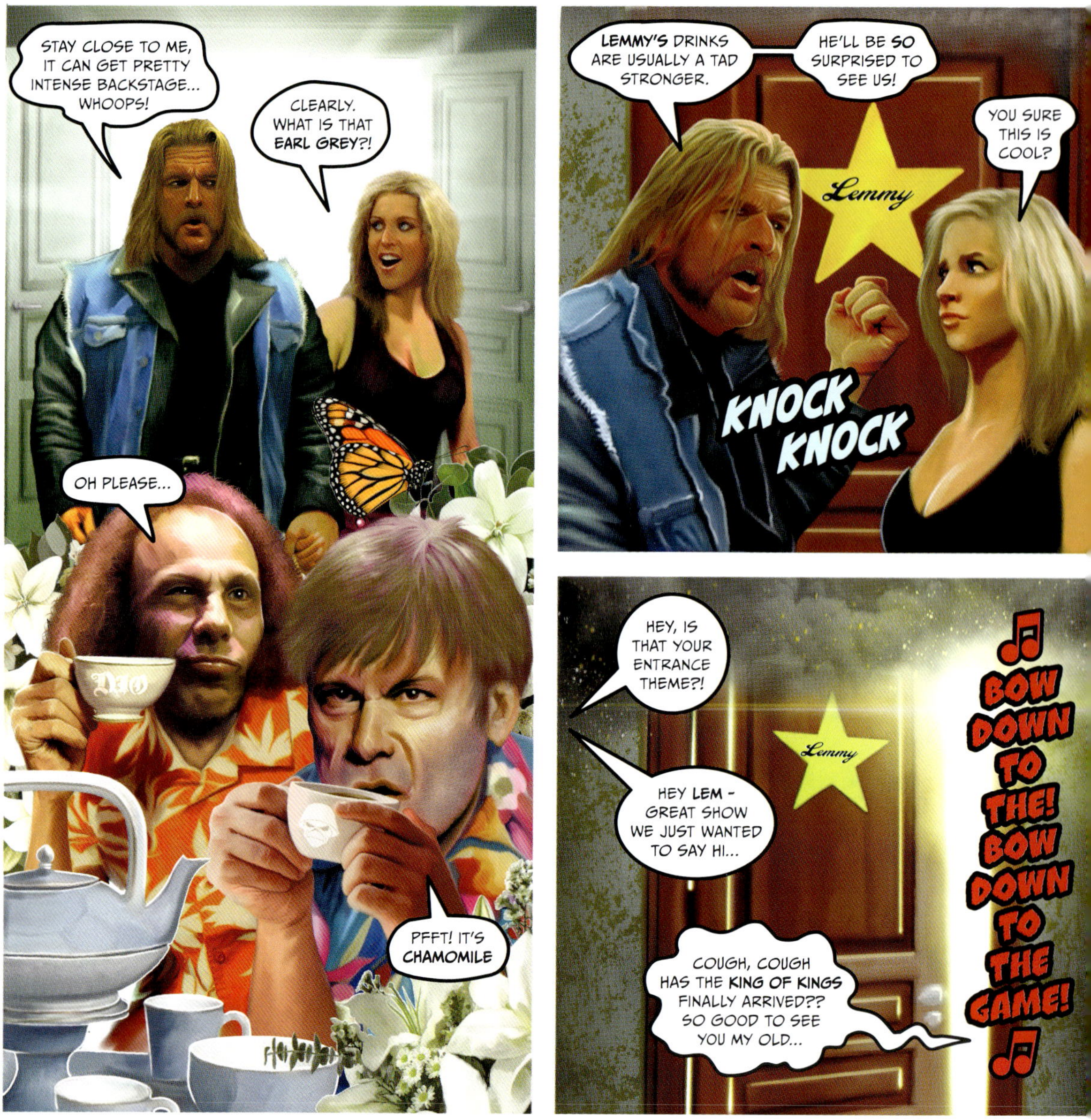
STAY CLOSE TO ME, IT CAN GET PRETTY INTENSE BACKSTAGE... WHOOPS!
CLEARLY. WHAT IS THAT EARL GREY?!
OH PLEASE...
PFFT! IT'S CHAMOMILE
LEMMY'S DRINKS ARE USUALLY A TAD STRONGER.
HE'LL BE SO SURPRISED TO SEE US!
YOU SURE THIS IS COOL?
Lemmy
KNOCK KNOCK
HEY, IS THAT YOUR ENTRANCE THEME?!
Lemmy
HEY LEM - GREAT SHOW WE JUST WANTED TO SAY HI...
COUGH, COUGH HAS THE KING OF KINGS FINALLY ARRIVED?? SO GOOD TO SEE YOU MY OLD...
BOW DOWN TO THE! BOW DOWN TO THE GAME!

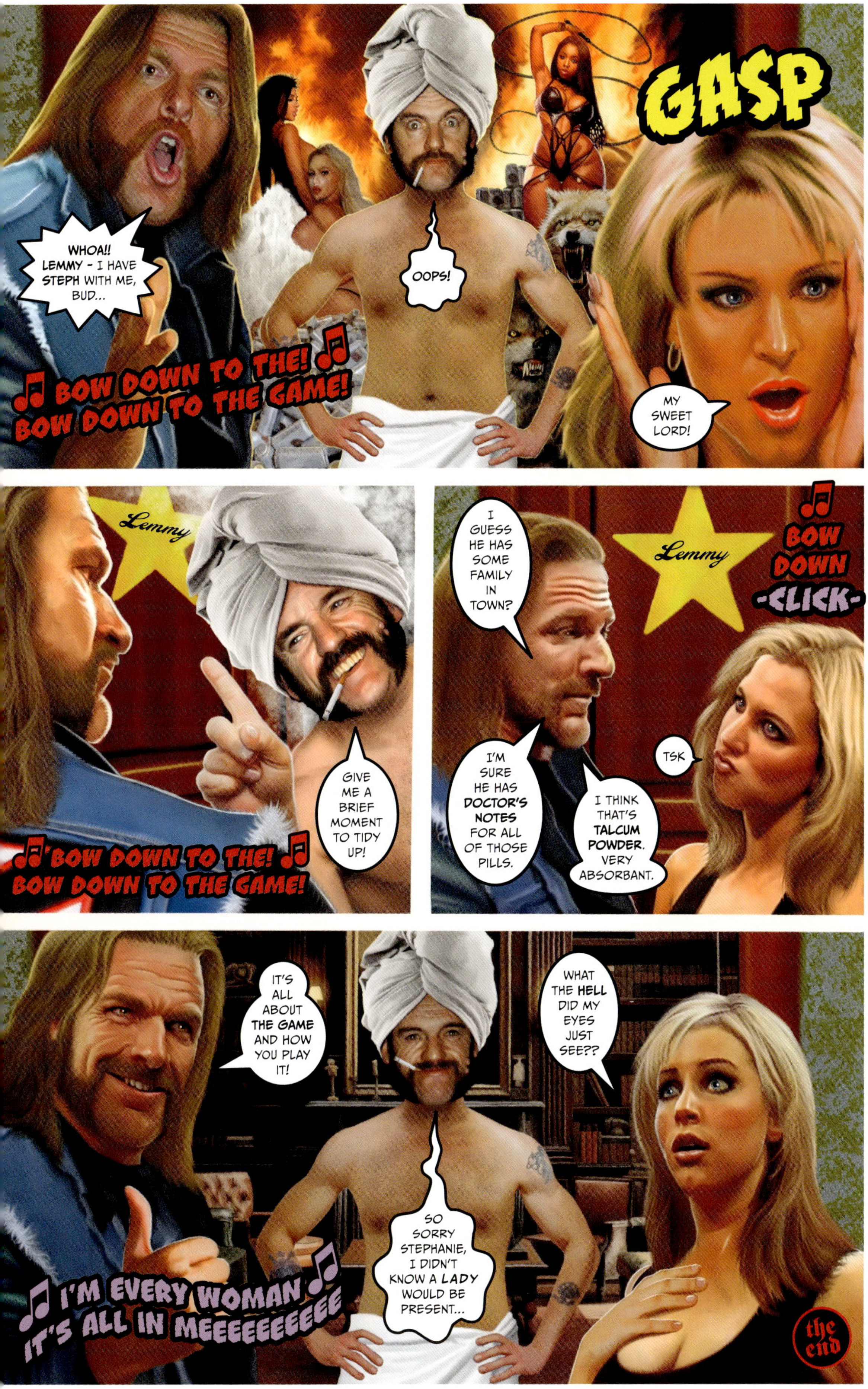
GASP
WHOA!! LEMMY - I HAVE STEPH WITH ME, BUD...
OOPS!
♫ BOW DOWN TO THE! ♫ BOW DOWN TO THE GAME!
MY SWEET LORD!
Lemmy
GIVE ME A BRIEF MOMENT TO TIDY UP!
♫ BOW DOWN TO THE! ♫ BOW DOWN TO THE GAME!
Lemmy
I GUESS HE HAS SOME FAMILY IN TOWN?
♫ BOW DOWN -CLICK-
I'M SURE HE HAS DOCTOR'S NOTES FOR ALL OF THOSE PILLS.
TSK
I THINK THAT'S TALCUM POWDER. VERY ABSORBANT.
IT'S ALL ABOUT THE GAME AND HOW YOU PLAY IT!
WHAT THE HELL DID MY EYES JUST SEE??
SO SORRY STEPHANIE, I DIDN'T KNOW A LADY WOULD BE PRESENT...
♫ I'M EVERY WOMAN ♫ IT'S ALL IN MEEEEEEEEEE
the end

"No excuses, no regrets and no apologies. Lemmy made himself at home, wherever he was."

FIRST MET
LEMMY
IN
2002

matt pinfield

LEGEND + HOST
120 MINUTES
THE POWER HOUR
FARMCLUB

STORY ILLUSTRATED BY SEAN PRYOR

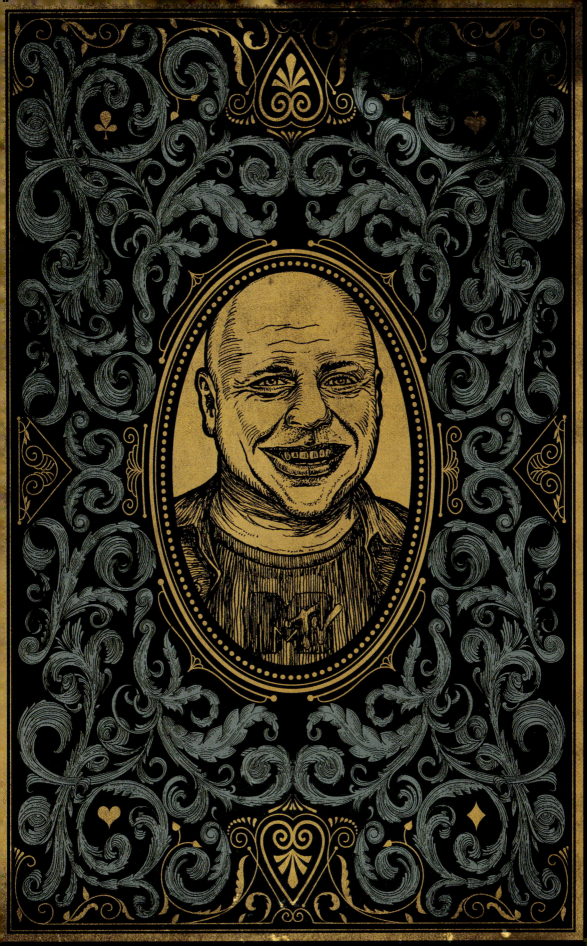

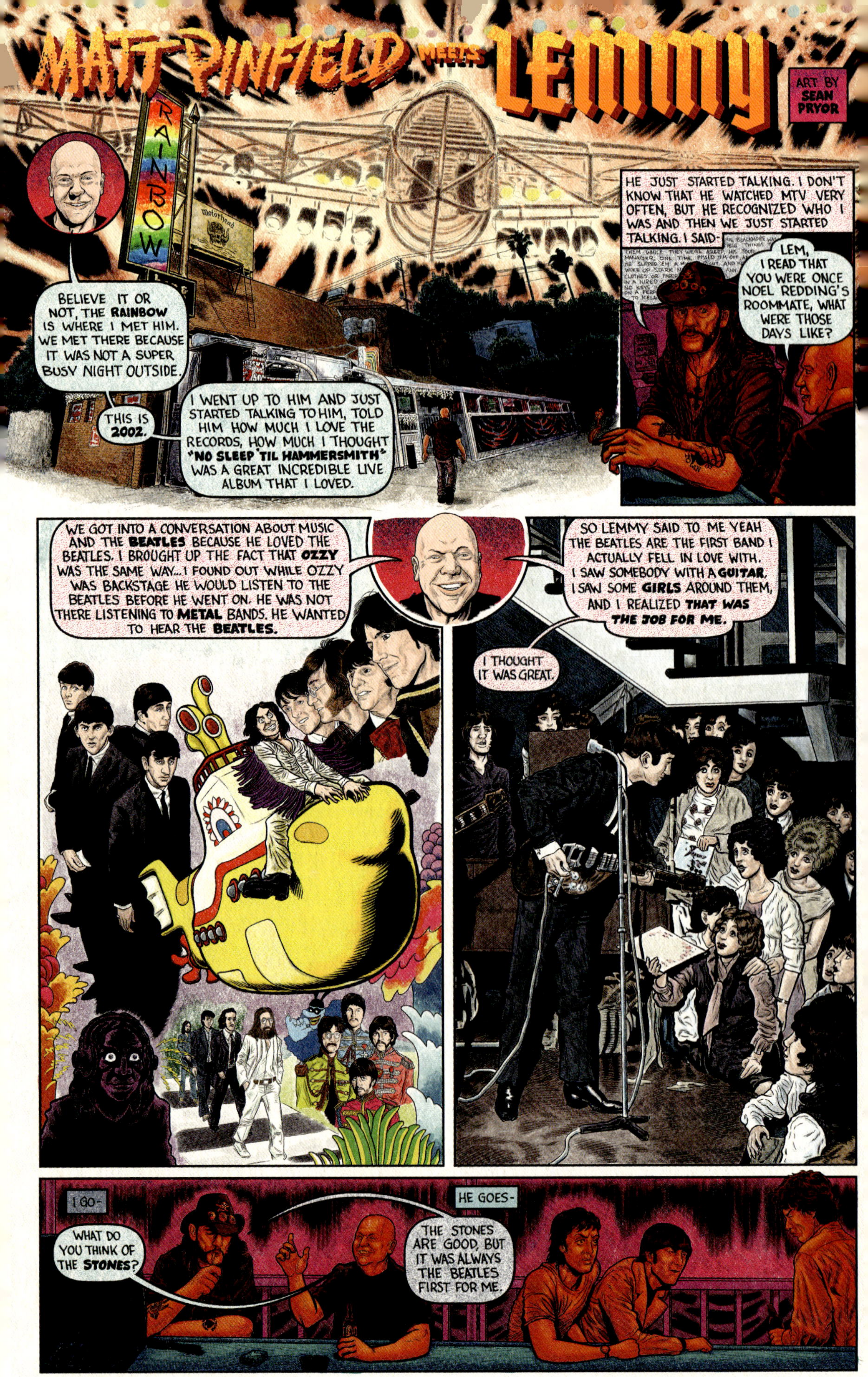
MATT PINFIELD MEETS LEMMY
ART BY SEAN PRYOR
RAINBOW
BELIEVE IT OR NOT, THE RAINBOW IS WHERE I MET HIM. WE MET THERE BECAUSE IT WAS NOT A SUPER BUSY NIGHT OUTSIDE.
THIS IS 2002.
I WENT UP TO HIM AND JUST STARTED TALKING TO HIM, TOLD HIM HOW MUCH I LOVE THE RECORDS, HOW MUCH I THOUGHT "NO SLEEP 'TIL HAMMERSMITH" WAS A GREAT INCREDIBLE LIVE ALBUM THAT I LOVED.
HE JUST STARTED TALKING. I DON'T KNOW THAT HE WATCHED MTV VERY OFTEN, BUT HE RECOGNIZED WHO I WAS AND THEN WE JUST STARTED TALKING. I SAID-
LEM, I READ THAT YOU WERE ONCE NOEL REDDING'S ROOMMATE, WHAT WERE THOSE DAYS LIKE?
WE GOT INTO A CONVERSATION ABOUT MUSIC AND THE BEATLES BECAUSE HE LOVED THE BEATLES. I BROUGHT UP THE FACT THAT OZZY WAS THE SAME WAY... I FOUND OUT WHILE OZZY WAS BACKSTAGE HE WOULD LISTEN TO THE BEATLES BEFORE HE WENT ON. HE WAS NOT THERE LISTENING TO METAL BANDS. HE WANTED TO HEAR THE BEATLES.
SO LEMMY SAID TO ME YEAH THE BEATLES ARE THE FIRST BAND I ACTUALLY FELL IN LOVE WITH. I SAW SOMEBODY WITH A GUITAR, I SAW SOME GIRLS AROUND THEM, AND I REALIZED THAT WAS THE JOB FOR ME.
I THOUGHT IT WAS GREAT.
I GO-
WHAT DO YOU THINK OF THE STONES?
HE GOES-
THE STONES ARE GOOD, BUT IT WAS ALWAYS THE BEATLES FIRST FOR ME.

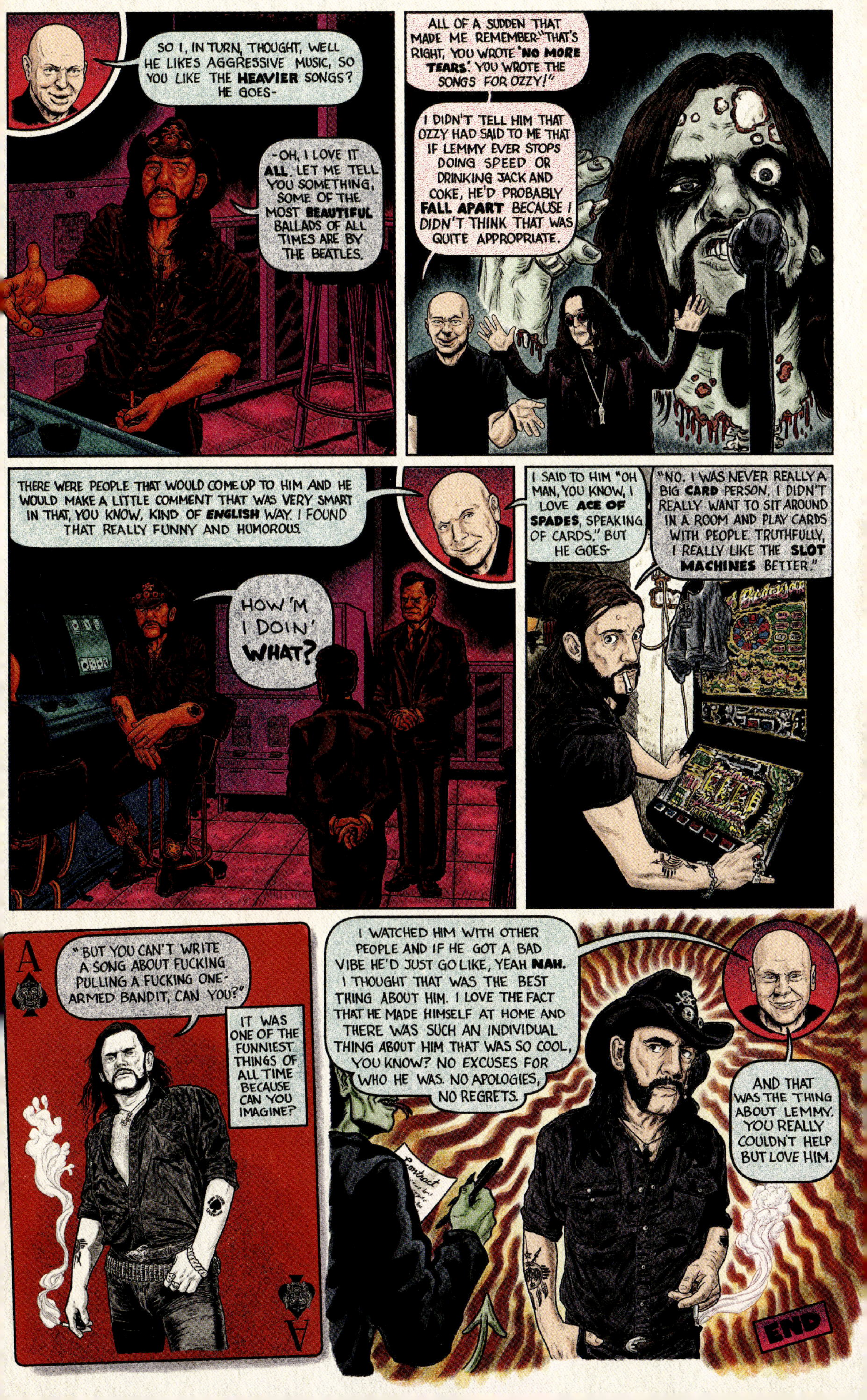

SO I, IN TURN, THOUGHT, WELL HE LIKES AGGRESSIVE MUSIC, SO YOU LIKE THE **HEAVIER** SONGS? HE GOES-
-OH, I LOVE IT **ALL**. LET ME TELL YOU SOMETHING, SOME OF THE MOST **BEAUTIFUL** BALLADS OF ALL TIMES ARE BY THE BEATLES.
ALL OF A SUDDEN THAT MADE ME REMEMBER- "THAT'S RIGHT, YOU WROTE '**NO MORE TEARS**'. YOU WROTE THE SONGS FOR OZZY!"
I DIDN'T TELL HIM THAT OZZY HAD SAID TO ME THAT IF LEMMY EVER STOPS DOING SPEED OR DRINKING JACK AND COKE, HE'D PROBABLY **FALL APART** BECAUSE I DIDN'T THINK THAT WAS QUITE APPROPRIATE.
THERE WERE PEOPLE THAT WOULD COME UP TO HIM AND HE WOULD MAKE A LITTLE COMMENT THAT WAS VERY SMART IN THAT, YOU KNOW, KIND OF **ENGLISH** WAY. I FOUND THAT REALLY FUNNY AND HUMOROUS.
HOW'M I DOIN' **WHAT?**
I SAID TO HIM "OH MAN, YOU KNOW, I LOVE **ACE OF SPADES**, SPEAKING OF CARDS." BUT HE GOES-
"NO. I WAS NEVER REALLY A BIG **CARD** PERSON. I DIDN'T REALLY WANT TO SIT AROUND IN A ROOM AND PLAY CARDS WITH PEOPLE. TRUTHFULLY, I REALLY LIKE THE **SLOT MACHINES** BETTER."
"BUT YOU CAN'T WRITE A SONG ABOUT FUCKING PULLING A FUCKING ONE-ARMED BANDIT, CAN YOU?"
IT WAS ONE OF THE FUNNIEST THINGS OF ALL TIME BECAUSE CAN YOU IMAGINE?
I WATCHED HIM WITH OTHER PEOPLE AND IF HE GOT A BAD VIBE HE'D JUST GO LIKE, YEAH **NAH**. I THOUGHT THAT WAS THE BEST THING ABOUT HIM. I LOVE THE FACT THAT HE MADE HIMSELF AT HOME AND THERE WAS SUCH AN INDIVIDUAL THING ABOUT HIM THAT WAS SO COOL, YOU KNOW? NO EXCUSES FOR WHO HE WAS. NO APOLOGIES, NO REGRETS.
AND THAT WAS THE THING ABOUT LEMMY. YOU REALLY COULDN'T HELP BUT LOVE HIM.
END

"*Every time I met Lemmy, I would nervously pee in my pants a little bit.*"

FIRST MET LEMMY IN 2003

josh bernstein

PRODUCER
THE GOLDEN GODS AWARDS
PRESIDENT
Z2

STORY ILLUSTRATED BY JOSH BERNSTEIN

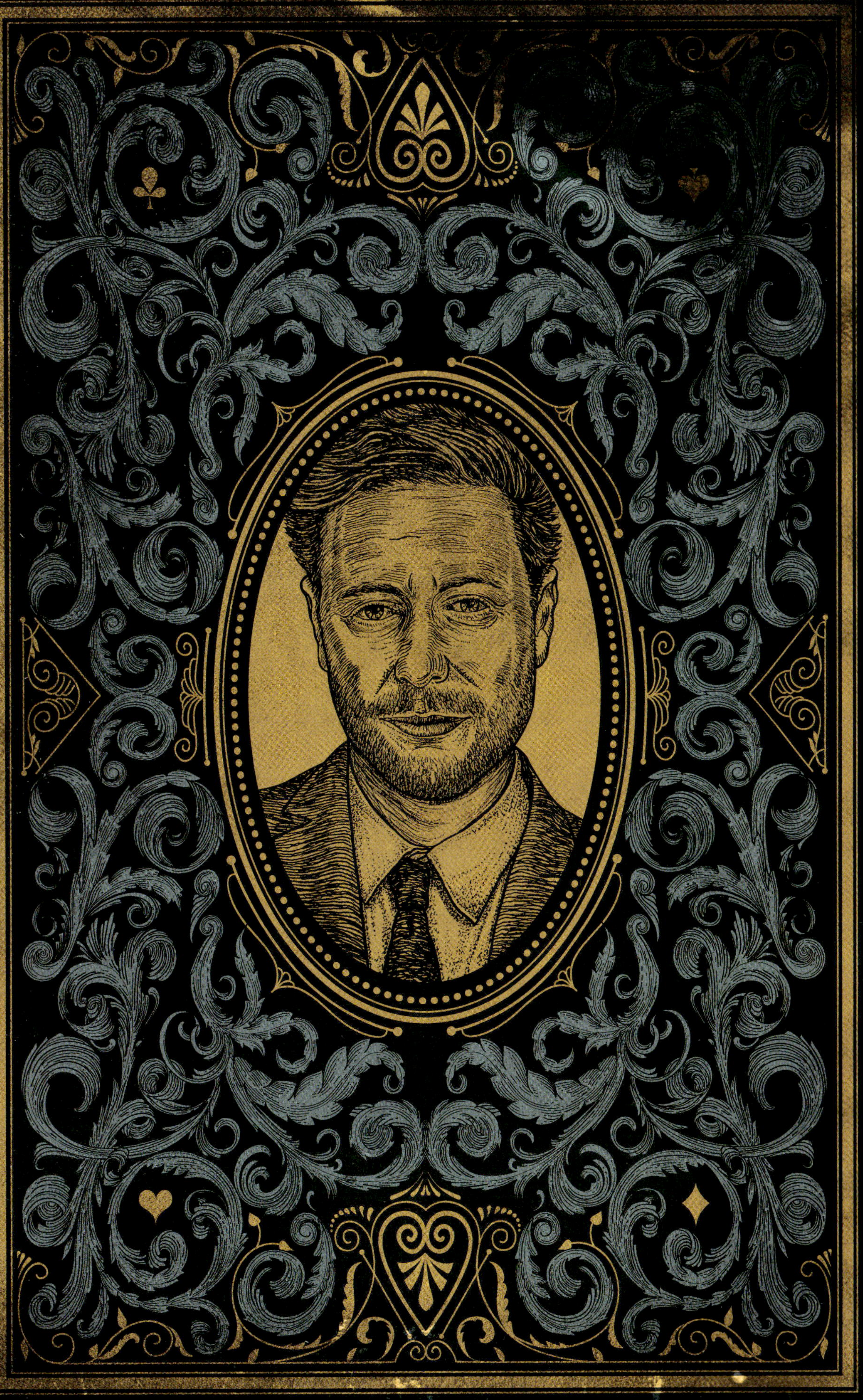

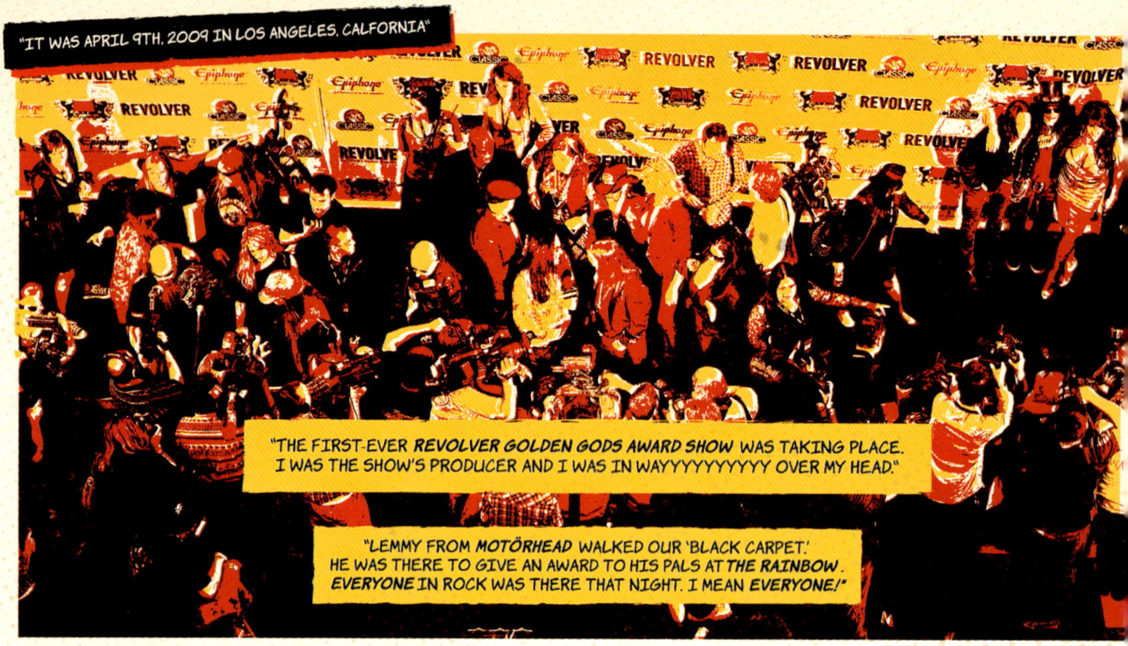
"IT WAS APRIL 9TH, 2009 IN LOS ANGELES, CALFORNIA"
"THE FIRST-EVER REVOLVER GOLDEN GODS AWARD SHOW WAS TAKING PLACE. I WAS THE SHOW'S PRODUCER AND I WAS IN WAYYYYYYYYYY OVER MY HEAD."
"LEMMY FROM MOTÖRHEAD WALKED OUR 'BLACK CARPET.' HE WAS THERE TO GIVE AN AWARD TO HIS PALS AT THE RAINBOW. EVERYONE IN ROCK WAS THERE THAT NIGHT. I MEAN EVERYONE!"

LEMMY'S BAR TAB

AS REMEMBERED BY JOSH BERNSTEIN

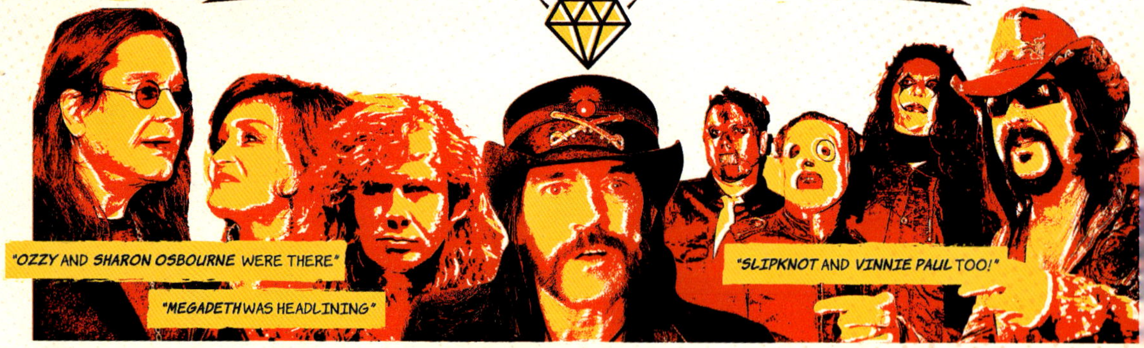
"OZZY AND SHARON OSBOURNE WERE THERE"
"MEGADETH WAS HEADLINING"
"SLIPKNOT AND VINNIE PAUL TOO!"

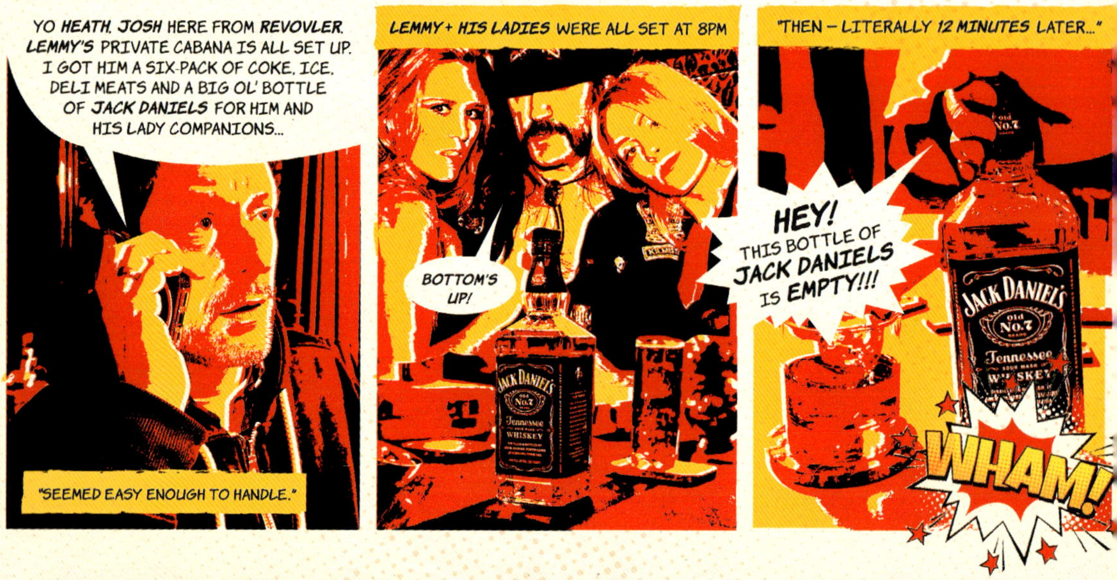
YO HEATH, JOSH HERE FROM REVOLVER. LEMMY'S PRIVATE CABANA IS ALL SET UP. I GOT HIM A SIX-PACK OF COKE, ICE, DELI MEATS AND A BIG OL' BOTTLE OF JACK DANIELS FOR HIM AND HIS LADY COMPANIONS...
"SEEMED EASY ENOUGH TO HANDLE."
LEMMY + HIS LADIES WERE ALL SET AT 8PM
BOTTOM'S UP!
"THEN – LITERALLY 12 MINUTES LATER..."
HEY! THIS BOTTLE OF JACK DANIELS IS EMPTY!!!
WHAM!

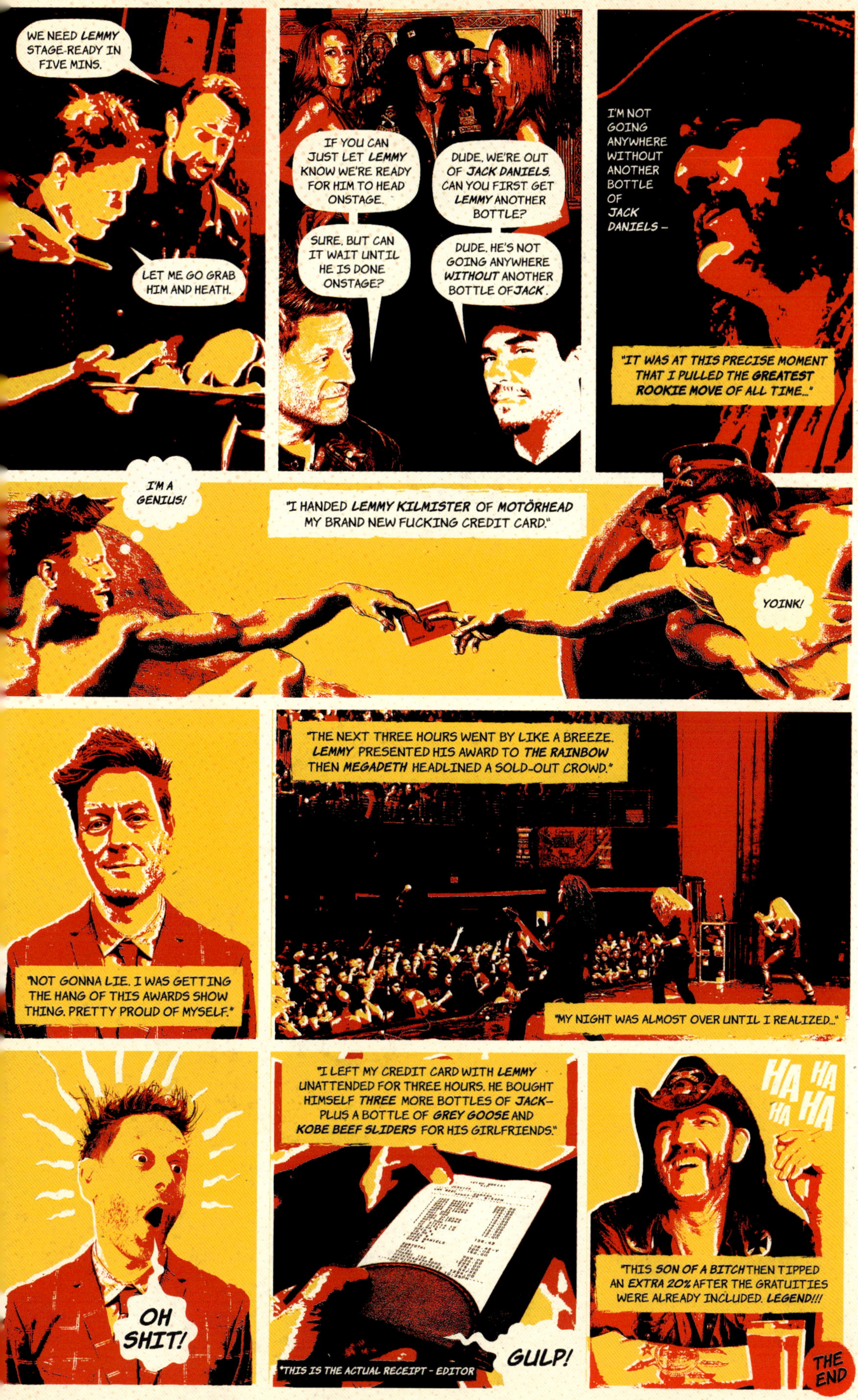
WE NEED LEMMY STAGE-READY IN FIVE MINS.
LET ME GO GRAB HIM AND HEATH.
IF YOU CAN JUST LET LEMMY KNOW WE'RE READY FOR HIM TO HEAD ONSTAGE.
SURE, BUT CAN IT WAIT UNTIL HE IS DONE ONSTAGE?
DUDE, WE'RE OUT OF JACK DANIELS. CAN YOU FIRST GET LEMMY ANOTHER BOTTLE?
DUDE, HE'S NOT GOING ANYWHERE WITHOUT ANOTHER BOTTLE OF JACK.
I'M NOT GOING ANYWHERE WITHOUT ANOTHER BOTTLE OF JACK DANIELS –
"IT WAS AT THIS PRECISE MOMENT THAT I PULLED THE GREATEST ROOKIE MOVE OF ALL TIME..."
I'M A GENIUS!
"I HANDED LEMMY KILMISTER OF MOTÖRHEAD MY BRAND NEW FUCKING CREDIT CARD."
YOINK!
"NOT GONNA LIE, I WAS GETTING THE HANG OF THIS AWARDS SHOW THING. PRETTY PROUD OF MYSELF."
"THE NEXT THREE HOURS WENT BY LIKE A BREEZE. LEMMY PRESENTED HIS AWARD TO THE RAINBOW THEN MEGADETH HEADLINED A SOLD-OUT CROWD."
"MY NIGHT WAS ALMOST OVER UNTIL I REALIZED..."
OH SHIT!
"I LEFT MY CREDIT CARD WITH LEMMY UNATTENDED FOR THREE HOURS. HE BOUGHT HIMSELF THREE MORE BOTTLES OF JACK–PLUS A BOTTLE OF GREY GOOSE AND KOBE BEEF SLIDERS FOR HIS GIRLFRIENDS."
*THIS IS THE ACTUAL RECEIPT - EDITOR
GULP!
HA HA HA HA
"THIS SON OF A BITCH THEN TIPPED AN EXTRA 20% AFTER THE GRATUITIES WERE ALREADY INCLUDED. LEGEND!!!
THE END

"Lemmy just wanted to do what he wanted to do. It wasn't about the money to him, it was about the music."

FIRST MET LEMMY IN 2004

steve luna

ROADIE
BASS TECH
ASSISTANT
MOTÖRHEAD

STORY ILLUSTRATED BY FRANK POWERS

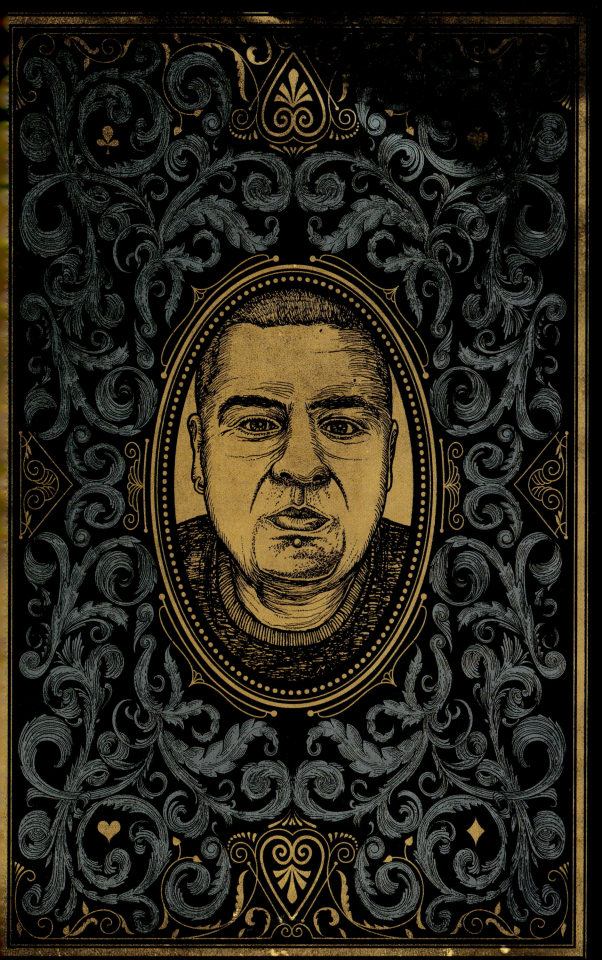

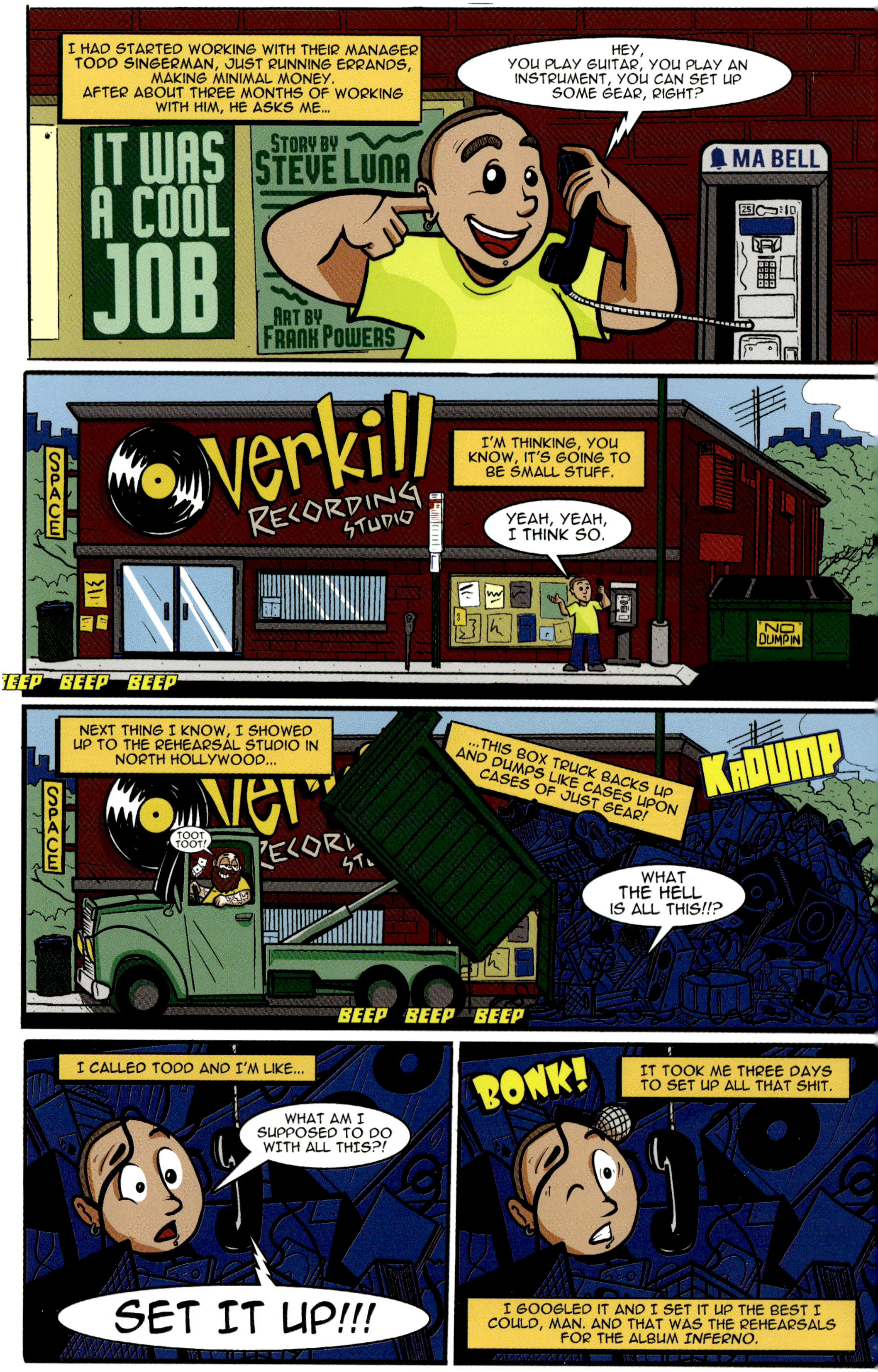
I HAD STARTED WORKING WITH THEIR MANAGER TODD SINGERMAN, JUST RUNNING ERRANDS, MAKING MINIMAL MONEY. AFTER ABOUT THREE MONTHS OF WORKING WITH HIM, HE ASKS ME...
IT WAS A COOL JOB
STORY BY STEVE LUNA
ART BY FRANK POWERS
HEY, YOU PLAY GUITAR, YOU PLAY AN INSTRUMENT, YOU CAN SET UP SOME GEAR, RIGHT?
MA BELL
SPACE
OVERKILL RECORDING STUDIO
I'M THINKING, YOU KNOW, IT'S GOING TO BE SMALL STUFF.
YEAH, YEAH, I THINK SO.
NO DUMPIN
BEEP BEEP BEEP
NEXT THING I KNOW, I SHOWED UP TO THE REHEARSAL STUDIO IN NORTH HOLLYWOOD...
...THIS BOX TRUCK BACKS UP AND DUMPS LIKE CASES UPON CASES OF JUST GEAR!
KADUMP
TOOT TOOT!
WHAT THE HELL IS ALL THIS!!?
BEEP BEEP BEEP
I CALLED TODD AND I'M LIKE...
WHAT AM I SUPPOSED TO DO WITH ALL THIS?!
SET IT UP!!!
BONK!
IT TOOK ME THREE DAYS TO SET UP ALL THAT SHIT.
I GOOGLED IT AND I SET IT UP THE BEST I COULD, MAN. AND THAT WAS THE REHEARSALS FOR THE ALBUM INFERNO.

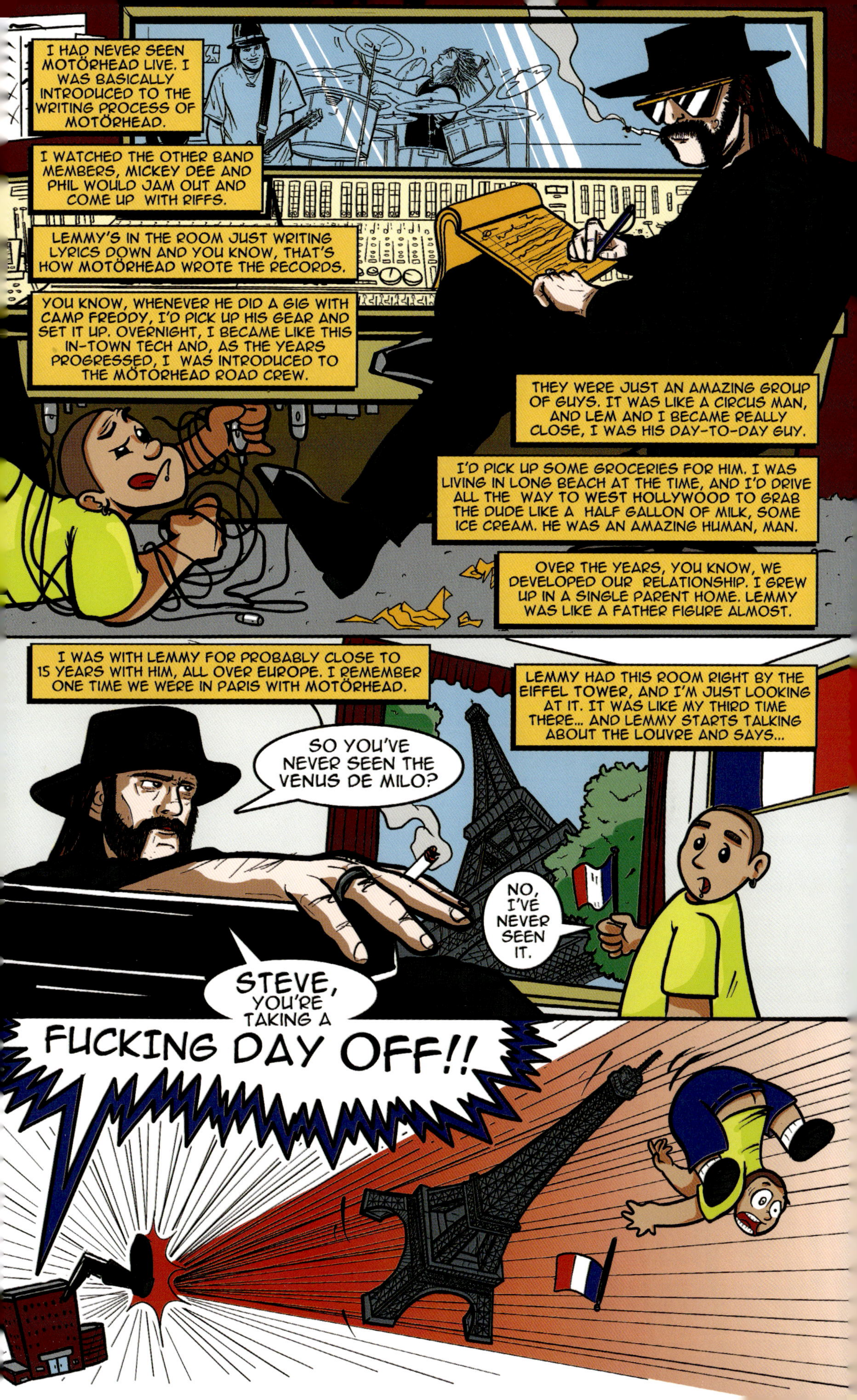
I HAD NEVER SEEN MOTÖRHEAD LIVE. I WAS BASICALLY INTRODUCED TO THE WRITING PROCESS OF MOTÖRHEAD.
I WATCHED THE OTHER BAND MEMBERS, MICKEY DEE AND PHIL WOULD JAM OUT AND COME UP WITH RIFFS.
LEMMY'S IN THE ROOM JUST WRITING LYRICS DOWN AND YOU KNOW, THAT'S HOW MOTÖRHEAD WROTE THE RECORDS.
YOU KNOW, WHENEVER HE DID A GIG WITH CAMP FREDDY, I'D PICK UP HIS GEAR AND SET IT UP. OVERNIGHT, I BECAME LIKE THIS IN-TOWN TECH AND, AS THE YEARS PROGRESSED, I WAS INTRODUCED TO THE MÖTORHEAD ROAD CREW.
THEY WERE JUST AN AMAZING GROUP OF GUYS. IT WAS LIKE A CIRCUS MAN, AND LEM AND I BECAME REALLY CLOSE, I WAS HIS DAY-TO-DAY GUY.
I'D PICK UP SOME GROCERIES FOR HIM. I WAS LIVING IN LONG BEACH AT THE TIME, AND I'D DRIVE ALL THE WAY TO WEST HOLLYWOOD TO GRAB THE DUDE LIKE A HALF GALLON OF MILK, SOME ICE CREAM. HE WAS AN AMAZING HUMAN, MAN.
OVER THE YEARS, YOU KNOW, WE DEVELOPED OUR RELATIONSHIP. I GREW UP IN A SINGLE PARENT HOME. LEMMY WAS LIKE A FATHER FIGURE ALMOST.
I WAS WITH LEMMY FOR PROBABLY CLOSE TO 15 YEARS WITH HIM, ALL OVER EUROPE. I REMEMBER ONE TIME WE WERE IN PARIS WITH MOTÖRHEAD.
LEMMY HAD THIS ROOM RIGHT BY THE EIFFEL TOWER, AND I'M JUST LOOKING AT IT. IT WAS LIKE MY THIRD TIME THERE... AND LEMMY STARTS TALKING ABOUT THE LOUVRE AND SAYS...
SO YOU'VE NEVER SEEN THE VENUS DE MILO?
NO, I'VE NEVER SEEN IT.
STEVE, YOU'RE TAKING A
FUCKING DAY OFF!!

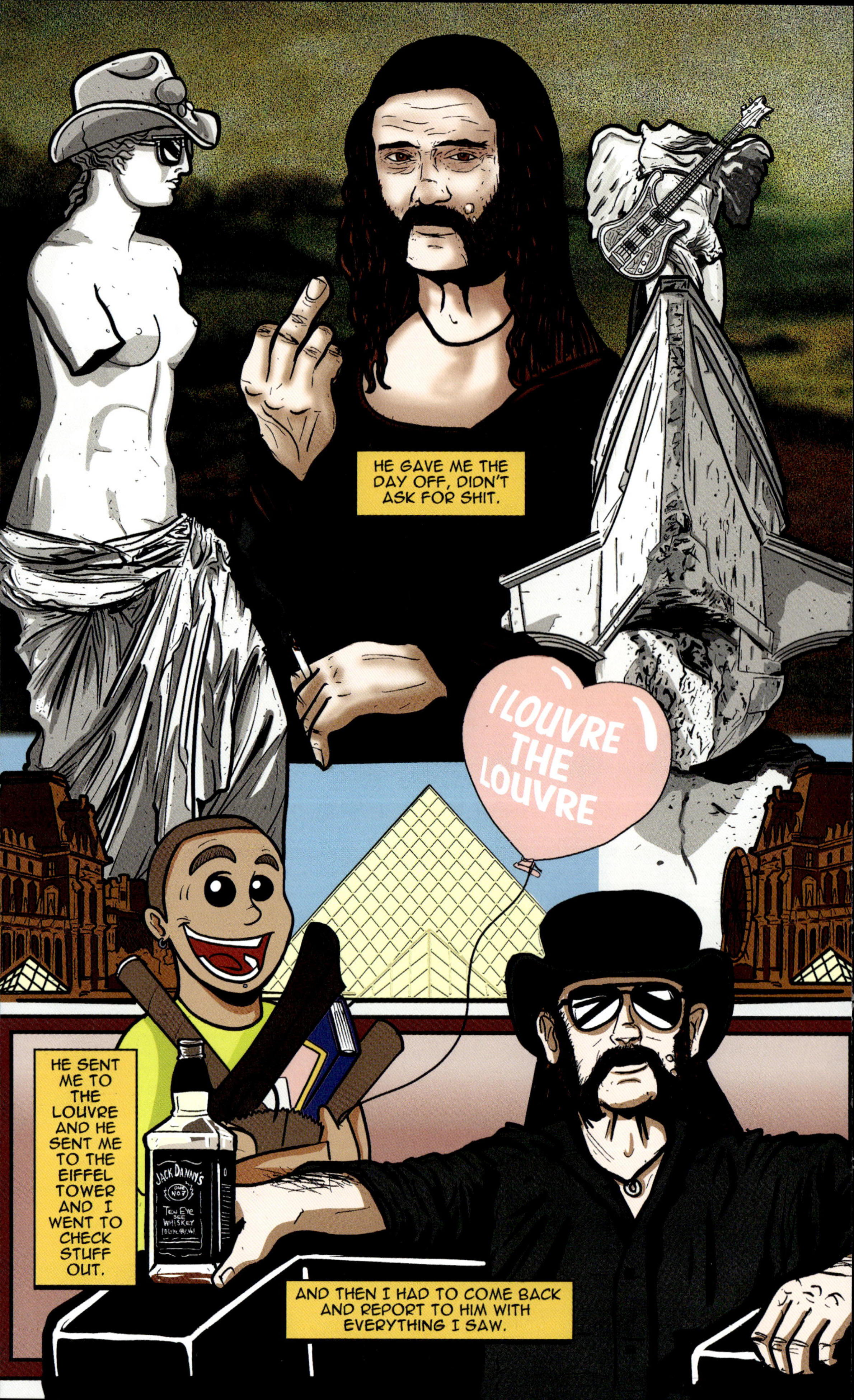
HE GAVE ME THE DAY OFF, DIDN'T ASK FOR SHIT.
I LOUVRE THE LOUVRE
HE SENT ME TO THE LOUVRE AND HE SENT ME TO THE EIFFEL TOWER AND I WENT TO CHECK STUFF OUT.
AND THEN I HAD TO COME BACK AND REPORT TO HIM WITH EVERYTHING I SAW.

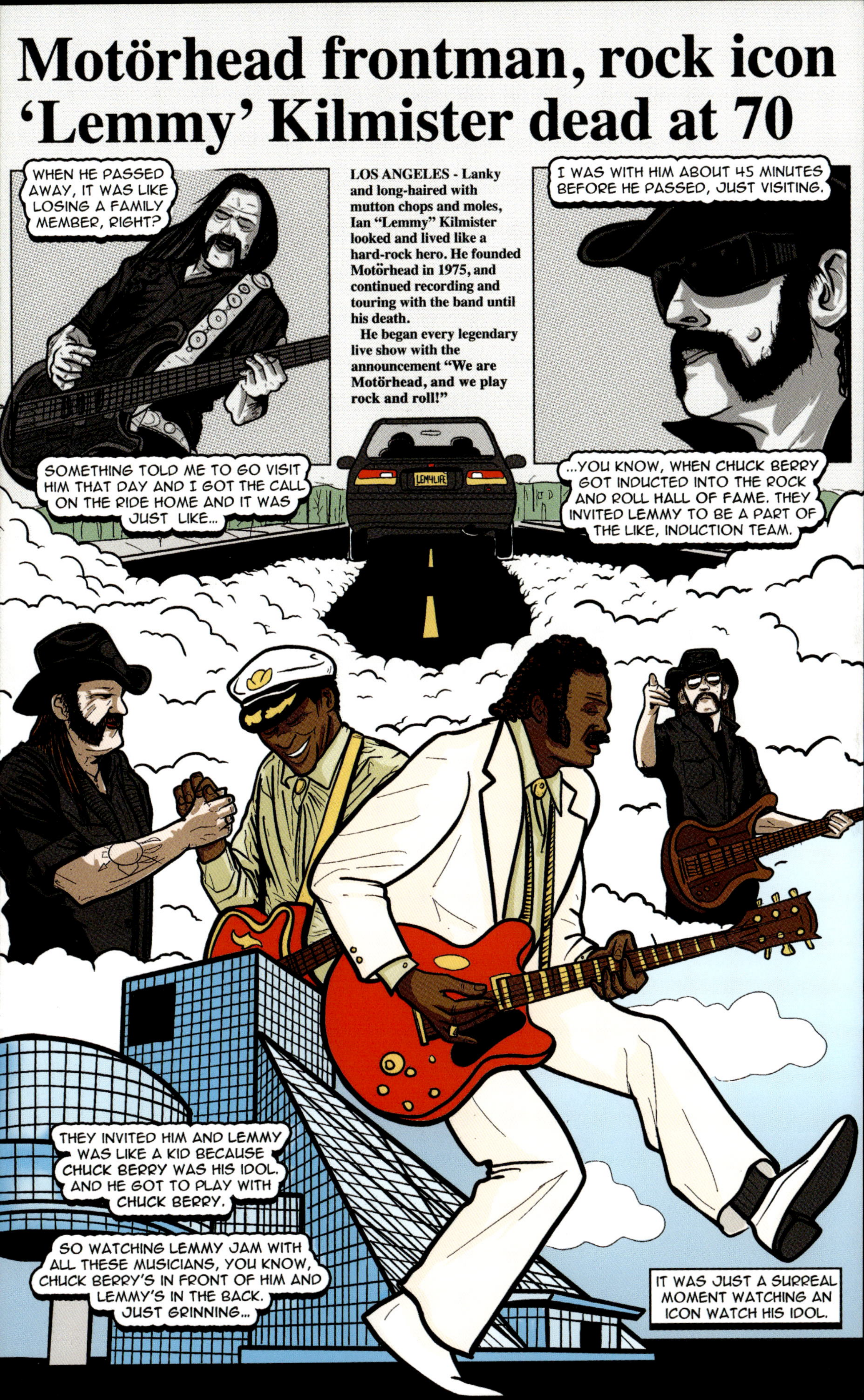

Motörhead frontman, rock icon 'Lemmy' Kilmister dead at 70
WHEN HE PASSED AWAY, IT WAS LIKE LOSING A FAMILY MEMBER, RIGHT?
LOS ANGELES - Lanky and long-haired with mutton chops and moles, Ian "Lemmy" Kilmister looked and lived like a hard-rock hero. He founded Motörhead in 1975, and continued recording and touring with the band until his death.
He began every legendary live show with the announcement "We are Motörhead, and we play rock and roll!"
I WAS WITH HIM ABOUT 45 MINUTES BEFORE HE PASSED, JUST VISITING.
SOMETHING TOLD ME TO GO VISIT HIM THAT DAY AND I GOT THE CALL ON THE RIDE HOME AND IT WAS JUST LIKE...
LEM4LIFE
...YOU KNOW, WHEN CHUCK BERRY GOT INDUCTED INTO THE ROCK AND ROLL HALL OF FAME. THEY INVITED LEMMY TO BE A PART OF THE LIKE, INDUCTION TEAM.
THEY INVITED HIM AND LEMMY WAS LIKE A KID BECAUSE CHUCK BERRY WAS HIS IDOL. AND HE GOT TO PLAY WITH CHUCK BERRY.
SO WATCHING LEMMY JAM WITH ALL THESE MUSICIANS, YOU KNOW, CHUCK BERRY'S IN FRONT OF HIM AND LEMMY'S IN THE BACK. JUST GRINNING...
IT WAS JUST A SURREAL MOMENT WATCHING AN ICON WATCH HIS IDOL.

"Even before I heard Motörhead I looked at Lemmy and went, 'that guy IS Rock & Roll.'"

FIRST MET LEMMY IN 2014

corey graves

THE VOICE OF WWE'S FRIDAY NIGHT SMACKDOWN

STORY ILLUSTRATED BY TONY PARKER

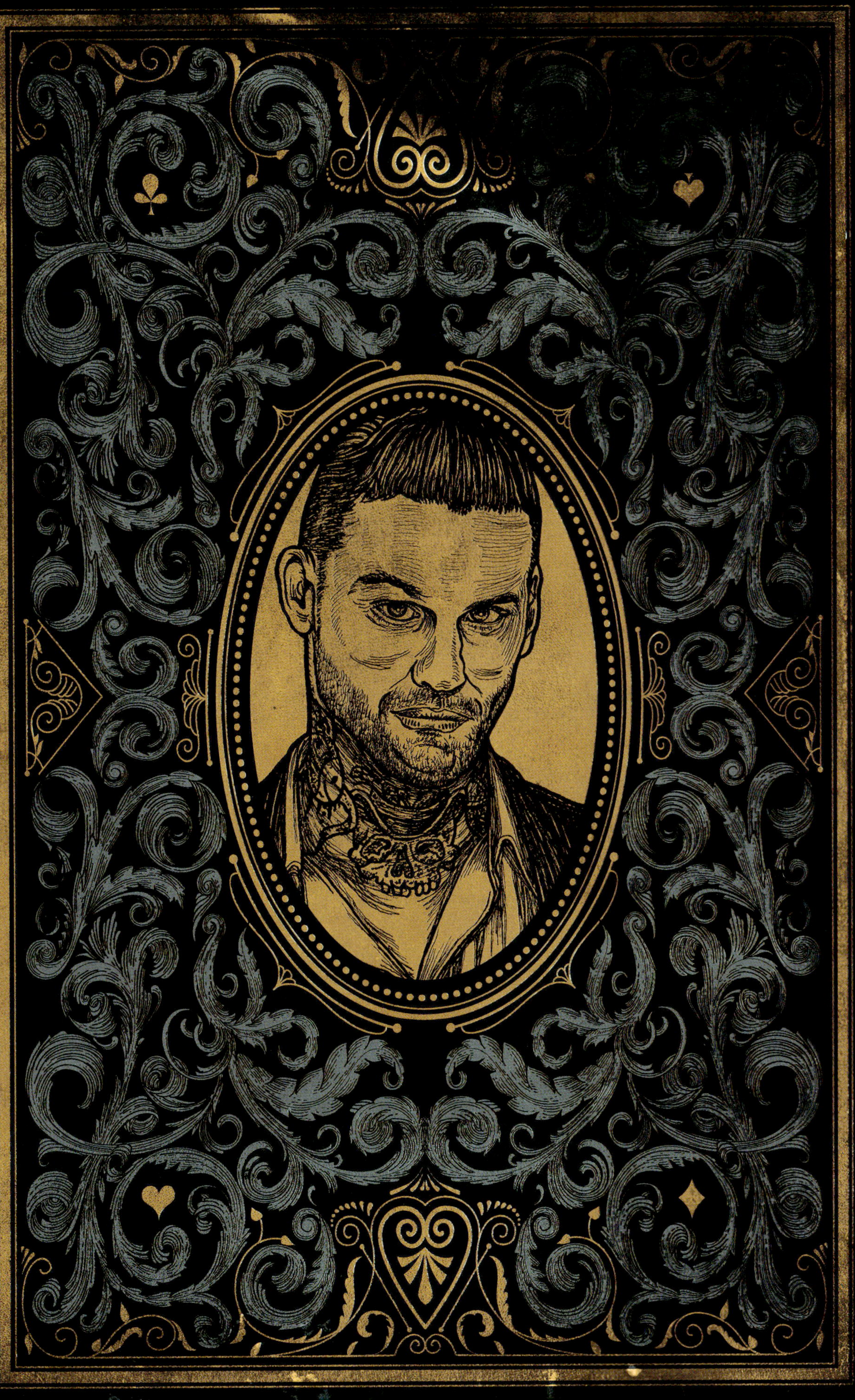

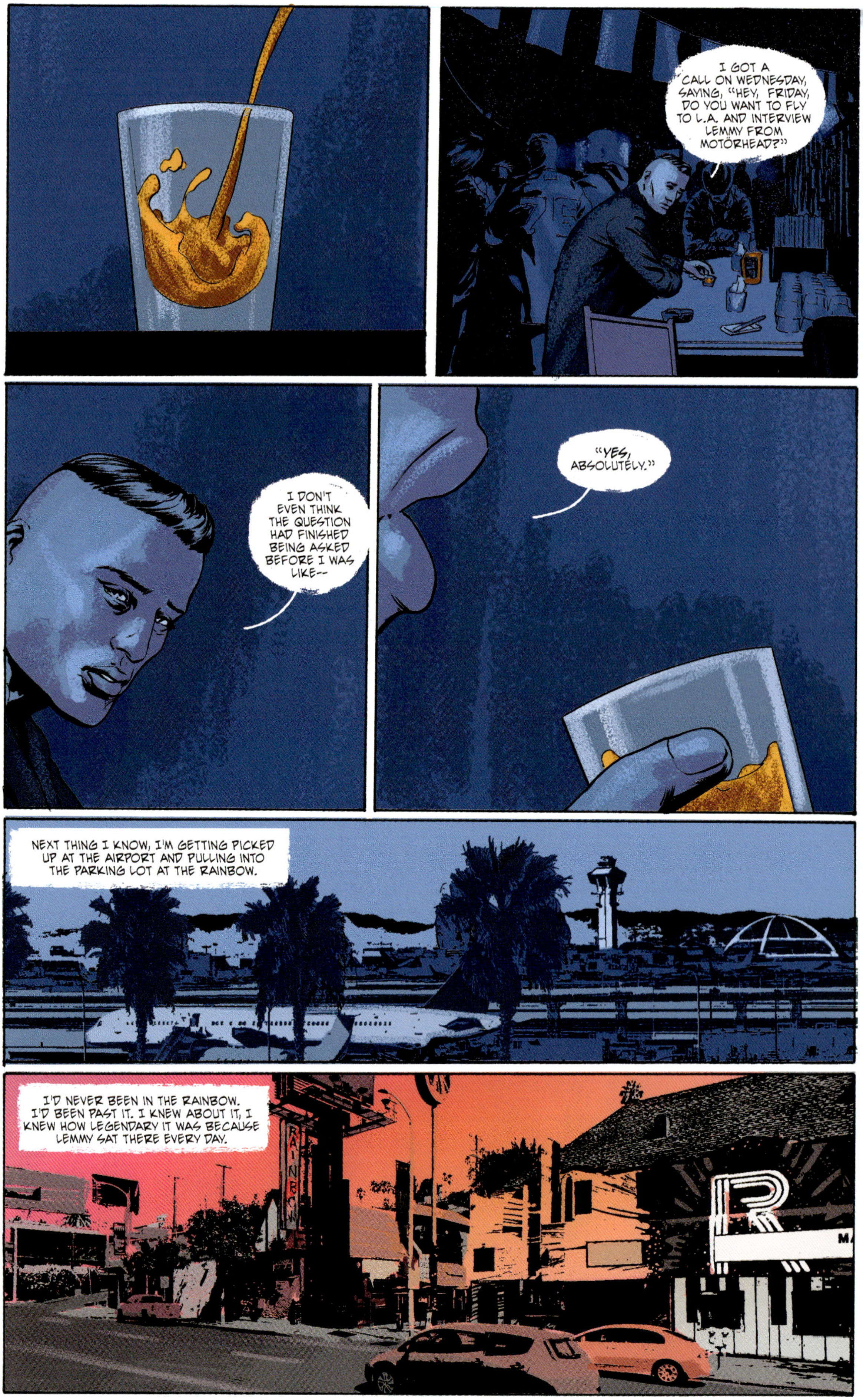
I GOT A CALL ON WEDNESDAY, SAYING, "HEY, FRIDAY, DO YOU WANT TO FLY TO L.A. AND INTERVIEW LEMMY FROM MOTÖRHEAD?"
I DON'T EVEN THINK THE QUESTION HAD FINISHED BEING ASKED BEFORE I WAS LIKE--
"YES, ABSOLUTELY."
NEXT THING I KNOW, I'M GETTING PICKED UP AT THE AIRPORT AND PULLING INTO THE PARKING LOT AT THE RAINBOW.
I'D NEVER BEEN IN THE RAINBOW. I'D BEEN PAST IT. I KNEW ABOUT IT, I KNEW HOW LEGENDARY IT WAS BECAUSE LEMMY SAT THERE EVERY DAY.
RAINBOW

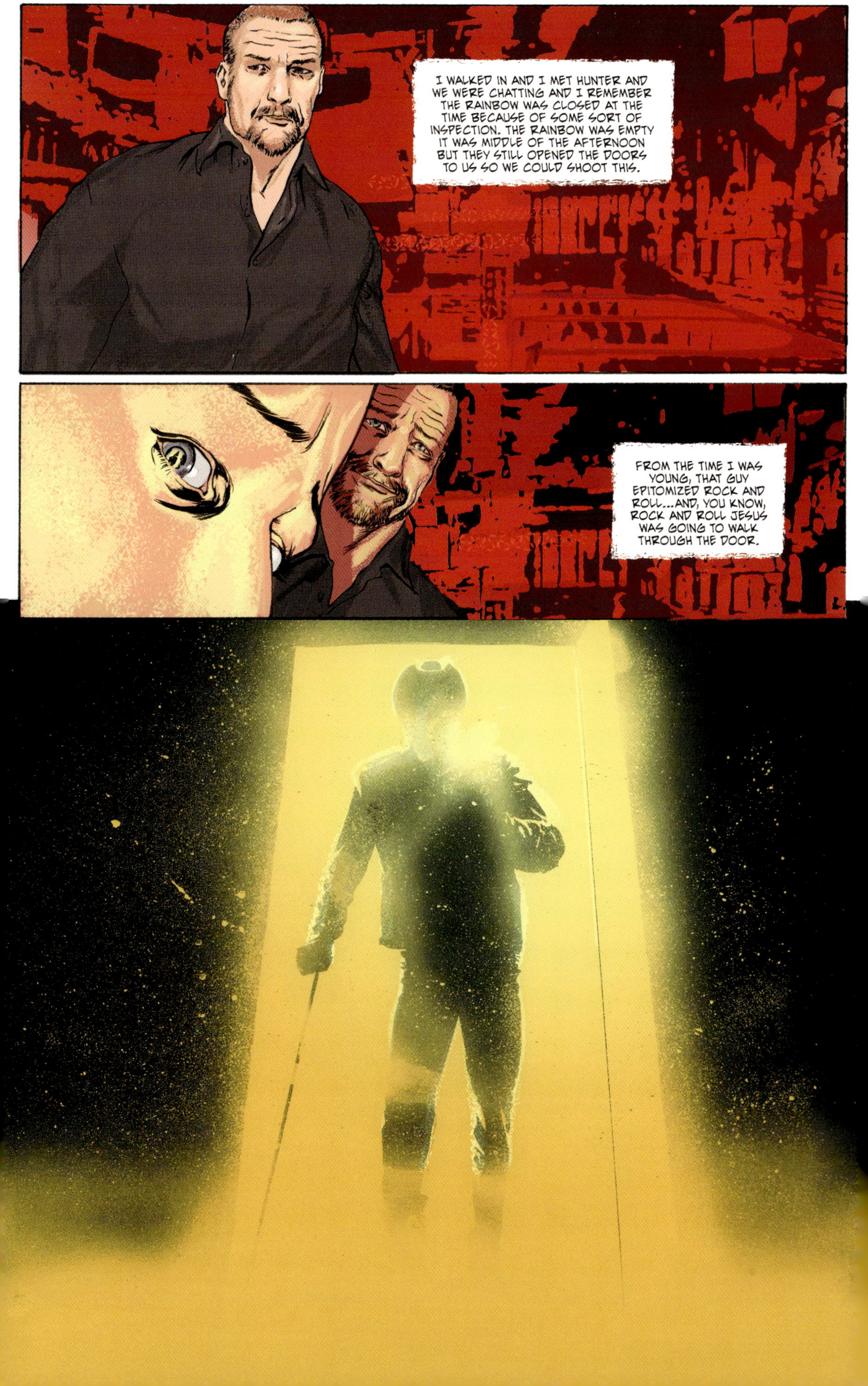
I WALKED IN AND I MET HUNTER AND WE WERE CHATTING AND I REMEMBER THE RAINBOW WAS CLOSED AT THE TIME BECAUSE OF SOME SORT OF INSPECTION. THE RAINBOW WAS EMPTY IT WAS MIDDLE OF THE AFTERNOON BUT THEY STILL OPENED THE DOORS TO US SO WE COULD SHOOT THIS.
FROM THE TIME I WAS YOUNG, THAT GUY EPITOMIZED ROCK AND ROLL...AND, YOU KNOW, ROCK AND ROLL JESUS WAS GOING TO WALK THROUGH THE DOOR.

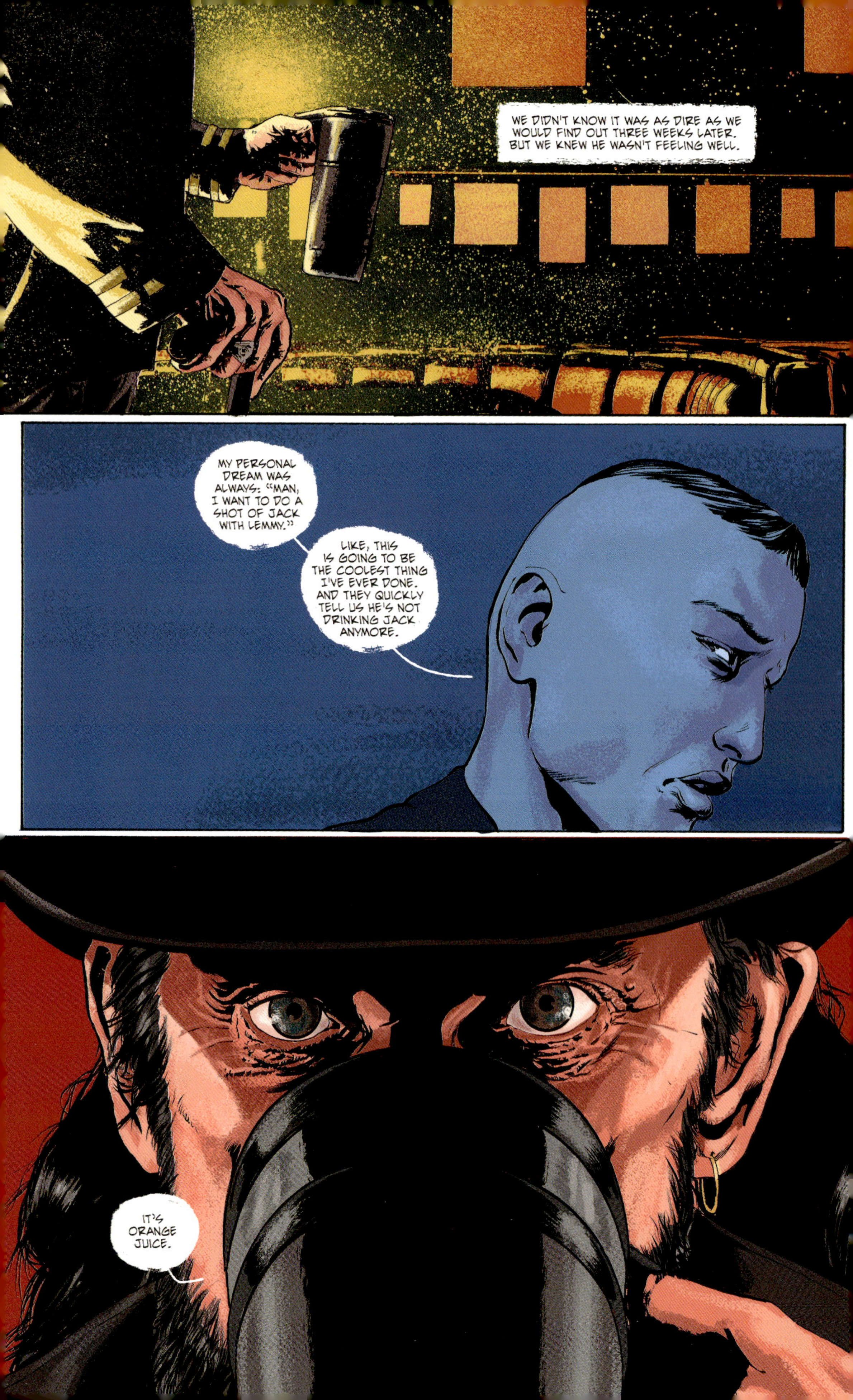
WE DIDN'T KNOW IT WAS AS DIRE AS WE WOULD FIND OUT THREE WEEKS LATER. BUT WE KNEW HE WASN'T FEELING WELL.
MY PERSONAL DREAM WAS ALWAYS: "MAN, I WANT TO DO A SHOT OF JACK WITH LEMMY."
LIKE, THIS IS GOING TO BE THE COOLEST THING I'VE EVER DONE. AND THEY QUICKLY TELL US HE'S NOT DRINKING JACK ANYMORE.
IT'S ORANGE JUICE.

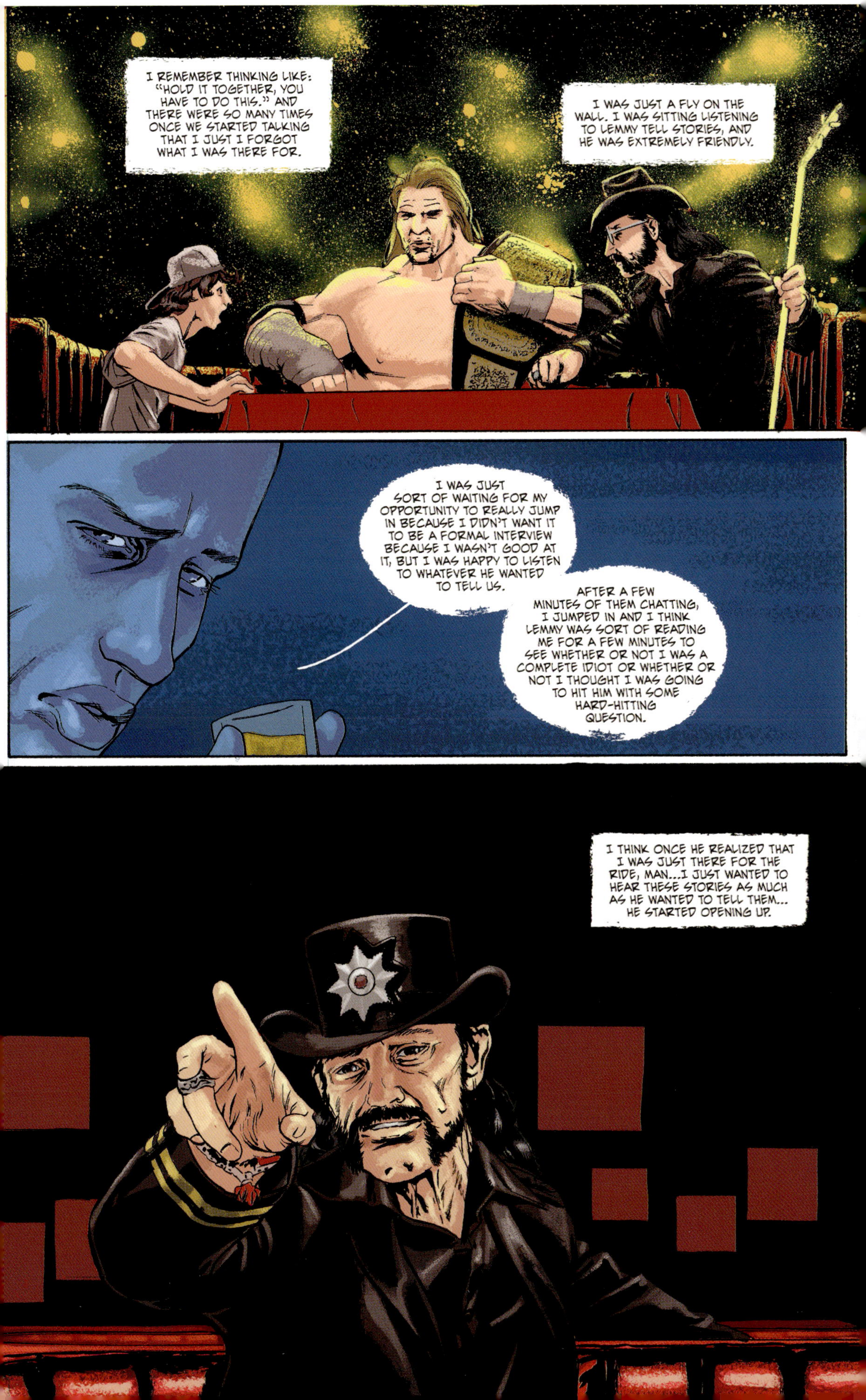

I REMEMBER THINKING LIKE: "HOLD IT TOGETHER, YOU HAVE TO DO THIS." AND THERE WERE SO MANY TIMES ONCE WE STARTED TALKING THAT I JUST I FORGOT WHAT I WAS THERE FOR.
I WAS JUST A FLY ON THE WALL. I WAS SITTING LISTENING TO LEMMY TELL STORIES, AND HE WAS EXTREMELY FRIENDLY.
I WAS JUST SORT OF WAITING FOR MY OPPORTUNITY TO REALLY JUMP IN BECAUSE I DIDN'T WANT IT TO BE A FORMAL INTERVIEW BECAUSE I WASN'T GOOD AT IT, BUT I WAS HAPPY TO LISTEN TO WHATEVER HE WANTED TO TELL US.
AFTER A FEW MINUTES OF THEM CHATTING, I JUMPED IN AND I THINK LEMMY WAS SORT OF READING ME FOR A FEW MINUTES TO SEE WHETHER OR NOT I WAS A COMPLETE IDIOT OR WHETHER OR NOT I THOUGHT I WAS GOING TO HIT HIM WITH SOME HARD-HITTING QUESTION.
I THINK ONCE HE REALIZED THAT I WAS JUST THERE FOR THE RIDE, MAN...I JUST WANTED TO HEAR THESE STORIES AS MUCH AS HE WANTED TO TELL THEM... HE STARTED OPENING UP.

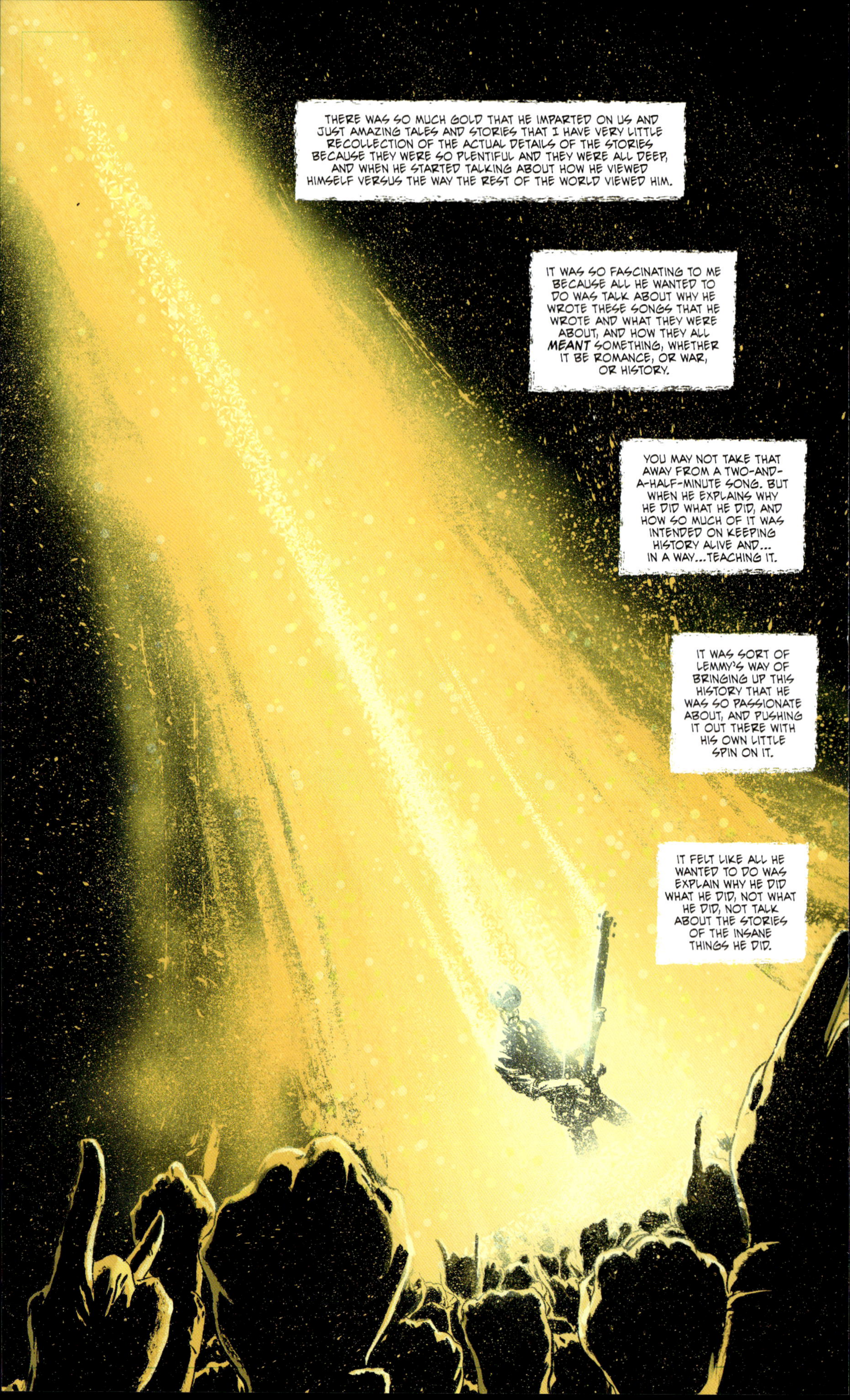
THERE WAS SO MUCH GOLD THAT HE IMPARTED ON US AND JUST AMAZING TALES AND STORIES THAT I HAVE VERY LITTLE RECOLLECTION OF THE ACTUAL DETAILS OF THE STORIES BECAUSE THEY WERE SO PLENTIFUL AND THEY WERE ALL DEEP, AND WHEN HE STARTED TALKING ABOUT HOW HE VIEWED HIMSELF VERSUS THE WAY THE REST OF THE WORLD VIEWED HIM.
IT WAS SO FASCINATING TO ME BECAUSE ALL HE WANTED TO DO WAS TALK ABOUT WHY HE WROTE THESE SONGS THAT HE WROTE AND WHAT THEY WERE ABOUT, AND HOW THEY ALL **MEANT** SOMETHING, WHETHER IT BE ROMANCE, OR WAR, OR HISTORY.
YOU MAY NOT TAKE THAT AWAY FROM A TWO-AND-A-HALF-MINUTE SONG. BUT WHEN HE EXPLAINS WHY HE DID WHAT HE DID, AND HOW SO MUCH OF IT WAS INTENDED ON KEEPING HISTORY ALIVE AND... IN A WAY...TEACHING IT.
IT WAS SORT OF LEMMY'S WAY OF BRINGING UP THIS HISTORY THAT HE WAS SO PASSIONATE ABOUT, AND PUSHING IT OUT THERE WITH HIS OWN LITTLE SPIN ON IT.
IT FELT LIKE ALL HE WANTED TO DO WAS EXPLAIN WHY HE DID WHAT HE DID, NOT WHAT HE DID, NOT TALK ABOUT THE STORIES OF THE INSANE THINGS HE DID.

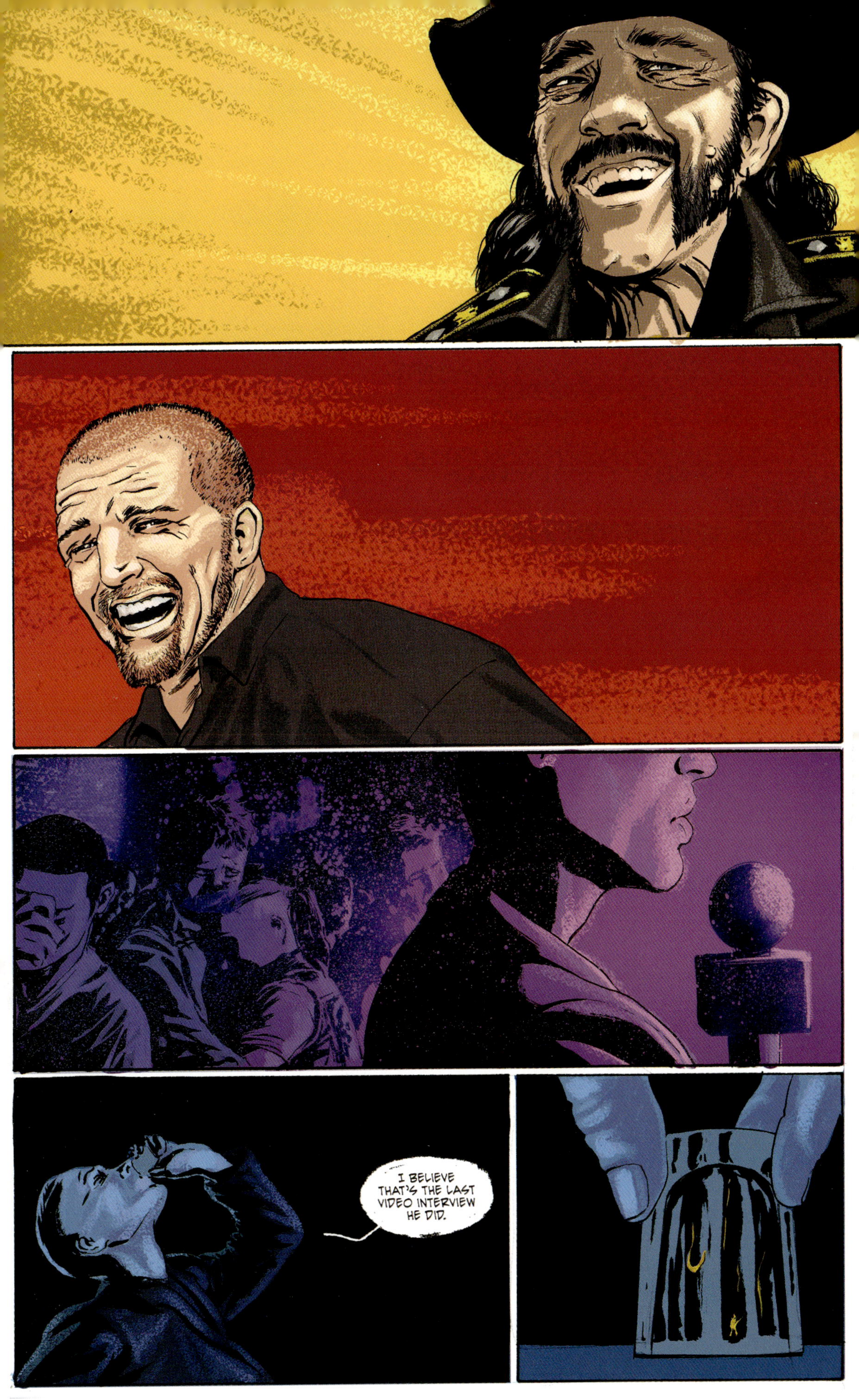
I BELIEVE THAT'S THE LAST VIDEO INTERVIEW HE DID.

"He was my hero. He was fucking great, a good friend. I'm missing him already. I'll never forget him."

FIRST MET
LEMMY
IN
1971

ozzy osbourne

FOUNDER
BLACK SABBATH
AND THE
PRINCE OF
DARKNESS

AFTERWORD AS TOLD TO KORY GROW

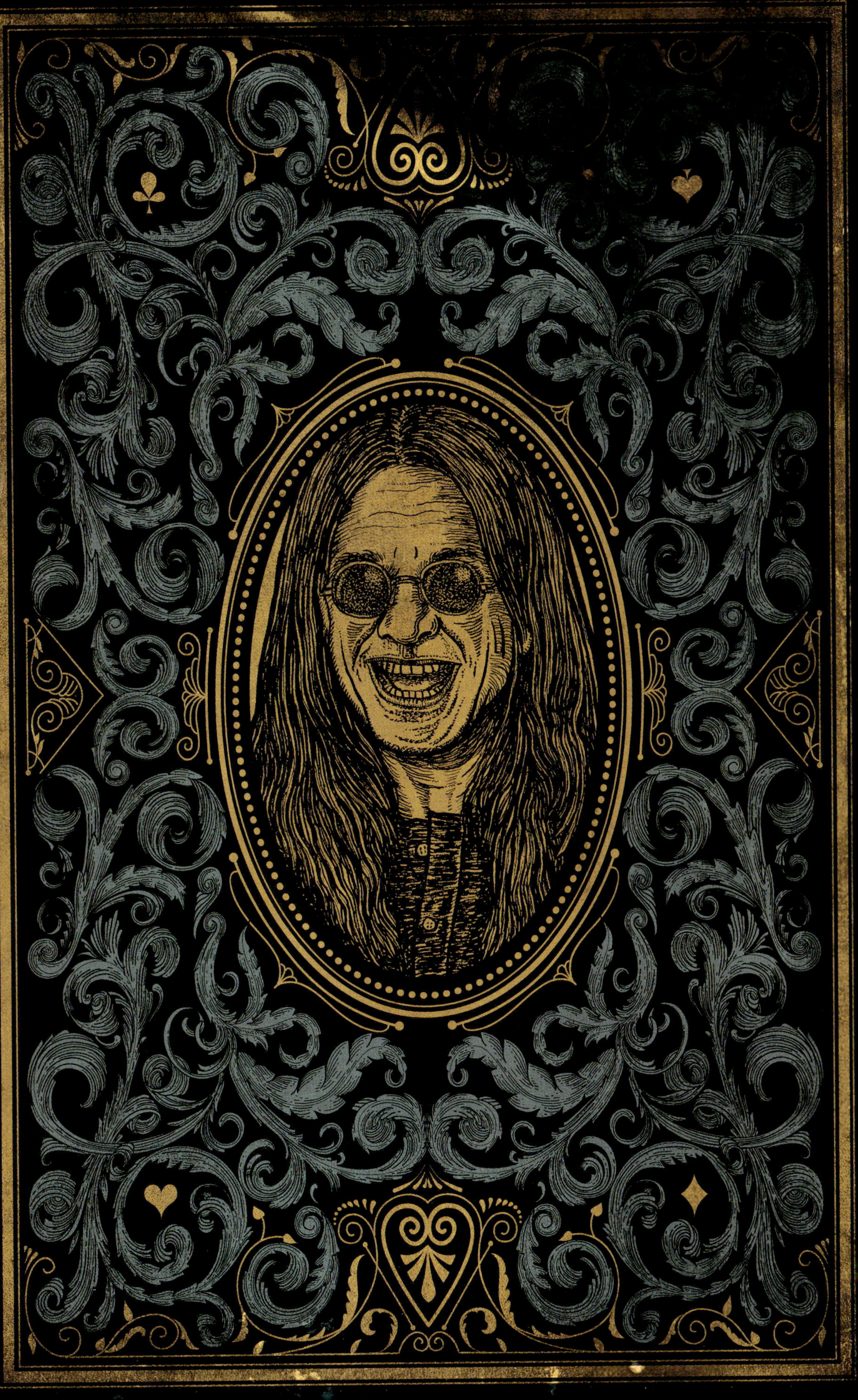

no more tears

AFTERWORD BY ozzy osbourne

ILLUSTRATIONS BY erik rodriguez & rantz a. hoseley

ME AND LEMMY GO BACK A LONG TIME. We used to have a standing joke with each other, "Which one of us is going to go first?" But I curbed my ways, staying up all night and all that shit, a long time ago. But Lemmy said to me one time, "What's the point of living to 99 if you're not enjoying it? It's my life and I want to have fun with it." And he lived to 70. And the way he lived, smoking cigarettes, drinking and all that, he knew he wouldn't be doing it. You can't live that lifestyle and live 'til 99. Very rarely, some people can. Most of us drop off along the way.

I MET LEMMY WHEN HE WAS IN Hawkwind. We used to rehearse in the same place in England. And then when he formed Motörhead, they were like the pirates of the rock business. I remember when I did my first solo tour of America, and they were opening up for us. We had a lot of fun together. They would be partying every day. On that tour, I remember saying to Lemmy at one point, "Do you ever sleep?" And he goes, "Well, not much." I go, "When was the last time you slept?" He said, "Let me think. Ten, 12 days ago." I said, "You're joking!" If I stayed awake for two days, I would be absolutely screaming, crazy. But they used to go for it.

He was the king of partying for a long while, but I'm sure he didn't keep it up forever. You could not do it. Lemmy was a fucking monster for it.

♠ ♣ ♥ ♦

WHEN THEY TOURED WITH ME, it was like Spinal Tap. They'd come off the stage, soaking with sweat, they'd get in the bus and just drive. They wouldn't shower. We were doing colleges, anywhere we could play. And their rider was like a case of Jack Daniel's, a case of vodka. Sharon says, "How much do you think we can afford to pay you?" Their rider was well more than we were paying them. They lived on vodka, orange juice, soda, and they'd walk around with bourbon all the time. I don't know how the fuck they drank that stuff. I got loaded on Jack Daniel's only one time, and I went, "You know what? It's fucking not for me."

Back in those days, I was hitting it pretty hard as well. But nothing like them. They put a new fucking meaning to partying. It was catastrophic. One of the guitar players went fucking insane. The stuff they used to use, that speed, whatever they fuck they used to use, it was fierce. They'd all be fucking wide-eyed and legless.

He stayed at our house for a while at one point. I remember when he arrived, this was back in the crazy days and I was hungover and wanted to crawl under a rock and die. He came to the door, and his face was fucking ashen. He looked like a ghost. He looked like he'd been under a slab for

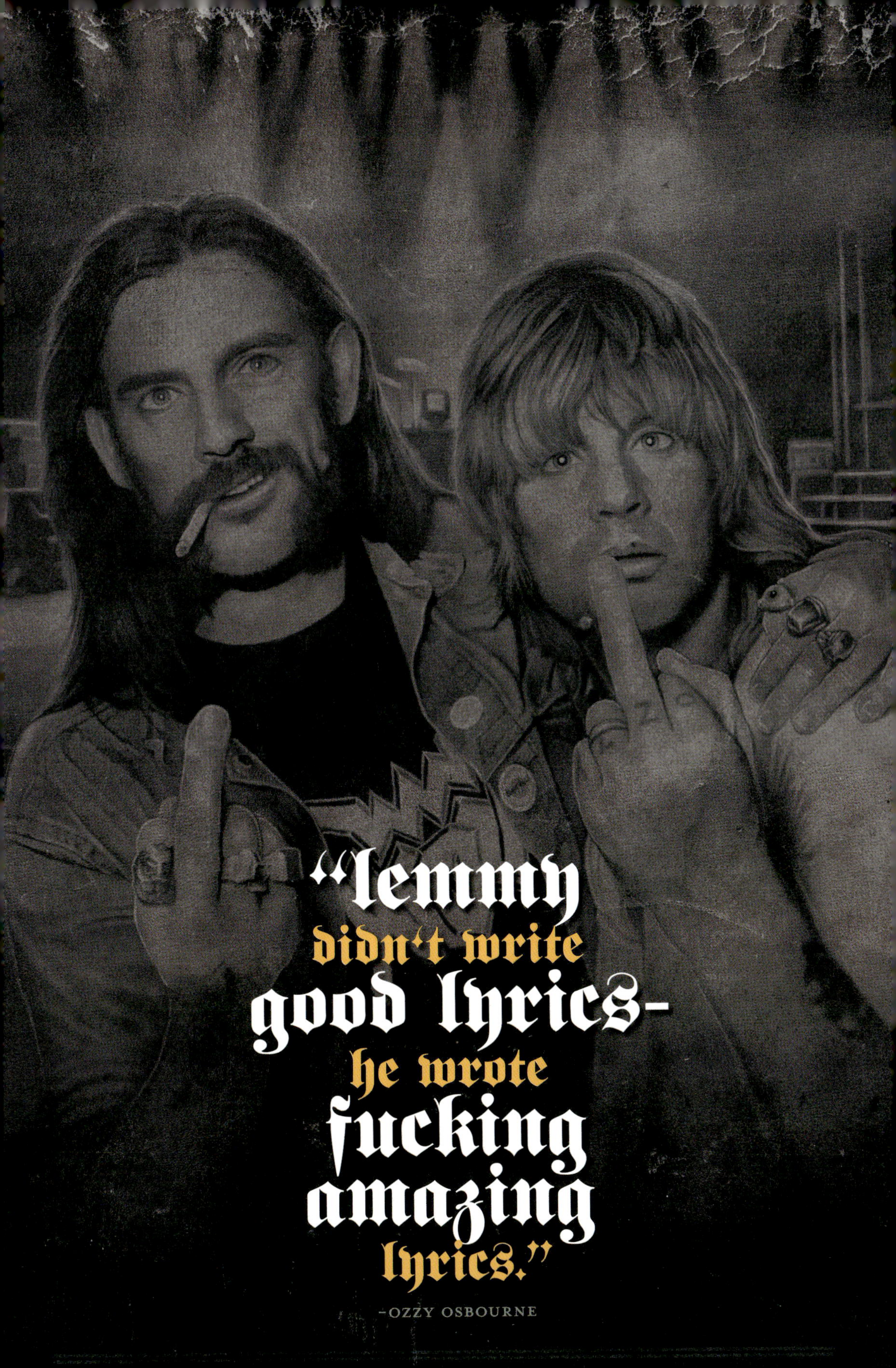

"lemmy didn't write good lyrics- he wrote fucking amazing lyrics."

-OZZY OSBOURNE

500 years. And he looked at me and he said, "Fuck me. I hope I don't look as bad as you." I go, "Fuck, if Lemmy Kilmister's saying that to me, I'm going back to bed." I went back to bed and called the gig.

It wasn't all partying, though. Lemmy and I did a lot of work together, too. I remember when he wrote some lyrics for me, I went over to his apartment. That place was unbelievable. There was more war memorabilia and things hanging off the wall than most museums. I've given him some swords and daggers over the years that I picked up. It was his hobby. We had an interest in that Second World War. But he was so intelligent about it. He knew so much about the history.

Anyway, I gave him a song that I wrote. He was great with lyrics, so I said to him, "Can you work on this?" I also gave him a book about the Second World War, about some general or something. He says, "Come back in two hours." So I come back and he not only wrote me a bunch of lyrics, he had three sets of lyrics and he said to me, "That book was crap also." I said, "What book?" "The one you gave me." He had read a book in an hour. I said, "Are you kidding me?" He said, "Do you like these lyrics?" And I think it was for "Mama, I'm Coming Home." And I said, "They're all right." And he goes, "What do you think about these?" He'd written me three sets of lyrics.

♣ ♠ ♥ ♦

HE WROTE MY SONG "SEE YOU ON the Other Side" with me. I came up with the idea and he wrote the lyrics. He wrote, "Mama, I'm Coming Home," "Hellraiser," "Desire," "I Don't Want to Change the World." I'd give him a song and think, "Where the fuck do you go from here?" And he'd write you like 15 other verses in such a short amount of time. I mean, if I was writing lyrics, most of the time, I go, "Well, she went to the door," and that's as far as I'd get. He just writes them as if he's writing a message. And it's like, "He wrote this in how long?" And they're not good lyrics – they're fucking amazing lyrics.

To look at Lemmy, you'd never think he was as educated as he was. People look at the music we do and the way we look, and they go, "Oh, this bunch is a bunch of yobbos. They don't know what they're doing. They're bad people." But it's not true. Lemmy looks like an old biker, but he was so well read. He was very up on a lot of things. He was a very clever guy. On his bus on the first tour, he had a plaid suitcase and all he had in there was a pair of knickers and a pair of socks, and the rest was books. When he stayed with us, he'd stay in the library for three days, reading fucking books. And if I got up to go to the bathroom in the middle of the night, he'd still be reading. And I'd go, "Why don't you sleep?"

He was a serious friend to us. He was very loyal. And if he had something to say to you, he wouldn't mince about it. He wouldn't yell at you. He'd just say, "That pissed me off." That was very rare. I don't think he said that to me, but he was just everybody's friend.

He had a great sense of humor, as well. One of his songs was called "Killed by Death," and that was an amazing title.

Lemmy discovered California and he moved out here a long while ago. He lived just around the corner from [West Hollywood bar] the Rainbow. He didn't drive and he could walk from his apartment to the Rainbow, and that's where he lived for the past 25, 30 years. The Rainbow, I believe, has a chair. It's part of the bar, which it has a plaque on saying, "Lemmy's chair." He sat in the same seat every day. He was local.

I saw him a few years ago at the Roxy. A friend of mine, Billy Morrison, was playing and I made a guest appearance. Lemmy was at the bar, as usual. I don't know if he was drinking or if he was just sitting in his place. He was very thin, very unwell, but he lived life the way he wanted and lived with the consequences. And I said to him, "Are you OK? Do you have kidney problems?" And he looked shocked. Nobody goes, "I'm going to die next year." I don't know why he kept going as long as he did.

♣ ♠ ♥ ♦

TO BE HONEST WITH YOU, I THINK doing the gigs kept him going. He worked until the very end. It gave him something to get out of bed for. He must have known he was very ill.

We did some gigs in South America with him in April of 2015, I remember my wife saying, "You should have seen Lemmy. He's lost a lot of weight and he really doesn't look too well." I was constantly texting him, saying, "If you need anything, call me." I was just looking at my phone, and there was a message from him that said, "Thanks for caring."

I'll miss him so much. We all will. There's a big hole in the music industry as far as I'm concerned.

He was a character. There ain't many characters in music today. I mean, you've got Miley Cyrus, OK, but there's not many characters in the game anymore. But he was definitely a character. An original. He lived the lifestyle. Sex, drugs and rock & roll, that was Lemmy.

You know what? There goes a hero for me. He was my hero. He was fucking great, a good friend. I'm missing him already. I'll never forget him. I don't think a lot of people will forget Lemmy. He'll be so missed in my camp. He was a good guy, a good man, a good friend of mine. He was just a fucking great dude, man. Not enough time for him.

God bless you, Lemmy. I'm so honored to have you a part of my life.

—— ozzy osbourne

we are the road crew

OUR INCREDIBLE STORYTELLERS
ALL PORTRAITS BY KELLEY SIMMS

neil warnock
AN MBE • THE HEAD OF UTA • FIRST HAWKWIND AGENT
SONG: we are the road crew

wayne kramer
FOUNDER/GUITARIST OF THE MC5 • WHITE PANTHER PARTY
SONG: ace of spades

michael moorcock
SCIENCE-FICTION AUTHOR AND HAWKWIND BANDMATE
SONG: ace of spades

ozzy osbourne
THE PRINCE OF DARKNESS • FOUNDER OF BLACK SABBATH
SONG: mama im coming home

phil campbell
MOTÖRHEAD GUITARIST SINCE 1984
SONG: overkill

chrissie hynde
FOUNDER/GUITARIST OF THE PRETENDERS
SONG: ace of spades

kim mcauliffe
FOUNDER/SINGER OF GIRLSCHOOL
SONG: please don't touch

slim jim phantom
FOUNDER/DRUMMER OF THE STRAY CATS
SONG: ace of spades

lars ulrich
FOUNDER/DRUMMER OF METALLICA
SONG: overkill

neil gaiman
WRITER/CREATOR OF SANDMAN • CORALINE
SONG: silver machine

dee snider
OUTSPOKEN SINGER OF TWISTED SISTER
SONG: born to raise hell

steffan chirazi
MOTÖRHEAD CREATIVE WRITER • FRIEND
SONG: the hammer

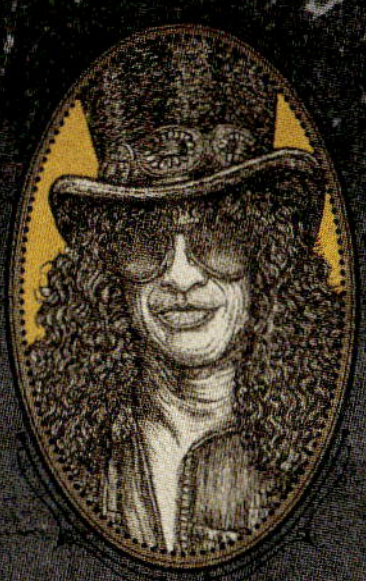

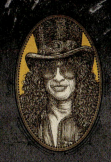

slash

FOUNDER/LEAD GUITARIST
OF GUNS N' ROSES

SONG: **we are the road crew**

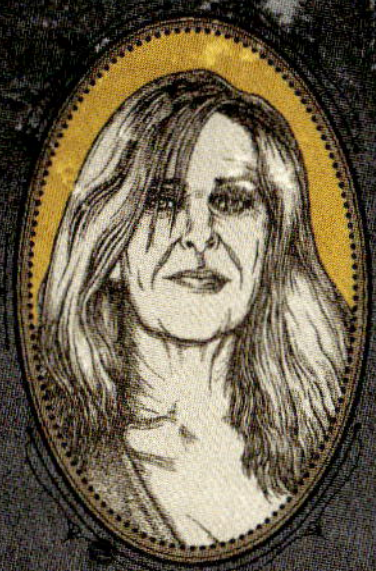

lita ford

FOUNDER/LEAD GUITARIST OF
THE RUNAWAYS + SOLO ARTIST

SONG: **can't catch me**

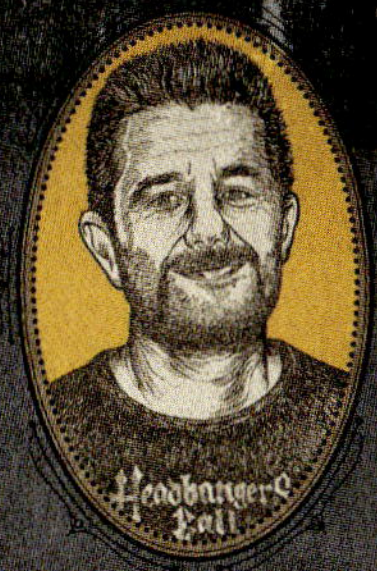
Headbangers
Ball

riki rachtman

OWNER OF THE CATHOUSE +
HOST OF HEADBANGER'S BALL

SONG: **in the name of tragedy**

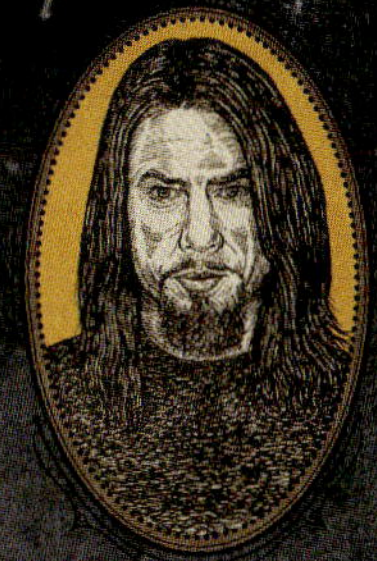

dave navarro

FOUNDER/GUITARIST
JANE'S ADDICTION

SONG: **ace of spades**

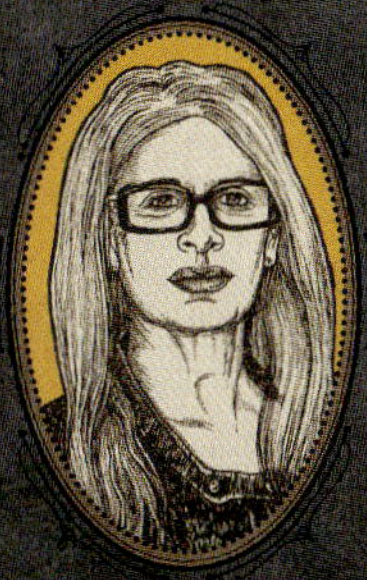

penelope shpeeris

DIRECTOR OF WAYNE'S WORLD +
DECLINE OF WESTERN CIVILIZATION

SONG: **ace of spades**

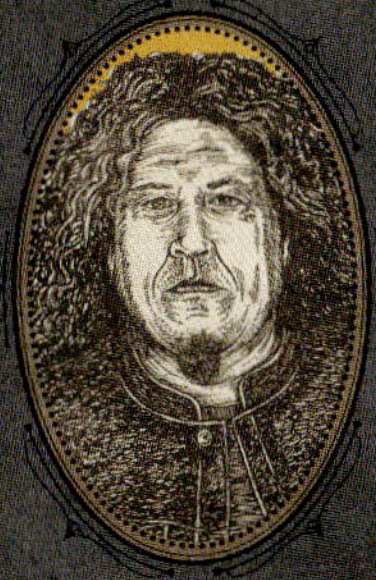

chuck billy

FOUNDER/SINGER
TESTAMENT

SONG: **ace of spades**

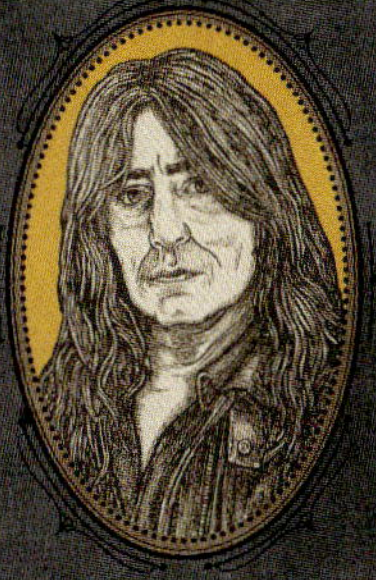

mikkey dee

DRUMMER FOR MOTÖRHEAD +
SCORPIONS + KING DIAMOND

SONG: **overkill**

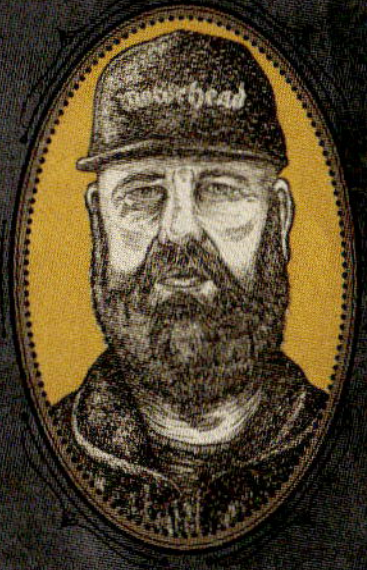
Motörhead

mikeal maglieri jr

OWNER, RAINBOW BAR & GRILL
+ THE WHISKY A GO-GO

SONG: **terrorizer**

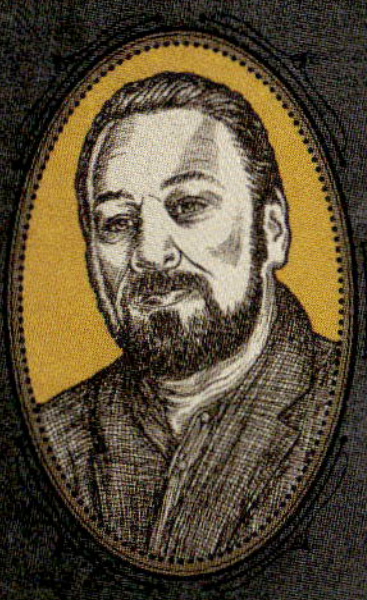

todd singerman

MANAGER OF
MOTÖRHEAD

SONG: **burner**

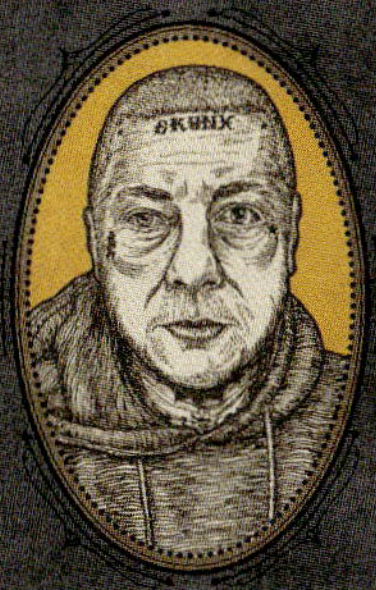
SKUNX

lars frederiksen

SINGER/GUITARIST
RANCID

SONG: **metropolis**

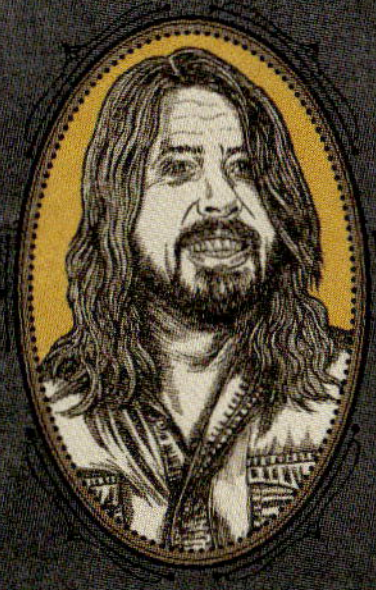

dave grohl

2X ROCK HALL OF FAMER
WITH NIRVANA + FOO FIGHTERS

SONG: **ace of spades**

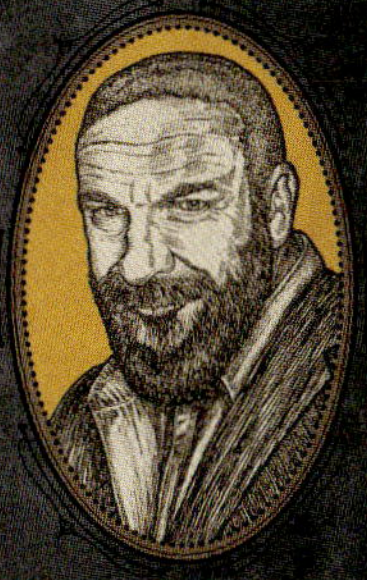

triple h

WWE HALL OF FAMER +
CHIEF CREATIVE OFFICER

SONG: **the game**

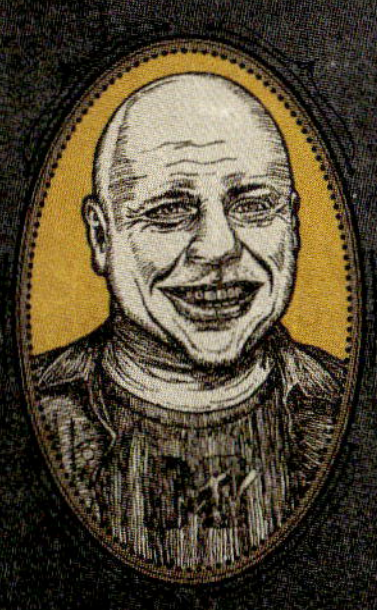

matt pinfield

MTV/VH1 BROADCAST LEGEND
+ HOST OF 120 MINUTES

SONG: **stay clean**

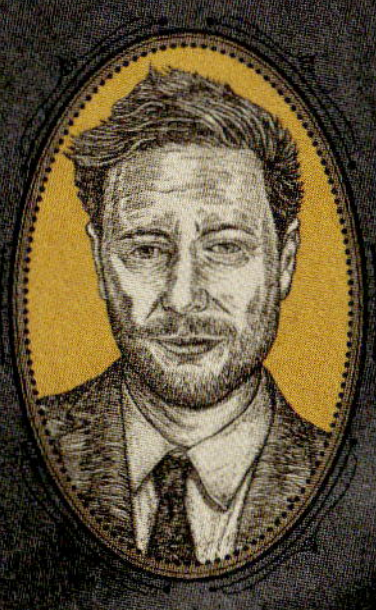

josh bernstein

Z2 PRESIDENT +
CREATOR OF THE GOLDEN GODS

SONG: **fast and loose**

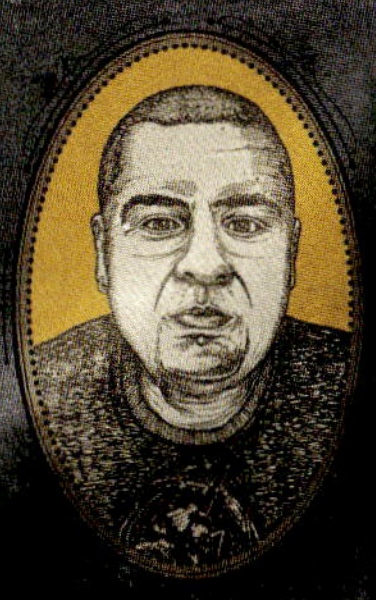

steve luna

MOTÖRHEAD
ROADIE

SONG: **killed by death**

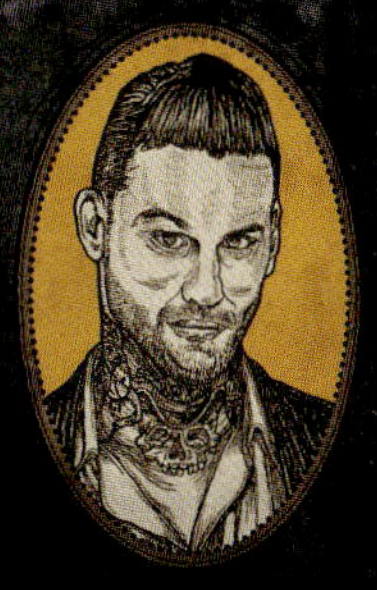

corey graves

HOST OF WWE'S
FRIDAY NIGHT SMACKDOWN

SONG: **hellraiser**

Shoot you in the back

A PEEK AT SOME OF THE INCREDIBLE ART FROM THE MAKING OF
NO REMORSE: THE ILLUSTRATED TRUE STORIES
OF LEMMY KILMISTER AND MOTÖRHEAD

COVER ILLUSTRATION
tim bradstreet

POSTER ILLUSTRATION
hydro74

CARD ILLUSTRATIONS
ed repka

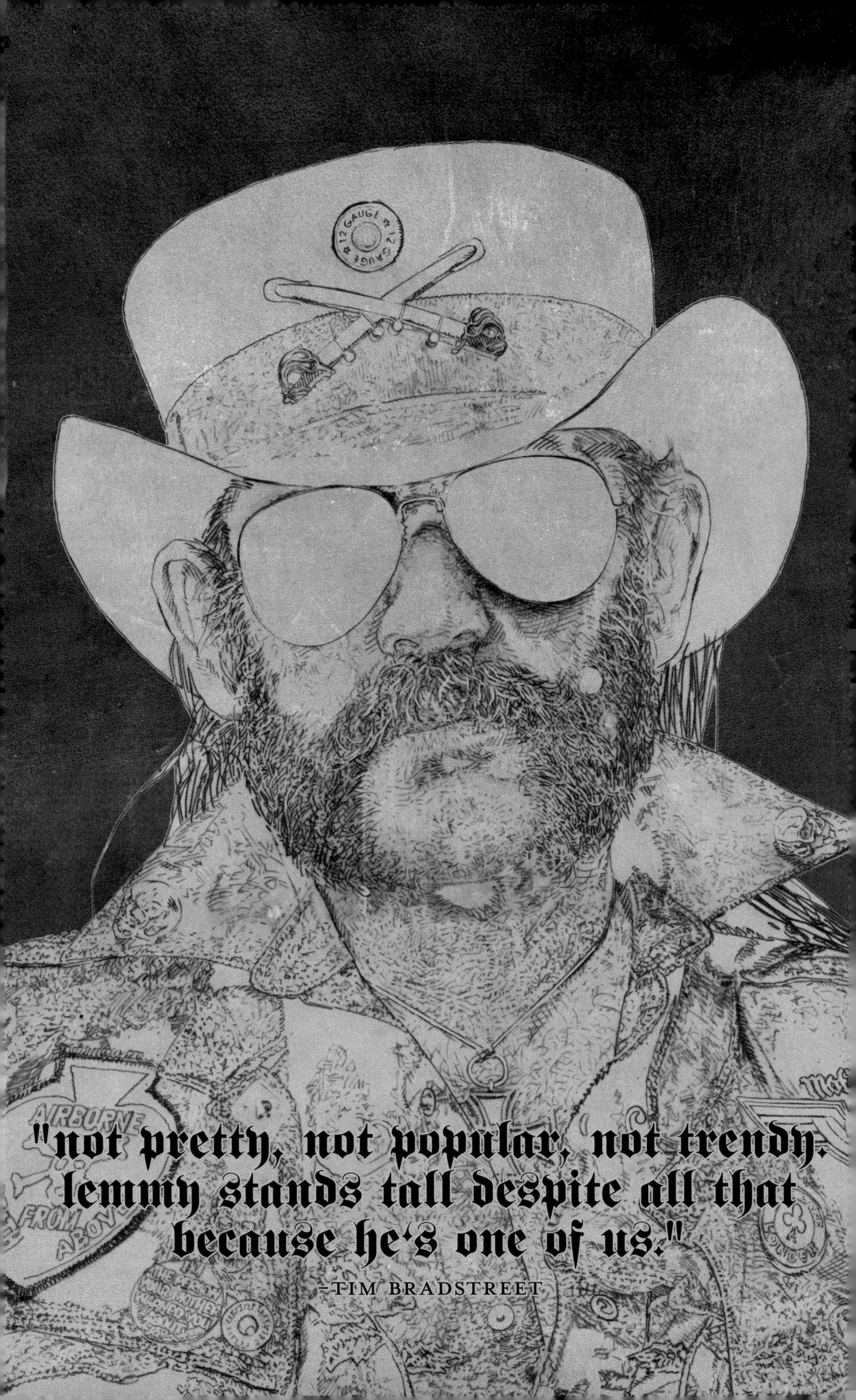
"not pretty, not popular, not trendy.
lemmy stands tall despite all that
because he's one of us."
–TIM BRADSTREET

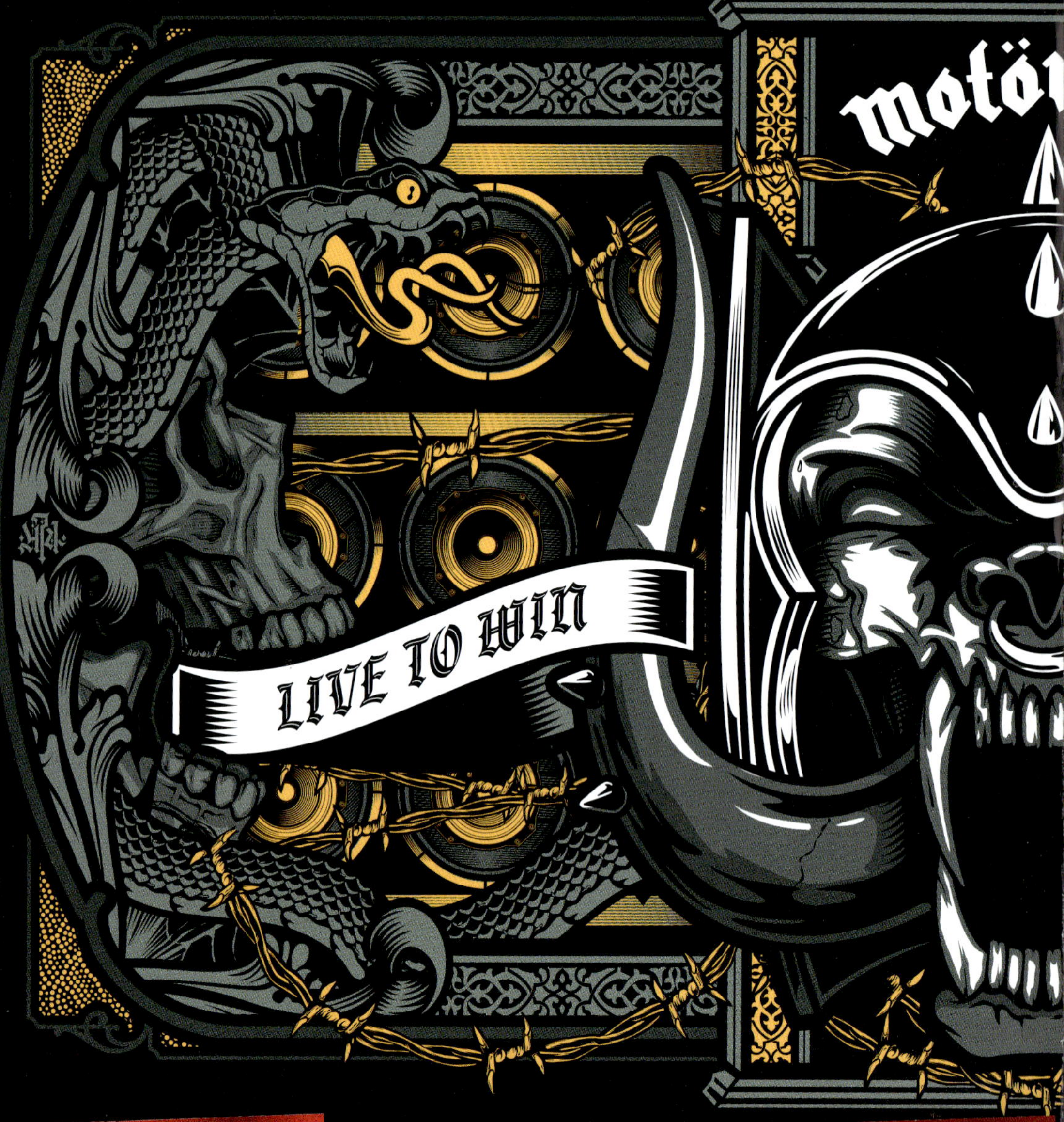
LIVE TO WIN

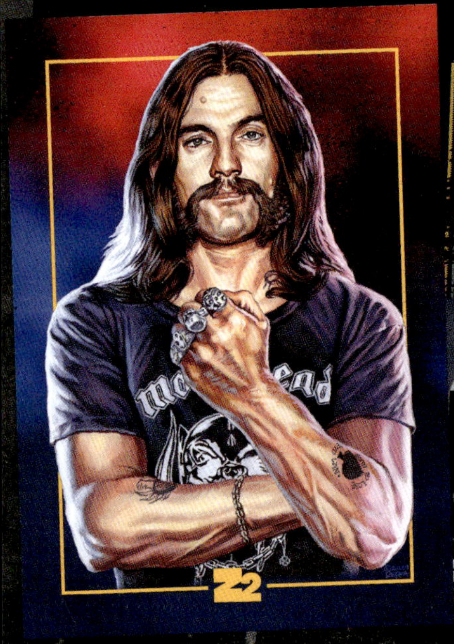

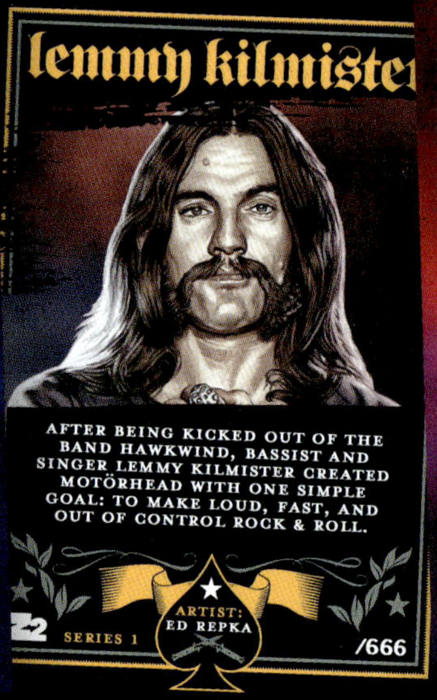
lemmy kilmister
AFTER BEING KICKED OUT OF THE BAND HAWKWIND, BASSIST AND SINGER LEMMY KILMISTER CREATED MOTÖRHEAD WITH ONE SIMPLE GOAL: TO MAKE LOUD, FAST, AND OUT OF CONTROL ROCK & ROLL.
SERIES 1
ARTIST: ED REPKA
/666

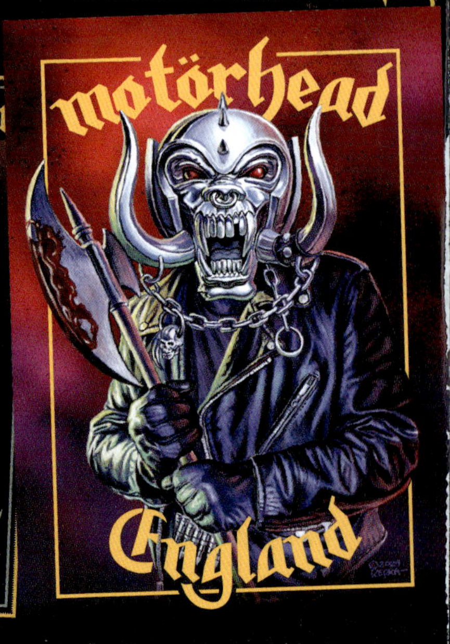
motörhead
England

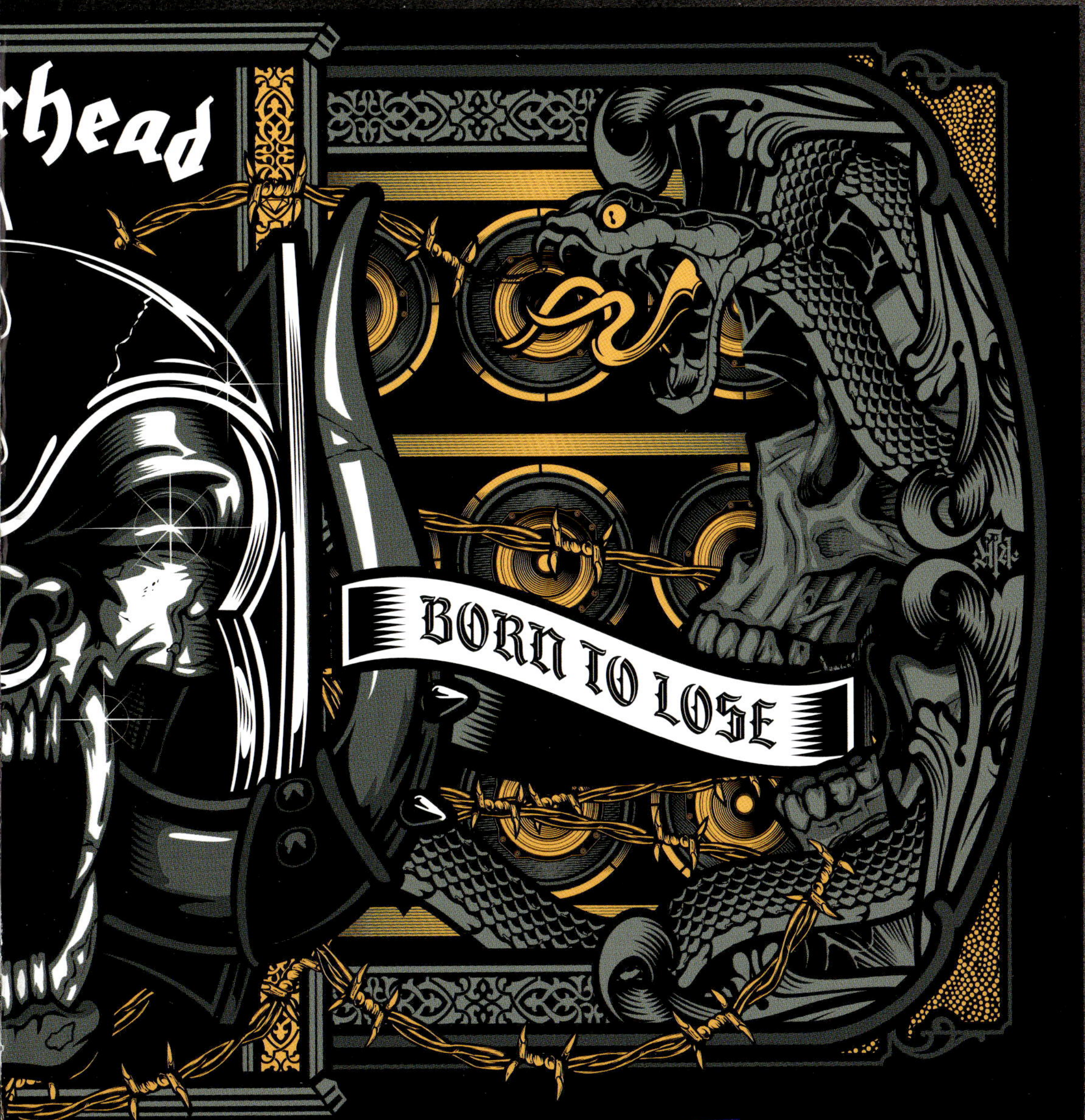
rhead
BORN TO LOSE

SPECIAL THANKS TO SUPER7

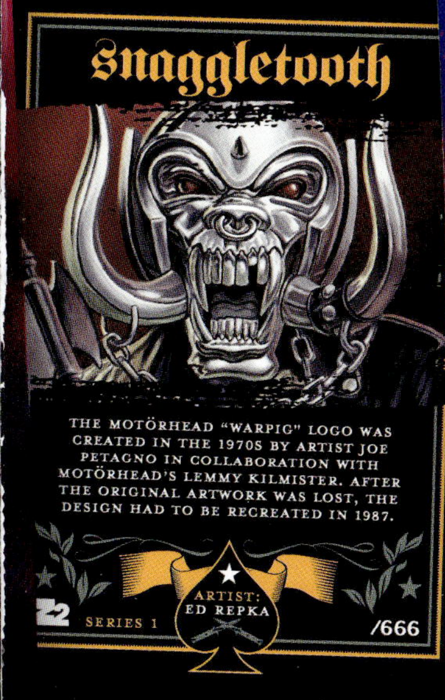
snaggletooth
THE MOTÖRHEAD "WARPIG" LOGO WAS CREATED IN THE 1970S BY ARTIST JOE PETAGNO IN COLLABORATION WITH MOTÖRHEAD'S LEMMY KILMISTER. AFTER THE ORIGINAL ARTWORK WAS LOST, THE DESIGN HAD TO BE RECREATED IN 1987.
ARTIST: ED REPKA
SERIES 1
/666

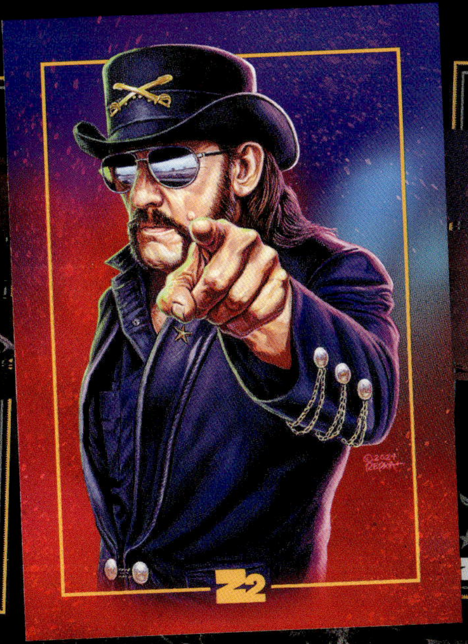

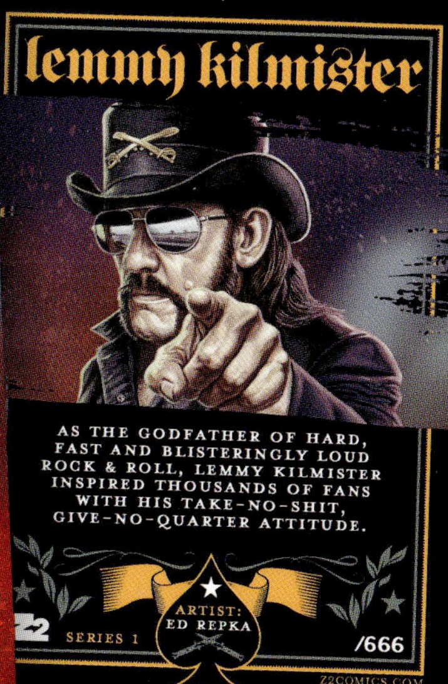
lemmy kilmister
AS THE GODFATHER OF HARD, FAST AND BLISTERINGLY LOUD ROCK & ROLL, LEMMY KILMISTER INSPIRED THOUSANDS OF FANS WITH HIS TAKE-NO-SHIT, GIVE-NO-QUARTER ATTITUDE.
ARTIST: ED REPKA
SERIES 1
/666

Z2COMICS.COM

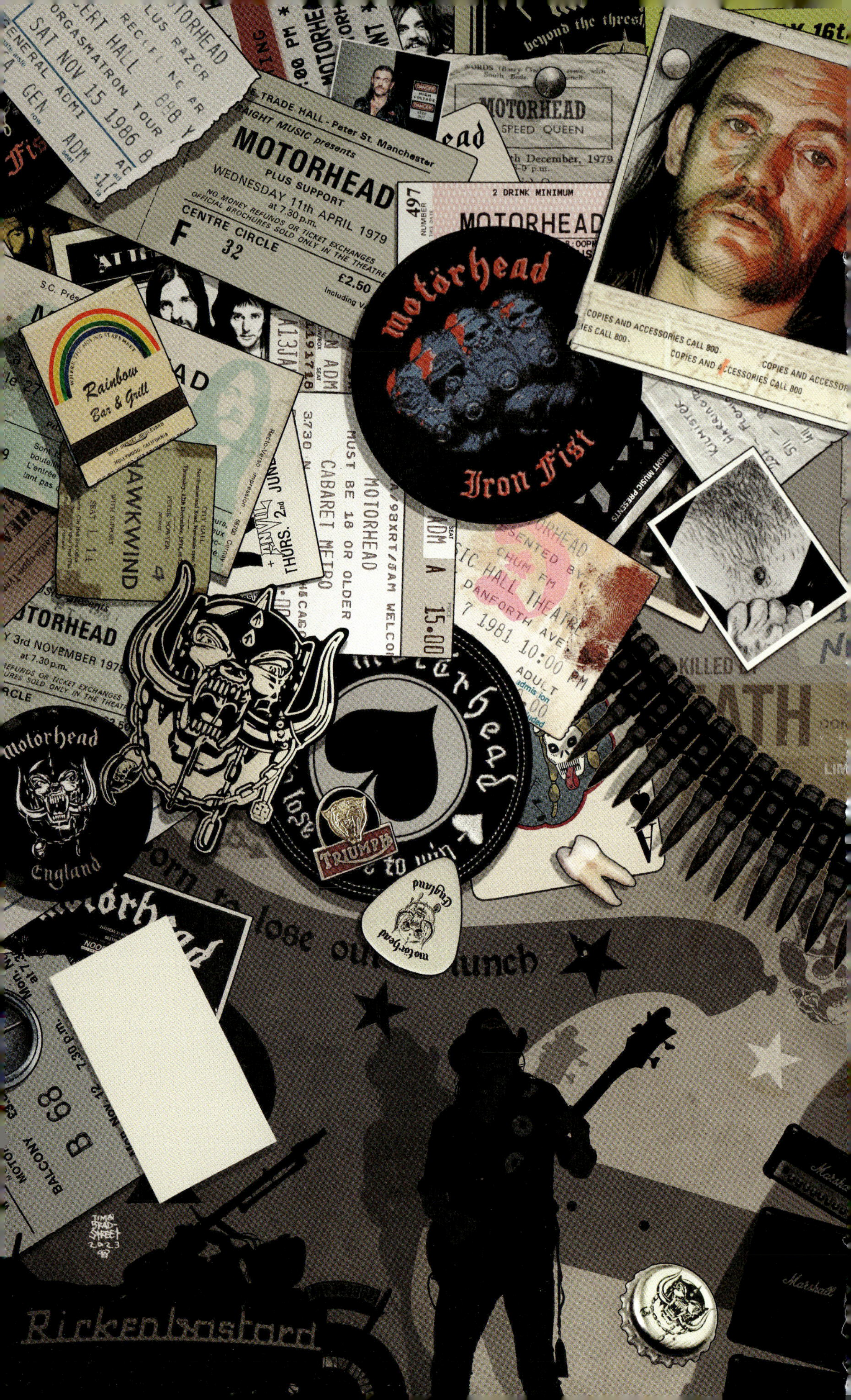
ORGASMATRON TOUR
SAT NOV 15 1986
GENERAL ADMISSION
FREE TRADE HALL - Peter St. Manchester
STRAIGHT MUSIC presents
MOTORHEAD
PLUS SUPPORT
WEDNESDAY 11th APRIL 1979
at 7.30 p.m.
NO MONEY REFUNDS OR TICKET EXCHANGES
OFFICIAL BROCHURES SOLD ONLY IN THE THEATRE
CENTRE CIRCLE
F 32
£2.50
MOTORHEAD
SPEED QUEEN
December, 1979
2 DRINK MINIMUM
MOTORHEAD
COPIES AND ACCESSORIES CALL 800
motörhead
Iron Fist
Rainbow
Bar & Grill
HAWKWIND
MOTORHEAD
MUST BE 18 OR OLDER
CABARET METRO
ADM A
15.00
CHUM FM
DANFORTH AVE
7 1981 10:00 PM
ADULT
MOTORHEAD
3rd NOVEMBER 1978
at 7.30 p.m.
KILLED BY
motörhead
England
TRIUMPH
born to lose
born to lose our lunch
motörhead
England
B 68
BALCONY
7.30 p.m.
TIM BRADSTREET 2023
Rickenbastard
Marshall